Fodor's 95 Montréal & Québec City

PRAISE FOR FODOR'S GUIDES

"Fodor's guides . . . are an admirable blend of the cultural and the practical."

—The Washington Post

"Researched by people chosen because they live or have lived in the country, well-written, and with good historical sections . . . Obligatory reading for millions of tourists."

—The Independent, *London*

"Usable, sophisticated restaurant coverage, with an emphasis on good value."

—Andy Birsh, Gourmet *restaurant columnist, quoted by Gannett News Service*

"Packed with dependable information."

—Atlanta Journal Constitution

"Fodor's always delivers high quality . . . thoughtfully presented . . . thorough."

—Houston Post

"Valuable because of their comprehensiveness."

—Minneapolis Star-Tribune

Reprinted from *Fodor's Canada '95*

Fodor's Travel Publications, Inc.
New York • Toronto • London • Sydney • Auckland

ISBN 0-679-02738-6

Grateful acknowledgment is made to Random House, Inc., Collins Publishers, and Hamish Hamilton, Ltd., for permission to reprint excerpts from *The Maple Leaf Rag* by Stephen Brook. Copyright © 1987 by Stephen Brook.

Fodor's Montréal & Québec City

Editor: Kristen D. Perrault
Contributors: Steven Amsterdam, Susan Brown, Echo Garrett, Dorothy Guinan, Helga Loverseed, Bevin McLaughlin, Scott McNeely, Linda K. Schmidt, Mary Ellen Schultz, Nancy van Itallie,
Creative Director: Fabrizio La Rocca
Cartographer: David Lindroth
Illustrator: Karl Tanner
Cover Photograph: Grant V. Faint/Image Bank

Design: Vignelli Associates

Special Sales

Fodor's Travel Publications are available at special discounts for bulk purchases for sales promotions or premiums. Special editions, including personalized covers, excerpts of existing guides, and corporate imprints, can be created in large quantities for special needs. For more information, contact your local bookseller or write to Special Marketing, Fodor's Travel Publications, 201 East 50th Street, New York, NY 10022. Inquiries from Canada should be directed to your local Canadian bookseller or sent to Random House of Canada, Ltd., Marketing Department, 1265 Aerowood Drive, Mississauga, Ontario L4W 1B9. Inquiries from the United Kingdom should be sent to Fodor's Travel Publications, 20 Vauxhall Bridge Road, London, England SW1V 2SA.

MANUFACTURED IN THE UNITED STATES OF AMERICA
10 9 8 7 6 5 4 3 2 1

Contents

Maps and Plans

Foreword

We wish to express our gratitude to those who helped prepare this guide: the Canadian Consulate General office in New York, particularly Lois Gerber and Barbara Cartwright; the Montréal Convention and Tourism Bureau; the Québec Government Ministry of Tourism, particularly Brian LeCompte, Pauline Roy, and Manon Lefebvre.

While every care has been taken to ensure the accuracy of the information in this guide, the passage of time will always bring change, and consequently, the publisher cannot accept responsibility for errors that may occur.

All prices and opening times are based on information supplied to us at press time. Hours and admission fees may change, however, and the prudent traveler will avoid inconvenience by calling ahead.

Fodor's wants to hear about your travel experiences, both pleasant and unpleasant. When a hotel or restaurant fails to live up to its billing, let us know and we will investigate the complaint and revise our entries where the facts warrant it. Send your letters to the editors of Fodor's Travel Publications, 201 East 50th Street, New York, NY 10022.

Highlights '95 and Fodor's Choice

Highlights '95

Montréal Montréal's first government-run casino, opened in October 1994, is located on Ile Notre-Dame in the former Palais de la Civilisation, the site of the French pavilion during Expo '67. The casino, a success from the start, cost more than $80 million to set up, and features 65 blackjack, mini-baccarat, and roulette tables; 1,200 slot machines; and a Keno betting room with a draw every five minutes. The casino attracts an average of 10,000 people daily, more on weekends, and houses a gourmet restaurant, Nuances. Further additions are planned for 1995.

Québec City In 1995, Québec City will step back 1,000 years in time to celebrate Médiévales de Québec—a colorful, animated five-day festival in mid-August. Hundreds of actors dressed in period costumes—as troubadours, warriors, artisans, and the like—will invade the Vieille Capitale, and activities will take place at 20 sites throughout the city. A cavalcade will involve some 250 people on horseback who will descend upon Québec from as far as Boston, Massachusetts. This will be the city's second time hosting the festival, which occurs annually, alternating between Québec City and Dinan, France. The event takes place August 9th–13th.

Due to the recession, Québec City saw little development during the past few years, but the few well-invested changes that did occur will grace the city for many years to come. The Château Frontenac—the city's landmark castle hotel—renovated all guest rooms and built a new wing (which includes a health spa) in preparation for its 100th birthday celebration in 1993. And the Capitole, a turn-of-the-century theater that reopened its doors in late 1992 after 20 years in ruin, is more successful than many people had anticipated: Big names like B.B. King, Kenny Rogers, and Québec's own Céline Dion have packed the spot since its opening, and more are expected for 1995.

Fodor's Choice

No two people will agree on what makes a perfect vacation, but it's fun and helpful to know what others think. We hope you'll have a chance to experience some of Fodor's Choices yourself in Montréal and Québec. For detailed information about each entry, refer to the appropriate chapter.

Montréal

Attractions

Pointe-à-Callière Museum of Archaeology and History

Montréal Museum of Fine Arts

Casino de Montréal

Shopping

Place Montréal Trust

Rue Faubourg Ste-Catherine

Notre-Dame Ouest for antiques

Marché aux puces (flea market), Vieux-Montréal

Les Promenades de la Cathédrale

Cultural Events

International Jazz Festival

L'Orchestre Symphonique de Montréal

Juste Pour Rire (Just for Laughs) Festival

Restaurants

Les Mignardises (*$$$$*)

Les Trois Tilleuls, Montérégie (*$$$$*)

Milos (*$$$$*)

Hotels

Le Westin Mont-Royal (*$$$$*)

Ritz-Carlton (*$$$$*)

Hôtel de la Montagne (*$$$*)

Château Versailles (*$$*)

Québec City

Attractions

Château Frontenac

Citadelle

Musée de la Civilisation

Shopping

Marché du Vieux-Port

La Trois Colombes, Inc.

Quartier Petit-Champlain

Cultural Events

Bibliothèque Gabrielle-Roy

Grand Théâtre de Québec

Le Théâtre Capitole

Restaurants À la Table de Serge Bruyère (*$$$$*)

Aux Anciens Canadiens (*$$$*)

L'Echaudée (*$$*)

Chez Temporel (*$*)

Hotels Hilton International Québec (*$$$$*)

Manoir d'Auteuil (*$$$*)

L'Auberge du Quartier (*$$*)

Montréal and Québec City

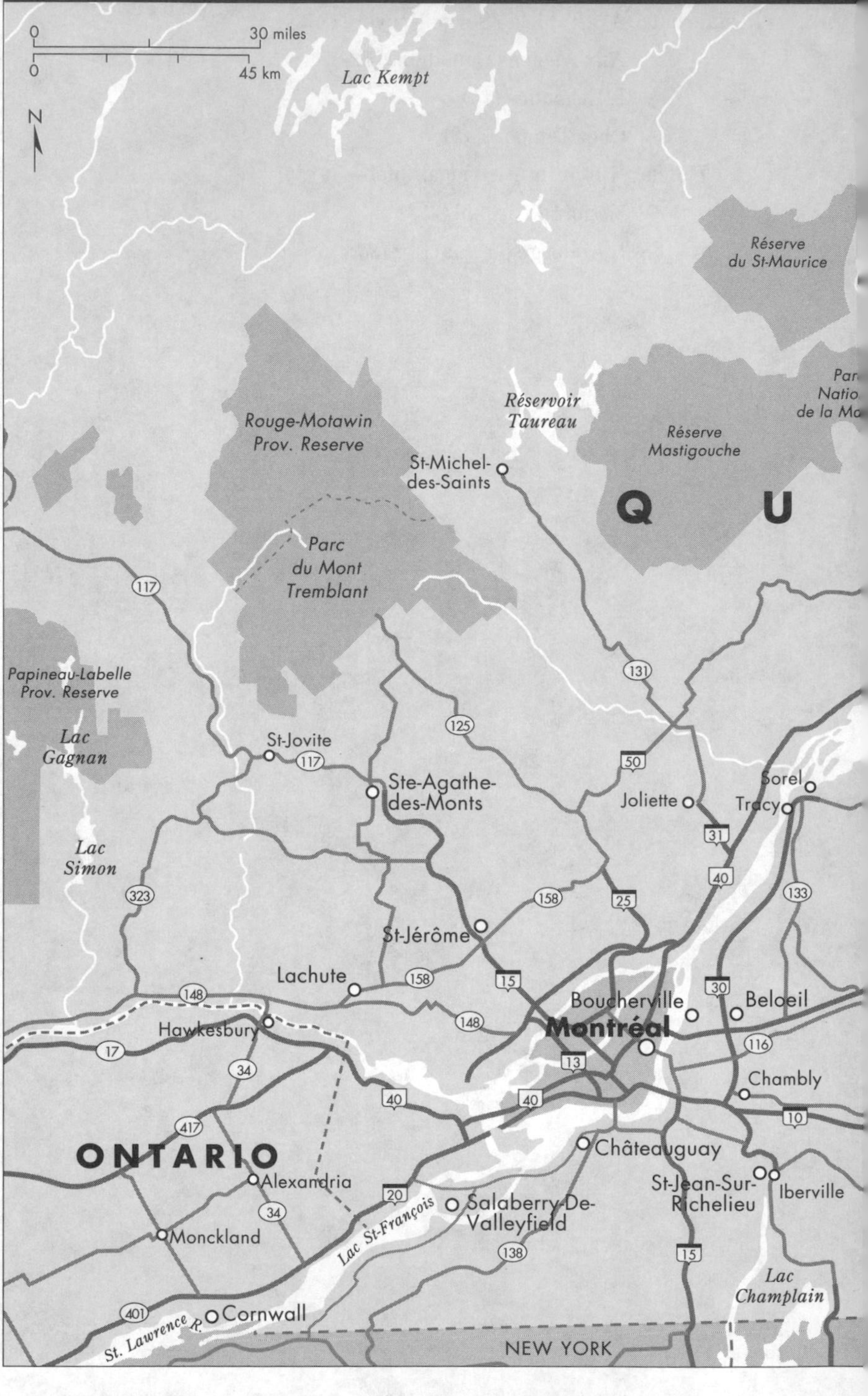
0
30 miles
0
45 km
N
Lac Kempt
Réserve du St-Maurice
Réservoir Taureau
Rouge-Motawin Prov. Reserve
St-Michel-des-Saints
Réserve Mastigouche
Par Natio de la Ma
Q U
Parc du Mont Tremblant
117
131
Papineau-Labelle Prov. Reserve
Lac Gagnan
125
St-Jovite
117
50
Ste-Agathe-des-Monts
Joliette
Sorel
Tracy
31
Lac Simon
40
323
158
25
133
St-Jérôme
Lachute
158
15
30
148
Boucherville
Beloeil
Hawkesbury
148
Montréal
17
116
34
13
Chambly
40
40
10
417
Châteauguay
ONTARIO
Alexandria
St-Jean-Sur-Richelieu
Iberville
20
Salaberry-De-Valleyfield
34
Lac St-François
Monckland
138
15
Lac Champlain
401
Cornwall
St. Lawrence R.
NEW YORK

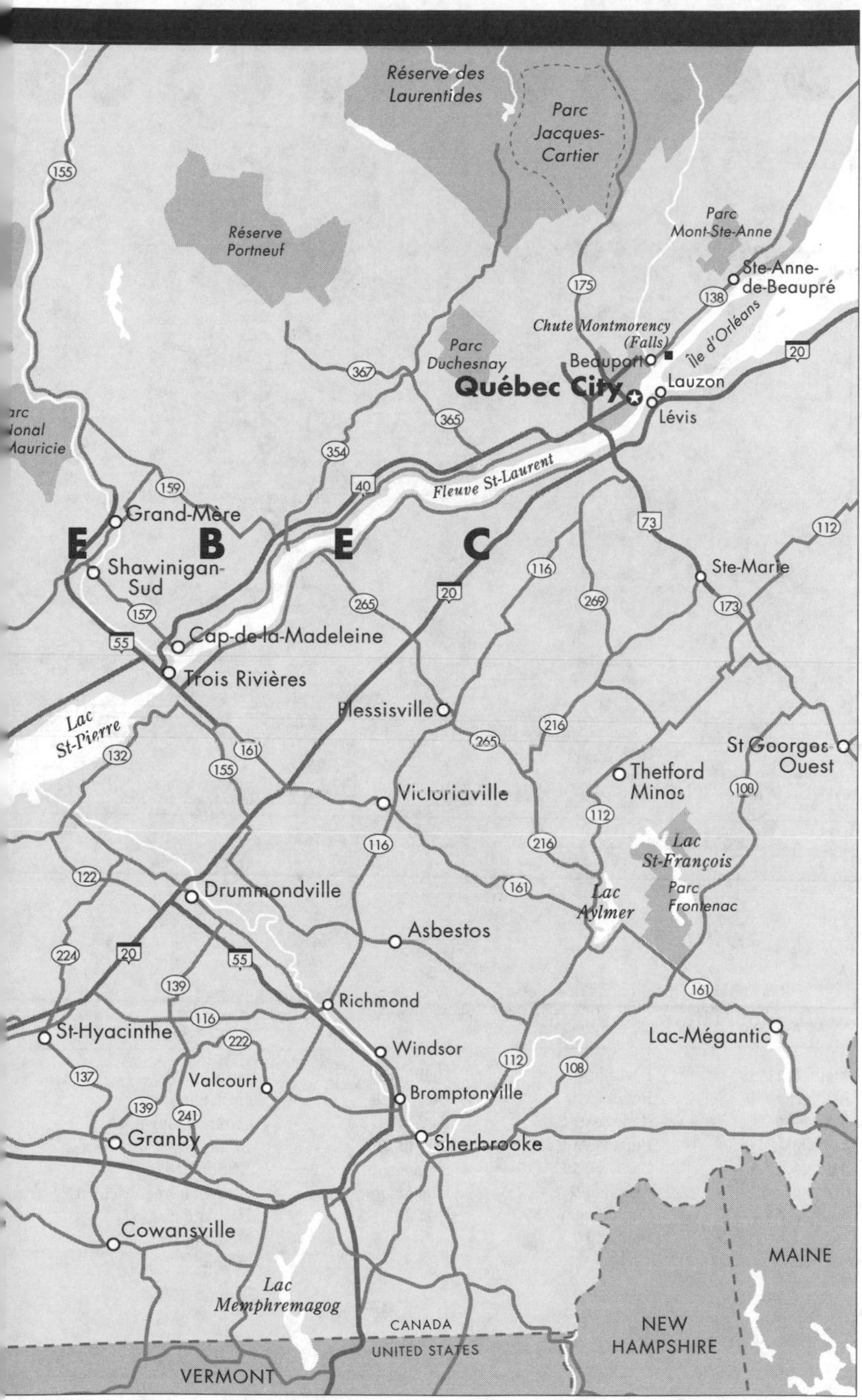
Réserve des Laurentides
Parc Jacques-Cartier
Réserve Portneuf
Parc Mont-Ste-Anne
Ste-Anne-de-Beaupré
Chute Montmorency (Falls)
Île d'Orléans
Parc Duchesnay
Beauport
Québec City
Lauzon
Lévis
Parc National Mauricie
Fleuve St-Laurent
Grand-Mère
Shawinigan-Sud
Cap-de-la-Madeleine
Trois Rivières
Ste-Marie
Plessisville
Lac St-Pierre
St Georges Ouest
Thetford Mines
Victoriaville
Lac St-François
Parc Frontenac
Lac Aylmer
Drummondville
Asbestos
Richmond
Lac-Mégantic
St-Hyacinthe
Windsor
Valcourt
Bromptonville
Granby
Sherbrooke
Cowansville
MAINE
Lac Memphremagog
CANADA
UNITED STATES
NEW HAMPSHIRE
VERMONT

World Time Zones

Numbers below vertical bands relate each zone to Greenwich Mean Time (0 hrs.). Local times frequently differ from these general indications, as indicated by light-face numbers on map.

Algiers, **29**
Anchorage, **3**
Athens, **41**
Auckland, **1**
Baghdad, **46**
Bangkok, **50**
Beijing, **54**

Berlin, **34**
Bogotá, **19**
Budapest, **37**
Buenos Aires, **24**
Caracas, **22**
Chicago, **9**
Copenhagen, **33**
Dallas, **10**

Delhi, **48**
Denver, **8**
Djakarta, **53**
Dublin, **26**
Edmonton, **7**
Hong Kong, **56**
Honolulu, **2**

Istanbul, **40**
Jerusalem, **42**
Johannesburg, **44**
Lima, **20**
Lisbon, **28**
London (Greenwich), **27**
Los Angeles, **6**
Madrid, **38**
Manila, **57**

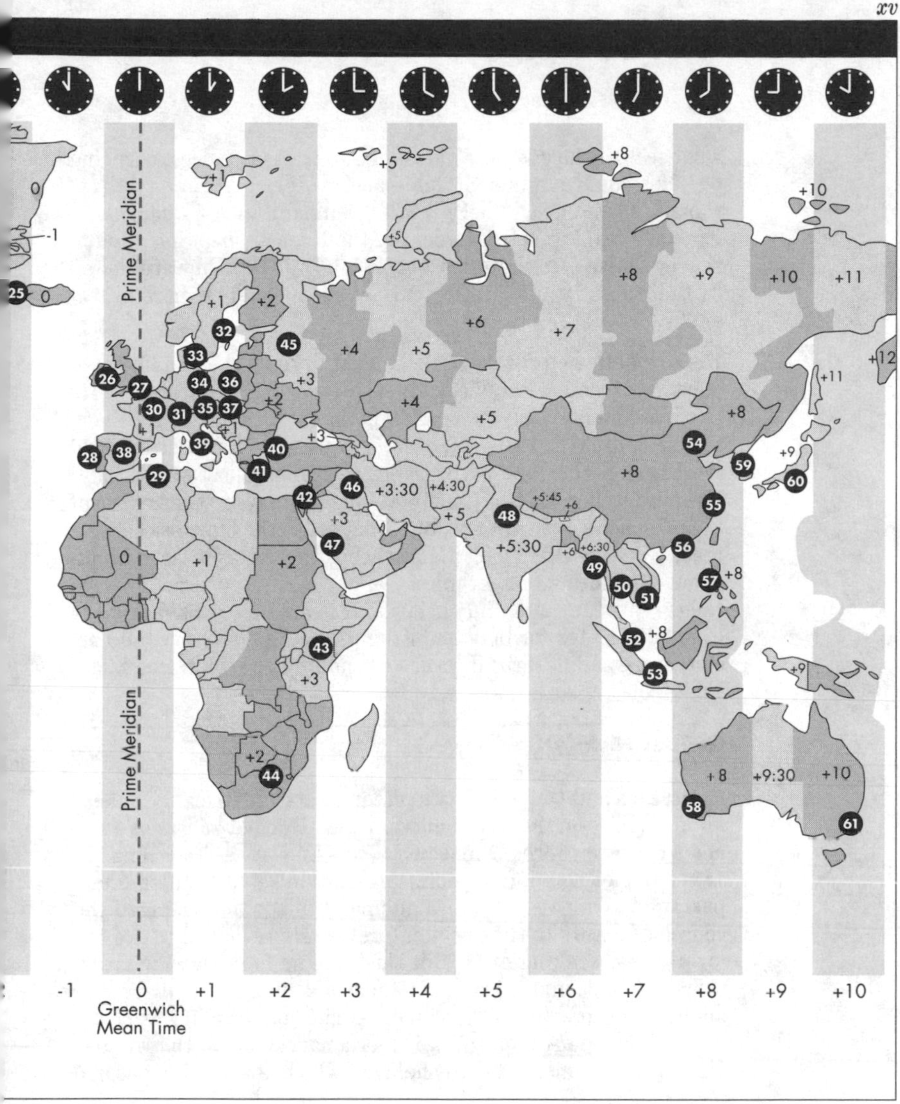

Mecca, **47**
Mexico City, **12**
Miami, **18**
Montréal, **15**
Moscow, **45**
Nairobi, **43**
New Orleans, **11**
New York City, **16**

Ottawa, **14**
Paris, **30**
Perth, **58**
Reykjavík, **25**
Rio de Janeiro, **23**
Rome, **39**
Saigon (Ho Chi Minh City), **51**

San Francisco, **5**
Santiago, **21**
Seoul, **59**
Shanghai, **55**
Singapore, **52**
Stockholm, **32**
Sydney, **61**
Tokyo, **60**

Toronto, **13**
Vancouver, **4**
Vienna, **35**
Warsaw, **36**
Washington, D.C., **17**
Yangon, **49**
Zürich, **31**

Introduction

Québec is the largest and oldest of Canada's provinces, covering 600,000 square miles of land and waterways, one-sixth of Canada's land. Of Québec's 6,627,000 inhabitants, 5,300,000 are French-speaking, 81.3 percent of the French-speaking population of Canada. Although Montréal and Québec City are linked by their history and culture, no two cities could be more different.

History buffs and romantics will want to roam the winding cobblestone streets of Québec City, the capital of the province. Its French colonial history is evident in its architecture, silver-spired churches, and grand cathedrals. In Montréal the Old World meets the New with French bistros and postmodern skyscrapers vying for the limelight. Québec may be the center of the province's government, but Montréal is the business center. Much like New York City, Montréal has attracted a large immigrant population. Its ethnic diversity can be seen in its wide range of restaurants and enclaves. It is not only considered the Canadian center for book publishing, the film industry, and architecture and design; it is also considered the unrivaled bagel capital of Canada.

Québec History

Montréal's and Québec City's histories are inextricably linked. Montréal sits on the site that was called Hochelaga by the Indians who lived there. Québec City was known as Stadacona. In 1534 Jacques Cartier, a young sea captain setting out to find a passage to China, instead came upon Canada and changed the course of events in that region forever. He returned in the following year seeking gold. But this time he found a wide river, sailed down it, and arrived at Stadacona, an Indian village. He admired the location of the village perched on the cliffs overlooking a *kebec*, the Algonquin word for a narrowing of the waters. He continued along to Hochelaga, which eventually became Montréal.

More than 1,000 surprised Iroquois greeted the Frenchman. It would take two centuries of fierce battles before the French made peace with the Iroquois people. Perhaps the violent meeting of the French explorers and the Canadian natives discouraged the French, because no more exploring was done until 1608, when Samuel de Champlain established a French settlement at Stadacona.

Throughout the 17th century, the French opened up Canada and some of what became the United States, using both Montréal and Québec City as convenient trading posts and strategic military locations. They discovered and mapped a vast area stretching from Hudson Bay to the Gulf of Mexico. *Coureurs de bois* (fur traders), missionaries, and explorers staked out this immense new territory.

During this time, France tamed and populated its new colonies across the ocean with the firm hand of *seigneurs,* aristocrats to whom the king distributed land. In turn, the seigneurs swore loyalty to the king, served in the military, maintained manor houses, ceded land to tenant farmers, and established courts to settle local grievances. Seigneuries were close knit, with sons and fathers able to establish farms within the same territory. In addition, the Roman Catholic Church's influence was strong in these communities. Priests and nuns acted as doctors, educators, and overseers of business arrangements among the farmers and between French-speaking traders and English-speaking merchants. An important doctrine of the church in Québec was *survivance,* the survival of the French people and their culture. Couples were told to have large families, and they did. Ten to 12 children in a family was the norm, not the exception.

The Seven Years' War between England and France marked the second half of the 18th century. In 1756, France sent the commander Louis-Joseph, Marquis de Montcalm, to secure the frontier of New France and consolidate the new territory of Louisiana. Although Montcalm, leading a French and Indian expedition, was able to secure the Ohio Valley, turn Lake Ontario into a French waterway, and secure Fort Carillon (now Ticonderoga) on Lake Champlain, the tides began to turn in 1759 with the arrival of a large British fleet to the shores of Québec City, commanded by James Wolfe.

After bombarding the city for several weeks, Wolfe and his 4,000 men decided the fate of Canada in a vicious battle that lasted 20 minutes. The British won, but both leaders were mortally wounded. Today, in Québec City's Governors Park, there is a unique memorial to these two army men—the only statue in the world commemorating both victor and vanquished of the same battle. A year later the French regained the city of Québec, but they were soon forced to withdraw when English ships arrived with supplies and reinforcements. The French were driven back to Montréal, where a large British army defeated them in 1760. In 1763, the Treaty of Paris ceded Canada to Britain. France preferred to give up the new country to preserve its sugar islands, which it believed were of greater value. At that time, all the French civil administrators, as well as the principal landowners and businessmen, returned to France. Of the leaders of New France, only the Roman Catholic clergy remained, and they became more important to the peasant farmers than ever before.

Québec's trouble was in no way over with the Treaty of Paris. In 1774, the British Parliament passed the Québec Act. It extended Québec's borders, hemming in the northernmost of the independence-minded British colonies to the south. The Roman Catholic Church's authority and the seigneurial landlord system were maintained under the act, leaving traditional

Québecois life fairly intact. But the American colonists were furious with the passing of the Québec Act and hoped to incite a revolt in Québec against British rule. After the American War of Independence broke out in 1775, Generals Richard Montgomery and Benedict Arnold led American troops that took over Montréal and set up headquarters in the Château de Ramezay, home of the British governor (and now a museum). The Americans then attempted to capture Québec City, but they had misunderstood the Catholic Royalist heritage of the Canadians. Québecois did not share the Americans' love of independence and republicanism. Rather than incite a revolt, the Americans managed to draw the Canadians and British together. The Canadians stood with the British in Québec City to fight off the invasions. Montgomery died in the attack and Arnold fled. The following year, British forces arrived and recaptured Montréal.

The Creation of Upper and Lower Canada

A number of British and American settlers left Albany in New York and settled in Montréal. They began to press the authorities, as did other British colonists west of the Ottawa River, to introduce representative government.

The British responded with the Constitutional Act of 1791, which divided Québec into two provinces, Upper and Lower Canada, west and east of the Ottawa. The act provided for nominated legislative councils and elected assemblies, like those that had existed in the English colonies. The first election was held the following year.

Elected government was a novelty to the French Canadians, who had never known democracy and had been shielded from the French Revolution of 1789. But democracy suited them well, and before long there was a rising demand for more rights. Heading the movement for greater rights was Louis Joseph Papineau, who was also leader of the French-speaking majority in the legislative assembly. He demanded that the English *château clique*, which made up the governor's council, should be subject to elections as the assembly was. In 1834, he and his associates issued a long list of grievances, "The 92 Resolutions." Papineau lost the support of many of his own associates, and that of the leaders of the church. The British responded with their own "10 resolutions" and refused elections to the council. That same year crops failed and unemployment spread. General unrest led to clashes between the English and young French *Patriotes* in Montréal. Soon a general insurrection broke out. Patriote irregulars fought British troops at St. Charles and St. Eustache near Montréal.

In spite of bad feelings, the upheavals led to major legislative changes in 1841. England passed the Act of Union, which produced a united Canada. Québec was now known as Canada East, while Upper Canada became Canada West. Each sent an equal number of representatives to the elected assembly; the governor was not responsible to the assembly, but rather to the Colonial Office in London. This continued to bridle both English and French members of the assembly.

The Growth of Montréal

Toward the end of the 1700s, the fur trade declined so much that Montréal almost faced economic disaster. But in Europe the demand for lumber increased, and Québec had lots of it. As a result, Montréal became the major trading center in British North America, helped by the fact that New York and New England had seceded from Britain.

Then the flood of immigration from Britain started, so much so that by the mid-1800s, Montréal was transformed into a predominantly English city. About 100,000 Irish immigrants came to work in Montréal's flour mills, breweries, and shipyards, which had sprung up on the shores of the river and the Lachine Canal, begun in 1821. By 1861, working-class Irish made up a third of Montréal's population. Within the next 80 years, Polish, Hungarian, Italian, Chinese, Ukrainian, Greek, Armenian, Spanish, Czech, Japanese, German, and Portuguese immigrants, escaping from poverty and political hardships, arrived by the thousands, seeking freedom in the New World. By 1867, more than a half-million immigrants had arrived from Europe, pushing Canada's population to more than 2 million. The demand for union came from all the provinces of British North America to increase trade and economic prosperity, to increase their military strength in case of attack from the United States, to create a government capable of securing and developing the Northwest (the vast lands west of Canada West), and to make possible the building of a railway that would contribute to the realization of all these ambitions.

The Dominion of Canada was created on July 1, 1867, by an act of the British Parliament, known as the British North America (BNA) Act. It divided the province of Canada into Québec and Ontario and brought in Nova Scotia and New Brunswick. Manitoba joined in 1870, British Columbia in 1871, Prince Edward Island in 1873, Alberta and Saskatchewan in 1905, and Newfoundland in 1949. The BNA Act also enshrined French as an official language. The province of Québec, like the other provinces, was given far-reaching responsibilities in social and civil affairs.

The Conscription Crisis

The entente between the French and the English in Canada was viable until World War I strained it. At the outbreak of the war, the two groups felt equally supportive of the two European motherlands. Many volunteered, and a totally French regiment, the Royal 22nd, was created. But two things ended the camaraderie.

On the battlefields of Europe, Canadians, along with Australians, formed the shock troops of the British Empire and died horribly, by the thousands. More than 60,000 Canadians died in the war, a huge loss for a country of 7½ million. In 1915, Ontario passed Regulation 17, severely restricting the use of French in its schools. It translated into an anti-French stand and created open hostility. The flow of French Canadians into the army became a trickle. Then Prime Minister Robert Borden ordered the conscription of childless males to reinforce the ailing Canadian corps. A wider conscription law loomed in Ottawa, resulting in an outcry in Québec led by nationalist, journalist, and politician Henri Bourassa (grandson of patriot Louis Joseph Papineau). The nationalists claimed that conscription was a device to diminish the French-speaking population. When, in 1917, conscription did become law, Québec was ideologically isolated from the rest of Canada.

The crisis led to the formation of the Union Nationale provincial party in 1936, initially a reformist party. Under its leader Maurice Duplessis, it held control until 1960 and was characterized by lavish patronage, strong-arm methods, fights with Ottawa, and nationalistic sloganeering. Duplessis believed that to survive, Québecois should remain true to their traditions. Duplessis deterred industrial expansion in Québec, which went to Ontario, and slowed the growth of reformist ideas until his death and the flowering of the Quiet Revolution.

The Quiet Revolution

The population of Québec had grown to 6 million, but the province had fallen economically and politically behind Canada's English majority. Under Duplessis and the Union Nationale party, French-language schools and universities were supervised by the church and offered courses in the humanities rather than in science and economics. Francophones (French-speaking Québeckers) were denied any chance of real business education unless they attended English institutions. As a result, few of them held top positions in industry or finance. On a general cultural basis, the country overwhelmingly reflected Anglo-Saxon attitudes rather than an Anglo-French mixture.

In 1960, the Liberal Party under Jean Lesage swept to power. Though initially occupied with social reform, it soon turned to economic matters. In 1962, Lesage's minister of natural resources, René Lévesque, called for the nationalization of most of the electricity industry, which up to then had been in private hands. This was the first step toward economic independence for Québec. The financiers of Montréal's St. James Street, the heart of the business district, opposed it, but ordinary Québecois were enthusiastic. In 1965, Lévesque's ministry established a provincial mining company to explore and develop the province's mineral resources.

Meanwhile U.S. capital poured into Québec, as it did everywhere else in Canada. With it came American cultural influence, which increased Québecois' expectations of a high standard of living. English-speaking citizens remained in firm control of the large national corporations headquartered in Montréal. Indeed it became clear that they had no intention of handing power over to the French. Few Francophones were promoted to executive status. Successive provincial governments became increasingly irritated by the lack of progress.

The discontent led to a dramatic radicalization of Québec politics. A new separatist movement arose that hoped to make Québec a distinct state by breaking away from the rest of the country. The most extreme faction of the movement was the Front de Libération du Québec (FLQ). It backed its demands with bombs and arson, culminating in the kidnapping and murder of Québec Cabinet Minister Pierre Laporte in October 1970.

The federal government in Ottawa, under Prime Minister Pierre Elliott Trudeau, himself a French-speaking Québecois, imposed the War Measures Act. This permitted the police to break up civil disorders and arrest hundreds of suspects and led to the arrest of the murderers of Laporte.

The political crisis calmed down, but it left behind vibrations that affected all of the country. The federal government redoubled its efforts to correct the worst grievances of the French Canadians. Federal funds flowed into French schools outside Québec to support French-Canadian culture in the other provinces. French Canadians were appointed to senior positions in the government and crown corporations. The federal government dramatically increased its bilingual services to the population.

In Québec from the mid-1970s, the Liberal government and then the Parti Québecois, elected in 1976 and headed by René Lévesque (who had left the Liberal party in 1967 and helped found the Parti Québecois), replaced the English language with the French language in Québec's economic life. In 1974, French was adopted as the official language of Québec. This promoted French-language instruction in the schools and made French the language of business and government. The Parti Québecois followed up in 1977 with the Charter of the French Language, which established deadlines and fines to help enforce the program to make French the chief language in all areas of Québec life. The charter brought French into the workplace; it also accelerated a trend for English companies to relocate their headquarters outside Québec, particularly in and near Toronto. The provincial government is working to attract new investment to Québec to replace those lost jobs and revenues.

The Parti Québecois proposed to go further by taking Québec out of the confederation, provided that economic ties with the rest of Canada could be maintained. Leaders in the other provinces announced that such a scheme would not be acceptable. A referendum was held in 1980 for the authority to negotiate a sovereignty association with the rest of Canada. Québec voters rejected the proposal by a wide margin. In 1985, the Parti Québecois government was defeated at the polls by the Liberal Party, headed by Robert Bourassa.

Bourassa was committed to keeping Québec within Canada until the collapse of the Meech-Lake Accord, a three-year attempt to integrate Québec into the Canadian constitution, in 1990. Bourassa then vowed to put the interests of the province before those of the country, even if this meant separation. The Québec Bélanger-Campeau commission, set up to study the future of Québec in Canada, concluded that the province should be recognized as a "sovereign state," although it will remain part of the Canadian Federation given certain conditions. However, the federal and provincial governments did not reach an agreement, so the debate has subsided for the moment. Most likely the issue will be re-ignited before 1994, the deadline for the next provincial election.

The People of Québec

Although French is the official language of Québec, Québec also has a large English-speaking population (676,000), particularly in Montréal, the Ottawa Valley, and l'Estrie. They are descendants of those English, Irish, and Scots who landed here after the conquest of New France, and of immigrants from other nations whose main language is English. English-speaking Montréalers founded and financed a variety of such great institutions as universities, museums, hospitals, orchestras, and social agencies, as well as a number of national and multinational corporations in the worlds of banking and finance, transportation, natural resources, and distilled spirits.

Half a million immigrants from Europe, Asia, Latin America, and the Caribbean also live in Québec. People from 80 different countries have made their new homes in the province. In proportion to its population, this land, along with the rest of Canada, has welcomed the greatest number of fugitives from political and economic unrest over the past 20 years. Between 1968 and 1982, for example, 60,000 immigrants arrived from Czechoslovakia, Haiti, Uganda, Lebanon, Chile, and Southeast Asia. A much larger wave of immigrants—from Italy, Greece, and Eastern Europe—had arrived following World War II.

The native people of Québec number more than 40,000. Nearly 30,000 of Québec's Amerindians live in villages within reserved territories in various parts of Québec, where they have exclusive fishing and hunting rights. The Inuit people (Eskimo) number over 5,000 and live in villages scattered along the shores of James Bay, Hudson Bay, Hudson Strait, and Ungava Bay. They have abandoned their igloos for prefabricated houses, but they still make their living by trapping and hunting.

The French Canadians of Québec, often called Latins of the North, have an ever-sparkling joie de vivre, especially at the more than 400 festivals and carnivals they celebrate each year. Even the long winter does not dampen their good spirits. The largest festival splash is on June 24, which was originally the Feast of Saint John the Baptist. Now it is called La Fête

Nationale (National Day). Everyone celebrates the long weekend by building roaring bonfires and dancing in the streets.

February brings Québec City's Winter Carnival, a two-week-long noisy and exciting party. Chicoutimi also has a winter carnival in which residents of the city celebrate and dress up in period costumes. In September international canoe races are held in Mauricie, and in August an international swim gets under way across Lac-Saint-Jean. Trois-Rivières celebrates the summer with automobile races through its streets, and Valleyfield is the scene of international regattas.

1 Essential Information

Before You Go

Government Tourist Offices

In the United States **Tourisme Québec** (C.P. 979, Montréal, Qué. HC3 2W3, tel. 800/363–7777).

U.S. Government Travel Briefings The U.S. Department of State's **Citizens Emergency Center** issues Consular Information Sheets, which cover crime, security, and health risks as well as embassy locations, entry requirements, currency regulations, and other routine matters. For the latest information, stop in at any passport office, consulate, or embassy; call the interactive hotline (tel. 202/647–5225); or, with your PC's modem, tap into the Bureau of Consular Affairs' computer bulletin board (tel. 202/647–9225).

In the United Kingdom Contact the **Canadian High Commission Department of Tourism,** Canada House, Trafalgar Square, London SW1Y 5BJ, tel. 071/258-6346; or **Québec Tourism** (59 Pall Mall, London SW1Y 5JH, tel. 071/930–8314).

Tours and Packages

Should you buy your travel arrangements to Canada packaged or do it yourself? There are advantages either way. Buying packaged arrangements saves you money, particularly if you can find a program that includes exactly the features you want. You also get a pretty good idea of what your trip will cost from the outset. Generally, you have two options: fully escorted tours and independent packages.

Escorted tours are most often via motorcoach, with a tour director in charge. They're ideal if you don't mind having limited free time and traveling with strangers. Your baggage is handled, your time rigorously scheduled, and most meals planned. Escorted tours are therefore the most hassle-free way to see a destination, as well as generally the least expensive. Independent packages allow plenty of flexibility. They normally include airline travel and hotels, with certain options available, such as sightseeing, car rental, and excursions. Independent packages are usually more expensive than escorted tours, but your time is your own.

Travel agents are your best source of recommendations for both tours and packages. They will have the largest selection, and the cost to you is the same as buying direct. Whatever program you ultimately choose, be sure to find out exactly what is included: taxes, tips, transfers, meals, baggage handling, ground transportation, entertainment, excursions, sports or recreation (and rental equipment if necessary). Ask about the level of hotel used, its location, the size of its rooms, the kind of beds, and the amenities, such as pool, room service, or programs for children, if they're important to you. Find out the operator's cancellation penalties. Nearly everyone charges them, and the only way to avoid it is to buy trip-cancellation insurance (*see* Trip Insurance, *below*). Also ask about the single supplement, a surcharge assessed to solo travelers. Some operators do not make you pay it if you agree to be matched up with a roommate of the same sex, even if one is not found by departure time. Remember that a program that has features you won't use, whether for rental sporting equipment or discounted museum admissions, may not be the most cost-wise choice for you.

Fully Escorted Tours

Escorted tours are usually sold in three categories: deluxe, first-class, and tourist or budget class. Some operators specialize in one category, while others offer a range.

Top operators include **Maupintour** (Box 807, Lawrence, KS 66044, tel. 913/843–1211 or 800/255–4266) and **Tauck Tours** (11 Wilton Rd., Westport, CT 06881, tel. 203/226–6911 or 800/468–2825) in the deluxe category; **Brendan Tours** (15137 Califa St., Van Nuys, CA 91411, tel. 818/985–9696 or 800/421–8446), **Domenico Tours** (751 Broadway, Bayonne, NJ 07002, tel. 201/823–8687 or 800/554–8687), **Gadabout Tours** (700 E. Tahquitz Way, Palm Springs, CA 92262, tel. 619/325–5556 or 800/952–5068), **Globus** (5301 South Federal Circle, Littleton, CO 80123, tel. 303/797–2800 or 800/221–0090), and **Princess Tours** (2815 Second Ave., Suite 400, Seattle, WA 98121, tel. 206/728–4215 or 800/426–0442) in the first-class category. In the budget category try **Cosmos Tourama,** a sister company of Globus (*see above*).

Most itineraries are jam-packed with sightseeing, so you see a lot in a short amount of time (usually one place per day). To judge just how fast-paced the tour is, review the itinerary carefully. If you are in a different hotel each night, you will be getting up early each day to head out, travel to your next destination, do some sightseeing, have dinner, and go to bed, then you'll start all over again. If you want some free time, make sure it's mentioned in the tour brochure; if you want to be escorted to every meal, confirm that any tour you consider does that. Also, when comparing programs, be sure to find out if the motorcoach is air-conditioned and has a rest room on board. Make your selection based on price and stops on the itinerary.

Independent Packages

Independent packages are offered by airlines, tour operators who may also do escorted programs, and any number of other companies from large, established firms to small, new entrepreneurs. Contact **Air Canada** (tel. 800/776–3000), **American Airlines Fly Away Vacations** (tel. 800/321–2121), **Delta Dream Vacations** (tel. 800/872–7786), **Supercities** (139 Main St., Cambridge, MA 02142, tel. 617/621–9988 or 800/333–1234), **United Vacations** (tel. 800/328–0877), and **USAir Vacations** (tel. 800/428–4322).

Their programs come in a wide range of prices based on levels of luxury and options—in addition to hotel and airfare, sightseeing, car rental, transfers, admission to local attractions, and other extras. Note that when pricing different packages, it sometimes pays to purchase the same arrangements separately, as when a rock-bottom promotional airfare is being offered, for example. Again, base your choice on what's available at your budget for the destinations you want to visit.

Special-Interest Travel

Special-interest programs may be fully escorted or independent. Some require a certain amount of expertise, but most are for the average traveler with an interest and are usually hosted by experts in the subject matter. When the program is escorted, it enjoys the advantages and disadvantages of all escorted programs; because your fellow travelers are apt to be passionate or knowledgeable about the subject, they can prove as enjoyable a part of your travel experience as the destination itself. The price range is wide, but the cost is usually higher—sometimes a lot higher—than for ordinary escorted tours and packages because of the expert guiding and special activities.

Bicycling

Classic Adventures (Box 153-P, Hamlin, NY 14464, tel. 716/964–8488 or 800/777–8090) has hiking and biking tours to Québec.

Canoeing **Battenkill Canoe, Ltd.** (Box 65, Arlington, VT 05250, tel. 802/362–2800) tours offer paddling in whitewater or more relaxed scenic trips, with lodgings at country inns or secluded riverside campsites throughout eastern Canada.

Fall Foliage Contact **Domenico Tours** (*see* Fully Escorted Tours, *above*), **Parker Tours** (218–14 Northern Blvd., Bayside, NY 11361, tel. 718/428–7800 or 800/833–9600), or **Trieloff Tours** (24301 El Toro Rd., Suite 140, Laguna Hills, CA 92653, tel. 800/248–6877 or 800/432–7125 in CA).

Skiing **Air Canada** (*see above*) and **United Vacations Ski Packages** (tel. 800/525–2052) have skiing programs to both eastern and Rockies resort areas.

When to Go

When to go will depend on your itinerary and your interests. Québec and Ontario have hot, steamy summers and severe winters, with snow lasting from mid-December to mid-March. The whole of eastern Canada enjoys blooming springs and brilliant autumns.

Climate The following are average daily maximum and minimum temperatures for Montréal and Québec City.

Montréal

Jan.	23F	– 5C	**May**	65F	18C	**Sept.**	68F	20C
	9	–13		48	9		53	12
Feb.	25F	– 4C	**June**	74F	23C	**Oct.**	57F	14C
	12	–11		58	14		43	6
Mar.	36F	2C	**July**	79F	26C	**Nov.**	42F	6C
	23	– 5		63	17		32	0
Apr.	52F	11C	**Aug.**	76F	24C	**Dec.**	27F	– 3C
	36	2		61	16		16	– 9

Québec City

Jan.	20F	– 7C	**May**	62F	17C	**Sept.**	66F	19C
	6	–14		43	6		49	9
Feb.	23F	– 5C	**June**	72F	22C	**Oct.**	53F	12C
	8	–13		53	12		39	4
Mar.	33F	1C	**July**	78F	26C	**Nov.**	39F	4C
	19	– 7		58	14		28	– 2
Apr.	47F	8C	**Aug.**	75F	24C	**Dec.**	24F	– 4C
	32	0		56	13		12	–11

Information Sources For current weather conditions for cities in the United States and abroad, plus the local time and helpful travel tips, call the **Weather Channel Connection** (tel. 900/932–8437; 95¢ per minute) from a touch-tone phone.

Government Holidays

Though banks, schools, and government offices close for national holidays, many stores remain open. As in the United States, certain holidays are observed on the Monday nearest the actual date, creating a long weekend.

National National holidays for 1995 are: New Year's Day (January 1), Good Friday (April 14), Easter Monday (April 17), Victoria Day (May 22), Canada Day (July 1), Labor Day (September 4), Thanksgiving (October 9), Remembrance Day (November 11), Christmas (December 25), and Boxing Day (December 26).

Provincial St. Jean Baptiste Day (June 24).

Festivals and Seasonal Events

You're likely to find a festival or special event whenever you travel to Montréal and Québec City, in winter and summer alike. Contact tourist boards to see what's in the offing for the time you'll be visiting, and inquire about any advance tickets you may need. The following are some of the top events.

January: La Fête des Neiges winter carnival in Montréal.
February: Winter Carnival, in Québec City, is an 11-day festival of winter sports competitions, ice-sculpture contests, and parades.
April: Sugaring-off parties throughout the province celebrate the beginning of the maple syrup season.
June: Molson Grand Prix, with some of the world's best drivers, takes place on the Gilles-Villeneuve Race Track, in Montréal; International Jazz Festival in Québec; International Children's Folklore Festival takes place in Beauport, Québec.
July: Festival International de Jazz de Montréal features more than 1,000 jazz musicians from all over the world for this 10-day series; Québec International Summer Festival offers entertainment in the streets and parks of old Québec City; Juste pour Rire (Just for Laughs) comedy festival features comics from around the world, in French and English; Drummondville World Folklore Festival brings troupes from more than 20 countries to perform in the streets and parks; Festival Orford features international artists performing at Orford Park's music center (through August); Matinée Ltd. International will spotlight best male tennis players in Montréal in 1995.
August: Montréal World Film Festival; Hot Air Balloon Festival in Saint-Jean-sur-Richelieu is the biggest gathering of hot air balloons in Canada.
September: Québec International Film Festival in Québec City.
October: Festival of Colors, throughout the province.

What to Pack

Clothing How you pack will depend on when you go and what you plan to do. Layering is the best defense against Canada's cold winters; a hat, scarf, and gloves are essential. For summer travel, loose-fitting natural-fiber clothes are best; bring a wool sweater and light jacket. If you're planning to spend time in Canada's larger cities, pack both casual clothes for day touring and more formal wear for evenings out. If your visit includes a stay at a large city hotel, bring a bathing suit in any season to take advantage of the indoor pool.

Miscellaneous If you plan on camping or hiking in the deep woods during the summer, particularly in northern Canada, insect repellent is a must, especially in June, which is blackfly season.

Bring an extra pair of eyeglasses or contact lenses. If you have a health problem that may require you to purchase a prescription drug, pack enough to last the duration of the trip, or have your doctor write a prescription using the drug's generic name, since brand names vary from country to country. And don't forget to pack a list of the addresses of offices that supply refunds for lost or stolen traveler's checks.

Luggage *Regulations* Free airline baggage allowances depend on the airline, the route, and the class of your ticket. In general, on domestic flights and on international flights between the United States and foreign destinations, you are entitled to check two bags—neither exceeding 62 inches, or 158 centimeters (length + width + height), or weighing more than 70 pounds (32 kilograms). A third piece may be brought aboard as a carryon; its total dimensions are generally limited to less than 45 inches (114 centimeters), so it will fit easily under the seat in front of you or in the overhead compartment. There are variations, so ask in advance. In the United States the Federal Aviation Administration (FAA) gives airlines broad latitude to limit carry-on allowances and tailor them to different aircraft and operational conditions. Charges for excess, oversize, or overweight pieces vary, so inquire before you pack.

Safeguarding Your Luggage Before leaving home, itemize your bags' contents and their worth in case they go astray. To minimize that risk, tag them inside and out with your name, address, and phone number. (If you use your home address, cover it so that potential thieves can't see it.) At check-in, make sure that the tag attached by baggage handlers bears the correct three-letter code for your destination. If your bags do not arrive with you, or if you detect damage, immediately file a written report with the airline before you leave the airport.

Money Matters

American money is readily accepted in much of Canada (especially in communities near the border), and traveler's checks and major U.S. credit cards are accepted in larger cities and resorts.

Traveler's Checks Traveler's checks are preferable in metropolitan centers, although you'll need cash in rural areas and small towns. The most widely recognized are **American Express, Citicorp, Diners Club, Thomas Cook,** and **Visa,** which are sold by major commercial banks. Both American Express and Thomas Cook issue checks that can be counter-signed and used by you or your traveling companion. Typically the issuing company or the bank at which you make your purchase charges 1% to 3% of the checks' face value as a fee. Some foreign banks charge as much as 20% of the face value as the fee for cashing travelers' checks in a foreign currency. Buy a few checks in small denominations to cash toward the end of your trip, so you won't be left with excess foreign currency. Record the numbers of checks as you spend them, and keep this list separate from the checks.

Currency Exchange Banks offer the most favorable exchange rates. If you use currency exchange booths at airports, rail and bus stations, hotels, stores, and privately run exchange firms, you'll typically get less favorable rates, but you may find the hours more convenient.

You can get good rates and avoid long lines at airport currency-exchange booths by getting a small amount of currency at **Thomas Cook Currency Services** (630 5th Ave., New York, NY 10111, tel. 212/757–6915 or 800/223–7373 for locations in major metropolitan areas throughout the U.S.) or **Ruesch International** (tel. 800/424–2923 for locations) before you depart. Check with your travel agent to be sure that the currency of the country you will be visiting can be imported.

Getting Money from Home

Cash Machines Many automated-teller machines (ATMs) are tied to such international networks as **Cirrus** and **Plus.** You can use your bank card at ATMs away from home to withdraw money from an account and get cash advances on a credit-card account if your card has been programmed with a personal identification number, or PIN. Check in advance on limits on withdrawals and cash advances within specified periods. Ask whether your bank-card or credit-card PIN number will need to be reprogrammed for use in the area you'll be visiting. Four digits are commonly used overseas. Note that Discover is accepted only in the United States. On cash advances you are charged interest from the day you receive the money from ATMs as well as from tellers. Although transaction fees for ATM withdrawals abroad will probably be higher than fees for withdrawals at home, Cirrus and Plus exchange rates tend to be good.

For specific Cirrus locations in the United States and Canada, call 800/424–7787 and press the area code and first three digits of the number you're calling from (or the calling area where you want an ATM).

Wiring Money You don't have to be a cardholder to send or receive a **MoneyGram from American Express** for up to $10,000. Go to a MoneyGram agent in retail and convenience stores and American Express travel offices, pay up to $1,000 with a credit card and anything over that in cash. You are allowed a free long-distance call to give the transaction code to your intended recipient, who needs only present identification and the reference number to the nearest MoneyGram agent to pick up the cash. MoneyGram agents are in more than 70 countries (call 800/926–9400 for locations). Fees range from 3% to 10%, depending on the amount and how you pay.

You can also use **Western Union.** To wire money, take either cash or a cashier's check to the nearest office or call and use your MasterCard or Visa. Money sent from the United States or Canada will be available for pickup at agent locations in Canada within minutes. Once the money is in the system it can be picked up at any one of 22,000 locations (call 800/325–6000 for the one nearest you).

Canadian Currency

The units of currency in Canada are the Canadian dollar (C$) and the cent, in almost the same denominations as U.S. currency ($2, $5, $10, $20, 1¢, 5¢, 10¢, 25¢, etc.)—the $1 bill is no longer used; instead it has been replaced by a $1 coin. The use of $2 paper currency is common here although rare in the United States. At press time the exchange rate was C$1.38 to US$1 and C$2.09 to £1. The Canadian dollar has decreased significantly in value relative to the U.S. dollar in recent months.

What It Will Cost

Throughout this guide, unless otherwise stated, prices are quoted in Canadian dollars.

With some exceptions, most food prices are higher in Canada than in the United States, but lower than in much of Western Europe. The biggest expense of the trip will be accommodations, but a range of choices, from economy to deluxe, is available in metropolitan areas, the country, and in resort areas.

Sample Prices The following prices are for Toronto (prices in other cities and regions are often lower): A soda (pop) costs $1–$1.25; a glass of beer, $3–$6; a sandwich, $3.50–$6; a taxi, as soon as the meter is turned on, $2.20, and $1 for every kilometer; a movie, about $8. (*See* Staying in Montréal and Québec City, GST and Sales Tax, *below*).

Passports and Visas

U.S. Citizens Because of the volume of border traffic between Canada and the United States, entry requirements are fairly simple. Citizens and legal residents of the United States do not need a passport or a visa to enter Canada, but proof of citizenship (a birth certificate, valid passport, or voter registration card) and proof of identity may be requested. Naturalized U.S. residents should carry their naturalization certificate or "green card." U.S. residents entering Canada from a third country must have a valid passport, naturalization certificate, or "green card." For more information, contact the **Canadian Embassy** (501 Pennsylvania Ave. NW, Washington, DC 20001, tel. 202/682–1740).

U.K. Citizens Citizens of the United Kingdom need a valid passport to enter Canada for stays of up to six months; all visitors must have a return ticket out of Canada. Applications for new and renewal passports are available from main post offices as well as at the six passport offices, located in Belfast, Glasgow, Liverpool, London, Newport, and Peterborough. You may apply in person at all passport offices, or by mail to all except the London office. Children under 16 may travel on a parent's passport when accompanying them. All passports are valid for 10 years. Allow a month for processing.

Customs and Duties

On Arrival American and British visitors may bring in the following items duty-free: 200 cigarettes, 50 cigars, and two pounds of tobacco; 1 bottle (1.14 litres or 40 imperial ounces) of liquor, or 24 355-milliliter (12-ounce) bottles or cans of beer for personal consumption; gifts up to the value of $60 per gift. A deposit is sometimes required for trailers (refunded upon return). Cats and dogs must have a certificate issued by a licensed veterinarian that clearly identifies the animal and certifies that it has been vaccinated against rabies during the preceding 36 months. Plant material must be declared and inspected. With certain restrictions (some fruits and vegetables), visitors may bring food with them for their own use, providing the quantity is consistent with the duration of the visit.

Returning Home

U.S. Customs Provided you've been out of the country for at least 48 hours and haven't already used the exemption, or any part of it, in the past 30 days, you may bring home US$400 worth of foreign goods duty-free. So can each member of your family, regardless of age; and your exemptions may be pooled, so one of you can bring in more if another brings in less. A flat 10% duty applies to the next US$1,000 of goods; above US$1,400, the rate varies with the merchandise. (If the 48-hour or 30-day limits apply, your duty-free allowance drops to US$25, which may not be pooled.) Please note that these are the *general* rules, applicable to most countries, including Canada.

Travelers 21 or older may bring back 1 liter of alcohol duty-free, provided the beverage laws of the state through which they reenter the United States allow it. In addition, 100 non-Cuban cigars and 200 cigarettes are allowed, regardless of your age. Antiques and works of art more than 100 years old are duty-free.

Gifts valued at less than US$50 may be mailed to the U.S. duty-free, with a limit of one package per day per addressee (do not send alcohol or tobacco products, nor perfume valued at more than US$50). These gifts do not count as part of your exemption, unless you bring them home with you. Mark the package "Unsolicited Gift" and include the nature of the gift and its retail value on the outside.

For a copy of "Know Before You Go," a free brochure detailing what you may and may not bring back to the United States, rates of duty, and other pointers, contact the **U.S. Customs Service** (Box 7407, Washington, DC 20044, tel. 202/927–6724).

U.K. Customs From countries outside the EU, such as Canada, you may import duty-free 200 cigarettes, 100 cigarillos, 50 cigars or 250 grams of tobacco; 1 liter of spirits or 2 liters of fortified or sparkling wine; 2 liters of still table wine; 60 milliliters of perfume; 250 milliliters of toilet water; plus £136 worth of other goods, including gifts and souvenirs.

For further information or a copy of "A Guide for Travellers," which details standard customs procedures as well as what you may bring into the United Kingdom from abroad, contact **HM Customs and Excise** (Dorset House, Stamford St., London SE1 9PY, tel. 071/928–3344).

Traveling with Cameras, Camcorders, and Laptops

Film and Cameras If your camera is new or if you haven't used it for a while, shoot and develop a few rolls of film before leaving home. Store film in a cool, dry place—never in the car's glove compartment or on the shelf under the rear window.

Airport security X-rays generally aren't harmful to film with ISO below 400. To protect your film, carry it with you in a clear plastic bag and ask for a hand inspection. Such requests are honored at U.S. airports, up to the inspector abroad. Don't depend on a lead-lined bag to protect film in checked luggage—the airline may increase the radiation to see what's inside. Call the Kodak Information Center (tel. 800/242–2424) for details.

Camcorders Before your trip, put camcorders through their paces, invest in a skylight filter to protect the lens, and check all the batteries.

Videotape Unlike still-camera film, videotape is not damaged by X-rays. However, it may well be harmed by the magnetic field of a walk-through metal detector. Airport security personnel may want you to turn the camcorder on to prove that that's what it is, so make sure the battery is charged.

Laptops Security X-rays do not harm hard-disk or floppy-disk storage, but you may request a hand-check, at which point you may be asked to turn on the computer to prove that it is what it appears to be. (Check your battery before departure.) Most airlines allow you to use your laptop aloft except during takeoff and landing (so as not to interfere with navigation equipment). For international travel, register your foreign-made laptop with U.S. Customs as you leave the country. If your laptop is U.S.-made, call the consulate of the country you'll be visiting to find out whether it should be registered with customs upon arrival. Before departure, find out about repair facilities at your destination.

Language

Canada's two official languages are English and French. Though English is widely spoken, it may be useful to learn a few French phrases if you plan to travel to the province of Québec or to the French Canadian communities in the maritime provinces (Nova Scotia, New Brunswick, and Prince Edward Island), northern Manitoba, and Ontario. Canadian French, known as Québecois or *joual*, is a colorful language often quite different from that spoken in France.

Canada, like the United States, has been settled by successive influxes of immigrants, from the British, Scottish, Irish, and French to the Germans, Scandinavians, Ukrainians, and Chinese. Many of these groups maintain their cultural identity through their native language, and ethnic daily and weekly newspapers are common. Immigration since the 1960s accounts for Asians, Arabs, East Indians, Italians, Hispanics, and Caribbean blacks. The native population of Canada now comprises less than 1% of the total population, yet it is possible to hear the languages of Native Canadians where these groups reside.

Insurance

U.S. Residents Most tour operators, travel agents, and insurance agents sell specialized health-and-accident, flight, trip-cancellation, and luggage insurance as well as comprehensive policies with some or all of these features. But before you make any purchase, review your existing health and homeowner policies to find out whether they cover expenses incurred while traveling.

Health-and-Accident Insurance Specific policy provisions of supplemental health-and-accident insurance for travelers include reimbursement for $1,000 to $150,000 worth of medical and/or dental expenses caused by an accident or illness during a trip. The personal-accident, or death-and-dismemberment, provision pays a lump sum to your beneficiaries if you die or to you if you lose one or both limbs or your eyesight; the lump sum awarded can range from $15,000 to $500,000. The medical-assistance provision may reimburse you for the cost of referrals, evacuation, or repatriation and other services, or it may automatically enroll you as a member of a particular medical-assistance company.

Flight Insurance Often bought as a last-minute impulse at the airport, flight insurance pays when a plane crashes a lump sum to either a beneficiary if the insured dies or sometimes to a surviving passenger who loses eyesight or a limb; it supplements the airlines' coverage described in the limits-of-liability paragraphs on your ticket. Charging an airline ticket to a major credit card often automatically entitles you to coverage and may also embrace travel by bus, train, and ship.

Baggage Insurance In the event of loss, damage, or theft on international flights, airlines' liability is US$20 per kilogram for checked baggage (roughly about US$640 per 70-pound bag) and US$400 per passenger for unchecked baggage. On domestic flights, the ceiling is US$1,250 per passenger. Excess-valuation insurance can be bought directly from the airline at check-in for about $10 per $1,000 worth of coverage. However, you cannot buy it at any price for the rather extensive list of excluded items shown on your airline ticket.

Trip Insurance **Trip-cancellation-and-interruption insurance** protects you in the event you are unable to undertake or finish your trip, especially if your airline ticket, cruise, or package tour does not allow changes or cancellations. The amount of coverage you purchase should equal the cost of your trip should you, a traveling companion, or a family member fall ill, forcing you to stay home, plus the nondiscounted one-way airline ticket you would need to buy if you had to return home early. Read the fine print carefully, especially sections defining "family member" and "preexisting medical conditions." **Default** or **bankruptcy insurance** protects you against a supplier's failure to deliver. Such policies often do not cover default by a travel agency, tour operator, airline, or cruise line if you bought your tour and the coverage directly from the firm in question. Tours packaged by one of the 33 members of the United States Tour Operators Association (USTOA, 211 E. 51 St., Suite 12B, New York, NY 10022; tel. 212/750–7371), which requires members to maintain $1 million each in an account to reimburse clients in case of default, are likely to present the fewest difficulties. Even better, pay for travel arrangements with a major credit card, so that you can refuse to pay the bill if services have not been rendered—and let the card company fight your battles.

Comprehensive Policies Companies supplying comprehensive policies with some or all of the above features include **Access America, Inc.** (Box 90315, Richmond, VA 23230, tel. 800/284–8300); **Carefree Travel Insurance** (Box 310, 120 Mineola Blvd., Mineola, NY 11501, tel. 516/294–0220 or 800/323–3149); **Tele-Trip** (Mutual of Omaha Plaza, Box 31762, Omaha, NE 68131, tel. 800/228–9792); **The Travelers Companies** (1 Tower Sq., Hartford, CT 06183, tel. 203/277–0111 or 800/243–3174); **Travel Guard International** (1145 Clark St., Stevens Point, WI 54481, tel. 715/345–0505 or 800/826–1300); and **Wallach and Company, Inc.** (107 W. Federal St., Box 480, Middleburg, VA 22117, tel. 703/687–3166 or 800/237–6615).

U.K. Residents Most tour operators, travel agents, and insurance agents sell specialized policies covering accident, medical expenses, personal liability, trip cancellation, and loss or theft of personal property. You can also purchase an annual travel-insurance policy valid for every trip you make during the year in which it's purchased (usually only trips of less than 90 days). Make sure you will be covered if you have a preexisting medical condition or are pregnant.

For advice by phone or a free booklet, "Holiday Insurance," that sets out what to expect from a holiday-insurance policy and gives price guidelines, contact the **Association of British Insurers** (51 Gresham St., London EC2V 7HQ, tel. 071/600–3333; 30 Gordon St., Glasgow G1 3PU, tel. 041/226–3905; Scottish Providence Bldg., Donegall Sq. W, Belfast BT1 6JE, tel. 0232/249176; call for other locations).

Car Rentals

All major car-rental companies are represented in Canada, including **Alamo** (tel. 800/327–9633); **Avis** (tel. 800/331–1212, 800/879–2847 in Canada); **Budget** (tel. 800/527–0700); **Hertz** (tel. 800/654–3001, 800/263-0600 in Canada); **National** (tel. 800/227–7368), affiliated with **Tilden Rent-a-Car** (tel. 514/842–9445). In cities, rates range from about $50 per day for an economy car to $70 for a large car; weekly rates range from $190 to $350. Unlimited mileage rentals are available only in limited areas. This does not include the 7% GST tax.

Requirements Any valid state or national driver's license is acceptable. If you have rented in the United States, be sure to keep the rental contract with you to indicate that use in Canada is authorized by the rental agency.

Extra Charges Picking up the car in one city or country and leaving it in another may entail substantial drop-off charges or one-way service fees. The cost of a collision or loss-damage waiver (*see below*) can be high, also. Fill the tank when you turn in the vehicle to avoid being charged for refueling at what you'll swear is the most expensive pump in town.

Cutting Costs Major international companies have programs that discount their standard rates by 15%–30% if you make the reservation before departure (anywhere from 24 hours to 14 days), rent for a minimum number of days (typically three or four), and prepay the rental. Ask about these advance-purchase schemes when you call for information. More economical rentals may come as part of fly/drive or other packages, even bare-bones deals that combine only the rental plus an airline ticket (*see* Tours and Packages, *above*).

Several companies that operate as wholesalers—they that do not own their own fleets but rent in bulk from those that do—offer advantageous rates to their customers. Rentals through such companies must be arranged and paid for before you leave the United States. Among them is **Auto Europe** (Box 1097, Camden, ME 04843, tel. 207/236–8235 or 800/223–5555, in Canada, 800/458–9503). You won't see these wholesalers' deals advertised; they're even better in summer, when business travel is down. Always ask whether the prices are guaranteed in U.S. dollars or foreign currency and if unlimited mileage is available. Find out about any required deposits, cancellation penalties, and drop-off charges, and confirm the cost of the Collision Damage Waiver.

Insurance and Collision Damage Waiver Until recently, standard rental contracts included liability coverage (for damage to public property, injury to pedestrians, and so on) and coverage for the car against fire, theft, and collision damage with a deductible. Due to law changes in some states and rising liability costs, several car rental agencies have reduced the type of coverage they offer. Before you rent a car, find out exactly what coverage, if any, is provided by your personal auto insurer. Don't assume that you are covered. If you do want insurance from the rental company, secondary coverage may be the only type offered. You may already have secondary coverage if you charge the rental to a credit card. Only Diner's Club (tel. 800/234–6377) provides primary coverage in the United States and worldwide.

Rail Passes

Although **VIA Rail,** Canada's major passenger carrier, has made considerable cuts in its services, it is still possible to travel coast to coast on its trains. The **Canrailpass** allows 12 days of coach-class travel within a 30-day period; sleeping cars are available, but they sell out very early and must be reserved at least a month in advance during the high season (June 1–Sept. 30) when the pass is C$510 for adults age 25–60, C$460 for travelers under 25 or over 60. Low season rates (Oct. 1–Dec. 14 and Jan. 6–May 31) are C$349 for adults and C$319 for youth and senior citizens. The pass is not valid during the Christmas period (Dec. 15–Jan. 5). The Canrailpass must be purchased prior to arrival in Canada; for more information and reservations, contact VIA Rail (tel. 800/665–0200 in the United States) or Compass Travel (Box 113, Peterborough, PE1 1LE, tel. 0733/51780, in the United Kingdom).

Student and Youth Travel

Travel Agencies **Council Travel Services (CTS),** a subsidiary of the nonprofit Council on International Educational Exchange (CIEE), specializes in low-cost travel arrangements abroad for students and is the exclusive U.S. agent for several discount cards. Also newly available from CTS are domestic air passes for bargain travel within the United States. CIEE's twice-yearly *Student Travels* magazine is available at the CTS office at CIEE headquarters (205 E. 42nd St., 16th Floor, New York, NY 10017, tel. 212/661–1450) and in Boston (tel. 617/266–1926), Miami (tel. 305/670–9261), Los Angeles (tel. 310/208–3551) and at 43 branches in college towns nationwide (free in person, $1 by mail). **Campus Connections** (1100 E. Marlton Pike, Cherry Hill, NJ 08034, tel. 800/428–3235) specializes in discounted accommodations and airline fares for students. The **Educational Travel Centre** (438 N. Frances St., Madison, WI 53703, tel. 608/256–5551) offers low-cost domestic and international airline tickets, mostly for flights departing from Chicago, and rail passes. Other travel agencies catering to students include **TMI Student Travel** (1146 Pleasant St., Watertown, MA 02172, tel. 617/661–8187 or 800/245–3672), and **Travel Cuts** (187 College St., Toronto, Ont. M5T 1P7, tel. 416/979–2406).

Discount Cards For discounts on transportation and on museum and attractions admissions, buy the **International Student Identity Card** (ISIC) if you're a bona fide student, or the **International Youth Card** (IYC) if you're under 26. In the United States the ISIC and IYC cards cost US$15 each and include basic travel accident and sickness coverage. Apply to **CIEE** (*see* address *above*, tel. 212/661–1414; the application is in *Student Travels*). In Canada the cards are available for C$15 each from **Travel Cuts** (*see above*). In the United Kingdom they cost £5 and £4 respectively at student unions and student travel companies, including Council Travel's London office (28A Poland St., London W1V 3DB, tel. 071/437–7767).

Hosteling A **Hostelling International** (HI) membership card is the key to more than 6,000 hostels in 70 countries; the sex-segregated, dormitory-style sleeping quarters, including some for families, go for US$7 to US$20 a night per person. Membership is available in the United States through **Hostelling International/American Youth Hostels** (AYH, 733 15th St. NW, Washington, DC 20005, tel. 202/783–6161), the American link in the worldwide chain, and costs US$25 for adults 18–54, US$10 for those under 18, US$15 for those 55 and over, and US$35 for families. Volume 2 of the *Guide to Budget Accommodation* lists hostels in Asia and Australia as well as in Canada and the United States (US$13.95 including postage). HI membership is available in Canada through **Hostelling International–Canada** (205 Catherine St., Suite 400, Ottawa, Ont. K2P 1C3, tel. 613/748–5638) for C$26.75, and in the United Kingdom through the **Youth Hostel Association of England and Wales** (Trevelyan House, 8 St. Stephen's Hill, St. Albans, Herts. AL1 2DY, tel. 0727/55215) for £9.

Traveling with Children

Publications
Newsletter ***Family Travel Times,*** published 10 times a year by **Travel With Your Children** (TWYCH, 45 W. 18th St., 7th Floor Tower, New York, NY 10011, tel. 212/206–0688; annual subscription $55), covers destinations, types of vacations, and modes of travel. TWYCH also publishes *Cruising with Children* and *Skiing with Children.*

Books *Traveling with Children—And Enjoying It,* by Arlene K. Butler (US$11.95 plus US$3 shipping; Globe Pequot Press, Box 833, Old Saybrook, CT 06475, tel. 800/243–0495, in CT, 800/962–0973), helps plan your trip with children, from toddlers to teens. Also from Globe Pequot is *Recommended Family Resorts in the United States, Canada, and the Caribbean,* by Jane Wilford with Janet Tice (US$12.95).

Tour Operators **Grandtravel** (6900 Wisconsin Ave., Suite 706, Chevy Chase, MD 20815, tel. 301/986–0790 or 800/247–7651) offers international and domestic tours for people traveling with their grandchildren. The catalogue, as charmingly written and illustrated as a children's book, positively invites armchair traveling with lap-sitters aboard.

Rascals in Paradise (650 5th St., Suite 505, San Francisco, CA 94107, tel. 415/978–9800, or 800/872–7225) specializes in programs for families.

Getting There
Air Fares
On international flights, the fare for infants under 2 not occupying a seat is generally 10% of the accompanying adult's fare; children ages 2–11 usually pay half to two-thirds of the adult fare. On domestic flights, children under 2 not occupying a seat travel free, and older children currently travel on the "lowest applicable" adult fare.

Baggage
In general, infants paying 10% of the adult fare are allowed one carry-on bag, not to exceed 70 pounds or 45 inches (length + width + height) and a collapsible stroller; check with the airline before departure, because you may be allowed less if the flight is full. The adult baggage allowance applies for children paying half or more of the adult fare.

Safety Seats
The FAA recommends the use of safety seats aloft and details approved models in the free leaflet **"Child/Infant Safety Seats Recommended for Use in Aircraft"** (available from the Federal Aviation Administration, APA–200, 800 Independence Ave. SW, Washington, DC 20591, tel. 202/267–3479). Airline policy varies. U.S. carriers allow FAA-approved models bearing a sticker declaring their FAA approval. Because these seats are strapped into a regular passenger seat, they may require that parents buy a ticket even for an infant under 2 who would otherwise ride free. Foreign carriers may not allow infant seats, may charge the child's rather than the infant's fare for their use, or may require you to hold your baby during takeoff and landing, thus defeating the seat's purpose.

Facilities Aloft
Some airlines do provide other services for children, such as children's meals and freestanding bassinets (to those sitting in seats at the bulkhead, where there's enough legroom). Make your request when reserving. The annual February/March issue of ***Family Travel Times*** gives details of the children's services of dozens of airlines (US$10; *see above*). "Kids and Teens in Flight" (free from the U.S. Department of Transportation, tel. 202/366–2220) offers tips for children flying alone.

Lodging
Although most major hotels in Canada welcome children, the policies and programs they offer are usually limited to a free stay for children under a certain age when sharing a room with their parents. For example, the Sheraton Hotels worldwide offer a free stay to children under the age of 17. At Best Westerns, the age limit ranges from 12 to 16, depending on the hotel. Baby-sitting services can often be arranged at the front desk of most hotels. In addition, priority for connecting rooms is often given to families. Inquire about programs and discounts when you make your reservation.

Hints for Travelers with Disabilities

Organizations
In Canada
Canadian Paraplegic Association National Office (520 Sutherland Dr., Toronto, Ont., M4G 3U9, tel. 416/422–5640) provides information about touring in Canada.

In the United States
Several organizations provide travel information for people with disabilities, usually for a membership fee, and some publish newsletters and bulletins. Among them are the **Information Center for Individuals with Disabilities** (Fort Point Pl., in MA, 27–43 Wormwood St., Boston, MA 02210, tel. 617/727–5540 or, in MA, 800/462–5015 between 11 and 4, or leave message; TDD 617/345–9743); **Mobility International USA** (Box 10767, Eugene, OR 97440, tel. and TDD 503/343–1284, fax 503/343–6812), the U.S. branch of an inter-

national organization based in Britain (*see below*) and present in 30 countries; **MossRehab Hospital Travel Information Service** (1200 W. Tabor Rd., Philadelphia, PA 19141, tel. 215/456–9603, TDD 215/456–9602); the **Travel Industry and Disabled Exchange** (TIDE, 5435 Donna Ave., Tarzana, CA 91356, tel. 818/368–5648, fax 818/344–0078); and **Travelin' Talk** (Box 3534, Clarksville, TN 37043, tel. 615/552–6670, fax 615/552–1182).

In the United Kingdom Main information sources include the **Royal Association for Disability and Rehabilitation** (RADAR, 25 Mortimer St., London W1N 8AB, tel. 071/637–5400), which publishes travel information for the disabled in Britain, and **Mobility International** (228 Borough High St., London SE1 1JX, tel. 071/403–5688), the headquarters of an international membership organization that serves as a clearinghouse of travel information for people with disabilities.

Travel Agencies and Tour Operators **Flying Wheels Travel** (143 W. Bridge St., Box 382, Owatonna, MN 55060, tel. 507/451–5005 or 800/535–6790) is a travel agency specializing in domestic and worldwide cruises, tours, and independent travel itineraries for people with disabilities. Adventurers should contact **Wilderness Inquiry** (1313 5th St. SE, Minneapolis, MN 55414, tel. and TDD 612/379–3838), which orchestrates action-packed trips like white-water rafting, sea kayaking, and dog sledding.

Publications In addition to the fact sheets, newsletters, and books mentioned above are several free publications available from the Consumer Information Center (Pueblo, CO 81009): "New Horizons for the Air Traveler with a Disability," a U.S. Department of Transportation booklet describing changes resulting from the 1986 Air Carrier Access Act and those still to come from the 1990 Americans with Disabilities Act (include Department 608Y in the address), and the Airport Operators Council's *Access Travel: Airports* (Dept. 5804), which describes facilities and services for people with disabilities at more than 500 airports worldwide.

Travelin' Talk Directory (*see* Organizations, *above*) was published in 1993. This 500-page resource book ($35) is packed with information for travelers with disabilities. Twin Peaks Press (Box 129, Vancouver, WA 98666, tel. 206/694–2462 or 800/637–2256) publishes the *Directory of Travel Agencies for the Disabled* ($19.95), listing more than 370 agencies worldwide and *Wheelchair Vagabond* ($14.95), a collection of personal travel tips. Add $2 per book for shipping.

Hints for Older Travelers

Organizations The **American Association of Retired Persons** (AARP, 601 E St. NW, Washington, DC 20049, tel. 202/434–2277) provides independent travelers who are members of the AARP (open to those age 50 or older; $8 per person or couple annually) with the Purchase Privilege Program, which offers discounts on lodging, car rentals, and sightseeing, and the AARP Motoring Plan, which furnishes domestic trip-routing information and emergency road-service aid for an annual fee of $39.95 per person or couple ($59.95 for a premium version). AARP also arranges group tours, cruises, and apartment living through AARP Travel Experience from American Express (400 Pinnacle Way, Suite 450, Norcross, GA 30071, tel. 800/927–0111 or 800/745–4567).

Two other organizations offer discounts on lodgings, car rentals, and other travel products, along with such nontravel perks as magazines and newsletters: the **National Council of Senior Citizens** (1331

F St. NW, Washington, DC 20004, tel. 202/347–8800; membership US$12 annually) and **Mature Outlook** (6001 N. Clark St., Chicago, IL 60660, tel. 800/336–6330; US$9.95 annually).

Note: Mention your senior-citizen identification card when booking hotel reservations for reduced rates, not when checking out. At restaurants, show your card before you're seated; discounts may be limited to certain menus, days, or hours. If you are renting a car, ask about promotional rates that might improve on your senior-citizen discount.

Educational Travel The nonprofit **Elderhostel** (75 Federal St., 3rd Floor, Boston, MA 02110, tel. 617/426–7788) has offered inexpensive study programs for people 60 and older since 1975. Held at more than 1,800 educational institutions in the United States, Canada, and 45 countries, courses cover everything from marine science to Greek myths and cowboy poetry. Participants generally attend lectures in the morning and spend the afternoon sightseeing or on field trips; they live in dorms on the host campuses. Fees for programs in the United States and Canada, which usually last one week, run about US$300, not including transportation.

Tour Operators **Saga International Holidays** (222 Berkeley St., Boston, MA 02116, tel. 800/343–0273), which specializes in group travel for people over 60, offers a selection of variously priced tours and cruises covering five continents. If you want to take your grandchildren, look into **Grandtravel** (*see* Traveling with Children, *above*).

Discounts **VIA Rail Canada** (tel. 800/665–0200) offers those 60 and over a 10% discount on basic transportation for travel any time and with no advance-purchase requirement. This 10% discount can also apply to off-peak reduced fares that have advance-purchase requirements.

Publications *The 50+ Traveler's Guidebook: Where to Go, Where to Stay, What to Do* by Anita Williams and Merrimac Dillon ($12.95; St. Martin's Press, 175 Fifth Ave., New York, NY 10010) is available in bookstores and offers many useful tips. "The Mature Traveler" (Box 50820, Reno, NV 89513, tel. 702/786–7419; $29.95), a monthly newsletter, contains many travel deals for older travelers.

Hints for Gay and Lesbian Travelers

Organizations The **International Gay Travel Association** (Box 4974, Key West, FL 33041, tel. 305-292-0217 or 800/999–7925 or 800-448-8550), which has 700 members, will provide you with names of travel agents and tour operators who specialize in gay travel. The **Gay & Lesbian Visitors Center of New York Inc.** (135 W. 20th St., 3rd Floor, New York, NY 10011, tel. 212/463–9030 or 800/395–2315; $100 annually) mails a monthly newsletter, valuable coupons, and more to its members.

Tour Operators and Travel Agencies The dominant travel agency in the market is **Above and Beyond** (3568 Sacramento St., San Francisco, CA 94118, tel. 415/922–2683 or 800/397–2681). Tour operator **Olympus Vacations** (8424 Santa Monica Blvd., Suite 721, West Hollywood, CA 90069; tel. 310/657–2220 or 800/965–9678) offers all-gay-and-lesbian resort holidays. **Skylink Women's Travel** (746 Ashland Ave., Santa Monica, CA 90405, tel. 310/452–0506 or 800/225-5759) handles individual travel for lesbians all over the world and conducts two international and five domestic group trips annually.

Publications The premiere international travel magazine for gays and lesbians is **Our World** (1104 N. Nova Rd., Suite 251, Daytona Beach, FL 32117, tel. 904/441–5367; $35 for 10 issues). **Out & About** (tel. 203/789-8518 or 800/929–2268; $49 for 10 issues) is a 16-page monthly newsletter with extensive information on resorts, hotels, and airlines that are gay-friendly.

Further Reading

Fiction Mordecai Richler is well known as the author of *The Apprenticeship of Duddy Kravitz*, a novel set in Montréal, which was made into a movie. His various collections of essays are also worth exploring. Joy Kogawa's first novel, *Obasan*, tells about the Japanese community of Canada during World War II.

Nonfiction Andrew Malcolm gives a cultural and historical overview of the country in *The Canadians*. Stephen Brook's *The Maple Leaf Rag* is a collection of idiosyncratic travel essays. *Why We Act Like Canadians: A Personal Exploration of Our National Character*, by Pierre Burton, is one of many popular nonfiction books by Burton focusing on Canada's history and culture. *Short History of Canada*, by Desmond Morton, is a recent historical account of the country.

Arriving and Departing

From North America by Plane

Flights are either nonstop, direct, or connecting. A **nonstop** flight requires no change of plane and makes no stops. A **direct** flight stops at least once and can involve a change of plane, although the flight number remains the same; if the first leg is late, the second waits. This is not the case with a **connecting** flight, which involves a different plane and a different flight number.

Airports and Airlines You can fly nonstop to Canada from most major U.S. cities; every major U.S. airline has nonstop service. The major international hubs are Montréal, Toronto, and Vancouver, but international flights also fly into Halifax, Calgary, and Edmonton. Some of the major airlines serving these hubs are **American** (tel. 800/433–7300), **Continental** (tel. 800/525–0280), **Delta** (800/221–1212), **Northwest** (tel. 800/225–2525), **United** (tel. 800/722–5243), and **USAir** (tel 800/428–4322).

Flying Time **To Montréal:** 1½ hours from New York, 2 hours from Chicago, 6 hours from Los Angeles, 6½ hours from London.

Cutting Flight Costs The Sunday travel section of most newspapers is a good source of deals. When booking, particularly through an unfamiliar company, call the Better Business Bureau or your local or state Consumer Protection Bureau to find out whether any complaints have been registered against the company, pay with a credit card if you can, and consider trip-cancellation and default insurance (*see* Insurance, *above*).

Promotional Airfares Less expensive fares, called promotional or discount fares, are round-trip and involve restrictions, which vary according to the route and season. You must usually buy the ticket—commonly called an APEX (advance purchase excursion) when it's for international travel—in advance (7, 14, or 21 days are usual), although some of the major airlines have added no-frills, cheap flights to compete with new bargain airlines on certain routes.

With the major airlines the cheaper fares generally require minimum- and maximum-stays (for instance, over a Saturday night or at least 7 and no more than 30 days). Airlines generally allow some return date changes for a $25 to $50 fee, but most low-fare tickets are nonrefundable. Only a death in the family would prompt the airline to return any of your money if you cancel a nonrefundable ticket. However, you can apply an unused nonrefundable ticket toward a new ticket, again with a small fee. The lowest fare is subject to availability, and only a small percentage of the plane's total seats will be sold at that price. Contact the U.S. Department of Transportation's Office of Consumer Affairs (I–25, Washington, DC 20590, tel. 202/366–2220) for a copy of "Fly-Rights: A Guide to Air Travel in the U.S." *The Official Frequent Flyer Guidebook* by Randy Petersen ($14.99 plus $3 shipping; 4715-C Town Center Dr., Colorado Springs, CO 80916, tel. 719/597–8899 or 800/487-8893, 800/485–8893) yields valuable hints on getting the most for your air travel dollars.

Consolidators Consolidators or bulk-fare operators—"bucket shops"—buy blocks of seats on scheduled flights that airlines anticipate they won't be able to sell. They pay wholesale prices, add a markup, and resell the seats to travel agents or directly to the public at prices that still undercut the airline's promotional or discount fares (higher than a charter ticket but lower than an APEX ticket, and usually without the advance-purchase restriction). Moreover, some consolidators sometimes give you your money back. Carefully read the fine print detailing penalties for changes and cancellations. If you doubt the reliability of a company, call the airline once you've made your booking and confirm that you do, indeed, have a reservation on the flight.

Charter Flights Charters usually have the lowest fares and the most restrictions. Departures are limited and seldom on time, and you can lose all or most of your money if you cancel. (The closer to departure you cancel, the more you lose, although sometimes you will be charged only a small fee if you supply a substitute passenger.) The charterer may legally cancel the flight for any reason up to 10 days before departure; within 10 days of departure, the flight may be canceled only if it is physically impossible to operate it. The charterer may also revise the itinerary or increase the price after you have bought the ticket, but if the new arrangement constitutes a "major change," you have the right to a refund. Before buying a charter ticket, read the fine print for the company's refund policy and details on major changes. Money for charter flights is usually paid into a bank escrow account, the name of which should be on the contract. If you don't pay by credit card, make your check payable to the escrow account (unless you're dealing with a travel agent, in which case, his or her check should be payable to the escrow account). The U.S. Department of Transportation's Office of Consumer Affairs (I–25, Washington, DC 20590, tel. 202/366–2220) can answer questions on charters and send you its "Plane Talk: Public Charter Flights" information sheet.

Charter operators may offer flights alone or with ground arrangements that constitute a charter package. You typically must book charters through your travel agent. One good source is **Charterlink** (988 Sing Sing Rd., Horseheads, NY 14845, tel. 607/739–7148 or 800/221–1802), a no-fee charter broker that operates 24 hours a day.

Discount Travel Clubs Travel clubs offer their members unsold space on airplanes, cruise ships, and package tours at nearly the last minute and at well below the original cost. Suppliers thus receive some revenue for their "leftovers," and members get a bargain. Membership generally includes a regular bulletin or access to a toll-free telephone hot line giving details of available trips departing anywhere from three or four days to several months in the future. Packages tend to be more common than flights alone, so if airfares are your only interest, read the literature before joining. Reductions on hotels are also available. Clubs include **Discount Travel International** (114 Forrest Ave., Suite 203, Narberth, PA 19072, tel. 215/668–7184; US$45 annually, single or family), **Entertainment Travel Editions** (Box 1014, Trumbull, CT 06611, tel. 800/445–4137; $28-$48 annually), **Great American Traveler** (Box 27965, Salt Lake City, UT 84127, tel. 800/548–2812; $29.95 annually), **Moment's Notice** (425 Madison Ave., New York, NY 10017, tel. 212/486–0503; US$45 annually, single or family), **Privilege Card** (3391 Peachtree Rd. NE, Suite 110, Atlanta, GA 30326, tel. 404/262–0222 or 800/236-9732; domestic annual membership $49.95, international, $74.95), **Travelers Advantage** (CUC Travel Service, 49 Music Sq. W, Nashville, TN 37203, tel. 800/548–1116; US$49 annually, single or family), and **Worldwide Discount Travel Club** (1674 Meridian Ave., Miami Beach, FL 33139, tel. 305/534–2082; US$50 annually for family, US$40 single).

Enjoying the Flight Fly at night if you're able to sleep on a plane. Because the air aloft is dry, drink plenty of beverages while on board; remember that drinking alcohol contributes to jet lag, as do heavy meals. Sleepers usually prefer window seats to curl up against; restless passengers ask to be on the aisle. Bulkhead seats, in the front row of each cabin, have more legroom, but since there's no seat ahead, trays attach awkwardly to the arms of your seat, and you must stow all possessions overhead. Bulkhead seats are usually reserved for people with disabilities, the elderly, and people traveling with babies.

Smoking Smoking is now banned on all domestic flights of less than six hours duration in the United States, and on all Canadian flights, including flights to and from Europe and the Far East. The U.S. ban also applies to domestic segments of international flights aboard U.S. and foreign carriers.

From the United States by Car

Drivers must have proper owner registration and proof of insurance coverage, which is compulsory in Canada. The Canadian Non-Resident Inter-Provincial Motor Vehicle Liability Insurance Card, available from any U.S. insurance company, is accepted as evidence of financial responsibility anywhere in Canada. Minimum insurance requirement in Canada is $200,000, except in Québec where the minimum is $50,000. For more information, contact the Insurance Bureau of Canada (181 University Ave., Toronto, Ont., M5H 3M7, tel. 416/362–2301). If you are driving a car that is not registered in your name, carry a letter from the owner that authorizes your use of the vehicle. (*See also* Getting around by Car, *below.*) The U.S. Interstate Highway System leads directly into Canada: I–95 from Maine to New Brunswick; I–91 and I–89 from Vermont to Québec; I–87 from New York to Québec; I–81 and a spur off I–90 from New York to Ontario; I–94, I–96, and I–75 from Michigan to Ontario; I–29 from North Dakota to Manitoba; I–15 from Montana to Alberta; and I–5 from Washington state to British Columbia. Most of these connections hook up with the Trans-Canada Highway within a few miles. There are many smaller highway crossings between the two countries as well.

From Alaska, take the Alaska Highway (from Fairbanks), the Klondike Highway (from Skagway), and the Top of the World Highway (to Dawson City).

From the United States by Train, Bus, and Ship

By Train **Amtrak** (tel. 800/872–7245) has service from New York to Montréal, New York and Buffalo to Toronto, and Chicago to Toronto. Amtrak's *Montrealer* departs from New York's Pennsylvania Station at 8:25 PM and arrives in Montréal the next day at about 10:45 AM. Sleepers are highly recommended for the overnight trip but must be booked well in advance. The *Montrealer* is the only Amtrak train to Canada that requires reservations.

A second Amtrak train to Montréal leaves New York from Pennsylvania Station in the morning and takes 10½ hours; the trip from New York to Toronto (passing through Buffalo) takes 11 hours and 45 minutes; travel from Chicago to Toronto takes 12 hours. In addition to these direct routes, there are connections from many major cities. At press time, Amtrak was scheduled to start daily rail service between Seattle and Vancouver by the end of 1994, providing connections in Seattle with Amtrak's U.S.-wide network and in Vancouver with VIA Rail's Canadian trans-continental routes.

By Bus **Greyhound** (tel. 800/231–2222) has the most widespread bus service to Canada, and you can get from almost any point in the United States to any point in Canada on its extensive network. One of the longest routes, from New York to Vancouver via Seattle, takes about 3½ days.

By Ship Many Canadian cities are also accessible by water on private yachts and boats. Local marine authorities can advise you about the necessary documentation and procedure.

From the United Kingdom by Plane

Airlines The major carriers between Great Britain and Canada are **Air Canada** (tel. 081/759–2331 in the London area, or 0800/181313 elsewhere), **British Airways** (tel. 081/897–4000), and **Canadian Airlines International** (tel. 071/930–3501). Air Canada has the most flights and serves the most cities, with at least one flight a day to Toronto, Vancouver, and Montréal from Heathrow, and considerably more at peak periods. Air Canada also flies to Calgary, Edmonton, Halifax, and St. John's from Heathrow; to Toronto from Birmingham and Manchester; and to Calgary, Halifax, Toronto, and Vancouver from Prestwick (Glasgow). British Airways has as many as 23 flights a week to Canada from Heathrow, serving Montréal, Toronto, and Vancouver. Canadian Airlines International serves Calgary, Edmonton, Ottawa, and Vancouver from London Gatwick, has at least one flight a day to Toronto, and has service from Manchester to Toronto.

Staying in Montréal and Québec City

Getting Around

By Plane **Air Canada** (tel. 800/776–3000) operates in every province. The other major domestic carrier is **Canadian Airlines International** (tel. 800/426–7000). Regularly scheduled flights to every major city and to most smaller cities are available on Air Canada or Canadian Airlines International or the domestic carriers associated with them: **Air Alliance** serves Québec; **Air Atlantic** and **Air Nova** serve Atlantic

Canada; and **Air Ontario** serves the Ontario region. These airlines can be contacted at local numbers within each of the many cities they serve. Check with the territorial tourist agencies for charter companies and with the District Controller of Air Services in the territorial (and provincial) capitals for the locations of air bases that allow private flights and for regulations.

By Train Transcontinental rail service is provided by **VIA Rail Canada** (tel. 800/665–0200). If you're planning on traveling to several major cities in Canada, the train may be your best bet. Routes run across the country as well as within individual provinces, with the exception of the Northwest Territories and the Yukon, Newfoundland, and Prince Edward Island.

You can choose either sleeping-car or coach accommodations on most trains. Both classes allow access to dining cars. Sleeping-car passengers can enjoy comfortable parlor cars, drawing rooms, bedrooms, and roomettes. First-class seats, sleeping-car accommodations, and Dayniter seats between Ontario, Québec, and the maritime provinces require reservations. VIA has a new "Silver and Blue" service on its transcontinental trains that provides first-class "cruise" comfort and amenities including exclusive use of their dome car. **Rocky Mountain Railtours** (*see* Compass Travel, *below*) operates spectacular two-day, all daylight rail trips through the Canadian Rockies to the west coast. In the United Kingdom, **Compass Travel** (Box 113, Peterborough, PE1 1LE, tel. 0733/51780) represents both VIA Rail and Rocky Mountain Railtours.

By Bus The bus is an essential form of transportation in Canada, especially if you want to visit out-of-the-way towns that do not have airports or rail lines. Two major bus companies, **Greyhound** (222 1st Ave. SW, Calgary, AB, T2P 0A6, tel. 403/265–9111) and **Voyageur** (505 E Boulevard Maisonneuve H2L 1Y4, Montréal, tel. 514/843–4231), offer interprovincial service. In the United Kingdom, contact **Greyhound World Travel Ltd.,** Sussex House, London Road, E. Grinstead, West Surrey, RH19 1LD (tel. 0342/317317).

By Car Canada's highway system is excellent. It includes the Trans-Canada Highway, the longest highway in the world, which runs about 5,000 miles from Victoria, British Columbia, to St. John's, Newfoundland, using ferries to bridge coastal waters at each end. The second-longest Canadian highway, the Yellowhead Highway, follows the old Indian route from the Pacific Coast and over the Rockies to the prairies. North of the population centers, roads become fewer and less developed.

You are required to wear seat belts (and use infant seats) except in the Yukon Territory. Some provinces have a statutory requirement to drive with vehicle headlights on for extended periods after dawn and before sunset.

Speed limits vary from province to province, but they are usually within the 90–100 kph (50–60 mph) range outside the cities. The price of gasoline varies more than the speed limit, from 40¢ to 72¢ a liter. (There are 3.8 liters in a U.S. gallon, 4.5 liters in a Canadian Imperial gallon.) Distances are now always shown in kilometers, and gasoline is always sold in liters. The Imperial gallon is seldom used.

Foreign driver's licenses are valid in Canada. The International Driving Permit is also valid but must be accompanied by the visitor's state or national driver's license. Members of the Automobile Association of America (AAA) can contact the **Canadian Automobile As**

sociation (1775 Courtwood Crescent, Ottawa, Ont. K2C 3J2, tel. 613/226–7631; emergency road service, tel. 800/336–4357). Members of the Automobile Association of Great Britain, the Royal Automobile Club, the Royal Scottish Automobile Club, the Royal Irish Automobile Club and the automobile clubs of the Alliance Internationale de Tourisme (AIT) and Fédération Internationale de l'Automobile (FIA) are entitled to all the services of the CAA on presentation of a membership card.

Telephones

Phones work as they do in the United States. Drop 25¢ in the slot and dial; pay phones accept American coins, unlike U.S. phones, which spit out Canadian money. There are no problems dialing direct to the United States; U.S. telephone credit cards are accepted. For directory assistance, dial 1, the area code, and 555–1212. To place calls outside Canada and the United States, dial "0" and ask for the overseas operator.

Mail

Postal Rates In Canada you can buy stamps at the post office or from automatic vending machines in most hotel lobbies, railway stations, airports, bus terminals, many retail outlets, and some newsstands. Within Canada, postcards and letters up to 30 grams cost 46¢; between 30 grams and a kilogram, the cost is $3.75. Letters and postcards to the United States cost 52¢ for up to 30 grams, and $3.40 for up to 250 grams. Prices include GST.

International mail and postcards run 92¢ for up to 30 grams, and $2.10 for up to 100 grams.

Telepost is a fast "next day or sooner" service that combines the CN/CP Telecommunications network with letter-carrier delivery service. Messages may be telephoned to the nearest CN/CP Public Message Centre for delivery anywhere in Canada or the United States. Telepost service is available 24 hours a day, seven days a week, and billing arrangements may be made at the time the message is called in. **Intelpost** allows you to send documents or photographs via satellite to many Canadian, American, and European destinations. This service is available at main postal facilities in Canada, and is paid for in cash.

Visitors may have mail sent to them c/o General Delivery in the town they are visiting, for pickup in person within 15 days, after which it will be returned to the sender.

Tipping

Tips and service charges are not usually added to a bill in Canada. In general, tip 15% of the total bill. This goes for waiters, waitresses, barbers and hairdressers, taxi drivers, etc. Porters and doormen should get about 50¢–$1 a bag ($1 or more in a luxury hotel). For maid service, $1 a day is sufficient ($2 in luxury hotels).

Opening and Closing Times

Stores, shops, and supermarkets are usually open Monday through Saturday from 9 to 6—although in major cities, supermarkets are often open from 7:30 AM until 9 PM. Blue laws are in effect in much of Canada, but a growing number of provinces have stores with limited

Sunday hours, usually from noon to 5 (shops in areas highly frequented by tourists are usually open on Sunday). Retail stores are generally open on Thursday and Friday evenings, most shopping malls until 9 PM. Most banks in Canada are open Monday through Thursday from 10 to 3, and from 10 to 5 or 6 on Friday. Some banks are open longer hours and are also open on Saturday morning. All banks are closed on national holidays. Drugstores in major cities are often open until 11 PM, and convenience stores are often open 24 hours a day, seven days a week.

GST and Sales Tax

A countrywide goods and services tax of 7% (GST) applies on virtually every transaction in Canada except for the purchase of basic groceries. Nonresidents can get a full GST refund on any purchase taken out of the country and on short-term accommodations (but not on food, drink, tobacco, car or motorhome rentals, or transportation); rebate forms, which must be submitted within 60 days of leaving Canada, may be obtained from certain retailers, duty-free shops, customs officials, or Revenue Canada (Visitor's Rebate Program, Ottawa, Ont. K1A 1J5, tel. in Canada 800/668-4748). Instant rebates are provided by some duty-free shops when leaving Canada, and most provinces do not tax goods that are shipped directly by the vendor to the purchaser's home. You'll need your sales slips.

In addition to the GST, all provinces except Alberta, the Northwest Territories, and the Yukon levy a sales tax from 5% to 12% on most items purchased in shops, on restaurant meals, and sometimes on hotel rooms.

Shopping

Antiques On the whole, prices for antiques are lower in Canada than in the United States. Shops along Montréal's rue Sherbrooke Ouest stock everything from ancient maps to fine crystal; Vieux-Montréal and the rue Notre-Dame sell antiques and collectibles ranging from Napoléonic-period furniture to 1950s bric-a-brac.

Arts and Crafts The craftspeople of Québec are known for producing beautiful wood carvings.

Native Canadian Art Interest has grown in the highly collectible art and sculpture of the Inuit, usually rendered in soapstone. For the best price and a guarantee of authenticity, purchase Inuit and other native crafts in the province where they originate. Many styles are now attributed to certain tribes and are mass-produced for sale in galleries and shops miles away from their regions of origin. At the very top galleries you can be assured of getting pieces done by individual artists, though the prices will be higher than in the provinces of origin. The Canadian government has registered the symbol of an igloo as a mark of a work's authenticity. Be sure this Canadian government sticker or tag is attached before you make your purchase. Many galleries and shops in the west also carry work done by Native Canadians of the Northwest, who have revived their ancient art. They are known for their highly stylized masks, totem poles, and canoes. Themes and images from nature, such as whales, bears, wolves, and eagles, are prominent in their work. Bright colors and geometric patterns distinguish their woven products: blankets, wall hangings, and clothing.

Algonkian and Iroquoian art survives mainly in the museums of eastern Canada.

Maple Syrup Eastern Canada is famous for its sugar maples. The trees are tapped in early spring, and the sap is collected in buckets to be boiled down into maple syrup. This natural confection is sold all year. Avoid the tourist shops and department stores; for the best prices and information, stop at farm stands and markets. A small can of syrup costs about $6–$9.

National Parks

Banff, the country's first national park, was established in 1885, and since then the national park system has grown to encompass 34 national parks and 112 national historic sites. Because of Canada's eagerness to preserve its environment, new lands are continually being added to this network. Almost every park offers camping—either primitive camping or campsites with various facilities that can accommodate recreational vehicles. Hiking trails weave their way through each of the parks. Environment Canada (Inquiry Center, Ottawa, Ont. K1A 0H3, tel. 819/997–2800) publishes *Canada's National Parks* and *Canada's National Historic Sites,* with descriptions and other key information.

Participant Sports and Outdoor Activities

Biking Eastern Canada offers some of the best bicycling terrain. Bikers favor the Gaspé Peninsula in Québec and the surrounding Atlantic provinces. The terrain varies from very hilly around the Gaspé to flat on Prince Edward Island, and varied in New Brunswick and Nova Scotia. Write to the provincial tourist boards for road maps (which are more detailed than the maps available at gas stations) and information on local cycling associations.

Boating With so much coastline—on the Atlantic and Pacific, the Great Lakes, major rivers, and thousands of smaller lakes—boating is extremely popular throughout Canada. Boat rentals are widely available, and provincial tourism departments can provide lists of companies.

Camping Canada's 2,000-plus campgrounds range from simple roadside turnoffs with sweeping mountain vistas to fully equipped facilities with groomed sites, trailer hookups, recreational facilities, and vacation village atmosphere. Many of the best sites are in Canada's national and provincial parks, with nominal overnight fees. Commercial campgrounds offer more amenities, such as electrical and water hookups, showers, and even game rooms and grocery stores. They cost more and are—some think—antithetical to the point of camping: getting a little closer to nature. Contact tourist offices for listings.

Canoeing and Kayaking Your degree of expertise and experience will dictate where you will canoe. Beginners will look for waterways in more settled areas; the pros will head north to the streams and rivers that flow into the Arctic Ocean. Provincial tourist offices and the federal Department of Northern Development and Indian Affairs (Ottawa, Ont. K1A OH4, tel. 819/997–0002) can be of assistance, especially in locating an outfitter to suit your needs. You can also contact the **Canadian Recreational Canoeing Association** (5–1029 Hyde Park Rd., London, Ont. N0M 1Z0, tel. 519/473–2109).

Fishing Anglers can find their catch in virtually any region of the country, though restrictions, seasons, license requirements, and bag limits vary from province to province. In addition, a special fishing permit is required to fish in all national parks; it can be obtained at any national park site, for a nominal fee. The lakes of Québec hold trout, bass, pike, and landlocked salmon, called ouananiche (pronounced *Wah*-nah-nish).

Golf Every province has something for the duffer, but British Columbia and Ontario dominate the golf scene. Because public courses are often overcrowded, if you are a member of a golf club, check to see if it has a reciprocal playing arrangement with any of the private clubs in the areas that you will be visiting.

Hiking Miles and miles of trails weave through all of Canada's national and provincial parks. Write to the individual provincial tourist offices (*see* Essential Information in individual chapters) or the Inquiry Center for the National Parks Department (*see* National Parks, *above*).

Hunting As with fishing, hunting is governed by federal, provincial, and territorial laws. You will need a hunting license from each province or territory in which you plan to hunt. A federal permit is required for hunting migratory game birds and is available at most Canadian post offices. Weapons of any type are prohibited in many of Canada's provincial parks and reserves and adjacent areas, and no hunting is permitted in Canada's national parks. Guides are required in many places and are available almost everywhere. Provincial tourist offices can provide specific information.

Skiing Skiing is probably the most popular winter sport in Canada. For downhill skiing there are slopes in every province, but those in Québec, Alberta, and British Columbia are the best. For cross-country skiing, almost any provincial or national park will do. (*See* the individual chapters.)

White-Water Rafting There are opportunities for rafting in almost every province, but the white waters of Ontario and British Columbia are especially inviting for thrill seekers. Commercial rafting companies offer a variety of trip packages.

Winter Sports Canadians flourish in winter, as the range of winter sports attests. In addition to the sports already mentioned, at the first drop of a snowflake Canadians will head outside to ice-skate, toboggan, snowmobile, dogsled, snowshoe, and ice-fish.

Spectator Sports

Baseball If you're missing a bit of Americana, don't fret. Baseball has been a favorite in Canada since the major leagues expanded into Montréal in 1969 with the Montréal Expos, and the Toronto Blue Jays formed a World Series–caliber club.

Curling For a true taste of Canadian sportsmanship you might want to watch a curling match, which is not unlike a shuffleboard game on ice. Two teams of four players each compete by sliding large polished granite stones toward the center of a bullseye, or "house."

Hockey Officially, Canada's national sport is lacrosse, but ice hockey is the national favorite. It's played by children and professionals alike, with leagues and teams organized everywhere. The National Hockey League teams in Canada include the Vancouver Canucks, Calgary Flames, Winnipeg Jets, Edmonton Oilers, Toronto Maple Leafs,

Ottawa Senators, Montréal Canadiens, and Québec Nordiques. The season runs from October to April.

Dining

The earliest European settlers of Canada—the British and the French—bequeathed a rather bland diet of meat and potatoes. But though there are few really distinct national dishes here, except in Québec, the strong ethnic presence in Canada makes it difficult not to have a good meal. This is especially true in the larger cities, where Greek, Italian, Chinese, Indian, and other immigrants operate restaurants. In addition, each province is well known for various specialties. Vestiges of what the European settlers learned from the Native Americans is evident in the hearty ingredients that make up the French Canadian cuisine, which thrives in Québec. To enjoy the best of the province's hearty meat pies and pâtés, head to Québec City; Montréal dining tends to be more classic French than French Canadian.

Lodging

Aside from the quaint hotels of Québec, Canada's range of accommodations more closely resembles that of the United States than Europe. In the cities you'll have a choice of luxury hotels, moderately priced modern properties, and smaller older hotels with perhaps fewer conveniences but a bit more charm. Options in smaller towns and in the country include large, full-service resorts; small, privately owned hotels; roadside motels; and bed-and-breakfast establishments. Canada's answer to the small European family-run hotel is the mom-and-pop motel, but even though Canada is as attuned to automobile travel as the United States, you won't find these motels as frequently. Even here you'll need to make reservations at least on the day on which you're planning to pull into town.

Chain Hotels There are two advantages to staying at a chain hotel. The first is that you'll be assured of standard accommodations, your own bathroom, and a range of services at the front desk. The second is the ease with which you can get information and make or change reservations, since most chains have toll-free booking numbers.

The major hotel chains in Canada include **Best Western International** (tel. 800/528–1234, in the U.K., 081/541–0033), **CP (Canadian Pacific) Hotels & Resorts** (tel. 800/828–7447, in the U.K., 071/798–9866), **Delta Hotels** (tel. 800/877–1133, in the U.K., 071/937–8033), **Four Seasons Hotels** (tel. 800/332–3442, in the U.K., 081/941–7941), **Holiday Inns** (tel. 800/465–4329, in the U.K., 071/722–7755), **Howard Johnson Hotels** (tel. 800/654–2000, in the U.K., 081/688–1640), **Radisson Hotels** (tel. 800/333–3333, in the U.K., 0992/441517), **Ramada** (tel. 800/228–2828, in the U.K., 071/235–5264), **Sheraton** (tel. 800/325–3535, in the U.K., 0800/353535), **Travelodge** (tel. 800/255–3050, in the U.K., 0345/404040), and **Westin Hotels** (tel. 800/228–3000, in the U.K., 071/408–0636).

Room Rates Expect accommodations to cost more in summer, peak tourist season, than in the off-season. But don't be afraid to ask about special deals and packages when reserving. Big city hotels that cater to business travelers often offer weekend packages, and many city hotels offer rooms at up to 50% off in winter. If you're planning to visit a major city or resort area during the high season, book well in advance. Also be aware of any special events or festivals that may coincide with your visit and block every room for miles around. For resorts and lodges, consider the winter ski-season high as well and plan accordingly (*See* GST and Sales Tax, *above*).

Bed-and-Breakfasts and Country Inns One way to save on lodging and spend some time with a native Canadian is to stay at a bed-and-breakfast establishment. They are gaining in popularity and are located in both the country and the cities. Every provincial tourist board either has a listing of B&Bs or can refer you to an association that will help you secure reservations. Rates range from $20 to upwards of $70 a night and include a Continental or a full breakfast. Because most bed-and-breakfasts are in private homes, you might not have your own bathroom. And some B&B hosts lock up early. Be sure to ask about your host's policies. Room quality varies from home to home as well, so don't be bashful about asking to see a room before making a choice. **Fodor's** guide *Canada's Great Country Inns* lists wonderful places to stay from coast to coast—from unpretentious houses with something special to the elegant Relais & Châteaux (*see below*). You can buy it in most bookstores or ask to have it ordered.

Farm Vacations Vacations on working farms and ranches are one way to enjoy the Canadian countryside. Depending on the size of the farm and the farmer's preferences, you'll be able to observe or even participate in daily activities. These stays include breakfast and some offer other meals and special family rates. For more information about farm vacations, contact the **Canadian Country Vacations Association** (525 Kylemore Ave., Winnipeg, Manitoba R3L 1B5, tel. 204/475-6624).

Dorms and Hostels There are a few alternatives to camping for those on a budget. Among them are hostels, which are open to young and old, families, and singles (*see* Student and Youth Travel, *above*) and university campuses, which open their dorms to travelers for overnight stays from May through August.

Relais & Châteaux Canada has 11 members of this prestigious association where rates run from $150 to $450 a night. Many of these small hotels and inns once served as private estates to the Canadian wealthy. One property is in the countryside, just 30 minutes from Montréal. Reservations must be made directly with each property; for a complete list contact **Relais & Châteaux** (tel. 800/743–8033; 800/677–3524 for reservations).

Home Exchange You can find a house, apartment, or other vacation property to exchange for your own by becoming a member of a home-exchange organization, which then sends you its annual directories listing available exchanges and includes your own listing in at least one of them. Arrangements for the actual exchange are made by the two parties to it, not by the organization. For more information contact the **International Home Exchange Association** (IHEA, 41 Sutter St., Suite 1090, San Francisco, CA 94104, tel. 415/673–0347 or 800/788–2489). Principal clearinghouses: **HomeLink International** (Box 650, Key West, FL 33041, tel. 800/638–3841), with thousands of foreign and domestic listings, publishes four annual directories plus updates; the $50 membership includes your listing in one book. **Intervac International** (Box 590504, San Francisco, CA 94159, tel. 415/435–3497) has three annual directories; membership is $62, or $72 if you want to receive the directories but remain unlisted. **Loan-a-Home** (2 Park La., Apt. 6E, Mount Vernon, NY 10552, tel. 914/664–7640) specializes in long-term exchanges; there is no charge to list your home, but the directories cost $35 or $45 depending on the number you receive.

Apartment and Villa Rentals If you want a home base that's roomy enough for a family and comes with cooking facilities, a furnished rental may be the solution. It's generally cost-wise a good solution, too, although not always—some rentals are luxury properties (economical only when your party is large). Home-exchange directories do list rentals—often second homes owned by prospective house swappers—and there are services that can not only look for a house or apartment for you (even a castle if that's your fancy) but also handle the paperwork. Some send an illustrated catalogue and others send photographs of specific properties, sometimes at a charge; up-front registration fees may apply.

Among the companies are **Property Rentals International** (1 Park West Circle, Suite 108, Midlothian, VA 23113, tel. 804/378–6054 or 800/220–3332) and **Rent a Home International** (7200 34th Ave. NW, Seattle, WA 98117, tel. 206/789–9377 or 800/488–7368). **Hideaways International** (15 Goldsmith St., Box 1270, Littleton, MA 01460, tel. 508/486–8955 or 800/843–4433) functions as a travel club. Membership (US$99 yearly per person or family at the same address) includes two annual guides plus quarterly newsletters; rentals are arranged directly between members, not by the club staff.

Provincial Ratings There is no national government rating system for hotels, but many provinces rate their accommodations.

Credit Cards

The following credit card abbreviations are used throughout this guide: AE, American Express; D, Discover; DC, Diners Club; MC, MasterCard; V, Visa. It's a good idea to call ahead to check current credit-card policies.

2 Portrait of Montréal and Québec City

Maple Leaf Rag: Two Excerpts

Naked City

By Stephen Brook

In Maple Leaf Rag, *author Stephen Brook describes his travels through Canada. Mr. Brook's other works include* New York Days and New York Nights *and* Honkytonk Gelato.

In my short-trouser years my best friend came from Montreal. His father exchanged cash for erudition on a British television quiz show, but the entire family was Canadian. So was his nanny, previously his mother's nanny, who affected to be severe in the best Scottish-Canadian manner, but was in truth kindly and humorous beneath it. Christopher, whose disposable pocket-money income eclipsed mine and whose upbringing had been less orderly than my own, helped push me into swaggering adolescence. At the age of 13 he was a heavy smoker, swore skillfully, took me to amusement arcades to burn a couple of shillings, used a Leica when I was still twirling a Brownie, and talked knowingly about girls at a time when I knew none. He was handsome and confident, and I moved rather in his shadow. He was a boy of strong opinions, all of which he voiced regularly. Although most of his closest friends were Jewish, he was not above the occasional anti-Semitic jibe, unthinkingly based on received opinion more than personal experience. He was virulently anti-Catholic, a prejudice fueled and bolstered by the redoubtable nanny, who riveted me with terrible tales of how Catholic mothers perish in childbirth in order that their newborn infants shall live. And so forth.

When Christopher was 14, he returned to Canada and four years went by before we met again, this time in his native city. The Montreal he showed me was an English Montreal. At no time was I aware that he or anyone in his family had more than a rudimentary knowledge of the French language. Christopher had matured with all his prejudices intact. He took me to St. Joseph's Oratory not to pray or admire but to pour scorn on Catholic credulousness. At the time I thought little of it, but revisiting the city after a gap of 20 years, it was not difficult to appreciate why French-Canadian nationalism had triumphed so decisively a decade ago. I don't think it ever occurred to Christopher, or to tens of thousands of other British-Canadian Montrealers, that their attitude was arrogant; they took it as given that they belonged to an educated elite, and that French Canadians, whatever their numerical status, didn't count for much and were somehow ineligible for full human consideration by virtue of their barbaric religion, incomprehensible dialect and insular culture.

The Montreal of his youth has certainly been modified, but it was essentially French even then and language laws and other recent developments have only altered the city in its degree of Frenchness. The English-speaking citizens may have controlled the economic life of the province, but they had never been able to dominate the tone of the city. Yet I was surprised, having heard so many tales of executive flight, to find how intact the English quarters of Montreal still are. Twenty years ago the inner suburb of Westmount was exclusively English-speaking; now French is heard on its steep streets and from behind the high fences of its grand houses. You'll still find here some of the few remaining road signs in Quebec that say STOP instead of ARRÊT, and on Greene Street you can have tea at the Café Oxford, buy your clothes at Carriage Trade, order a catered meal from By George, and stop at the Avenue Bookshop to tickle the chin of Orwell the marmalade cat. On the same street I watched a dignified old lady parking a Jaguar which sported the following bumper sticker: LET ME TELL YOU ABOUT MY GRANDCHILDREN. I ran after her, imploring her to satisfy my curiosity, but the old tease wouldn't tell me a thing, not even whether they were legitimate.

A few blocks away, on Lansdowne, a condominium development is dangled before the moneyed public in a manner that suggested the matter-of-fact Canadians, when pushed, can exhibit as much vulgarity as any coven of copywriters in the United States: "In search of excellence? Finally. A luxury condominium that delivers your personal statement. Success. Unmatched anywhere in the city. Le 200 Lansdowne in Westmount. Beyond elite." The British style still gasps along at some of the old clubs in downtown Montreal on and near Sherbrooke Street; here all the rituals of London clubland have been embalmed in their North American setting. Perhaps there are French-Canadian members, but I heard no French spoken during the enjoyable claret-drenched evening I spent at the University Club, and I imagine that any Francophone Québecois would with some justification fail to see what purpose could possibly be served by joining such an institution.

Even though the walls between French and English have crumbled in recent years, Montreal is still a city of enclaves. Mordecai Richler's novels portray the Jewish quarters of the city that existed in his childhood. Of that thickly populated district little remains, for many Jews prospered sufficiently to allow them to move to more sedate suburbs, but their place has been taken by other, more recent arrivals. One Saturday morning I drove up the avenue du Parc, with its string of Greek restaurants, and then east along Laurier; these blocks along Laurier used to be unprepossessing, but now they are being smartened up, and bright shopfronts dazzle among less colorful facades. I turned up boulevard St-Laurent, which everyone in the city calls the Main, through what's left of the Jewish quarter, and soon found myself in the Italian quarter.

From rue Mozart, where I parked, it was just a few paces to the Marché du Nord, which resembles a display of prize fruits and vegetables suddenly invaded by the general public. There were huge sooty black plums the size of tennis balls, green and yellow watermelons stacked beneath the stalls, bulbs of garlic plaited on their stalks, a smell of ripe cantaloupes mugging occasional whiffs of greeny mint, peppers enthusiastically marked DOLCI DOLCI DOLCI!, bunches of basil hanging from chains suspended between the concrete pillars of the market square, a battalion of honeys, baby Italian aubergines erupting from green stalks with the texture of aged skin, green and yellow haricot beans, buckets of lumpish broad beans going cheap, scrubbed potatoes, fresh corn skinned back to reveal pale yellow grains (*"très sucré!"*), riotous spinach curling in on itself (*"Bueno, bueno,"* murmured a woman approvingly as she fingered the leaves), white radishes like mandrake roots, pale green "white" zucchini, lizardy sage, 2-foot-long wispy dill, orange zucchini blossoms destined to frolic with glistening wet cos lettuces in salads. And weaving their way between the crowded stalls were West Indians in straining shorts and hair curlers, determined Italians with shopping baskets that bulged as capaciously as their paunches, thoughtful chin-stroking invaders from Westmount, burly French-Canadians with packs of Craven A tucked beneath the shoulder straps of their white T-shirts. Officialdom's attempt to force a metric system on Canada was in disarray here for, though some stalls had signs scrawled in kilos as well, almost all gave equal prominence to the old system. The Mulroney government had given the nod to relaxations of enforced metrication, and in large cities and conservative rural townships alike, kilos and meters began to be displaced by the archaic yet familiar mysteries of pounds and yards.

The European profusion of the Marché du Nord was in vibrant contrast to the decorum of the Atwater Market, situated closer to the English-speaking districts on the other side of the city. Earlier that morning produce had been stacked onto the stalls with a bricklayer's precision, as though the goods were too lovely and precious to be sold or even fingered by jowly matrons feeling their way toward a ratatouille. Fruit and vegetables were scrubbed so as to extinguish any associations with such lowly elements as earth and compost. If the northern Montreal market was a marvelous mélange of Paris, Naples, and Lisbon, Atwater was more American in style; its teeth had been capped and there were no gray hairs. . . .

The pleasures of stuffing yourself with food were first elevated to the art of gastronomy in 19th-century Paris. The Canadian equivalent of bourgeois prosperity founded on the pursuit of trade and commerce had its roots in Vieux-Montréal. When Christopher had taken me there two decades ago at the midnight hour, it had been dark and sinister; bulky massive warehouses and commercial buildings glowered over deserted streets. Here and there dim yellow lights indicated that a restaurant or bar was still open, but for the most part the old town was still and forbidding. It's somber still, for the heavy gray stone buildings continue to overshadow the narrow lanes, but there are places among the network of austere commercial streets that reveal now, as they must have done a century ago, the grandeur of Vieux-Montréal. Where the Lower Town of Quebec City is archly quaint in its re-creation of bustling 17th-century small businesses and maritime trading offices, Vieu-Montréal affirms the solidity and ambition of 19th-century commercialism. True, there are older churches and seminaries from the 17th century, together with 18th-century houses such as the Château Ramezay, but the mighty commercial buildings mostly date from a period of Victorian prosperity. As the city moved to preserve its most ancient quarter, new uses had to be found for these imposing buildings, and inevitably restaurants and studios and loft flats were carved out of spaces once taken up by winches and ledgers and bales.

Many sneer at such prosperous middle-class invasions of once dilapidated downtown areas, but I applaud adaptations that allow old districts to be preserved without being fossilized. Vieux-Montréal still feels alive, and its character has not been violated by the injection of new blood along the long handsome streets such as St. Paul. Vieux-Montréal succeeds where the Lower Town of Quebec City fails because there has been no programmatic zeal to remove "unhistorical" later accretions. The essentially 19th-century character of the old town, with its mighty church and massive municipal buildings—even the City Hall of 1926 resembles a French Renaissance extravaganza more typical of the previous century—is intact. While the Lower Town of Quebec City has been re-created essentially as a tourist attraction—admittedly a successful one—Vieux-Montréal remains integral to the city that has grown around it.

Quebec City is irretrievably provincial, which is in large part its charm. Vieux-Montréal, on the evidence of its architecture, always aspired to greater things. The scale is altogether more grandiose, reflecting Montreal's standing in the mid-19th century as a colonial capital and a major center of communications and finance. Take the neo-Gothic church of Notre Dame that dominates the spacious Place d'Armes. Here the fervour of institutional Catholicism blends happily with civic pride. Lavishly ornamented with wood carvings and gold leaf and polychrome decoration, there is little echo here of the Jansenism and cloistered piety of the Quebec City churches (a severity that can, however, be conveniently recaptured at the austere seminary of 1685 adjoining the church); the spirit here is closer to the proud splendor of Italian Baroque, where the worldly is used, with varying degrees of success, as a vehicle for the spiritual. The nave and the double-decker galleries overlooking it were built to seat 3,000, a remarkable number when one recalls that when the church was built in the 1820s the population of Montreal was no more than 15,000.

The Place d'Armes is not the only spot where the urban pride of old Montreal lives on. A few hundred yards to the east are two more squares, named after Cartier and Vauquelin; both are spacious and invigorating, since even on hot days a breeze often wafts up from the St. Lawrence. (It was Cartier who first came to what was then the Indian village of Hochelaga in 1535, though the Europeans didn't settle here until a century later, when Montreal proved a well-situated base for the French fur trade.) Shoppers and visitors congregate here, and there's always somebody around who has unpacked a guitar at the base of

Canada's version of Nelson's Column and is strumming tunelessly to the accompaniment of cigarette or marijuana smoke, while tourists enjoy an overpriced ice cream or beer at a café before ambling down to the rue Bonsecours and its famous sailors' church. Fewer tourists stroll as far west as the loveliest spot in Vieux-Montréal, and indeed one of the most enchanting groups of buildings in Canada: the Youville Stables. A gate leads into a beautiful courtyard overlooked by dignified early 19th-century buildings, their walls awash with ivy; stately gravel paths flow across the lawns and tubs packed with flowers provide a welcome burst of color amid the restraint of gray stone and clipped green lawn.

Unconsummated Divorce

When, 15 years ago, I lived in Boston, I would occasionally drive up through Maine to Quebec City for a long weekend. Boston was a congenial city but an American one, and I missed Europe. I missed the texture of old stone and the scrawled *plat du jour* on a menu, and I could find both of those in Quebec. On returning to the city after a long absence my former affection welled up once again. Not that Quebec is an especially attractive city, despite its splendid site high over the St. Lawrence River. With its gray stone and raucous climate, it reminds me of Old Aberdeen—only physically, I hasten to add, for the atmosphere of Quebec City is almost hedonistic, and no one could say that about Aberdeen. Within its partially reconstructed walls, the old city covers a small area, and the bulk of the municipality spreads out through a string of modern suburbs such as Ste-Foy.

Quebec City is no Paris, and that is its very charm. It is unequivocally provincial. With its ancient university, its churches and convents, its hotels and restaurants, it is urban, but not cosmopolitan. It is, however, European, with that density of habitation that packs together public buildings and churches, boutiques and convents, into a thickly jumbled profusion of squares and streets, alleys and terraces. To me the appeal of Quebec City lies less in its superficial picturesque quality than in its austerity, and I dislike many of the attempts now being made to prettify the old town: the quaint signs, the colorful windowboxes, the heightening of antique architectural features. Streets such as Ste-Anne that cater to the tourists—and admittedly do it well—are not half as expressive as, say, rue Ste-Famille. This lane descends a hill and is flanked on the right by a harsh authoritarian building that is part of Laval University. The structure is relatively recent—it dates from 1920—but its uncompromising, unlovely bulk is closer to the grim Jansenist spirit of the town than the ardent but obsequious crowd-pleasing of many of the main streets. At the foot of rue Ste-Famille stands a row of cottages dating from the 1750s that bring some modest charm to the austere street. More characteristic of Quebec as a whole are the tall stone town houses, entered through raised doorways so that the ground-floor windows are often just above snooping level. On rue St-Louis most tourists walk straight past the fine Maison Maillou, for with its navy blue shutters set against rough gray stone walls, the house does not call attention to itself, but it is very French and very handsome. The townhouse interiors are guarded not only by stern doorways, but by shutters that fold over double glazing that shields a layer of starched lace curtains. Block-faced old women still lift a corner of those curtains to peer out at the weather. This is a city of exteriors; the houses are not welcoming but excluding.

An ecclesiastical atmosphere permeates the city like incense, for although the Catholic Church has lost its former stranglehold, the old town still seems packed with nuns. The ancient seminary is as severe as the houses, though the bright white-washed walls around the courtyard modify an austerity that would be oppressive were it not for the wealth of details that have accrued over the centuries. Most visitors rightly admire the great panoramas from the terraces overlooking the river and from the ancient citadel, but they are not what makes the town unique. Quebec, unlike a modern city, exalts the idiosyncratic. A chimney stack or a doorway or a previously unnoticed alley keeps one's interest alive, and though the city is small, it never seems to pall. There are still quiet spots frequented only by cats and tourists who have put the guidebooks away and allowed themselves to stray. At the end of rue Mont Carmel, for instance, is a small park, scarcely more than a garden, but the view is fine and the mood somber but tranquil, in contrast to its aura three centuries ago when a windmill supported a three-gun battery. The old fortifications of the city, which date from the late 17th century, have been more or less rebuilt, and it's possible to walk their length for about 3 miles.

The churches in this very ecclesiastical city are resplendent. The Anglican cathedral of 1804 has a magnificent interior, complete with box pews and wood gallery; its broad but shallow apse is, like any English church of the same vintage, lined with memorial tablets. A few streets away stands, in complete contrast, Notre Dame de Québec. There has been a church on this site since the 1640s, though the present structure dates from 1925. The conservative citizens didn't adopt a modern idiom when the church was rebuilt, and the interior is resolutely Baroque, with voluptuous gilt furnishings. Another rebuilt church is the equally sumptuous chapel of the Ursuline convent, adorned with a pulpit and reredos in luxurious black, white and gold. An elaborate screen divides the nuns' choir from the public area of the chapel. More grilles—how rigidly the laity was kept at bay!—fence off the founder's burial chapel. This is a historical spot, for Montcalm is buried here, and a notice sternly informs visitors, RESPECTUOUS CLOTHES REQUIRED. Another contrast to Catholic elaboration is provided at St. Andrew's Church of 1810, the oldest Presbyterian church in Canada, though the country has certainly made up for lost time since. Here, in contrast with the more stratified disposition of the Anglican Cathedral, an appropriately nonconformist note is sounded by having the pews curved so that the entire congregation can face the elevated pulpit behind the altar.

The provincial motto is *Je me souviens* (I remember), though a translation of "I haven't forgotten" catches the hint of aggrieved menace I always detect in the words. Ironically, the motto was taken from a Loyalist poem. History was not kind to the people of Quebec. The Frenchman Champlain was astute enough to nail this site as a future colonial center in 1608, and the settlement grew rapidly. Bishop Laval, after whom the university is named, arrived in 1659 and initiated the unremitting ecclesiastical control that strangled Quebec for three centuries. When, during the 18th century, Britain and France began to battle it out for control of the strategically crucial river, it was inevitable that Quebec City would be much fought over. The decisive encounter took place in 1759. The British general James Wolfe began to besiege the city in July. Late on September 12 the British forces crept up on to the Plains of Abraham, the broady grassy plateau adjoining the present-day citadel. The following day the French commander Montcalm led his troops into battle against the encroaching besiegers. For Wolfe as well as Montcalm it was a fatal encounter, and the outcome was a rout of the French forces. This was the end of New France, and the beginning of the French-Canadian mentality enshrined in the motto *Je me souviens*.

Although the battle heralded the beginning of the end of French rule, it certainly wasn't the end of French influence. To this day Quebec City remains resolutely French in language and culture. Its half million inhabitants are, unlike the population of Montreal, overwhelmingly of French descent. As Montreal became increasingly important as a cultural and commercial center within Canada, the influence of Quebec City began to diminish. Montreal had to participate, at least commercially, in the life of the rest of North America, leaving Quebec free to retreat into the certainties of French-Canadian culture, an ethos dominated by the church. As recently as 30 years ago the province was, notoriously, a society ruled by demagogues in league with the power of the church; the *curé* and the *notaire*, as the only educated citizens of innumerable small towns and villages, exercised a powerful, and usually reactionary, influence. Education rarely proved intellectually liberating, since it reiterated the largely authoritarian values current when the province was originally colonized. In the 1960s, with what became known as the Quiet Revolution, these traditional cultural arbiters rapidly lost influence, and within a decade or so Quebec had become more outward-looking, more sophisticated, more liberal. The schools and universities no longer supplied a constant stream of smalltown priests, doctors and lawyers, but began to educate scientists and engineers as well. Churchgoing is no longer ubiquitous, and, most astonishing of all, the birthrate is decreasing for the first time. The Quiet Revolution also brought political changes. The province gained the confidence to assert its identity within the larger Canadian confederation, even though it chose to do so by insisting on the irreconcilable differences between its culture and that of the predominantly English culture that enveloped it. Political separatism gathered force and in 1968 the Parti Québecois was founded. Just eight years later, to the astonishment not only of the rest of Canada but of the Parti's own leaders, it was elected into office, and for nine years the province was ruled by a party that officially espoused separatism. . . .

Québecois worry about their identity almost as much as other Canadians do, though with less justification. French Canada is instantly identifiable as a place apart. Glancing through the visitors' book at Louisburg, I easily identified the French-Canadian signatories, because their handwriting differs from that of their British-Canadian compatriots. It would surely be impossible to distinguish between the handwriting of Americans or Germans from different parts of their respective countries, but here in Canada this minor cultural indicator signified the almost total cultural separation of French Canadians. There are other such indicators. French Canadians seem, and I say this on the basis of observations in crowded cafés rather than on statistical evidence, to be far heavier smokers than their compatriots outside the province. . . .

The events that brought about the downfall of French Quebec are most easily recalled at the citadel, positioned on a formidably fortified hill on the edge of the old town. The ramparts that surround it include outer walls spacious enough to enclose a tennis court. Before touring the citadel, which was built in the 1820s and is still in use, visitors are compelled to attend the Changing of the Guard. The soldiers' uniforms are essentially British in design: red coats and bearskin hats. But all commands are issued in French, which I found culturally dislocating. An excellent band wandered about the parade ground, and the pounding of the drums and the growl of the brass reverberated thunderously off the barrack walls. One soldier gripped a leash attached to a goat with gilded horns, and at various times during the long ceremony, the goat was tugged around the parade ground and, despite the splendor of its outfit, did not seem to be enjoying itself. How unsoldierly these French Canadians were! While at ease, they grinned and smirked, mostly in the direction of teenage girls in tight shorts. The drills were of a high standard, but there was no sense of military preparedness, and without any doubt a platoon of halberdiers could have taken the citadel that morning with a minimum of casualties. Myself, I'd have had that guard changed and back at work in half the time. Almost without exception, the soldiers were mustachioed. Mustaches are common in Quebec but here they seemed almost part of the uniform. When I questioned a soldier about this urgent matter, he confirmed my observation but couldn't explain it. During the tedious moments on the parade ground, I could at least admire the views: of the Château Frontenac, which like most buildings named Château in Canada turns out to be a luxurious Canadian Pacific hotel, and, in another direction, of the typically undistinguished Hilton tower. The best view of all unfurls itself from the Prince of Wales bastion, which overlooks the St. Lawrence and the Plains of Abraham, now a park.

Back in the city, the most popular panorama is enjoyed from the Terrasse Dufferin, a boardwalk that carpets the clifftop in front of the Château Frontenac. The spot is overlooked by a statue of Champlain, who is depicted as stamping his foot with impatience ("Merde! Vaincu encore"), though more probably he was just feeling the cold. While the bulky Frontenac looks splendid from a distance, a closer view reveals it as pastiche, and brings into focus the dull caramel brick of which it is built. Steep flights of steps lead down from the Terrasse to the lower town, for old Quebec thrived at two levels, the lower of which huddles around the port. During the 19th century the Lower Town, which architecturally must have equaled the Upper, became a slum. In recent years it has been renovated at a cost of over $30 million. Without the efforts of the restorers, there's little doubt that the entire area would have been razed and replaced by container warehouses and car parks, so it seems churlish to carp at what has been done here. But I'll carp anyway, for the restoration struck me as extreme, and lacking in the sensitivity displayed at Louisburg. In the Lower Town features not deemed "authentic"—post 17th and 18th century, in other words—were simply removed. Extra stories built on to older houses in later decades were dismantled, and new "authentic" roofs have taken their place. Brand-new dormer windows and rearranged fenestration contort the ramshackle old structures into pattern-book shape. Old buildings and their accretions eventually become stylistically coherent, with occasional exceptions. By ignoring this principle, the restorers of the Lower Town have preserved the letter and throttled the spirit. As a tourist attraction it works well, for some of the old mansions have been converted into excellent small museums; and the Place Royale, the ancient square surrounded by former merchants' houses in the heart of the Lower Town and the very spot where in 1608 Champlain founded French North America, is always crowded. Notre-Dame des Victoires, founded here in 1688 and rebuilt in the same style in 1759, is the most charming of Quebec's churches, with its cream and gold interior and the castlelike construction of the High Altar. By wandering down some of the less tampered-with streets, such as rue St-Pierre and rue St-Paul, toward the Vieux-Port, I filtered through my mind a better sense of what the old Lower Town must have been like, say, a century ago. The old houses along these streets have been less fanatically restored than those around the Place Royale. Small restaurants, chic and high-priced, as well as design and crafts boutiques, keep the lights burning, more, I suspect, in anticipation of a steady influx of lucre than in response to a present demand. Even more off the tourist beat are the streets beyond the fortifications that slope down to the Lower Town. Here, along Olivier, Richelieu, and D'Aiguillon are tucked-in houses and artisans' cottages, vestiges of old Quebec that lie midway between the walled city and the sprawling suburbs.

Quebec reserves its greatest charm for nighttime. The terraces of cafés and bars are crowded with people sipping an aperitif or a brandy. The vigorous rooflines of Château Frontenac and some of the large public buildings are floodlit. Down in the Lower Town a string quartet had found a vacant corner and was sending a divertimento by Mozart spinning into the night. In the Upper Town, near the central Place d'Armes, musicians—playing a mouth organ, a variety of banjo, and a clackety castanet tapped against the thigh—sang out fast and lively Québecois songs, and passersby joined in the choruses. In front of the musicians an old man, his white hair spilling out from beneath a well-chewed panama, danced a stately jig. From the Terrasse Dufferin, the lights of the town of Lévis, on the opposite bank of the St. Lawrence, twinkled brightly, and I could see the fat little ferry chugging its way across the river.

3 Montréal

By Patricia Lowe

Updated by Helga Loverseed

"Plus ça change, plus c'est la même chose," like other travel clichés, no longer applies to Montréal, which marked its 350th anniversary in 1992. For years, as Québec's largest city and the world's second-largest French-speaking metropolis, Montréal clung to an international reputation attained in the heyday of former Mayor Jean Drapeau, who brought his beloved hometown the 1967 World's Fair (Expo '67), the Métro subway, its Underground City, and the 1976 Summer Olympics. During his nearly three decades in power, Drapeau's entrepreneurial spirit added pizzazz to this transportation and financial capital at the gateway to the St. Lawrence Seaway.

But with the arrival of a nationalist provincial government in 1976, the mayor and Montréal were forced to rest on their laurels as the province agonized over its place in Canada. Separation from the rest of the country was seriously considered. The provincial government passed the controversial Bill 101, which makes French the official language of business and public communication. For the city it was a wrenching ideological change; the only difference that visitors saw was that English or bilingual billboards and public signs were replaced by French ones. Bill 101 was replaced by the more conciliatory Bill 178 in January, 1994, which permits English and other languages to be used in certain public areas and on road signs.

Nearly 60% of the province's population opted in 1980 to remain in the federal family, but a decade later, French-speaking Québecois' old animosities regarding English Canada were rekindled when former Prime Minister Mulroney attempted to unite all 10 provinces through a constitutional agreement called the Meech Lake accord. However, the legislatures of two provinces did not ratify the accord. In 1992, Mulroney came up with a more elaborate plan, this time allowing the Canadian people to decide in a referendum. On October 26, six provinces rejected a deal that would have radically changed the country's 125-year-old constitution. Today the problem remains unresolved.

The melding of old and new architecture that characterizes this city is no more apparent than in the flamboyant office tower of La Maison des Coopérants. Even though the design of this 35-story pink glass structure imitates the Gothic-style Christ Church Cathedral it overshadows, it was not what the earnest French missionaries who founded Montréal envisioned. What today is a metropolis of 3.1 million—some 15% of English mother tongue—began as 54 dedicated souls from France who landed on Montréal island in 1642 to convert the Indians to Christianity.

For nearly 200 years city life was confined to a 95-acre walled community, today's Vieux-Montréal and a protected historic site. Ville-Marie became a fur-trading center, the chief embarkation point for the voyageurs setting off on discovery and trapping expeditions. This business quickly usurped religion as the settlement's raison d'être, along with its role as a major port at the confluence of the St. Lawrence and Ottawa rivers.

The Old Montréal of the French regime lasted until 1760, when, during one of the battles of the Seven Years' War, British troops easily forced the poorly fortified and demoralized city to surrender. The Treaty of Paris ended the war in 1763, and Québec became one of Great Britain's most valuable colonies. British and Scottish settlers poured in to take advantage of Montréal's geography and economic potential. When it was incorporated as a city in 1832, it was a leading colonial capital of business, finance, and transportation.

Montréal Exploring *(Boxes Refer to Detail Maps)*

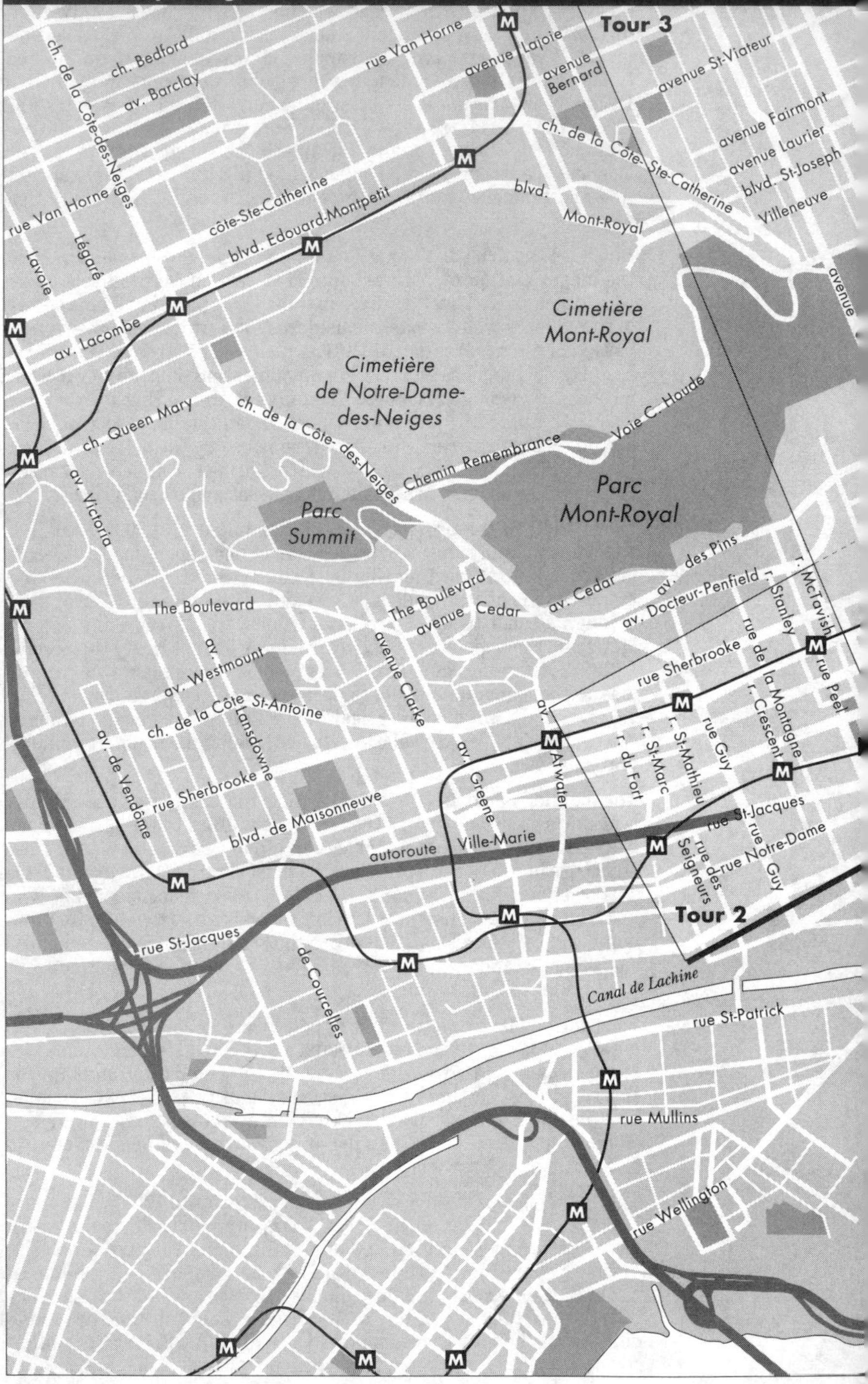
Tour 3
rue Van Horne
avenue Lajoie
avenue Bernard
avenue St-Viateur
ch. Bedford
av. Barclay
ch. de la Côte-des-Neiges
avenue Fairmont
avenue Laurier
blvd. St-Joseph
Villeneuve
ch. de la Côte-Ste-Catherine
blvd. Mont-Royal
côte-Ste-Catherine
blvd. Edouard-Montpetit
rue Van Horne
Légaré
Lavoie
av. Lacombe
avenue
Cimetière Mont-Royal
Cimetière de Notre-Dame-des-Neiges
ch. Queen Mary
ch. de la Côte-des-Neiges
Voie C. Houde
Chemin Remembrance
Parc Mont-Royal
Parc Summit
av. Victoria
av. des Pins
av. Cedar
av. Docteur-Penfield
r. Stanley
r. McTavish
The Boulevard
The Boulevard
avenue Cedar
avenue Clarke
av. Westmount
rue Sherbrooke
rue de la Montagne
rue Peel
ch. de la Côte St-Antoine
Lansdowne
av. Atwater
r. St-Mathieu
r. St-Marc
r. du Fort
rue Guy
r. Crescent
av. de Vendôme
rue Sherbrooke
av. Greene
blvd. de Maisonneuve
rue St-Jacques
rue Guy
autoroute Ville-Marie
rue des Seigneurs
rue Notre-Dame
Tour 2
rue St-Jacques
de Courcelles
Canal de Lachine
rue St-Patrick
rue Mullins
rue Wellington

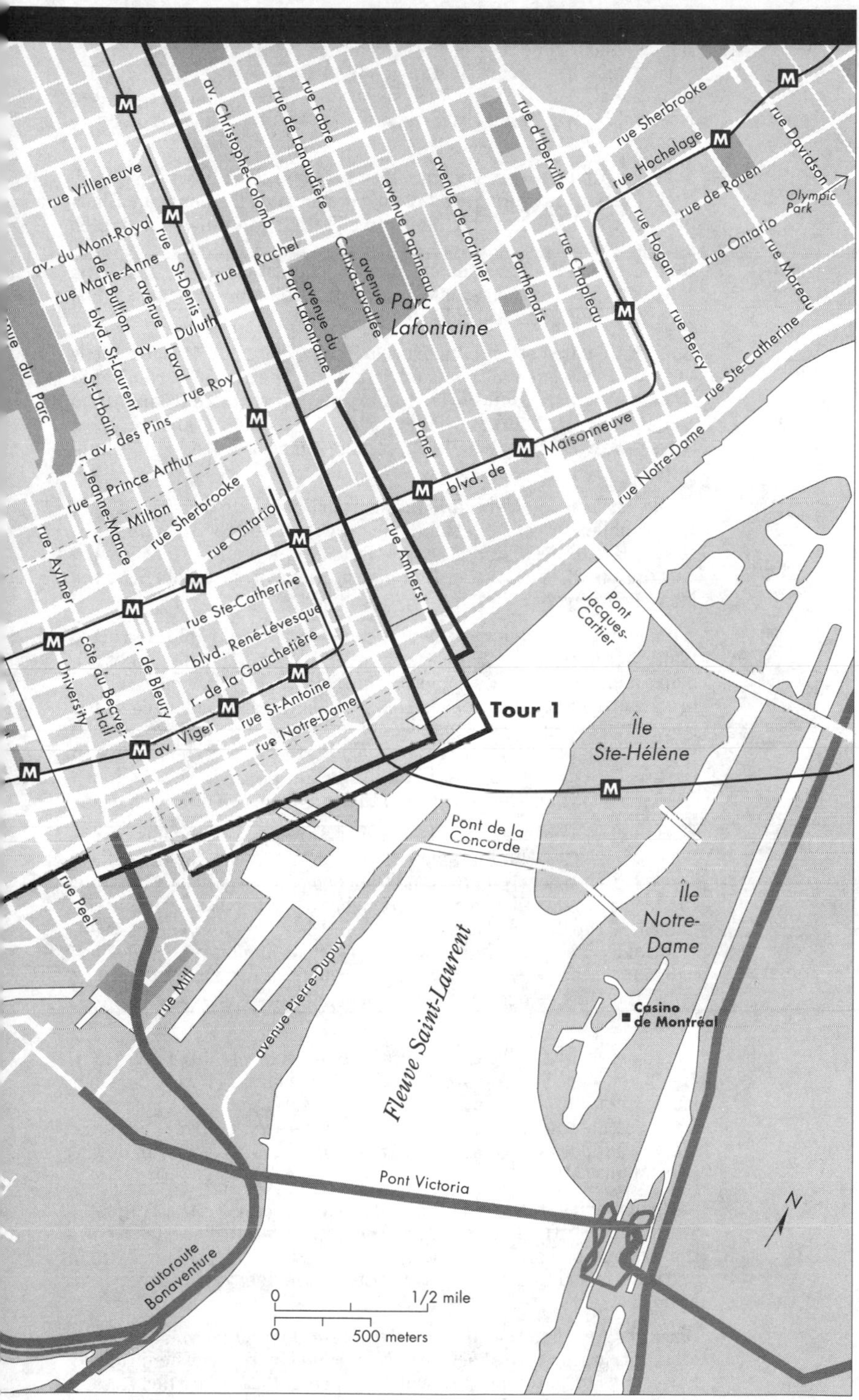
Tour 1
rue Villeneuve
av. du Mont-Royal
rue Marie-Anne
de Bullion
blvd. St-Laurent
St-Urbain
avenue Laval
rue St-Denis
av. Duluth
rue Rachel
rue Roy
av. des Pins
rue Prince Arthur
r. Jeanne-Mance
r. Milton
rue Sherbrooke
rue Ontario
rue Aylmer
rue Ste-Catherine
blvd. René-Lévesque
r. de la Gauchetière
rue St-Antoine
rue Notre-Dame
av. Viger
r. de Bleury
côte du Beaver Hall
University
rue Peel
rue Mill
av. Christophe-Colomb
rue de Lanaudière
rue Fabre
avenue du Parc Lafontaine
avenue Calixa-Lavallée
avenue Papineau
avenue de Lorimier
Parc Lafontaine
rue d'Iberville
Parthenais
rue Chapleau
Panet
rue Amherst
blvd. de Maisonneuve
rue Sherbrooke
rue Hochelage
rue de Rouen
rue Hogan
rue Ontario
rue Bercy
rue Davidson
Olympic Park
rue Moreau
rue Ste-Catherine
rue Notre-Dame
Pont Jacques-Cartier
Île Ste-Hélène
Pont de la Concorde
Île Notre-Dame
Casino de Montréal
avenue Pierre-Dupuy
Fleuve Saint-Laurent
Pont Victoria
autoroute Bonaventure
0
1/2 mile
0
500 meters
N
M

Montréal is still Canada's transport hub: It is home to the national railway and airline, the largest private rail company (Canadian Pacific), Canada's version of Amtrak (VIA Rail), Air Canada, the International Air Transport Association (IATA), and the United Nations' International Civil Aviation Organization (ICAO) on Sherbrooke.

Solidly established by the late 19th century, downtown today still reminds visitors of its grand old days, particularly along rue Sherbrooke, the lifeline of chic Montréal. The busy flower-lined stretch between rues Guy and University takes in the de la Montagne–Crescent–Bishop–Mackay sector, where sophisticated restaurants, cafés, and bars share canopied facades with haute-couture salons, antiques shops, and art galleries.

Rue Peel, between rue Sherbrooke and Place du Canada, rolls through the Montréal most tourists visit. The recently renovated Dominion Square Building is the art deco home of tourism offices and information bureaus. Bus tours, taxi guides, and *calèches* (horse-drawn carriages) all depart from some point around this public park.

To the east, rue St-Denis and the surrounding Latin Quarter attract Francophiles; a more ethnic flavor characterizes the Chinese, Greek, Portuguese, and other districts around Prince Arthur's pedestrian mall, boulevard St-Laurent (known to locals as "the Main"), and avenue du Parc.

A bohemian atmosphere pervades rue Prince Arthur, blocked off to traffic between boulevard St-Laurent and Carré St-Louis. What the mall's many restaurants sometimes lack in quality they make up for in ethnic diversity—Chinese, Greek, Italian, Polish, Québecois, and Vietnamese—and price, especially at establishments where you supply the liquor (BYO). Some 12,000 Portuguese residents live in the area's St-Louis district, and their bright pastel houses and lush front gardens have contributed to the neighborhood's renaissance.

Early in this century, rue St-Denis cut through a bourgeois neighborhood of large, comfortable residences. After a period of decline, it revived in the early 1970s, and then boomed, largely as a result of the 1969 opening of Université du Québec's Montréal campus and the launch of the International Jazz Festival in the summer of 1980. Rows of French and ethnic restaurants, charming bistros, and chess hangouts cater to Franco and Anglo academics; stylish intellectuals prowl the Québec designer boutiques, antiques shops, and art galleries.

Activity reaches its peak during the 10 days in late June and early July when some 500,000 jazz buffs descend upon the city to hear such music giants as Pat Metheny and Montréal-born Oscar Peterson. Theaters hosting the 1,000 or so performers range from sidewalk stages to Place des Arts, the main performing arts center in downtown Montréal.

The popularity of the jazz festival is rivaled only by the August's World Film Festival (also featured near this area at Place des Arts), the lively Just For Laughs Comedy Festival in the St-Denis area, and the Cinéma Le Parisien on rue Ste-Catherine, among other venues.

Place des Arts and the adjacent Complexe Desjardins constitute another intriguing hive of activity. Now joined by the new home of the Musée d'Art Contemporain, which opened in 1992, Place des Arts is really three separate halls built around a sweeping plaza overlooking rue Ste-Catherine.

One often-overlooked sector of the city requires a Métro ride but is worth the fare for a varied tour of Olympic and de Maisonneuve parks, the Château Dufresne Decorative Arts Museum, the Botanical Garden, and the Biodome—all located at or near the corner of boulevard Pie-IX (Métro station of the same name) and rue Sherbrooke Est.

This triangle in the east end is distinguished by the flying-saucer design of the Olympic Stadium, completed by the world's "tallest inclined tower." The stadium's latest attraction is the funicular cable car that speeds sightseers to its observation deck for a spectacular view of the island of Montréal.

Essential Information

Arriving and Departing by Plane

Airports Montréal is served by two airports: **Dorval International,** 22½ kilometers (14 miles) west of the city, handles domestic and most U.S. flights; **Mirabel International,** 54½ kilometers (34 miles) northwest of the city, is a hub for the rest of the international trade.

Airlines From the United States: **Air Canada** (tel. 514/393–3333 or 800/361–8620) has nonstop service from New York, Miami, and Tampa; nonstop from Boston via Air Canada's connector airline, **Air Alliance;** direct service is available from Los Angeles and San Francisco. **American Airlines** (tel. 800/433–7300) has nonstop service from Chicago with connections from the rest of the United States. **British Airways** (tel. 514/287–9133; in Québec province, 800/668–1059) has nonstop service from Detroit to Montréal. **Canadian Airlines International,** (tel. 514/847–2211; in Canada, 800/363–7530; in U.S., 800/420–7000) formerly CP Air, has a nonstop charter from Fort Lauderdale and direct or connecting service from Hawaii and Los Angeles. **Delta Air Lines** (tel. 514/337–5520, in Québec Province, 800/361–1970; in U.S., 800/221–1212) has nonstops from Boston, Hartford, Connecticut, and Miami and connecting service from most major U.S. cities. **USAir** (tel. 800/428–4322) has services from Buffalo and Syracuse, New York, and from Pittsburgh.

Flying Time From New York, 1½ hours; from Chicago, two hours; from Los Angeles, 6½ hours (with a connection).

Between the Airports and Center City Dorval Airport is about a 20- to 30-minute drive from downtown Montréal, and Mirabel International is about a 45-minute drive away.

By Taxi A taxi from Dorval to downtown will cost $25. The taxi rates from Mirabel to the center of Montréal average $56, depending on traffic, and you can count on about the same cost for a taxi between the two airports. All taxi companies in Montréal must charge the same rates by law. It is best to have Canadian money with you, because the exchange rate for U.S. dollars is at the driver's discretion.

By Bus **Autobus Connaisseur** (tel. 514/934–1222) provides a much cheaper alternative into town from Mirabel. For $14 a van will take you into the city, with stops at Le Reine Elizabeth (Queen Elizabeth)—next to Gare Centrale—and the Voyageur bus station. It runs every hour from 4 AM until noon and 8 PM until 2 AM, and every half hour between 12:30 and 7:30. Bus service between Mirabel and Dorval is also available for $12, every hour from 9:20 AM until 11:20 AM and 8:20 PM until 11:20 PM. Between 11:40 AM and 8 PM the bus runs every 20 minutes.

Grayline (tel. 514/934–1222) offers bus transportation between Dorval and downtown Montréal for $9. On weekdays it runs every 20 minutes between 7:30 AM and 12:30 AM; on weekends every half hour between 7:30 AM and 12:30 AM.

Arriving and Departing by Train, Bus, and Car

By Train The Gare Centrale (Central Station), on rue de la Gauchetière between rues University and Mansfield (behind La Reine Elizabeth—Queen Elizabeth Hotel—on boulevard René-Lévesque Ouest), is the rail terminus for all trains from the United States and from other Canadian provinces. It is connected by underground passageway to the Métro's Bonaventure stop (schedule information, tel. 514/871–1331).

Amtrak (tel. 800/USA–RAIL) runs the overnight *Montrealer* (reservations necessary), which gives travelers in the Northeast the option of day or night transportation. It has a dining car with snacks and full dinners. Sleepers are available; make reservations well in advance. The unreserved *Adirondack* departs New York's Penn Station every morning and takes 10½ hours to reach Montréal. It has a snack car but no dinner service or sleepers. A round-trip ticket on either train is cheaper than two one-way fares, except during major holidays.

VIA Rail (tel. 514/871–1331; in Québec province, 800/361–5390; in the United States, 800/561–3949) connects Montréal by train with all the major cities of Canada, including Québec City, Halifax, Ottawa, Toronto, Winnipeg, Edmonton, and Vancouver.

By Bus **Greyhound** has coast-to-coast service and serves Montréal with buses arriving from and departing for various cities in North America. **Voyageur** and **Voyageur-Colonial** service destinations primarily within Québec and Ontario. **Vermont Transit** (tel. 514/842–2281) also serves Montréal via Boston, New York, and other points in New England. Both lines use the city's downtown bus terminal, Terminus Voyageur (tel. 514/842–2281), which connects with the Berri-UQAM Métro station in downtown.

By Car Montréal is accessible from the rest of Canada via Trans-Canada Highway 401, which enters the city from the east and west via Highways 20 and 40. The New York State Thruway (I–87) becomes Highway 15 at the Canadian border, and then it's 47 kilometers (30 miles) to the outskirts of Montréal. U.S. I–89 becomes two-lane Route 133 at the border, which is Highway 10 at St-Jean. From I–91 from Boston, you must take Highways 55 and 10 to reach Montréal. At the border you clear Canadian Customs, so be prepared with proof of citizenship and your vehicle's ownership papers. On holidays and during the peak summer season, expect waits of a half hour or more at the major crossings.

Once you're in Québec, the road signs will be in French (this will change as Bill 178 takes effect), but they're designed so you shouldn't have much trouble understanding them. The speed limit is posted in kilometers; on highways the limit is 100 kph (about 62 mph). There are extremely heavy penalties for driving while intoxicated, and drivers and front-seat passengers must wear over-the-shoulder seat belts. Gasoline is sold in liters (3.75 liters equal 1 U.S. gallon), and lead-free is called *sans plomb*. If you're traveling in winter, remember that your car may not start on extra-cold mornings unless it has been kept in a heated garage. All Montréal parking signs are in French, so brush up on your *gauche* (left) and *droit* (right).

You should be aware that Montréal police have a diligent tow-away and fine system for cars double-parked or stopped in no-stopping zones in downtown Montréal during rush hours and business hours. The penalty will cost between $35 and $40. If your car is towed away while illegally parked, it will cost an additional $35 to retrieve it. New York State, Maine, and Ontario residents should drive with extra care in Québec: Traffic violations in the province (and vice versa) are entered on their driving records.

Getting Around

By Métro and Bus You should be armed with a few maps to see Montréal, but you won't need a car; public transit will do quite well, thank you. The Métro is clean, quiet (it runs on rubber wheels), and safe, and it's heated in winter and cooled in summer. Métro hours are from 5:30 AM to 12:58 AM Monday through Friday, 5:30 AM to 1:28 AM on Saturday, and 5:30 AM to 1:58 AM on Sunday. The Blue Line runs daily from 5:30 AM to 11 PM. Trains run as often as every three minutes on the most crowded lines. The Métro is also connected to the 29 kilometers (18 miles) of the Underground City, so you may not need to go outside during bad weather. Each of the 65 Métro stops has been individually designed and decorated; Berri-UQAM has stained glass, and at Place d'Armes a small collection of archaeological artifacts is exhibited. The stations between Snowdon and Jean-Talon on the Blue Line are worth a visit, particularly Outremont, with its glass-block design. Each station connects with one or more bus routes, which cover the rest of the island. The STCUM (Société de Transport de la Communauté Urbaine de Montréal) administers both the Métro and the buses, so the same tickets and transfers are valid on either service. You should be able to go within a few blocks of anywhere in the city on one fare. At press time rates were: $1.75; six tickets, $7, monthly pass, $43.

Free maps may be obtained at Métro ticket booths. Try to get the *Carte Réseau* (system map); it's the most complete. Transfers from Métro to buses are available from the dispenser just beyond the ticket booth inside the station. Bus-to-bus and bus-to-Métro transfers may be obtained from the bus driver. Information on reaching your destination can be had by dialing 514/AUTOBUS (288–6287).

By Taxi Taxis in Montréal all run on the same rate: $2.25 minimum and $1 a kilometer (at press time). They're usually prompt and reliable, although they may be hard to find on rainy nights after the Métro has closed. Each carries on its roof a white or orange plastic sign that is lit when available and off when occupied.

Important Addresses and Numbers

Tourist Information **Greater Montreal Convention and Tourism Bureau,** 1555 rue Peel, Suite 600, Montréal, Québec H3A 1X6 (tel. 514/844–5400 or 800/363–7777) or **Tourisme-Québec** (tel. 514/873–2015).

Stop by the downtown headquarters for Info-Touriste, the home of Tourisme-Québec (tel. 514/873–2015 or 800/363–7777), on the north side of Square Dorchester. It's run by the Greater Montreal Convention and Tourism Bureau, and is open daily, June 10–Labor Day, 8:30–7:30; Labor Day–June 9, 9–6. Info-Touriste also operates a smaller tourist information center at 174 rue Notre-Dame Est (tel. 514/873–2015) in Vieux-Montréal, at the corner of Place Jacques-

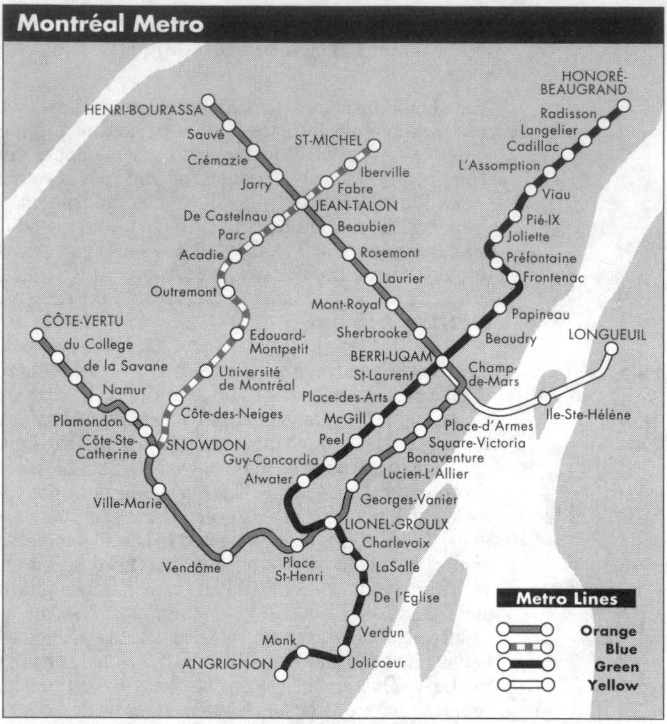

Cartier, and is open Labor Day–mid-May, daily 9–1 and 2–5; mid-May–Labor Day, daily 9–7.

Consulates **United States** (1155 St-Alexandre, Métro Place des Arts, tel. 514/398–9695).

United Kingdom (1155 rue University, Métro McGill, tel. 514/866–5863).

Emergencies Dial 911 to reach the **police, fire,** and **ambulance.**

Doctors and Dentists The U.S. Consulate cannot recommend specific doctors and dentists but does provide a list of various specialists in the Montréal area. Call in advance (tel. 514/398–9695) to make sure the consulate is open.

Dental clinic (tel. 514/342–4444) open 24 hours, Sunday emergency appointments only; **Montréal General Hospital** (tel. 514/937–6011); the **Québec Poison Control Centre** (800/463–5060); **Touring Club de Montréal-AAA, CAA, RAC** (514/861–7111).

Late-night Pharmacies Many pharmacies are open weeknights until 11 PM, weekends until 10, including: **Jean Coutu** (501 Mt. Royal E, tel. 514/521–3481; 5510 Côte-des-Neiges, tel. 514/344–8338).

Travel Agencies **American Express** (1141 boul. de Maisonneuve O, tel. 514/284–3300). **Thomas Cook** (1155 rue University, Suite 314, tel. 514/398–0555).

Opening and Closing Times

Banks are open weekdays from 10 to 4, with some banks open until 5 on weekdays (until 8 on Thursday) and on Saturday morning. Many Montréal banks also have 24-hour banking-machine services.

A law that passed in December 1992 allows shops to stay open weekdays 9–9 and weekends 9–5. However, many merchants close Monday–Wednesday evenings and on Sunday. You'll find many specialty service shops closed on Monday, particularly in predominantly French neighborhoods. Stores in designated tourist zones, such as Vieux-Montréal, remain open on Sunday.

Guided Tours

Orientation **Gray Line** (tel. 514/934–1222) has nine different tours of Montréal in the summer, and one tour during the winter. It offers pickup service at the major hotels, or you may board the buses at Info-Touriste (1001 Square Dorchester).

Amphi Tour Ltée (tel. 514/386–1298) offers a unique tour of Vieux-Montréal (Old Montréal) and the Vieux-Port (Old Port) on both land and water in an amphibious bus. The one-hour tours run from May 1 to October 31.

Boat Tours **Montreal Harbour Cruises** (tel. 514/842–3871) runs two-hour and day-long harbor cruises daily, between May 1 and mid-October. Vessels have room for up to 400 passengers, and evening dinner cruises are available. Boats leave several times a day from the Clock Tower Pier at the foot of rue Berri in the Vieux-Port next to Vieux-Montréal (Métro Champs-de-Mars).

Calèche Rides Open horse-drawn carriages—fleece-lined in winter—leave from Place Jacques-Cartier, Square Dorchester, Place d'Armes and rue de la Commune. An hour-long ride is about $50 (tel. 514/653–0751).

Exploring Montréal

By Andrew Coe

Updated by Dorothy Guinan

When you explore Montréal, there will be very little to remind you that it's an island. It lies in the St. Lawrence River roughly equidistant (256 kilometers, or 160 miles) from Lake Ontario and the point where the river widens into a bay. For its entire length, the St. Lawrence is flanked by flat, rich bottomland for 48 kilometers (30 miles) or more on each side. The only rise in the landscape is the 233-meter (764-foot) Mont Royal, which gave Montréal its name. The island itself is 51 kilometers (32 miles) long and 14 kilometers (9 miles) wide and is bounded on the north by the narrow Rivière des Prairies and on the south by the St. Lawrence. Aside from Mont Royal, the island is relatively flat, and because the majority of attractions are clustered around this hill, most tourists don't visit the rest of the island.

Head to the Mont Royal Chalet Belvedere (lookout) for a panoramic view of the city. You can drive most of the way, park, and walk ½ kilometer (¼ mile) or hike all the way up from avenues Côte-des-Neiges or Côte des Pins. If you look directly out—southeast—from the belvedere, at the foot of the hill will be the McGill University campus and, surrounding it, the skyscrapers of downtown Montréal. Just beyond, along the banks of the St. Lawrence, are the stone houses of Vieux-Montréal. Hugging the opposite banks are the Iles Ste-Hélène and Notre-Dame (St. Helen's and Notre-Dame islands), sites of La Ronde amusement park, the Biosphere, the Montréal Casino, acres of parkland, and the Lac de l'Ile Notre-Dame public beach.

There are a host of attractions that you can see on all-day and half-day trips. The most popular are the amusement park complex on Ile St-Hélène and the Olympic Stadium and its neighbor, the Botanical Garden. The 500 forested acres of Parc du Mont-Royal are busy with joggers and strollers year-round, and skaters in winter. Beyond the city limits are the Eastern Townships and the Laurentians for day trips or weekends in the country.

Montréal is easy to explore. Street signs, subways, and bus lines are clearly marked. The city is divided by a grid of streets roughly aligned east–west and north–south. (This grid is tilted about 40 degrees off—to the left of—true north, so west is actually southwest and so on.) North–south street numbers begin at the Fleuve St-Laurent (St. Lawrence River) and increase as you head north. East–west street numbers begin at boulevard St-Laurent, which divides Montréal into east and west halves. The city is not so large that seasoned walkers can't see all the districts around the base of Mont Royal on foot.

Highlights for First-time Visitors

Botanical Garden/Olympic Park complex (*see* Parks and Gardens, *below*)
Historic Montréal, Tour 1: Vieux-Montréal
Mont Royal (*see* Parks and Gardens, *below*)
Rue St-Denis, Tour 3: St-Denis, Prince Arthur, and North
Rue Sherbrooke Ouest, Tour 2: Downtown Montréal

Tour 1: Vieux-Montréal (Old Montréal)

Numbers in the margin correspond to points of interest on the Tour 1: Vieux-Montréal map.

The Fleuve St-Laurent was the highway on which the first settlers arrived in 1642. Just past the island of Montréal are the Lachine Rapids, a series of violent falls over which the French colonists' boats could not safely travel. It was natural for them to build their houses just above the rapids, near the site of an old Iroquois settlement on the bank of the river nearest Mont Royal. In the mid-17th century Montréal consisted of a handful of wood houses clustered around a pair of stone buildings, the whole flimsily fortified by a wood stockade. For the next three centuries this district—bounded by rues Berri and McGill on the east and west, rue St-Antoine on the north, and the river to the south—was the financial and political heart of the city. Government buildings, the largest church, the stock exchange, the main market, and the port were there. The narrow but relatively straight streets were cobblestone and lined with solid, occasionally elegant houses, office buildings, and warehouses—also made of stone. Exiting the city meant using one of four gates through the thick stone wall that protected against Indians and marauding European powers. Montréal quickly grew past the bounds of its fortifications, however, and by World War I the center of the city had moved toward Mont Royal. The new heart of Montréal became Dominion Square (now Square Dorchester). For the next two decades Vieux-Montréal, as it became known, was gradually abandoned, the warehouses and offices emptied. In 1962 the city began studying ways to revitalize Vieux-Montréal, and a decade of renovations and restorations began.

Today, Vieux-Montréal is a center of cultural life and municipal government, if not of commerce and politics. Most of the summer activities revolve around Place Jacques-Cartier, which becomes a pedestrian mall with street performers and outdoor cafés spilling out of restaurants. This lovely square is a good place to view the fireworks festival, and it's adjacent to the Vieux-Port exhibition grounds and the docks for the harbor cruises. Classical music concerts are staged all year long at the Notre-Dame Basilica, which possesses one of the finest organs in North America, and plays are staged in English by the Centaur Theatre in the old stock-exchange building. This district has six museums devoted to history, religion, and decorative and fine arts.

To begin your tour of Vieux-Montréal, take the Métro to the Place d'Armes station, beneath the Palais des Congrès convention center,
1 and walk 1½ blocks south on rue St-Urbain to **Place d'Armes.** In the 1600s, Place d'Armes was the site of battles with the Iroquois and later became the center of Montréal's "Upper Town." In the middle of the square is a statue of Paul de Chomedey, Sieur de Maisonneuve, the founder of Montréal. In 1644 he was wounded here in a battle with 200 Indians. Historians recently uncovered a network of tunnels beneath the square; they connected the various buildings, and one tunnel ran down to the river. These precursors of the Underground City protected the colonists from the extremes of winter weather and provided an escape route should the city be overrun. Unfortunately, the tunnels are too small and dangerous to visit. Calèches are available at the south end of the square.

2 The north side of the square is dominated by the **Bank of Montréal,** an impressive building with Corinthian columns, built in 1847 (remodeled by renowned architects McKim, Mead & White in 1905), that houses a small, interesting numismatics museum. *129 rue St-Jacques. Admission free. Open weekdays 9–5.*

The office building to the west of the square is the site of the old Café Dillon, a famous gourmet restaurant frequented by members of the fur traders' Beaver Club (*see* Dining, *below*). Two extremely important edifices form the south end of Place d'Armes: the Sulpician Seminary, the oldest building in Montréal, and the imposing Notre-Dame Basilica.

The first church called Notre-Dame was a bark-covered structure built within the fort in 1642, the year the first settlers arrived. Three times it was torn down and rebuilt, each time in a different spot, each time larger and more ornate. The enormous (3,800-seat)
3 neo-Gothic **Notre-Dame Basilica,** which opened in 1829, is the most recent. The twin towers, named Temperance and Perseverance, are 227 meters (69 feet) high, and the western one holds one of North America's largest bells, the 12-ton Gros Bourdon. The interior of the church was designed in medieval style by Victor Bourgeau, with stained-glass windows, a stunning blue vault ceiling with gold stars, and pine and walnut wood carving in traditional Québec style. The church has many unique features: It is rectangular rather than cruciform in shape; it faces south rather than east; the floor slopes down 4 meters (1¼ feet) from back to front; and it has twin rows of balconies on each side. The Casavants, a Québec family, built the 6,800-pipe organ, one of the largest on the continent. Notre-Dame has particularly excellent acoustics and is often the site of Montréal Symphony (tel. 514/842–9951) concerts, notably, Handel's *Messiah* during the week before Christmas and the Mozart Plus Festival in July. Behind the main altar is the Sacré-Coeur Chapel, which was destroyed by fire in 1978 and rebuilt in five different styles. Also in

Tour 1: Vieux-Montréal

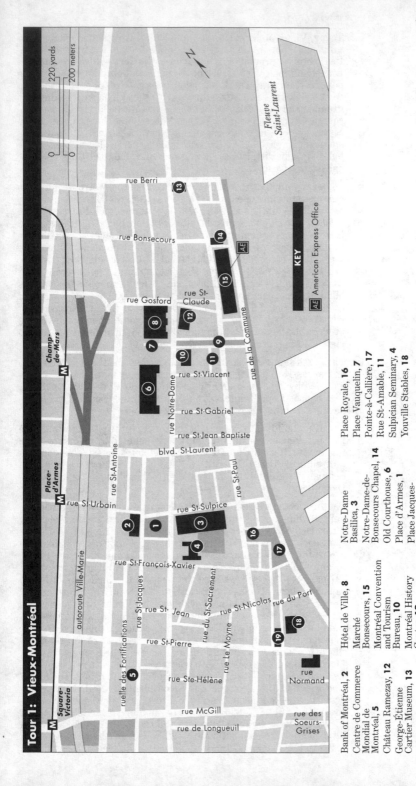

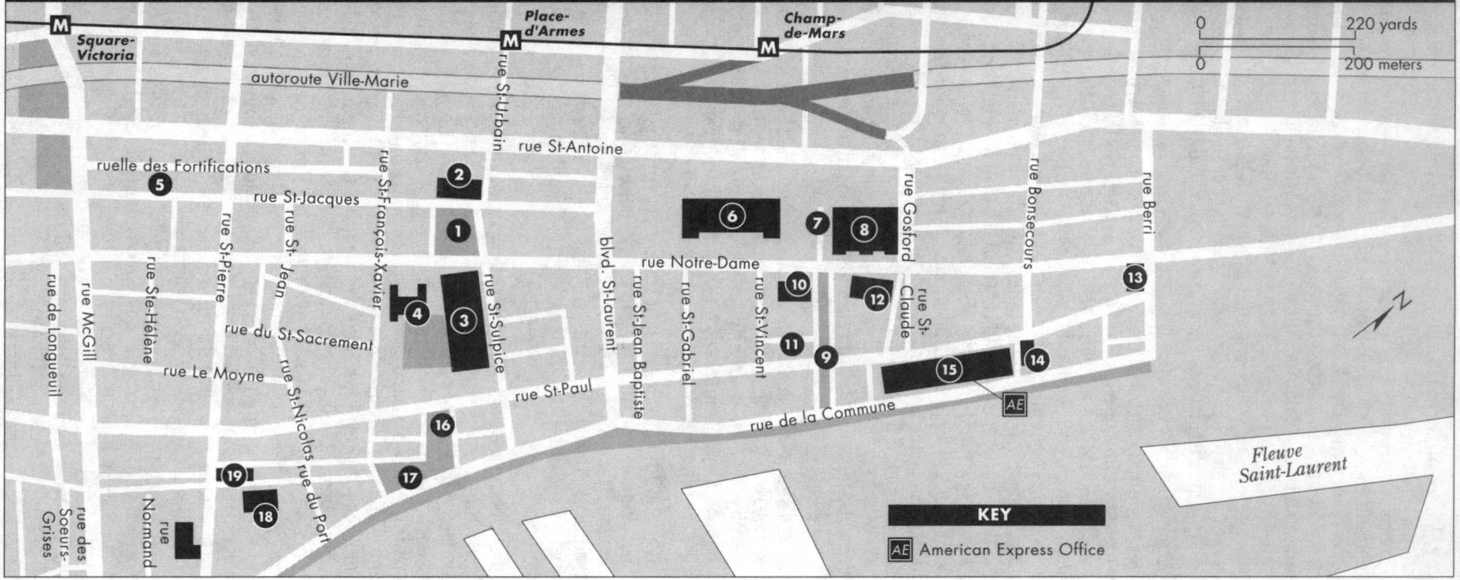

Bank of Montréal, **2**

Centre de Commerce Mondial de Montréal, **5**

Château Ramezay, **12**

George-Étienne Cartier Museum, **13**

Hôtel de Ville, **8**

Marché Bonsecours, **15**

Montréal Convention and Tourism Bureau, **10**

Montréal History Center, **19**

Notre-Dame Basilica, **3**

Notre-Dame-de-Bonsecours Chapel, **14**

Old Courthouse, **6**

Place d'Armes, **1**

Place Jacques-Cartier, **9**

Place Royale, **16**

Place Vauquelin, **7**

Pointe-à-Callière, **17**

Rue St-Amable, **11**

Sulpician Seminary, **4**

Youville Stables, **18**

the back of the church is a small museum of religious paintings and historical objects. *116 rue Notre-Dame O. Basilica: tel. 514/849-1070. Open Labor Day–June 24, daily 7–6; June 25–Labor Day, daily 7 AM–8 PM. Guided tours daily (except Sun. morning) May–June 24, 9–4; June 24–Labor Day, 8:30–4:30; Labor Day–mid-Oct., 9–4. Museum: tel. 514/842–2925. Admission: $1 adults, 50¢ children. Open weekends 9:30–5.*

The low, more retiring stone building behind a wall to the west of the
4 basilica is the **Sulpician Seminary.** This is Montréal's oldest building, built in 1685, and is still a residence for the Sulpician order (unfortunately, it's closed to the public). For almost two centuries, until 1854, the Sulpicians were *the* political power in the city, because they owned the property rights to the island of Montréal. They were also instrumental in recruiting and equipping colonists for New France. The building itself is considered the finest, most elegant example of rustic 17th-century Québec architecture. The clock on the roof over the main doorway is the oldest (pre-1701) public timepiece in North America. Behind the seminary building is a small garden, another Montréal first.

Take a right on rue St-François-Xavier to rue St-Jacques and turn
5 left to reach the new **Centre de Commerce Mondial de Montréal** (World Trade Centre of Montréal), an ambitious block-long complex that combines old and new. It's home to the new Inter-Continental Hotel in Montréal, a retail mall, and office space. Developers of this innovative complex have gambled that they can attract businesses back from downtown to rue St-Jacques, which, when it was known as St. James Street, was the financial center of Canada.

Moving back toward the Basilica, visit **rue St-Sulpice,** the first street in Montréal. On the eastern side of the street there's a plaque marking where the Hôtel-Dieu, the city's first hospital, was built in 1644. Now cross rue St-Sulpice—the Art Deco **Aldred Building** sits on the far left corner—and take rue Notre-Dame Est. One block farther, just past boulevard St-Laurent, on the left, rises the black-glass-sheathed **Palais de Justice** (1971), which houses the higher courts for both the city and the province. (Québec's legal system is based on the Napoleonic Code for civil cases and on British common law for criminal cases.)

The large domed building at 155 rue Notre-Dame Est is the classic
6 revival–style **Old Courthouse** (1857), now municipal offices. Across the street, at 160 rue Notre-Dame Est, is the **Maison de la Sauvegarde** (1811), one of the oldest houses in the city and now home to the European sausage restaurant, Chez Better (*see* Dining, *be-*
7 *low*). The Old Courthouse abuts the small **Place Vauquelin,** named after the 18th-century naval hero who is memorialized by a statue in its center. North of this square is **Champs-de-Mars,** the former site of a colonial military parade ground and now a public park. The ornate building on the east side of Place Vauquelin is the Second Em-
8 pire–style **Hôtel de Ville** (City Hall, 1878). On July 24, 1967, French President Charles de Gaulle stood on the central balcony of the hotel and made his famous "*Vive le Québec libre*" speech.

9 You are in a perfect spot to explore **Place Jacques-Cartier,** the heart of Vieux-Montréal. This two-block-long square opened in 1804 as a municipal market, and every summer it is transformed into a flower market. The 1809 monument at the top of the square celebrates Lord Nelson's victory at Trafalgar. At the western corner of rue Notre-Dame is a small building (1811), site of the old Silver Dollar Saloon, so named because there were 350 silver dollars nailed to the

10 floor. Today it's the home of the **Greater Montreal Convention and Tourism Bureau** (*see* Important Addresses and Numbers, *above*). Both sides of the square are lined with two- and three-story stone buildings that were originally homes or hotels.

Time Out **Le St-Amable** (188 rue St-Amable, tel. 514/866–3471) features a businessmen's lunch weekdays from noon to 3, but you don't have to be an executive or even be dressed like one to sample such classics as fresh poached salmon or grilled New Zealand lamb chops.

11 In the summer, the one-block **rue St-Amable** becomes a marketplace for local jewelers, artists, and craftspeople. From the bottom of Place Jacques-Cartier you can stroll out into the **Port of Montreal Exhibition Ground,** where from summer through the Winter Carnival there is always something going on. At the foot of boulevard St-Laurent and rue de la Commune are the port's major exhibitions: **Images du Futur, IMAX Super Cinema,** and **Expotec.**

Retrace your steps to the north end of Place Jacques-Cartier, then continue east on rue Notre-Dame. At the corner of rue St-Claude on
12 the right is **Château Ramezay** (1705), built as the residence of the 11th governor of Montréal, Claude de Ramezay. In 1775–76 it was the headquarters for American troops seeking to conquer Canada. Benjamin Franklin stayed here during that winter occupation. One of the most elegant colonial buildings still standing in Montréal, the château is now a museum, and it has been restored to the style of Governor de Ramezay's day. The ground floor is furnished like a gentleman's residence of New France, with dining room, bedroom, and office. *280 rue Notre-Dame E, tel. 514/861–3708. Admission: $5 adults, $3 students and senior citizens, $10 families. Visitors using wheelchairs are advised to reserve 1 day in advance. Open Tues.–Sun. 10–4:30.*

At the end of rue St-Paul are two houses built by Sir George-Étienne Cartier, a 19th-century Canadian statesman. They recently have
13 been opened as the **George-Étienne Cartier Museum.** Downstairs displays focus on the political career of this Québec-born Father of Canadian Confederation. Upstairs rooms are furnished as they would have been in the 1850s and 1860s when the Cartiers lived here. *458 rue Notre-Dame E, tel. 514/283–2282. Admission free. Open summer, daily 9–5; fall–winter, Wed.–Sun. 10–noon and 1–5.*

One block back on rue St. Paul is rue Bonsecours, one of the oldest streets in the city. At the end of rue Bonsecours is the small but
14 beautiful **Notre-Dame-de-Bonsecours Chapel.** Marguerite Bourgeoys, who was canonized in 1983, helped found Montréal and dedicated this chapel to the Virgin Mary in 1657. It became known as a sailor's church, and small wood models of sailing ships are suspended from the ceiling just above the congregation. In the basement there is a small, strange museum honoring the saint that includes a story of her life modeled by little dolls in a series of dioramas. A gift shop sells Marguerite Bourgeoys souvenirs. From the museum you can climb to the rather precarious bell tower (beware of the slippery metal steps in winter) for a fine view of Vieux-Montréal and the port. *400 rue St-Paul E, tel. 514/845–9991. Admission: $2 adults, 50¢ children. Chapel and museum open May–Oct., Tues.–Sun. 9–4:30; Nov.–Apr., Tues.–Sun. 10:30–2:30.*

At the corner of rues St-Paul and Bonsecours is the historic **Maison du Calvet,** now a charming café. Double back and head west on rue
15 St-Paul. The long, large, domed building to the left is the **Marché**

Bonsecours (1845), for many years Montréal's main produce, meat, and fish market and now municipal offices. The market has been transformed into a permanent cultural center with temporary exhibits on Montréal.

Rue St-Paul is the most fashionable street in Vieux-Montréal. For almost 20 blocks it is lined with fine restaurants, shops, and even a few nightclubs. Québecois handcrafts are a specialty here, with shops at 88, 136, and 272 rue St-Paul Est. **L'Air du Temps,** at 191 rue St-Paul Ouest, is one of the city's top jazz clubs. Nightly shows usually feature local talent, with occasional international name bands. Take rue St-Paul eight short blocks west of Place Jacques-Cartier,
16 and you will come to **Place Royale,** the site of the first permanent settlement in Montréal.

17 Behind the Old Customs House you will find **Pointe-à-Callière,** a small park that commemorates the settlers' first landing. A small stream used to flow into the St. Lawrence here, and it was on the point of land between the two waters that the colonists landed their four boats on May 17, 1642. After they built the stockade and the first buildings at this site, the settlement was almost washed away the next Christmas by a flood. When it was spared, de Maisonneuve placed a cross on top of Mont Royal as thanks to God. The new **Pointe-à-Callière Museum of Archaeology and History** has been built around the excavated remains of structures dating back to Montréal's beginnings, including the city's first Catholic cemetery. The museum is a labyrinth of stone walls and corridors, illuminated by spotlights and holograms of figures from the past. An audiovisual show gives a historical overview of the area. *350 Place Royale, tel. 514/872–9150. Admission: $6 adults, $5 senior citizens, $4 students, children under 12 free. Open June 24–Sept. 5, Tues.–Sun. 10–8; Sept. 6–June 23, Tues.–Sun. 10–5.*

18 A 1½-block walk down rue William takes you to the **Youville Stables** on the left. These low stone buildings enclosing a garden were originally built as warehouses in 1825 (they never were stables). A group of businesspeople renovated them in 1968, and the buildings now house offices, shops, and a restaurant.

19 Across rue William from the stables is the **Montréal History Centre.** Visitors to this high-tech museum are led through a series of audiovisual environments depicting the life and history of Montréal. *335 Place d'Youville, tel. 514/872–3207. Admission: $4.50 adults, $2.75 senior citizens and students 6–17, children under 6 free (Jan. 5–Apr.); $4.50 adults, $3 senior citizens and students 6–17, children under 6 free (May–Dec.). Open Jan. 5–May 2, Tues.–Sun. 10–5; May 3–July 4, daily 9–5; July 5–Sept. 6, daily 10–6; Sept. 7–Dec. 12, Tues.–Sun. 10–5.*

Tour 2: Downtown

Numbers in the margin correspond to points of interest on the Tour 2: Downtown Montréal map.

Downtown is a sprawling 30- by 8-block area bounded by avenue Atwater and boulevard St-Laurent on the west and east, respectively, avenue des Pins on the north, and rue St-Antoine on the south.

After 1700, Vieux-Montréal wasn't big enough for the rapidly expanding city. In 1701 the French administration signed a peace treaty with the Iroquois, and the colonists began to feel safe about building outside Montréal's fortifications. The city inched northward, toward Mont Royal, particularly after the English conquest in 1760. By the end of the 19th century, rue Ste-Catherine was the main commercial thoroughfare, and the city's elite built mansions on the slope of the mountain. Since 1960 city planners have made a concerted effort to move the focus eastward. With the opening of Place des Arts (1963) and the Complexe Desjardins (1976), the city center shifted in that direction. It hasn't landed on any one corner yet, although some Montréalers will tell you it's at the intersection of avenue McGill College and rue Ste-Catherine.

A major development of the past 30 years is the inauguration of the **Underground City**, an enormous network of passages linking various shopping and office complexes. These have served to keep the retail trade in the downtown area, as well as to make shoppers and workers immune to the hardships of the Canadian winter.

Our tour of downtown begins at the McGill Métro station. The corner of rue University and boulevard de Maisonneuve has recently been the center of intensive development. Two huge office buildings, **2020 University** and **Galleries 2001**, with malls at street and basement levels, rise from the north side of the intersection. The southwest
20 corner, indeed the entire block, is taken up by **Eaton** (*see* Shopping, *below*), one of the Big Three department stores in the city. Aside from many floors of mid-priced clothing and other merchandise, the real attraction of Eaton is the ninth-floor art deco dining room.

Time Out **Eaton le 9e** was modeled after the dining room of the luxury liner *Ile-de-France*, Lady Eaton's favorite cruise ship. Elegant marble columns hold up the ceiling, and the walls are decorated with two art deco murals featuring willowy ladies at leisure. The patrons are usually shoppers, of course, dining on pasta, fish, and meat dishes. The service is practical and fast; the decor's the thing. *677 rue Ste-Catherine O, tel. 514/284–8421. AE, MC, V. Open Mon.–Wed. 11:30–3, Thurs. and Fri. 11:30–3 and 4:30–7, Sat. 11:30–3.*

Eaton is connected to the **Eaton Centre** shopping complex via passageways; it is also linked to the McGill Métro and Les Promenades de la Cathédrale and La Baie (The Bay) eastward, and Place Montréal Trust westward.

21 Across rue University from Eaton stands **Christ Church Cathedral** (1859), the main church of the Anglican Diocese of Montréal. In early 1988 this building was a sight. Plagued by years of high maintenance costs and declining membership, the church fathers leased their land and air rights to a consortium of developers for 99 years. All the land beneath and surrounding the cathedral was removed, and the structure was supported solely by a number of huge steel stilts. The glass 34-story office tower behind the cathedral, **La Maison des Coopérants,** and Les Promenades de la Cathédrale retail complex beneath it, are the products of that agreement.

22 **Place Ville-Marie** is an office, retail, and mall complex that signaled a new era for Montréal when it opened in 1962. It was the first link in the huge chain of the Underground City, which meant that people could have access to all the services of the city without setting foot outside. It was also the first step Montréal took to claiming its place as an international city. The labyrinth that is the Underground City now includes six hotels, thousands of offices, 30 movie theaters, more than 1,000 boutiques, hundreds of restaurants, and almost 18 kilometers (10.8 miles) of passageways.

23 From Place Ville-Marie head south via the passageways toward **Le Reine Elizabeth (Queen Elizabeth)** hotel. You can reach the **Gare**

Tour 2: Downtown Montréal

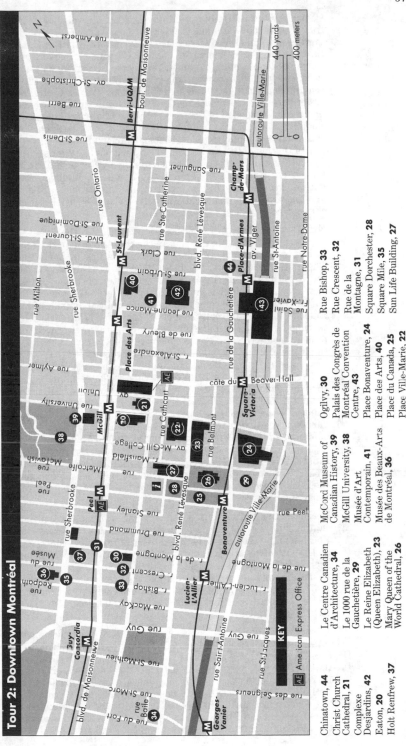

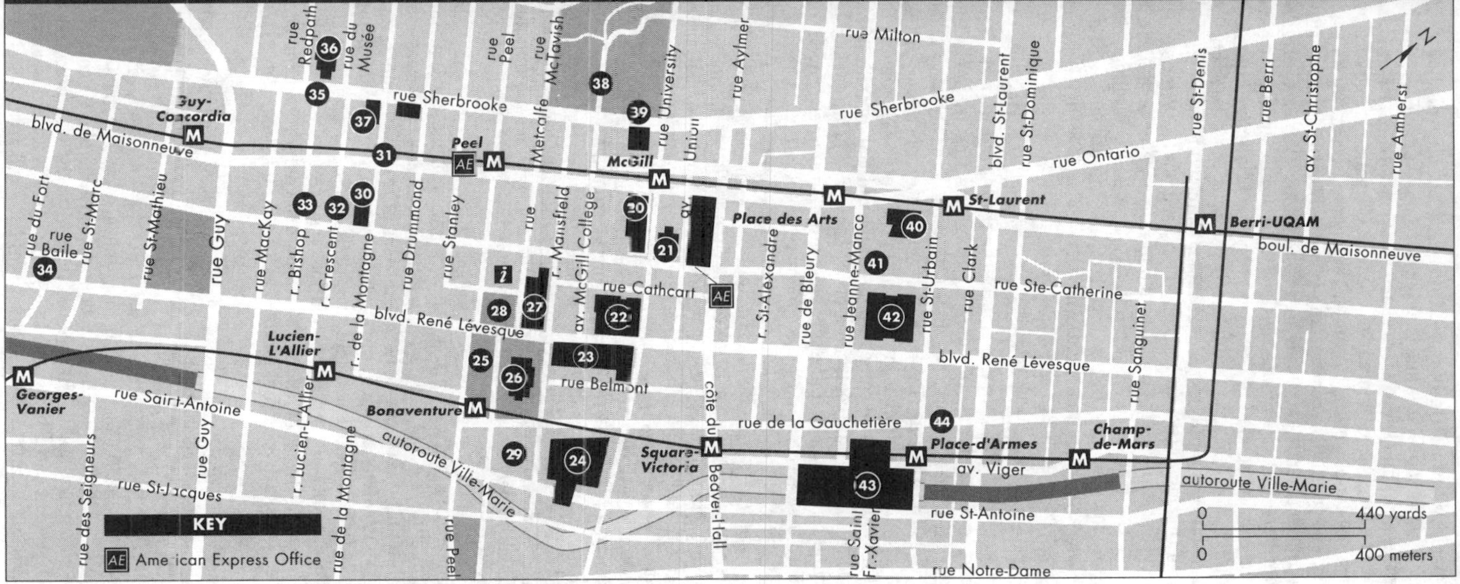

Chinatown, **44**
Christ Church Cathedral, **21**
Complexe Desjardins, **42**
Eaton, **20**
Holt Renfrew, **37**
Le Centre Canadien d'Architecture, **34**
Le 1000 rue de la Gauchetière, **29**
Le Reine Elizabeth (Queen Elizabeth), **23**
Mary Queen of the World Cathedral, **26**
McCord Museum of Canadian History, **39**
McGill University, **38**
Musée d'Art Contemporain, **41**
Musée des Beaux-Arts de Montréal, **36**
Ogilvy, **30**
Palais des Congrès de Montréal Convention Centre, **43**
Place Bonaventure, **24**
Place des Arts, **40**
Place du Canada, **25**
Place Ville-Marie, **22**
Rue Bishop, **33**
Rue Crescent, **32**
Rue de la Montagne, **31**
Square Dorchester, **28**
Square Mile, **35**
Sun Life Building, **27**

Centrale (Central Railway Station) just behind the hotel. Trains
from the United States and the rest of Canada arrive here. Then fol-
24 low the signs marked "Métro/Place Bonaventure" to **Place Bonaventure,** the largest commercial building in Canada. On the lower floors
there are shops and restaurants, then come exposition halls and offices, and finally the whole thing is topped by the Bonaventure Hilton International (*see* Lodging, *below*) and 2½ acres of gardens.
From here take the route marked "Place du Canada," which will
bring you to the mall in the base of the **Le Château Champlain** (*see*
Lodging, *below*). This building is known as the Cheesegrater because of its rows and rows of half-moon-shape windows. Our exploration of this leg of the Underground City will end at **Windsor Station**
(follow the signs). This was the second railway station built in Montréal by the Canadian Pacific Railway Company. Windsor Station,
with its massive rustic stone exterior holding up an amazing steel-
and-glass roof over an arcade, was designed in 1889 by New York architect George Price.

Exit at the north end of Windsor Station and cross the street to the
25 park known as **Place du Canada.** In the center of the park there is a
statue to Sir John A. Macdonald, Canada's first prime minister.
26 Then cross the park and rue de la Cathédrale to the **Mary Queen of
the World Cathedral** (1894), which you enter on boulevard René-
Lévesque. This church is modeled after St. Peter's Basilica in Rome.
Victor Bourgeau, the same architect who did the interior of Notre-
Dame in Vieux-Montréal, thought the idea of the cathedral's design
terrible but completed it after the original architect proved incom-
petent. Inside there is even a canopy over the altar that is a miniature copy of Bernini's *baldacchino* in St. Peter's. The massive gray
granite edifice across boulevard René-Lévesque from the cathedral
27 is the **Sun Life Building** (1914), at one time the largest building in the
British Commonwealth. During World War II much of England's financial reserves and national treasures were stored in Sun Life's
vaults. The park that faces the Sun Life building just north of boule-
28 vard René-Lévesque is **Square Dorchester,** for many years the heart
of Montréal. Until 1870 a Catholic burial ground occupied this block
(and there are still bodies buried beneath the grass), but with the
rapid development of the area, the city fathers decided to turn it into
a park. The statuary of Square Dorchester includes a monument to
the Boer War in the center and a statue of the Scottish poet Robert
Burns near rue Peel.

In the large skyscraper just south of Square Dorchester is an indoor
29 skating rink, **Le 1000 rue de la Gauchetière,** that is open year-round.
Located in the 1000 rue de la Gauchetière office tower, the $5 million
rink is bathed in natural light and surrounded by a host of amenities,
such as cafés, a food court, and a winter garden. It's open to all levels
of skaters, and skate rentals and lockers are available. There are
also a regular program of ice shows, Saturday-night skating to rock
music, and skating lessons. *1000 rue de la Gauchetière, tel. 514/499–
2001.*

A block north of Square Dorchester is rue Ste-Catherine, the main
retail shopping street of Montréal. Three blocks west, at 1307 rue
30 Ste-Catherine Ouest and rue de la Montagne, is **Ogilvy,** the last of
the Big Three department stores. The store has been divided into
individual name boutiques that sell generally pricier lines than does
La Baie or Eaton. Most days at noon a bagpiper plays Scottish airs
31 as he circumnavigates the ground floor. **Rue de la Montagne,** and
32 33 rues **Crescent** and **Bishop,** the two streets just west of it, constitute
the heart of Montréal's downtown nightlife and restaurant scene.

This area once formed the playing fields of the Montréal Lacrosse and Cricket Grounds, and later it became an exclusive suburb lined with millionaires' row houses. Since then these three streets between rues Sherbrooke and Ste-Catherine have become fertile ground for trendy bars, restaurants, and shops ensconced in those old row houses.

While you're in the vicinity, take in one of downtown's newest at-
34 tractions, **Le Centre Canadien d'Architecture (Canadian Centre for Architecture),** just four blocks west at rue St-Marc on rue Baile. The lifelong dream of its founding director, Phyllis Lambert (of the Bronfman fortune), the CCA opened in May 1989 and houses one of the world's premier architectural collections. *1920 rue Baile, tel. 514/939–7000. Admission free to children under 12 and Thurs. evening to adults; otherwise, $5 adults, $3 senior citizens and students. Group rates available. Open Wed. and Fri. 11–6, Thurs. 11–8, weekends 11–5. Reservations required.*

Now that you're in the mood for historic pursuits, backtrack to rues Ste-Catherine and Bishop. By walking two blocks north on rue Bishop to rue Sherbrooke, you enter a very different environment:
35 the exclusive neighborhood known as the **Square Mile.**

36 Directly across the street from the end of rue Bishop is the **Musée des Beaux-Arts de Montréal (Montreal Museum of Fine Arts),** the oldest established museum in Canada (1860). The present building was completed in 1912 and holds a large collection of European and North American fine and decorative art; ancient treasures from Europe, the Near East, Asia, Africa, and America; art from Québec and Canada; and Native American and Eskimo artifacts. From June through October there is usually one world-class exhibition, such as the inventions of Leonardo da Vinci or the works of Marc Chagall.

The Museum of Fine Arts has a gift shop, an art-book store, a restaurant and cafeteria, and a gallery from which you can buy or rent paintings by local artists. *1380 rue Sherbrooke O, tel. 514/285–1600. Admission: permanent collection, $4.75 adults, $3 students, $1 children 12 and under and senior citizens; visiting exhibitions, $9.50 adults, $4.75 students and senior citizens, $2 children 12 and under; audio guides, $4. Open Tues., Thurs., Fri., and Sun. 11–6; Wed. and Sat. 11–9.*

Walking east on rue Sherbrooke brings you to the small and exclu-
37 sive **Holt Renfrew** department store, perhaps the city's fanciest, at the corner of rue de la Montagne (*see* Shopping, *below*). A few blocks farther east along rue Drummond stands the **Ritz-Carlton,** the grande dame of Montréal hotels. It was built in 1912 so the local millionaires' European friends would have a suitable place to stay. Take a peek in the elegant Café de Paris restaurant. It's Montréal's biggest power dining spot, and you just might see the prime minister dining here. (For more on the Ritz-Carlton and its restaurants, *see* Lodging and Dining sections, *below.*) The Ritz-Carlton's only real competition in town is the modern and elegant **Le Westin Mont-Royal** two blocks west at rues Sherbrooke and Peel. Just beyond this hotel
38 on the other side of the street begins the grassy **McGill University** campus. James McGill, a wealthy Scottish fur trader, bequeathed the money and the land for this institution, which opened in 1828 and is perhaps the finest English-language school of higher education in the nation. The student body numbers 15,000, and the university is best known for its medical and engineering schools.

39 Just across rue Sherbrooke from the campus is the **McCord Museum of Canadian History.** The quality and extent of the McCord collec-

tions, which date primarily from the 18th century, make it one of the best history museums in Canada. The collections document the environment of Canadian native peoples and feature costumes and textiles, decorative arts, paintings, prints and drawings, and the 700,000-print-and-negative Notman Photographic Archives, which highlights 19th-century life in Montréal. The McCord is the only museum in Canada with a permanent costume gallery. There are guided tours (call for times), a reading room and documentation center, a gift shop and bookstore, and a tearoom. *690 rue Sherbrooke O, tel. 514/398–7100. Admission: $5 adults, $3 senior citizens, $2 students, $8 families, $3 per person in groups, children under 12 free. Open Tues., Wed., and Fri. 10–6; Thurs. 10–9; weekends 10–5. Closed Mon., except statutory holidays.*

Turn right on rue University and walk a block to the McGill Métro station. Take the train one stop in the direction of Honoré-Beaugrand to the Place des Arts station.

Montréal's Métro opened in 1966 with well-designed stations—many decorated with works of art—and modern trains running on quiet pneumatic wheels. Today there are 65 stations on four lines with 65 kilometers (40 miles) of track. The 759 train cars carry more
40 than 700,000 passengers a day. When you exit at **Place des Arts,** follow the signs to the theater complex of the same name. From here you can walk the five blocks to Vieux-Montréal totally underground. Place des Arts, which opened in 1963, is reminiscent of New York's Lincoln Center in that it is a government-subsidized complex of three very modern theaters. The largest, Salle Wilfrid Pelletier, is the home of the Orchestre Symphonique de Montréal (Montreal Symphony Orchestra), which has won international raves under the baton of Charles Dutoit. The Orchestre Métropolitain de Montréal, Grands Ballets Canadiens, and the Opéra du Québec also stage productions here.

41 The complex also houses the **Musée d'Art Contemporain,** the city's modern art museum, which moved here from Cité du Havre in 1991. The museum's large permanent collection represents works by Québecois, Canadian, and international artists in every medium. The museum often features weekend programs, with many child-oriented activities, and almost all are free. There are guided tours, though hours vary and groups of more than 15 are asked to make a reservation. *185 rue Ste-Catherine O, tel. 514/847–6226. Admission: $4.75 adults, $3.75 senior citizens, $2.75 students, children under 12 free. Wed. evenings free. Open Tues. and Thurs.–Sun. 11–6, Wed. 11–9.*

42 While still in Place des Arts, follow the signs to the **Complexe Desjardins.** Built in 1976, this is another office building, hotel, and mall development along the lines of Place Ville-Marie. The luxurious Meridien Hotel (*see* Lodging, *below*) rises from its northwest corner. The large galleria space is the scene of all types of performances, from lectures on Japanese massage techniques to pop music, as well as avid shopping in the dozens of stores. The next development south is the **Complexe Guy-Favreau,** a huge federal office building named after the Canadian Minister of Justice in the early
43 '60s. If you continue in a straight line, you will hit the **Palais des Congrès de Montréal Convention Centre** above the Place d'Armes Métro stop. But if you take a left out of Guy-Favreau onto rue de la
44 Gauchetière, you will be in **Chinatown,** a relief after all that artificially enclosed retail space.

The Chinese first came to Montréal in large numbers after 1880, following the construction of the transcontinental railroad. They settled in an 18-block area between boulevard René-Lévesque and avenue Viger to the north and south, and near rues Hôtel de Ville and Bleury on the east and west, an area that became known as Chinatown, where there are many restaurants, food stores, and gift shops.

Tour 3: St-Denis, Prince Arthur, and North

Numbers in the margin correspond to points of interest on the Tour 3: St-Denis, Prince Arthur, and North map.

After a long day of fulfilling your touristic obligations at the historical sites and museums of downtown and Vieux-Montréal, it's good to relax and indulge in some primal pleasures, such as eating, shopping, and nightlife. For these and other diversions, head to the neighborhoods east and north of downtown. Our tour begins in the Latin Quarter, the main student district, then wends its way north.

The southern section of this area, around the base of rue St-Denis, was one of the city's first residential neighborhoods, built in the 19th century as the city burst the bounds of Vieux-Montréal. Then known as Faubourg St-Laurent, it was the home of many wealthy families. The lands to the north of present-day rue Sherbrooke were mostly farms and limestone quarries.

Begin at the **Berri-UQAM** Métro stop, perhaps the most important in the whole city, because three lines intersect here. This area, particularly along **rue St-Denis** on each side of boulevard de Maisonneuve, is known as the **Latin Quarter** and is the site of the **Université du Québec à Montréal** and a number of other educational institutions. Rue St-Denis is lined with cafés, bistros, and restaurants that attract the academic crowd. On rue Ste-Catherine there are a number of low-rent nightclubs popular with avant-garde rock-
45 and-roll types. Just west of rue St-Denis you find the **Cinémathèque Québecoise,** a museum and repertory movie house. For $3 you can visit the permanent exhibition on the history of filmmaking equipment and see two movies. The museum also houses one of the largest cinematic reference libraries in the world. *335 boul. de Maisonneuve O, tel. 514/842–9763. Admission free; movies $3. Library, museum, and theater open June–Aug., weekdays 12:30–4:30; Sept.–May, Mon. and Fri. 12:30–5, Tues.–Thurs 12:30–8:30.*

Around the corner and half a block north on rue St-Denis stands the
46 2,500-seat **Théâtre St-Denis,** the second-largest auditorium in Montréal (after Salle Wilfrid Pelletier in Place des Arts). Sarah Bernhardt and numerous other famous actors have graced its stage. It currently is the main site for the summertime concerts of the Montréal International Jazz Festival. On the next block north you see the Beaux Arts **Bibliothèque Nationale du Québec** (1915), a library that houses Québec's official archives (1700 rue St-Denis; open Tues.–Sat. 9–5). If you have a lot of money and some hours set aside for dining, try **Les Mignardises** at 2035–37 rue St-Denis just south of rue Sherbrooke (*see* Dining, *below*).

Continue north on rue St-Denis past rue Sherbrooke. On the right, above the Sherbrooke Métro station, is the **Hôtel de l'Institut,** the hands-on training academy of the government *hôtelier* school. To the
47 left is the small **Square St-Louis,** once considered among the most beautiful in Montréal; unfortunately, now it is a haven for neighborhood panhandlers. In its heyday, this was the focal point of the com-

Tour 3: St-Denis, Prince Arthur, and North

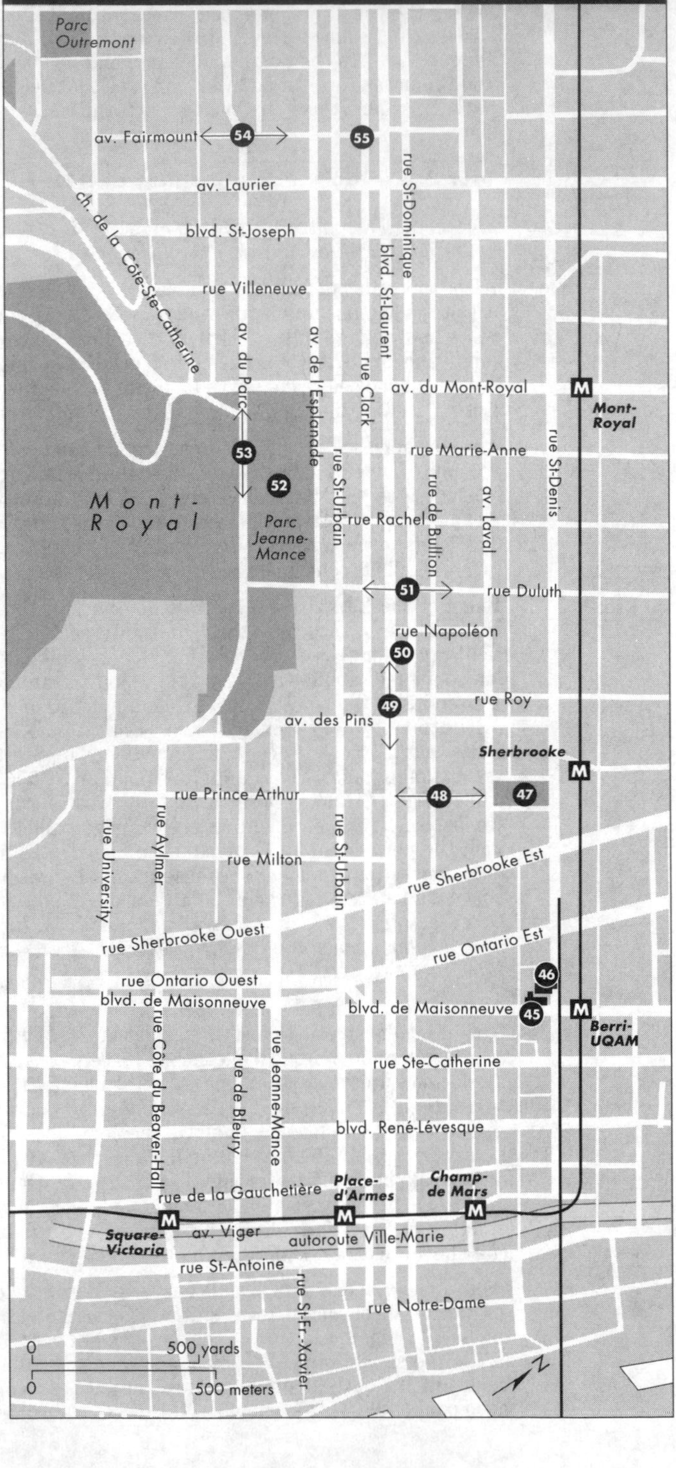

munity, and the surrounding neighborhood takes its name from the once grand square. Originally a reservoir, these blocks became a park in 1879 and attracted upper-middle-class families and artists to the area. French Canadian poets were among the most famous creative people to occupy the houses back then, and the neighborhood is the home today for Montréal painters, filmmakers, musicians, and writers. On the wall of 336 Square St-Louis you can see—and read, if your French is good—a long poem by Michel Bujold.

48 **Rue Prince Arthur** begins at the western end of Square St-Louis. In the '60s the young people who moved to the neighborhood transformed the next few blocks into a small hippie bazaar of clothing, leather, and smoke shops. It remains a center of youth culture, although it's much tamer and more commercial. In 1981 the city turned the blocks between avenue Laval and boulevard St-Laurent into a pedestrian mall. Hippie shops live on today as inexpensive Greek, Vietnamese, Italian, Polish, and Chinese restaurants and boîtes of the singles-bar variety.

49 When you reach **boulevard St-Laurent,** take a left and stroll south on the street that cuts through Montréal life in a number of ways. First, this is the east–west dividing street; like the Greenwich meridian, boulevard St-Laurent is where all the numbers begin. The street is also lined with shops and restaurants that represent the incredible ethnic diversity of Montréal. Until the late 19th century this was a neighborhood first of farms and then of middle-class Anglophone residences. It was on boulevard St-Laurent in 1892 that the first electric tramway was installed that could climb the slope to Plâteau Mont-Royal. Working-class families, who couldn't afford a horse and buggy to pull them up the hill, began to move in. In the 1880s the first of many waves of Russian-Jewish immigrants escaping the pogroms arrived and settled here. Boulevard St-Laurent became known as the Main, as in "main street," and Yiddish was the primary language spoken along some stretches. The Russian Jews were followed by Greeks, Eastern Europeans, Portuguese, and, most recently, Latin Americans.

The 10 blocks north of rue Sherbrooke are filled with delis, junk stores, restaurants, luncheonettes, and clothing stores, as well as fashionable boutiques, bistros, cafés, bars, nightclubs, bookstores, and galleries exhibiting the work of the latest wave of "immigrants" to the area—gentrifiers and artists. The block between rues Roy and Napoléon is particularly rich in delights. Just east at 76 rue Roy is **Waldman's Fish Market,** reputed to be the largest wholesale/retail fish market in North America. **Warshaw's Supermarket** at 3863 boulevard St-Laurent is a huge Eastern European–style emporium that sells all sorts of delicacies.

A few doors up the street from Warshaw's—at No. 3895—is
50 **Schwartz's Delicatessen.** Among the many contenders for the "smoked-meat king" title in Montréal, Schwartz's is most frequently at the top. Smoked meat is just about all it serves, but the meat comes in lean, medium, or fatty cuts. The waiters give you your food and take your money, and that's that.

A block north is **Moishe's** (*see* Dining, *below*), home of the best, but priciest, steaks in Montréal as well as the noisiest atmosphere. The
51 next corner is **rue Duluth,** where merchants are seeking to re-create rue Prince Arthur. If you take a walk to the right all the way to rue St-Denis, you will find Greek and Vietnamese restaurants and boutiques and art galleries on either side of the street. A left turn on rue
52 Duluth and a three-block walk brings you to **Parc Jeanne-Mance,** a

flat, open field that's a perfect spot for a picnic of delicacies purchased on the Main. The park segues into the 2 wooded, hilly square kilometers (494 acres) of **Parc Mont-Royal.**

53 **Avenue du Parc** forms the western border of Parc Jeanne-Mance. To get there either cut through the park or take a left on avenue du Mont-Royal at the north end. No. 93 avenue du Mont-Royal Ouest is the home of **Beauty's,** a restaurant specializing in bagels, lox, pancakes, and omelets. Expect a line weekend mornings. Turn right and head north to **avenue Laurier.** All along this avenue, from Côte Ste-Catherine to boulevard St-Laurent, are some of the fanciest fur stores, boutiques, pastry shops, and jewelers in the city. For a quick chocolate eclair bracer or two, go to **Le Nôtre,** at 1050 avenue Laurier O, a branch of the Parisian shop of the same name.

Time Out **La Petite Ardoise** is a casual, slightly arty café that serves soups, quiches, sandwiches, and more expensive daily specials. The onion soup is lovingly overdosed with cheese, bread, and onions. Whether it's breakfast, lunch, or dinner, the best accompaniment for your meal is a big, steamy bowl of creamy café au lait. This café is a perfect place to take a breather from shopping. *222 av. Laurier O, tel. 514/495–4961. AE, MC, V. Open daily 8 AM–midnight, later on weekends.*

The next three blocks of avenue du Parc form the heart of the Greek district. Try **Symposium,** at No. 5334, or the neighboring **Milos** at 5357 avenue du Parc (*see* Dining, *below*) for some of the best Greek appetizers, grilled seafood, and atmosphere you'll find in this hemisphere.

54 **Avenue Fairmount,** a block north of avenue Laurier, is the site of two small but internationally known culinary landmarks. The **Fairmount Bagel Factory,** at 74 avenue Fairmount Ouest, claims to make the best bagels in the world.

Half a block east, on the corner of avenue Fairmount and rue Clark,
55 stands the famous **Wilensky's Light Lunch** (*see* Dining, *below*). Moviegoers will recognize this Montréal institution from *The Apprenticeship of Duddy Kravitz,* based on the Mordecai Richler novel of the same name. Lunch is all that's served here, and it certainly is light on the wallet. A couple of dollars will get you a hot dog or a bologna, salami, and mustard pretzel-roll sandwich with a strawberry soda. Books are available for perusing. The atmosphere is free.

Parks and Gardens

Numbers in the margin correspond to points of interest on the Olympic Park and Botanical Garden map.

Of Montréal's three major parks, **Lafontaine** is the smallest (the other two are Parc Mont-Royal and Ile Ste-Hélène). Parc Lafontaine, founded in 1867, is divided into eastern and western halves. The eastern half is French style; the paths, gardens, and lawns are laid out in rigid geometric shapes. There are two public swimming pools on the north end, along rue Rachel. In the winter the park is open for ice skating. The western half is designed on the English system, in which the meandering paths and irregularly shaped ponds follow the natural contours of the topography. Pedal boats can be rented for a paddle around one of two man-made lakes. Its band shell is the site of many free outdoor summertime concerts, performances by dance and theater groups, and film screenings. Take the Métro to the Sherbrooke station and walk eight blocks east along rue Cherrier until avenue Parc Lafontaine. *3933 av. Parc Lafontaine, tel. 514/872–6211. Open dialy 9 AM–10 PM.*

The giant, mollusk-shape **Olympic Stadium** and the tilted tower that supports the roof are probably the preeminent symbols of modern Montréal. Planning for the Olympic Stadium complex began in 1972, and construction in the old Parc Maisonneuve started soon afterward. The Olympics took place in 1976, but the construction of the stadium's roof and tower was not completed until 1989. Many Montréalers were proud of what they had—at least until the summer of 1991, when a 55-ton concrete beam in the stadium came crashing to the ground, and the stadium was forced to close for several months.
56 The Olympic Park includes the 70,000-seat **Olympic Stadium,** the
57 58 **Olympic Tower,** six swimming pools, the **Aréna Maurice-Richard,** and the Olympic Village. Daily guided tours (tel. 514/252–8687) of the entire complex leave from Tourist Hall at 11, 12:40, 2, and 3:40; two are in English, two are in French. Perhaps the most popular visitor activity is a ride up to the tilted tower's observatory on the Funicular, the exterior cable car. The two-level cable car holds 90 people and takes two minutes to climb the 270 meters (890 feet) to the observatory, from which you can see up to 80 kilometers (50 miles) on clear days.

59 The **Biodôme,** in the former Olympic Park Velodrome, opened in June of 1992. This natural sciences museum combines four ecosystems—the boreal forest, tropical forest, polar world, and St. Lawrence River—under one climate-controlled dome. Visitors follow protected pathways through each environment, observing indigenous flora and fauna of each of the ecosystems. Animals from the former zoo at Angrignon Park and the now closed aquarium on Ile Ste-Hélène have been incorporated into this center. *4777 av. Pierre-de-Coubertin, tel. 514/868–3000. Admission: $8.50 adults, $6 senior citizens over 65 and students, $4.25 children 6–17, children under 5 free. Open June 18–Sept. 9, daily 9–8; Sept. 10–June 17, daily 9–6.*

60 If you've brought your swimsuit and towels, take a dip at the **Aquatic Center** (tel. 514/252–4622 for hours). There are also a cafeteria and a souvenir shop on the grounds. You can reach the **Olympic Park** via the Pie-IX or Viau Métro stations (the latter is nearer the stadium entrance).

Continuing your back-to-nature experience, cross rue Sherbrooke to the north of the Olympic Park (or take the free shuttle bus) to
61 reach the **Botanical Garden** (closest Métro stop is Pie-IX). Founded in 1931, this garden is said to be one of the largest in the world. During the summer you can visit the 73 hectares (181 acres) of outdoor gardens—a favorite is the poisonous-plants garden; the 10 exhibition greenhouses are open year-round. There are more than 26,000
62 species of plants here. When the 5-acre **Montréal-Shanghai Dream Lake Garden** opened here in June 1991, it became the site of the largest Chinese garden outside Asia. The authentic Ming-style garden has seven elegant pavilions, including a large exhibition hall featuring changing exhibitions and a 30-foot rockery around a central reflecting pool. There is also an impressive collection of penjings or
63 Chinese bonsais (miniature trees). A **Japanese Garden** and its pavilion, where guests may join a formal tea ceremony, are next to the
64 Dream Lake. The **Insectarium,** a bug-shape building, houses more than 250,000 insect specimens collected by Montréal entomologist Georges Brossard. *4101 rue Sherbrooke E, tel. 514/872–1400. Admission to the greenhouses and the Insectarium May–Oct.: $7*

Aquatic Center, **60**
Aréna Maurice-Richard, **58**
Biodôme, **59**
Botanical Garden, **61**
Insectarium, **64**
Japanese Garden, **63**
Montréal-Shanghai Dream Lake Garden, **62**
Olympic Stadium, **56**
Olympic Tower, **57**

Olympic Park and Botanical Garden

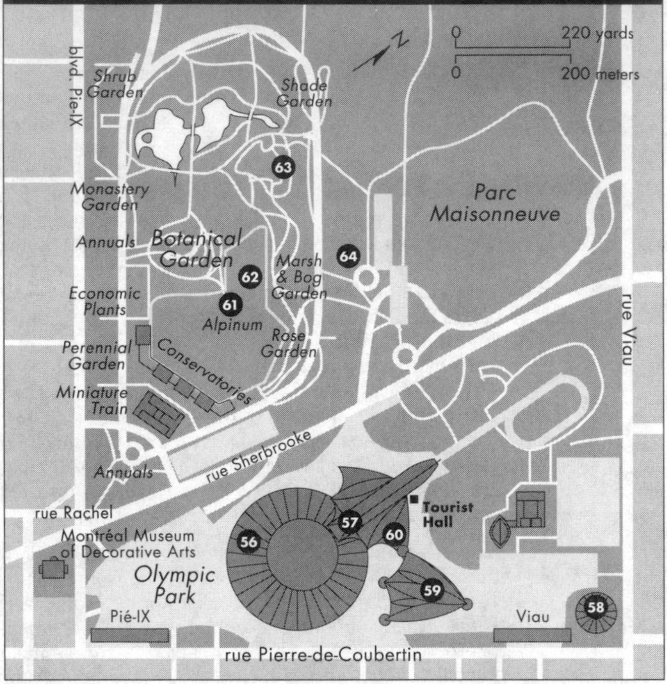

adults, $3.50 children 6–17, $5 senior citizens; Nov.–Apr.: $5 adults, $2.50 children 6–17, $3.50 senior citizens.

Ile Ste-Hélène (along with Ile Notre-Dame, the former site of the Expo '67 World's Fair), opposite Vieux-Montréal in the middle of the St. Lawrence River, draws big crowds, particularly during the warm months. You can reach it via either the de la Concorde or Jacques-Cartier bridges, via the Métro to the Ile Ste-Hélène station, or by city bus (summer only) from downtown. Ile Ste-Hélène is a wooded, rolling park perfect for picnicking in the summer and cross-country skiing and ice skating during the snow season. The former 1967 World's Fair site on the island has been upgraded. Buckminster Fuller's biosphere (the world's largest geodesic dome when the famous architect and engineer built it for Expo '67, but since ravaged by fire) is scheduled to reopen in 1995 as a permanent water and environment interpretation center.

La Ronde was created as part of the Expo celebration. This world-class amusement park boasts a huge new roller coaster (the second-highest in the world), water slides with incredible drops, an international circus, Ferris wheels, boat rides, and rides, rides, rides. La Ronde is also the site of the annual Benson & Hedges International Fireworks Competition, on Saturday or Sunday nights during June and July. A ticket, which includes a reserved seat for the show and an amusement park pass, costs $22.75. *Ile Ste-Hélène, tel. 514/872-6222 or 800/361-7178 for La Ronde; 514/790-1245 or 800/361-4595 for fireworks. Admission: $19.25 adults, $9.50 children, $44.50 families. Open May and early June, weekends; mid-June–Aug., Sun.–Thurs. 11 AM–midnight, Fri. and 11 AM–1 AM.*

A stroll back along the north side of the island brings you to the **Old Fort** just under the Jacques-Cartier Bridge. This former British arsenal has been turned into the **David M. Stewart Museum** and a dinner theater called **Le Festin du Gouverneur.** The latter is a re-creation of a 17th-century banquet, complete with balladeers and comedy skits. In the military museum are displays of old firearms, maps, scientific instruments, uniforms, and documents of colonial times. During the summer the parade ground is the scene of mock battles—cannons and all—by the Compagnie Franche de la Marine and bagpipe concerts by the 78th Fraser Highlanders. *Tel. 514/861-6701. Admission: $3 adults, $2 children and senior citizens. Open summer, Wed.–Mon. 10–6; winter, Wed.–Mon. 10–5.*

In mid-June, **Ile Notre-Dame** is the site of the Molson Grand Prix du Canada, a top Formula I international circuit auto race at the Gilles Villeneuve Race Track.

Just west of de la Concorde Bridge is the futuristic **Casino de Montréal.** Since it opened in October 1993, the government-owned gaming hall—the site of the French Pavilion during Expo '67—has been a roaring success. Over 10,000 people a day stream in to try their hand at the 65 gaming tables and more than 1,200 slot machines. Restaurants and gift shops are on the premises. *1 av. du Casino, tel. 514/392-2746 or 800/665-2274. Admission (minimum age is 18) and parking free. No jeans, shorts, or jogging shoes. Open daily 11 AM–3 AM.*

Another former Expo building, the Québec Pavilion, opened a **Dinasaurium** in June 1994. Visitors enter a time tunnel to take a "safari" through landscapes depicting Earth 200 million years ago, complete with giant beasts. Hands-on exhibits, interpretive talks, and dinosaur films are part of the program. *Tel. 514/861-3462 for hours and admission fees.*

Ile Notre-Dame is also site of the city's only natural beach on **Lac de l'Ile Notre-Dame.** Opened in the summer of 1990, it was an immediate success and is now packed on every hot, sunny day. Just a Métro stop away (Ile Ste-Hélène Métro) from downtown, the beach is an oasis, with clear lake water filtered by a treatment system that relies on aquatic plants, and an inviting stretch of lawn and trees rimmed with sand. Lifeguards are on duty; there is a shop that rents swimming and boating accessories, and there are picnic areas and a restaurant on the premises. There is also a moderate admission fee.

The **Parc Mont-Royal,** the finest in the city, is not easy to overlook. These 494 acres of forest and paths at the heart of the city were designed by Frederick Law Olmsted, the celebrated architect of New York's Central Park. He believed that communion with nature could cure body and soul. The park is designed following the natural topography and accentuating its features, as in the English mode. You can go skating on Beaver Lake in the winter, visit one of the two lookouts and scan the horizon, or study the park interpretation center in the chalet at the Mont Royal belvedere. Horse-drawn transport is popular year-round: sleigh rides in winter and calèche rides in summer. On the eastern side of the hill stands the 30-meter (100-foot) steel cross that is the symbol of the city.

Shrines

St. Joseph's Oratory, on the northwest side of Mont Royal, is a Catholic shrine on a par with Lourdes or Fatima. Take the blue Métro line to the Côte-des-Neiges station, then walk three blocks uphill on the chemin de la Côte-des-Neiges. You can't miss the enormous church up on the hillside. Brother André, a member of the Society of the Brothers of the Holy Cross, constructed a small chapel to St. Joseph, Canada's patron saint, in 1904. Brother André was credited with a number of miracles and was beatified in 1982. His chapel became a pilgrimage site, the only one to St. Joseph in the world (St. Joseph is the patron saint of healing). The dome is among the world's largest, and while the interior is of little aesthetic interest, there is a small museum dedicated to the life of the Holy Family and containing many displays, including thousands of crutches discarded by the formerly disabled faithful. From early December through February the museum features a display of crèches (nativity scenes) from all over the world. Carillon, choral, and organ concerts are held weekly at the oratory during the summer, and you can still visit Brother André's original chapel and tomb at the side of the massive basilica. *3800 chemin Queen Mary, tel. 514/733–8211. Open Sept.–May, daily 6 AM–9:30 PM; June–Aug., daily 6 AM—10 PM.*

Montréal for Free

The Saidye Bronfman Centre hands-on fine arts school has open-house activities, gallery exhibitions, and public affairs lectures (*see* Off the Beaten Track, *below*).

Classical and pop concerts, dance performances, and theater are held at **Parc de Lafontaine,** rue Rachel.

Picnic in **Parc Mont-Royal,** sail miniature boats in its Beaver Lake during the summer, and skate on it during the winter (*see* Parks and Gardens, *above*).

Bicycle along Montréal's waterfront to the Lachine Canal, atop its mountain, or through the Vieux-Port (*see* Participant Sports, *below*).

Le Centre Canadien d'Architecture is free on Thursday evening (*see* Tour 2, *above*).

What to See and Do with Children

Biodôme de Montréal at Olympic Park (*see* Parks and Gardens, *above*).

At the Old Fort on Ile Ste-Hélène, now the site of the **David M. Stewart Museum,** mock battles, military drills, military-history exhibitions, and bagpipe concerts take place all summer long (*see* Parks and Gardens, *above*).

Dow Planetarium. The heavens are reproduced with the aid of a giant Zeiss projector on the inside of the planetarium's vaulted dome. *1000 rue St-Jacques, tel. 514/872–4530. Admission: $4 adults, $2.50 children and senior citizens; prices may vary. Open Tues.–Sun. 12:30–8:30.*

Images du Futur has futuristic art and science exhibits, and interactive displays highlighting new technologies—laser images, holograms, computer graphics, videos and electronic music. *Vieux-Port at boul. St-Laurent and rue de la Commune, tel. 514/849–1612. Open mid-May–mid-Sept., daily 10 AM–11 PM.*

IMAX Super Cinema shows films on a seven-story-tall screen. Next to Images du Futur is **Expotec,** a hands-on scientific exhibition. *Vieux-Port, Shed No. 7, tel. 514/496–IMAX for information, 514/*

790–1245 for tickets. Admission: $11.50 adults, $9.50 students and senior citizens, $7 children; prices may vary. Open daily 10–10.

The Botanical Garden's Insectarium (*see* Parks and Gardens, *above*).

La Ronde's Amusement Park (*see* Parks and Gardens, *above*).

Olympic Tower. Zoom up the "tallest-inclined-tower-in-the-world" on the funicular for a 50-mile panorama of Montréal and its environs (*see* Parks and Gardens, *above*).

Indoor skating year-round at the **Le 1000 rue de la Gauchetière** (*see* Tour 2, *above*).

Off the Beaten Track

Just two blocks west of Victoria and the Métro Côte-Ste-Catherine station is the Saidye Bronfman Centre. This multidisciplinary institution has long been recognized as a focus of cultural activity for the Jewish community in particular and for Montréal as a whole. The center was a gift from the children of Saidye Bronfman in honor of their mother's lifelong commitment to the arts. In fact, the Mies van der Rohe-inspired building was originally designed by Mrs. Bronfman's daughter, Montréal architect Phyllis Lambert. Accessible by car, just one block east of the Décarie Expressway and about four blocks north of chemin Queen Mary, the center is well worth the trip.

Many of its activities, such as gallery exhibits, lectures on public and Jewish affairs, performances, and concerts, are free to the public. The center, open year-round, is home to the Yiddish Theatre Group, one of the few Yiddish companies performing today in North America. The theater also stages English works, often by local playwrights. Many an artist has passed through the doors of the center's School of Fine Arts. *5170 Côte Ste-Catherine, tel. 514/739–2301; box office 514/739–7944. Admission to gallery free; theater ticket prices vary. Open Mon.–Thurs. 9–9, Fri. 9–3, Sun. 10–5. Closed Jewish holidays.*

Accessible by Métro and bus is **Maison Saint-Gabriel,** which dates back to 1668, when it served as a boarding school for Les Filles du Roy—the young women, many of them orphans, who were brought over to New France to marry the predominantly male settlers. Here Montréal's first teacher (and Canada's first female saint), Marguerite Bourgeoys, patiently trained the "King's wards" to take on their duties as wives and mothers. The house was renovated in 1960. A typical "habitant" farmhouse, it displays furnishings and household objects from the 17th, 18th, and 19th centuries, as well as a kitchen much like the one Les Filles would have learned to bake in before setting off for their new homes. You can see the exhibits by guided tour only mid-April to mid-December. It is advisable to call beforehand. *2146 Place Dublin (Square-Victoria Métro, then transfer to Bus 61), tel. 514/935–8136. Admission: $3 adults, $2 students 8–16 and senior citizens. Tours Tues.–Sat., 1:30 and 3; Sun. 1:30, 2:30, and 3:30.*

Shopping

By Patricia Lowe

Montréalers *magasinent* (go shopping) with a vengeance, so it's no surprise that the city has 160 multifaceted retail areas encompassing some 7,000 stores.

Visitors usually reserve at least one day to hunt for either exclusive fashions along rue Sherbrooke or bargains at the Vieux-Montréal flea market. But there are specific items that the wise shopper seeks out in Montréal.

Montréal is one of the fur capitals of the world. Close to 85% of Canada's fur manufacturers are based in the city, as are many of their retail outlets: **Alexandor** (2025 rue de la Montagne), **Shuchat** (402 boul. de Maisonneuve O), **Grosvenor** (400 boul. de Maisonneuve O), **McComber** (440 boul. de Maisonneuve O), and **Birger Christensen at Holt Renfrew** (1300 rue Sherbrooke O) are a few of the better showrooms.

Fine English bone china, crystal, and woolens are more readily available and cheaper in metropolitan stores than in their U.S. equivalents, thanks to Canada's tariff status as a Commonwealth country. There are three **Jaeger** boutiques (Holt Renfrew, Centre Rockland in the town of Mount Royal, and Centre Fairview in the West Island) selling classical woolen sweaters, along with $700 pure-wool suits. Collectors of china and crystal will find reasonable prices at **Caplan Duval** (Côte-St-Luc's Cavendish Mall and Montréal's Plaza Côte-des-Neiges), which offers an overwhelming variety of patterns.

Today, only dedicated connoisseurs can uncover real treasures in traditional pine Canadiana, but scouting around for Québec *antiquités* and art can be fun and rewarding, especially along increasingly gentrified rue Notre-Dame Ouest.

The Montréal area has six major retail districts: the city center (or downtown), Vieux-Montréal, rue Notre-Dame Ouest, the Plâteau Mont-Royal–St-Denis area, the upper St-Laurent–Laurier Ouest areas of Outremont, and the city of Westmount.

Just about all stores, with the exception of some bargain outlets and a few selective art and antiques galleries, accept major credit cards. Buy your Canadian money at a bank or exchange bureau beforehand to take advantage of the latest rates on the dollar. Most purchases are subject to a federal goods and services tax of 7% as well as a provincial tax of 8%.

If you think you might be buying fur, it is wise to check with your country's customs officials before leaving to find out which animals are considered endangered and cannot be imported. Do the same if you think you might be buying Eskimo carvings, many of which are made of whalebone and ivory and cannot be brought into the United States.

(For general opening times, *see* Opening and Closing Times in Essential Information, *above.*)

City Center

Central downtown is Montréal's largest retail district. It takes in rue Sherbrooke, boulevard de Maisonneuve, rue Ste-Catherine, and the side streets between them. Because of the proximity and variety of shops, it's the best shopping bet for visitors in town overnight or over a weekend.

Faubourg Ste-Catherine

Several complexes have added glamour to the city-center shopping scene. A good place to start is the **Faubourg Ste-Catherine,** Montréal's answer to Boston's Quincy Market. At the corner of rues Ste-Catherine Ouest and Guy, it is a vast bazaar housed in a former parking and auto-body garage abutting the Grey Nuns' convent grounds. Three levels of clothing and crafts boutiques, as well as food counters selling fruits and vegetables, pastry, baked goods, and meats, surround the central atrium of tiered fountains and islands of café tables and chairs where food-fair kiosks sell such snacks as egg rolls, pizza, souvlaki, and sushi. This is the place to pick up Québec maple syrup and maple candy, at the pine-decorated boutique at street level, or a fine French wine, about $30, at the government-run **Société d'Alcools du Québec.** Prices at most stores are generally reasonable here, especially if you're sampling the varied ethnic cuisine at any of the snack counters.

Les Cours Mont-Royal Continuing east on rue Ste-Catherine, the *très élégant* **Les Cours Mont-Royal** dominates the east side of rue Peel between this main shopping thoroughfare and boulevard de Maisonneuve. This mall caters to expensive tastes, but even bargain hunters find it an intriguing spot for window shopping.

Place Montréal Trust Just two blocks away, **Place Montréal Trust** at McGill College is the lively entrance to an imposing glass office tower. Shoppers, fooled by the aqua and pastel decor, may think they have stumbled into a California mall. Prices at the 110 outlets range from hundreds (for designs by **Alfred Sung,** haute couture at **Gigi** or **Rodier,** or men's high fashion at **Bally**) to mere dollars (for sensible cotton T-shirts, or beef-and-kidney pies or minced tarts at the British dry goods and food store **Marks & Spencer**). These imported goodies share the floor space with moderately ticketed ladies' suits, menswear, lingerie, and children's clothing.

Les Cours Mont-Royal and Place Montréal Trust compete with the **Centre Eaton** and **Les Promenades de la Cathédrale.** All four of these centers are linked to the Underground City retail network. Always a favorite with visitors, the nearly 29-kilometer (17.4-mile) "city below" draws large crowds to its shop-lined corridors honeycombing between Les Promenades de la Cathédrale, Place Ville-Marie, Place Bonaventure, and Complexe Desjardins.

Les Promenades de la Cathédrale Nestled between Eaton and La Baie department stores, this underground retail complex is popular with Montréalers. Its unusual location makes it a sightseeing adventure as well: It's connected to the McGill Métro and located directly beneath the stately and historic Christ Church Cathedral. A highlight (some say a travesty) of the retail mall's design is the replication of architectural details found in the cathedral above. Among its 150 boutiques and chain stores, Les Promenades boasts Canada's largest Linen Chest outlet, with hundreds of bedspreads and duvets draped over revolving racks plus aisles of china, crystal, linen, and silver.

Place Ville-Marie Weatherproof shopping began in 1962 beneath the 42-story cruciform towers of Place Ville-Marie on boulevard René-Lévesque (formerly Dorchester Boulevard) at rue University. (Take the corridor from Centre Eaton, south, to Place Ville-Marie.) A recent renovation has opened Place Ville-Marie up to the light, creating a more cheerful ambience as well as adding stores.

Stylish women head to Place Ville-Marie's 100-plus retail outlets for the clothes: haute couture at **Tristan, Iseut, JC Creations, Cactus,** and **Danier.** Traditionalists will love **Aquascutum.** More affordable clothes shops include **Dalmy's, Marie Claire, Reitman's,** and, for shoes, **Mayfair, Brown's, François Villon,** and **French.**

Place Bonaventure From here it's an easy underground trip through Gare Centrale (the train station) to Place Bonaventure's mall beneath one of Canada's largest commercial buildings. It houses some 120 stores, ranging from the trendy (**Au Coton** and **Bikini Village**) to the exclusive (**Armand Boudrias** boutique). There are also a number of fun shops: **Aldo** for trendy leather wear; and **Ici-Bas** for outrageous hose.

Complexe Desjardins Still in the downtown area but a bit farther east on boulevard René-Lévesque is Complexe Desjardins. It's a fast ride via the Métro at Bonaventure station; just get off at Place des Arts and follow the tunnels to Desjardins' multitiered atrium mall. Filled with splashing fountains and exotic plants, Desjardins exudes a Mediterranean joie de vivre, even when it's below freezing outside. Roughly 80 stores include budget outlets like Le Château for fashion as well as the exclusive Redeor, where wool and jersey-knit ensembles start at about $150.

Department Stores **Eaton** is the city's leading department store and part of Canada's largest chain. Founded in Toronto by Timothy Eaton, the first Montréal outlet appeared in 1925. It now sells everything—from the art decorating the top-floor restaurant entrance to zucchini loaves in the basement bakery. The main restaurant is an unusual art deco replica of the dining room aboard the old *Ile-de-France* ocean liner, once Lady Eaton's favorite cruise ship.

The nearby sandstone building housing **La Baie** opened in 1891, although the original Henry Morgan Company that founded it moved to Montréal in 1843. Morgan's was purchased in 1960 by the Hudson Bay Company, which was founded in 1670 by famous Montréal voyageurs and trappers Radisson and Grosseilliers. La Baie is known for its Hudson Bay red-, green-, and white-stripe blankets and duffel coats. It also sells the typical department store fare.

Exclusive **Holt Renfrew,** at 1300 rue Sherbrooke Ouest, is known for its furs. The city's oldest store, it was established in 1837 as Henderson, Holt and Renfrew Furriers and made its name supplying coats to four generations of British royalty. When Queen Elizabeth II married Prince Phillip in 1947, Holt's created a priceless Labrador mink as a wedding gift. Holt's carries the exclusive and pricey line of furs by Denmark's Birger Christensen, as well as the haute-couture and prêt-à-porter collections of Yves St-Laurent.

Around the corner and two blocks down rue de la Montagne, at **Ogilvy** (1307 rue Ste-Catherine O), a kilted piper regales shoppers every day at noon. An institution with Montréalers since 1865, the once-homey department store has undergone a miraculous face-lift. Fortunately, it has preserved its delicate pink glass chandeliers and still stocks traditional apparel—Aquascutum, Jaeger, tweeds for men, and smocked dresses for little girls.

This area—bounded by rues Sherbrooke and Ste-Catherine, and rues de la Montagne and Crescent—also boasts antiques and art galleries as well as designer salons. Rue Sherbrooke is lined with an array of art and antiques galleries as well as tony clothing stores. Rue Crescent is a tempting blend of antiques, fashions, and jewelry boutiques displayed beneath colorful awnings.

Vieux-Montréal

The second major shopping district, historic Vieux-Montréal, can be a tourist trap, but a shopping spree there can be a lot less expensive and more relaxing than shopping downtown. Both rues Notre-Dame and St-Jacques, from rue McGill to Place Jacques-Cartier, are lined with low to moderately priced fashion boutiques, garish souvenir shops slung with thousands of Montréal T-shirts, and shoe stores.

Along the edge of Vieux-Montréal is Montréal's rejuvenated waterfront, the Vieux-Port, which hosts a sprawling flea market, the **Marché aux Puces,** on Quai King Edward (King Edward Pier). Dealers and pickers search for secondhand steals and antique treasures as they prowl through the huge hangar that is open Wednesday through Sunday from spring through early fall.

Notre-Dame Ouest

The place for antiquing is the city's third shopping sector, beginning at rue Guy and continuing west to avenue Atwater (a five-minute walk south from the Lionel-Groulx Métro station). Once a shabby strip of run-down secondhand stores, this area has blossomed beyond its former nickname of Attic Row. It now has the highest concentration of antiques, collectibles, and curiosity shops in Montréal. Collectors can find Canadian pine furniture—armoires, cabinets, spinning wheels, rocking chairs—for reasonable prices here. Consider a Sunday tour, beginning with brunch at **Salon de Thé Ambiance,** a charming restaurant that also sells antiques (No. 1874).

Plateau Mont-Royal and St-Denis

Popular with students, academics, and journalists, this easterly neighborhood embraces boulevard St-Laurent, the longtime student ghetto surrounding the Prince Arthur mall, St-Denis and its Latin Quarter near the Université du Québec à Montréal campus, and the Plateau district. Plateau Mont-Royal and St-Denis attract a trendier, more avant-garde crowd than the determined antiquers along Notre-Dame.

Boulevard St-Laurent—dubbed "the Main" because it divides the island of Montréal into east and west—has always been a lively commercial artery. It was first developed by Jewish merchants who set up shop here in the early 1900s. Cutting a broad swath across the island's center, this long boulevard has an international flavor, with its mélange of stores run by Chinese, Greek, Latin American, Portuguese, Slav, and Vietnamese immigrants. Lower boulevard St-Laurent is lined with discount clothing and bric-a-brac stores, secondhand shops, electronics outlets, and groceries selling kosher meats, Hungarian pastries, Peking duck, and natural foods.

While boulevard St-Laurent's personality is multi-ethnic, rue St-Denis's is distinctly French. (Both are lengthy arteries, so make use of Bus 55 for boulevard St-Laurent, Buses 31 and 30 along rue St-Denis.) More academic in makeup, the boulevard has awnings that shelter bookstores (mostly French), art galleries, antiques stores, and a range of boutiques.

Upper St-Laurent and Laurier Ouest

Upper boulevard St-Laurent (for our purposes, roughly from avenue du Mont-Royal north to rue St-Viateur), intersecting with avenue Laurier Ouest and climbing the mountain to rue Bernard, has blossomed into one of Montréal's chicest *quartiers* in recent years. It's not entirely surprising, given that much of this area lies within or adjacent to Outremont, traditionally the enclave for wealthy Francophone Montréalers, with restaurants, boutiques, nightclubs, and bistros catering to the upscale visitor. In addition, the influx of a new generation of multi-ethnic professionals, artists, and entrepreneurs is making its mark on the area. It now rivals St-

Denis, downtown, and Laurier Ouest as a cultural hot spot, and it is reminiscent of New York City's SoHo.

Avenue Laurier Ouest, from boulevard St-Laurent to chemin de la Côte-Ste-Catherine, is roughly an eight-block stretch; you'll crisscross it many times as you explore its Québec-style shops, which carry everything from crafts and clothing to books and paintings.

Square Westmount and Avenue Greene

Visitors with time to shop or friends in the elegant residential neighborhood of Westmount, a separate municipality in the middle of the island of Montréal, should explore Square Westmount and adjacent avenue Greene. Next door to downtown, these malls are on the Angrignon Métro line, easily accessible via the Atwater station, which has an exit at Square Westmount. Just follow the tunnel to this mall's 90 or so exclusive shops.

The square's plaza opens onto avenue Greene's two-block shopping area, which is lined with trees and flowers. Its redbrick row houses and even the renovated old post office are home to a wealth of boutiques and shops.

Sports and Fitness

The range of sporting activities available in Montréal is testament to Montréalers' love of the outdoors. With world-class skiing in the Laurentians and the Eastern Townships less than an hour away and dozens of skating rinks within the city limits, they revel in winter. When the last snowflake has melted, they store away skis, poles, and skates and dust off their bikes, tennis rackets, and fishing poles. And year-round they watch the pros at hockey matches, baseball games, car races, and tennis tournaments.

Participant Sports

Bicycling The island of Montréal—except for Mont Royal itself—is quite flat, and there are more than 20 cycling paths around the metropolitan area. Among the most popular are those on Ile Ste-Hélène, along the Lachine Canal, and in Angrignon and Vieux-Port parks. You can rent 10-speed bicycles at **Cyclo-Touriste** at the Centre Info-Touriste (1001 Sq. Dorchester, tel. 514/393–1528).

Parks Canada conducts guided cycling tours along the historic **Lachine Canal** (1825) every summer weekend. For more details, call 514/283–6054 or 514/637–7433.

Golf For a complete listing of the many golf courses in the Montréal area, call **Tourisme-Québec** at 514/873–2015.

Hunting and Fishing Québec's rich waters are filled with fish, but before you begin the chase, you need to purchase a license from the Ministère des Loisirs, de la Chasse et de la Pêche or from an authorized agent. The lakes and rivers around Montréal teem with fish, and a number of guides offer day trips. For complete information, call **Tourisme-Québec** (tel. 514/873–2015).

Ice Skating There are at least 195 outdoor and 21 indoor rinks in the city. You'll probably find one in the nearest park. Call parks and recreation (tel. 514/872–6211).

Jogging Montréal became a runner's city following the 1976 Olympics. There are paths in most city parks, but for running with a panoramic view, head to the dirt track in **Parc du Mont-Royal** (take rue Peel, then the steps up to the track).

Rafting Montréal is the only city in the world where you can step off a downtown dock and minutes later be crashing through Class V white water in a sturdy aluminum jet boat. The Lachine Rapids, just south of Vieux-Montréal, were responsible for the founding of Montréal. The roiling waves were too treacherous for the first settlers to maneuver, so they founded Ville-Marie, the forerunner of Vieux-Montréal. Modern voyageurs suit up for the 45-minute jet-boat trip in multiple layers of wool and rain gear, but it's nearly impossible to stay dry—or to have a bad time. *Lachine Rapids Tours Ltd., 105 rue de la Commune, Vieux-Montréal, tel. 514/284–9607. 5 trips daily, departing from Quai Victoria May–Sept., 10, noon, 2, 4, and 6. Trips are narrated in French and English and reservations are necessary. Rates: $45 adults, $40 senior citizens, $35 children 13–18, $25 children 6–12. Special group and family rates are available.*

Skiing
Downhill For the big slopes you'll have to go northwest to the Laurentians or south to the Eastern Townships, an hour or two away by car. There is a small slope in Parc du Mont-Royal. Pick up the Ski-Québec brochure at one of the Tourisme-Québec offices.

Cross-country Trails crisscross most of the city's parks, including Notre-Dame and Ile Ste-Hélène, Angrignon, Maisonneuve, and Mont-Royal.

Squash You can reserve court time for this fast-paced racquet sport at **Nautilus Centre St-Laurent Côte-de-Liesse Racquet Club** (8305 chemin Côte-de-Liesse, tel. 514/739–3654).

Swimming There is a large indoor pool at the **Olympic Park** (Métro Viau, tel. 514/252–4622) and another at the **Centre Sportif et des Loisirs Claude-Robillard** (1000 av. Emile Journault, tel. 514/872–6900). The outdoor pool on Ile Ste-Hélène is an extremely popular (and crowded) summer gathering place, open June–Labor Day. The new city-run beach at Ile Notre-Dame is the only natural swimming hole in Montréal (tel. 514/872–6211).

Tennis There are public courts in the Jeanne-Mance, Kent, LaFontaine, and Somerled parks. For details, call Montréal Sports and Recreation (tel. 514/872–6211).

Windsurfing and Sailing Sailboards and small sailboats can be rented at **L'École de Voile de Lachine** (2105 boul. St-Joseph, Lachine, tel. 514/634–4326) and the **Société de l'Ile Notre-Dame** (Ile Notre-Dame, tel. 514/872–6093).

Spectator Sports

Baseball The National League **Montréal Expos** play at the Olympic Stadium from April through September. For information and reservations, call 514/253–3434 or 800/463–9767.

Cycling **Le Tour de l'Ile de Montréal** has made the *Guinness Book of World Records* for attracting the greatest number of participants. More than 30,000 amateur cyclists participate in "North America's most important amateur cycling event" each June, wending their way 70 kilometers (38 miles) through the streets and parks of Montréal (514/847–8687).

Grand Prix The annual **Molson Grand Prix du Canada,** which draws top Formula 1 racers from around the world, takes place every June at the Gilles Villeneuve Race Track on Ile Notre-Dame (tel. 514/392–0000 for tickets, tel. 514/392–4731 for information).

Hockey The **Montréal Canadiens,** winners of 23 Stanley Cups, meet National Hockey League rivals at the Forum (2313 rue Ste-Catherine O, tel. 514/932–2582) from October to April.

Dining

The promise of a good meal is easily satisfied in Montréal. Les Montréalais don't "eat out"; they "dine." And they are passionate about dining. The city has more than 4,500 restaurants of every price representing more than 75 ethnic groups. It has such culinary institutions as Les Mignardises, Le Paris, and the Beaver Club, which emphasize classic cuisine and tradition. Delicatessens such as Briskets, Schwartz's, and Wilensky's are mainstays for budget dining. In between there are ethnic eateries featuring the foods of China, Greece, India, Morocco, and Italy. Then there are the ubiquitous inexpensive fast-food outlets and coffee shops. But above all, Montréal is distinguished by the European ambience of its restaurants. Catch a glimpse of the eateries' terraces from midday to 2 PM for a look at the hours that Montréal diners take most seriously. Each of the city's well-known bistros is more Parisian than the last. The challenge of dining in Montréal is choosing from among the thousands of restaurants and the varieties of inexpensive fast-food outlets and coffee shops.

Many expensive French and Continental restaurants offer two options, which can be a blessing or a burden to your wallet. Either choice guarantees you a great meal. Instead of ordering à la carte—you select each dish—you can opt for the table d'hôte or the *menu de dégustation*. The table d'hôte is a complete two- to four-course meal chosen by the chef. It is less expensive than a complete meal ordered à la carte and often offers interesting special dishes. It also may take less time to prepare. If you want to splurge with your time and money, indulge yourself with the *menu de dégustation*, a five- to seven-course dinner executed by the chef. It usually includes, in this order, salad, soup, a fish dish, sherbet, a meat dish, dessert, and coffee or tea. At the city's finest restaurants, this menu for two and a good bottle of wine can cost $170 and last three or four hours. But it's worth every cent and every second.

Montréal restaurants are refreshingly relaxed. Although many of the hotel restaurants require a jacket and tie, neatness (no torn T-shirts and scruffy jeans) is appreciated in most other restaurants. Lunch hour is generally from noon to 2:30 and dinner from 6 to 11 or midnight. (Montréalers like to dine late, particularly on summer weekends.) Some restaurants are closed on Sunday or Monday. Because there is no consistent annual closing among Montréal eateries—some will take time off in August, while others will close around Christmas and January—call ahead to avoid disappointment.

Highly recommended restaurants in each price category are indicated by a star ★.

Category	**Cost***
$$$$	over $30
$$$	$20–$30

$$	$10–$20
$	$5–$10

**per person without tax (combined GST of 7% and provincial tax of 4% on all meals), service, or drinks*

Chinese

$$–$$$ **Zen.** At press time this mod establishment in the basement of Le Westin Mont-Royal (*see* Lodging, *below*) was offering a $19 fixed-price menu that should not be missed. Called the Zen Experience, the meal is a kind of all-you-can-eat extravaganza, except that instead of helping yourself to a buffet of precooked dishes, you are presented with a menu of 41 items and asked to select one at a time until you can't possibly eat any more. The food is delicate Chinese with some Thai, Malaysian, and Indonesian dishes mixed in for variety. Try the fillet of chicken with crispy spinach, eggplant croquettes with sweet-and-sour sauce, and Mother Ma's shredded zucchini with spicy garlic sauce. This is very fine Chinese cuisine, and you'll pay for it. Check to make sure the Zen Experience is still being offered. *Le Westin Mont-Royal, 1050 Sherbrooke St. W, tel. 514/499–0801. Reservations advised. Dress: casual but neat. AE, DC, MC, V.*

$$ **Cathay Restaurant.** Hong Kong investors, fearful of their city's future, are pouring money into Montréal's Chinatown, among other Chinatowns in North America. They're opening slick, Hong Kong–style restaurants and competing with the older Chinese eateries. The consumer wins in these restaurant wars. The 15-year-old Cathay was remodeled and expanded in 1985, and is now the most popular and largest dim sum restaurant in the city. The two floors are both huge rooms with institutional dropped ceilings and the usual red and gold Chinese stage decorations. From 11 AM to 2:30 PM, waitresses emerge from the kitchen pushing carts laden with steaming beef dumplings in bamboo steamers, spicy cuttlefish, shrimp rice noodles, bean-curd rolls, and on and on. *73 rue de la Gauchetière O, Chinatown, tel. 514/866–3131. Reservations accepted. Dress: casual. AE, MC, V.*

Continental

$$$ ★ **Nuances.** One of the best and classiest new restaurants is in, of all places, the Casino de Montréal. Gaming halls aren't normally known for their elegance and good taste, but this establishment is not only ritzy, its menu is sophisticated. The setting, too, is stunning: Diners sit amidst burnished rosewood paneling and dusky pink upholstery and drapes, eating off pretty Bosch and Villeroy porcelain plates displayed on a sea of starched white linen. The clientele is as elegant as the decor. The casino has a strict dress code; high rollers turn up in gowns and tuxedos. Less flamboyant types can get away with a jacket and tie. Starters include a sautée of fresh foie gras served on a bed of braised cabbage, a heavenly mussel soup flavored with pesto, and venison paté encased in filo pastry. The main dishes include coriander flavored rabbit stuffed with scampi, medaillions of salmon topped with a scallop mousse, and smoked duck with cardamom sauce. More conservative diners can opt for tenderloin of beef, veal chops, or roast rack of lamb. *1 av. de Casino, tel. 514/392–2708. Reservations required. Jacket and tie required. AE, DC, MC, V. Closed weekend lunch.*

Auberge le Vieux St-Gabriel, **13**
Basha, **20**
Beaver Club, **19**
Bens, **22**
Bocca d'Oro, **30**
Bonaparte, **14**
Cathay, **18**
Chez Better, **12**
Chez Delmo, **17**
Katsura, **27**
La Charade, **11**
La Chartreuse, **9**
La Sucrerie de la Montagne, **1**
Le Café de Paris, **25**
Le Cercle, **23**
Le Lutetia, **26**
Le Mitoyen, **2**
Le Taj, **24**
Le Tramway, **21**
Les Halles, **29**
Les Mignardises, **10**
Les Trois Tilleuls, **16**
L'Express, **8**
Milos, **4**
Moishe's, **6**
Nuances, **15**
Pizzaiole, **3, 28**
Toqué, **7**
Wilensky's Light Lunch, **5**
Zen, **23**

Montréal Dining

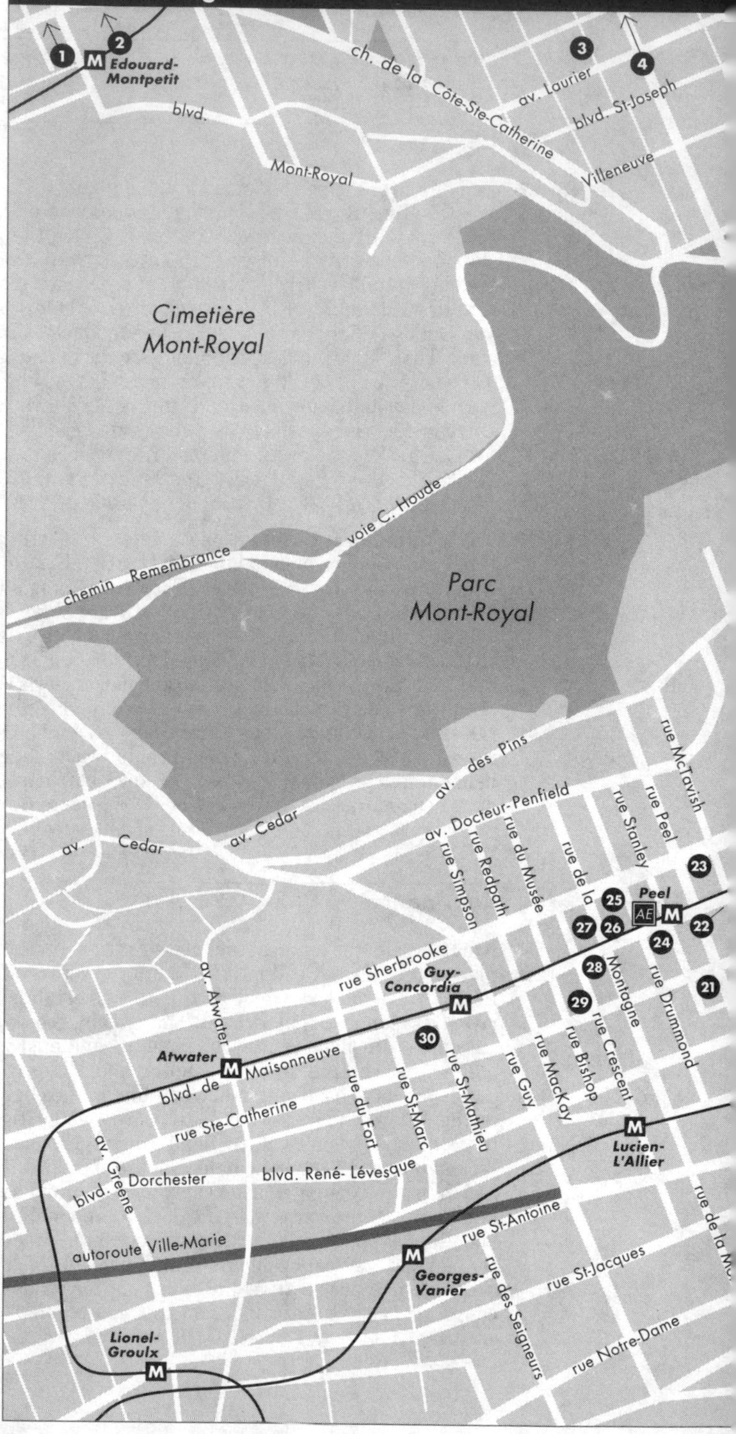

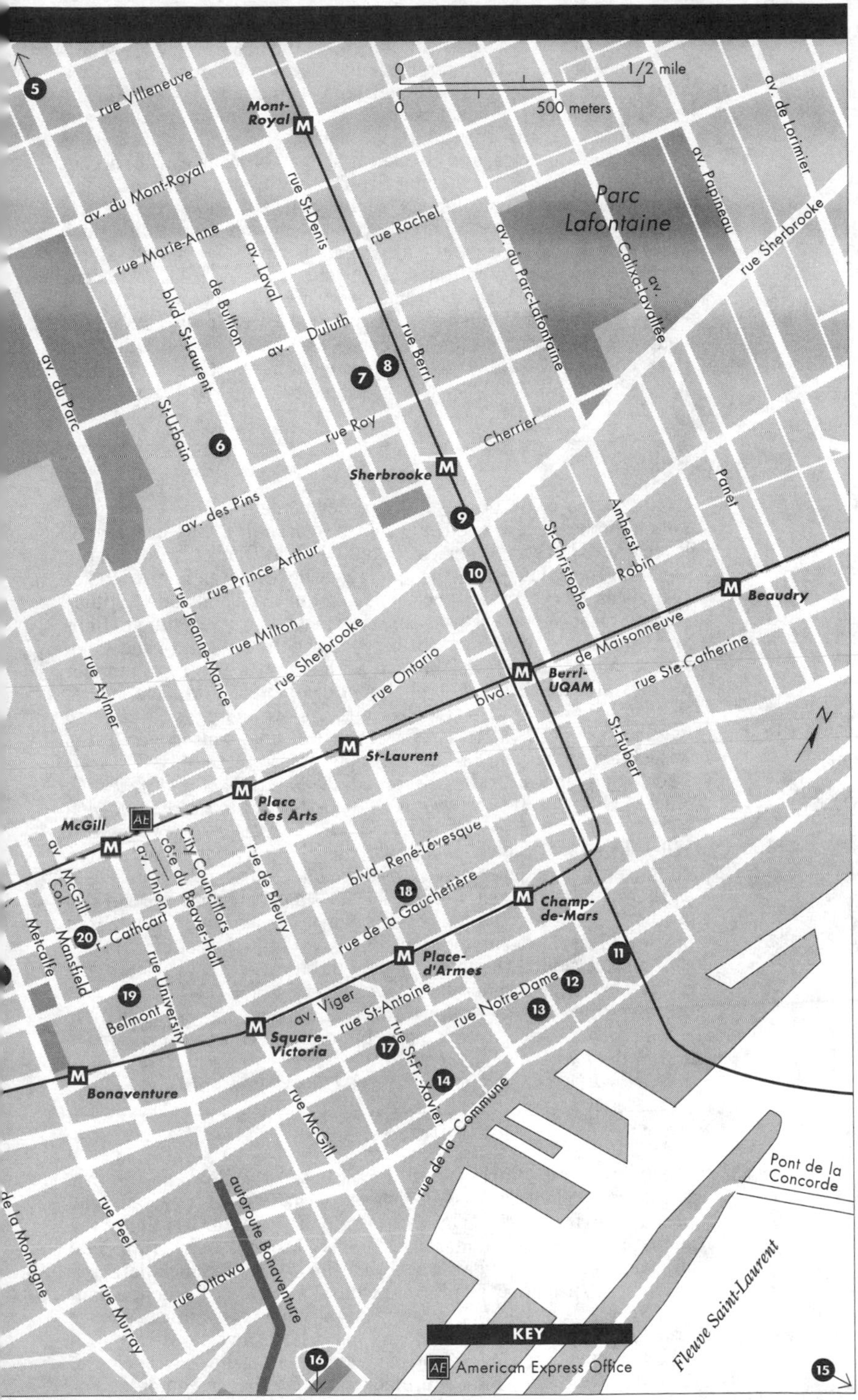
0
1/2 mile
0
500 meters
Mont-Royal
rue Villeneuve
av. du Mont-Royal
rue Marie-Anne
rue Rachel
rue St-Denis
av. Laval
de Bullion
blvd. St-Laurent
av. Duluth
rue Berri
av. du Parc
St-Urbain
rue Roy
Cherrier
Sherbrooke
Parc Lafontaine
av. du Parc-Lafontaine
av. Calixa-Lavallée
av. Papineau
av. de Lorimier
rue Sherbrooke
av. des Pins
rue Prince Arthur
rue Milton
rue Jeanne-Mance
rue Aylmer
rue Sherbrooke
rue Ontario
St-Christophe
Amherst
Robin
Panet
Beaudry
de Maisonneuve
blvd.
Berri-UQAM
rue Ste-Catherine
St-Hubert
St-Laurent
Place des Arts
McGill
av McGill Col.
av. Union
côte du Beaver-Hall
City Councillors
rue de Bleury
blvd. René-Lévesque
rue de la Gauchetière
Champ-de-Mars
Place-d'Armes
r. Cathcart
Metcalfe
Mansfield
rue University
Belmont
av. Viger
rue St-Antoine
rue Notre-Dame
Square-Victoria
rue St-Fr.-Xavier
Bonaventure
rue McGill
rue de la Commune
Pont de la Concorde
de la Montagne
rue Peel
autoroute Bonaventure
rue Ottawa
rue Murray
Fleuve Saint-Laurent
KEY
American Express Office
N

$ **La Charade.** A short walk east from City Hall on rue Notre-Dame Est, this storefront restaurant is a gathering place for civil servants and some of the more budget-minded city councillors. The restaurant is cozy, and the food, although not gourmet fare, is plentiful and varied, served by a pleasant staff. The menu features Italian and French dishes, with a sprinkling of such other choices as paella with a tangy tomato sauce, and chicken or shrimp brochettes. The accent is definitely on pasta, offering five or six different linguine selections, and there are a hearty veal Parmesan, one of the tastier dishes, and *coq au vin,* a hefty portion of chicken stewed in a thick wine sauce with onions and mushrooms. Lighter eaters may sample seafood stews of *moules* (mussels) and shrimp or a Caesar salad. The table d'hôte offers a choice of meals with soup, a main course, and coffee, many of which come to less than $15 (excluding taxes). Of course, ordering up a carafe of house wine or a bottle of imported beer adds to the bill. *358 rue Notre-Dame E (Champ-de-Mars Métro), tel. 514/861–8756. Reservations not required. Dress: casual. MC, V.*

Delicatessens

$ **Bens.** On the menu of this large, efficient deli, all the items with "Bens" in the name are red or are covered in red: "Bens Cheesecake" is smothered in strawberries; "Bens Ice Cold Drink" is the color of electric cherry juice; and the specialty, the "Big Ben Sandwich," is two slices of rye bread enclosing a seductive, pink pile of juicy smoked meat (Montréal's version of corned beef). According to Bens lore, the founder, Ben Kravitz, brought the first smoked-meat sandwich to Montréal in 1908. The rest, as they say, is history. A number of the walls are devoted to photos of celebrities who have visited Bens. The decor is strictly '50s, with yellow and green walls and vaguely art deco, institutional furniture. The waiters are often wisecracking characters but are nonetheless incredibly efficient. Beer, wine, and cocktails are served. *990 boul. de Maisonneuve O, downtown, tel. 514/844–1000. No reservations. Dress: casual. MC, V.*

$ **Wilensky's Light Lunch.** Since 1932 the Wilensky family has served up its special: Italian-American salami on a kaiser roll, generously slathered with mustard. Served hot, it's a meal in itself. You can also get hot dogs or a grilled sandwich, which comes with a marinated pickle and an old-fashioned sparkling beverage. The regulars at the counter are among the most colorful in Montréal. A visit here is a must. This neighborhood haunt was a setting for the film *The Apprenticeship of Duddy Kravitz,* from the novel by Mordecai Richler. The service does not prompt one to linger, but the prices make up for it. *34 Fairmount O, tel. 514/271–0247. No reservations. Dress: casual. No credit cards. No liquor license. Closed weekends.*

French

$$$$ **The Beaver Club.** Early fur traders started the Beaver Club in a shack during Montréal's colonial days. In the 19th century it became a social club for the city's business and political elite. It still has the august atmosphere of a men's club devoted to those who trap: Pelts of bear, buffalo, and beaver still line the walls with members' engraved copper plates. The Beaver Club is a gourmet French restaurant open to anyone with a reservation who arrives in the proper attire. Master chef John Cordeaux has a large and devoted following. The luncheon table d'hôte includes such dishes as terrine of duckling with pistachios and onion, and cranberry compote. For

more mundane tastes, the restaurant also specializes in such meaty dishes as roast prime rib of beef au jus. The Beaver Club always offers one or two low-fat, low-salt, low-calorie plates. The waiters are veteran (Charles, the maître d', has worked here for more than 20 years), and the service is as excellent as the food. *La Reine Elizabeth, 900 boul. René-Lévesque O, downtown, tel. 514/861–3511. Reservations required. Jacket and tie required. AE, D, DC, MC, V.*

$$$$ **Le Lutetia.** This magnificent restaurant is worth a little detour, if only for the piano bar happy hour. The plethora of styles—rococo, renaissance, empire, fin de siècle, and baroque—is a spectacle in itself. This outrageously romantic restaurant is the perfect choice for a tête-à-tête by candlelight. The French cuisine, sometimes nouvelle, sometimes classic, is always served under a silver cover. Behind their glass partition, the cooks busy themselves and give the clientele an appetizing show, even at the busiest moments. The *menu gastronomique* changes each week according to the market and the seasons. The menu changes frequently as well, with such creative dishes as shrimp with fennel in puff pastry, ballotine of pheasant in a brioche dough, noisettes of veal *périgourdine* (with truffles), or medaillions of beef with coarse mustard, all preceding the cheese or the dessert cart. There is a very good wine list and champagne. *1430 rue de la Montagne, tel. 514/288–5656. Reservations advised. Dress: casual but neat. Terrace on the roof in summer. AE, D, DC, MC, V.*

$$$$ ★ **Les Halles.** Definitely French, this restaurant took its name from the celebrated Parisian market. Its old-France character is enhanced by mirrors and typical bistro inscriptions, and fussy waiters, with their white aprons and towels on their arms, seem to come straight out of a '40s French film. The wine cellar is exceptional and contains about 250 different bottles, with prices ranging from $20 to $540 a bottle. The menu shows a lot of imagination without ignoring the classics: Grapefruit Marie-Louise with scallops and lobster, poêlée d'escargots, or duck with pears sit comfortably beside the chef's ventures into nouvelle cuisine, such as his lobster with ginger and coconut. The desserts are classic, delicious, and remarkably fresh. The Paris-Brest, a puff pastry with praline cream inside, is one of the best in town. *1450 rue Crescent, tel. 514/844–2328. Reservations advised. Dress: casual but neat. AE, DC, MC, V. Closed Sun. lunch, Mon. lunch, and some holidays.*

$$$$ ★ **Les Mignardises.** Chef Jean-Pierre Monnet used to run the kitchen at Les Halles. Now that he has his own place, his talents are given free range. Les Mignardises is considered the finest and certainly the most expensive restaurant in town. You enter via the bar and climb up one flight to the simple, elegant dining room decorated with copper pans hanging from the exposed-brick walls. The dining area holds only about 20 tables, so reservations are a must. If your wallet is full, you can choose the six-course *menu de dégustation* ($68.50). But if you're on a budget, it's still possible to enjoy a full meal. The three-course table d'hôte lunch menu allows you to sample such delicious dishes as fish salad on gazpacho or marinated duck breast with vinegar sauce. In the evening, the chef's creations include *panaché de poisson* (salmon and lotte served with a tangy lime sauce) and *noisette de faux filet* (tender beef medaillions in sherry wine). The presentation always takes a back seat to the taste. As you would expect, the wine list is large and pricey. The waiters and waitresses are prompt, knowledgeable, and friendly. *2035–37 rue St-Denis, near Berri and Sherbrooke métros, tel. 514/842–1151. Reservations required. Dress: casual, but no jeans or T-shirts. AE, DC, MC, V.*

$$$ **Auberge le Vieux St-Gabriel.** Established in a big stone house in 1754, this restaurant claims to be part of the oldest inn in North America. The interior is lined with rough stone walls, and enormous old beams hold up the ceilings. The fare is hearty yet unadventurous French, with a bit of local Québecois flavor: You may want to start off with the maple smoke salmon, followed by sautéed shrimp on a bed of buttered leeks, although the rack of lamb seasoned with fresh thyme is the chef's specialty. For the brave diner, the Unforgettable 1754 is an old-fashioned Québecois experience: a steaming bowl of pea soup à la Canadienne for starters, then tortière (meat pie), baked beans, pigs knuckles, and homemade ketchup. The restaurant seats close to 500 people, but you'd never guess it because there are so many separate dining rooms. *426 rue St-Gabriel, Vieux-Montréal, tel. 514/878-3561. Reservations advised. Dress: casual but neat. AE, DC, MC, V. Closed Sat. lunch.*

$$$ **Le Café de Paris.** This restaurant, a study in atmosphere, seats patrons at large, well-spaced tables in a room ablaze with flowers and with light streaming through the French windows. Renovated in 1991, the Ritz garden, with its picturesque duck pond, is open for summer dining alfresco. Inside or outside the waiters provide perfect, unobtrusive service. The menu opens with a selection of fresh caviar flown in from Petrossian's in New York City. You can choose from such classics as calf sweetbreads with a slightly bitter endive sauce or the flambéed fillet of buffalo with green peppercorns. At meal's end the waiter will trundle over the dessert cart; the crème brûlée with raisins is a favorite. The wine list includes everything from reasonably priced bottles to extremely expensive vintages. The table to the right rear of the dining room as you enter is where the prime minister dines when in town. If the prime minister is not there, you are likely to see other national political and financial figures supping or schmoozing among the tables. *Hôtel Ritz-Carlton, 1228 rue Sherbrooke O, tel. 514/842-4212. Reservations required. Jacket required at lunch and dinner. AE, D, DC, MC, V.*

$$$ **Le Cercle.** Le Cercle has the power look. The choicest seats are on a raised circular platform, encircled by a white Hellenistic colonnade. In these impressive surroundings Québec's political and business leaders dine on first-class nouvelle cuisine. Many must suffer from high blood pressure, because the menu features "alternative cuisine" dishes with reduced salt, cholesterol, and calories. The grilled lamb chops with mint dressing are not on this list. If you are on a budget, stop in for lunch and have the onion soup with a ham and cheese sandwich on French bread. Power breakfasts start at 6:30 AM. The standard of service here, as in the rest of the hotel, is high. The wine list is expensive and excellent, of course. *Le Westin Mont-Royal, 1050 rue Sherbrooke O, tel. 514/284-1110. Reservations advised. AE, DC, MC, V.*

$$$ **Toqué.** One of the zaniest restaurants on the Montréal scene, this eatery has been a hit from the moment it opened its doors in the spring of '93. Its name means "a bit crazy." Montréalers call it *flyée*, an expression meaning "slightly off the wall." Both descriptions fit the bill. Its appeal lies not just in its market-fresh ingredients whipped into dazzling combinations and colors, but also in its stark, futuristic decor. Toqué looks like a cross between an art gallery and an airport terminal, but the ambience is funky and eccentric. Passersby along the trendy St-Denis are stopped short by the sight of Toqué's chefs preparing food behind a wall of plate glass. The young and innovative chef-owner, thirty-something Normand Laprise, who trained with Jean-Pierre Bulloux of Dijon, France, is considered to be one of the best chefs in the city. Such entrées as venison medaillions, swordfish steaks, smoked salmon, and warm fois gras

are flavored with such fresh ingredients as red peppers, raspberry vinaigrette, thinly shredded leeks, celery roots, and Québec goat cheese. The portions don't look big but they are suprisingly filling. *3842 rue St-Denis, tel. 514/499–2084. Reservations required at least a day ahead. Dress: casual. MC, V. Closed Sun.*

$$–$$$ ★ **L'Express.** The crowd is elbow to elbow, and the animated atmosphere is reminiscent of a Paris train station. L'Express has earned the title "best bistro in town." Popular media figures come here to be seen, a task made easier by the mirrored walls. The atmosphere is smoky, and the noise level at its peak on weekend evenings. The cuisine is always impeccable, the service is fast, and the prices are very good. L'Express has one of the best and most original wine cellars in town. Wine and champagne are available by the glass as well as by the bottle. The steak tartare with french fries, the salmon with sorrel, the calves' liver with tarragon, the first course of chicken livers with pistachios, or even the modest smoked salmon are all marvelous year-round. There are specials of the day to give the many regulars a change of pace. Jars of gherkins and fresh *baguettes*, cheeses aged to perfection, and quality eaux-de-vie make the pleasure last longer. *3927 rue St-Denis, tel. 514/845–5333. Reservations required. Dress: casual but neat. AE, DC, MC, V.*

$$ **Bonaparte.** This classical French eatery is situated in the heart of Vieux-Montréal, a stone's throw from the Centaur, Montréal's English language theater. Piped Mozart serenades diners surrounded by exposed brick walls hung with pictures of soldiers from Napoléon's era. Chef Nicolas Carrere comes from Paris and prepares French dishes that, while traditional, have a light touch. Starters include fresh oysters (when in season) served on a bed of ice, salmon smoked on the premises, and game pâté with pistachios. The entrées run the gamut from tuna steak marinated in Vermouth, to veal sweetbreads served with wine sauce. *443 rue St-François-Xavier, tel. 514/844–4368. Reservations required (except winter). Dress: casual. AE, MC, V. Closed Sat. morning.*

Greek

$$$$ **Milos.** Nets, ropes, floats, and lanterns—the usual cliché symbols of the sea—hang from Milos's walls and ceilings. The real display, however, is in the refrigerated cases and on the beds of ice in the back by the kitchen, fresh fish from all over the world: octopus, squid, and shrimp; crabs, oysters, and sea urchins; lamb chops, steaks, and chicken; and vegetables, cheese, and olives. The seafood is flown in from wholesalers in Nova Scotia, New York, Florida, and Athens. A meal can start out with chewy, tender, hot octopus, or, if you're adventurous, the cool and creamy roe scooped from raw sea urchins. The main dish at Milos is usually fish—pick whatever looks freshest—grilled over charcoal and seasoned with parsley, capers, and lemon juice. It's done to a turn and is achingly delicious. The fish are priced by the pound, and you can order one large fish to serve two or more. The bountiful Greek salad (enough for two) is a perfect side dish or can be a meal itself. For dessert you might try the traditional baklava, or for something lighter, the fresh fruit plate. The waiters are professional but not always knowledgeable about the array of exotic seafood available. Milos is a healthy walk from Métro Laurier. You can also take Bus 51 from the same Métro stop and ask the driver to let you off at avenue du Parc; Milos is halfway up the block to the right. *5357 av. du Parc, tel. 514/272–3522. Reservations required. Dress: casual. AE, MC, V.*

Indian

$$–$$$ **Le Taj.** One of the rare Indian restaurants in town in which the decor and the music are appropriate. The cuisine of the north of India is honored here, less spicy and more refined than that of the south. The tandoori ovens seal in the flavors of the grilled meat and fish, the *naan* bread comes piping hot to the table, and behind a glass partition the cook retrieves the skewers from the hot coals with his bare hands, just like an experienced fakir. There are a few vegetarian specialties on the menu; for example, the *taj-thali*, consisting of lentils, chili *pakoras*, *basmati* rice, and *saag panir*—spicy white cheese with spinach. The tandoori quail and the nan stuffed with meat go well together, as does a whole series of dry curries, from lamb to chicken and beef with aromatic rice. A nine-course buffet is served daily at lunch for under $10. The desserts, coconut ice cream, or mangoes (canned) are sometimes decorated with pure silver leaves. The tea scented with cloves is delicious; it cleans the palate, warms in winter, and cools in summer. *2077 rue Stanley, tel. 514/845–9015. Reservations advised weekend. Dress: casual but neat. AE, MC, V.*

Italian

$$$ **Bocca d'Oro.** This Italian restaurant next to Métro Guy has a huge menu offering a wide variety of appetizers, pastas, veal, and vegetarian dishes. One pasta specialty is *tritico di pasta,* which is one helping each of spinach ravioli with salmon and caviar, shellfish marinara, and spaghetti primavera. A good choice from the dozen or so veal dishes is scaloppine *zingara* (with tomatoes, mushrooms, pickles, and olives). The *tajiolini misteriosi* combines pasta, avocado, and shrimp in white wine. With the dessert and coffee, the waiters bring out a big bowl of walnuts for you to crack at your table (nutcrackers provided). The two floors of dining rooms are decorated with brass rails, wood paneling, and paintings, and Italian pop songs play in the background. The staff is extremely friendly and professional; if you're in a hurry, they'll serve your meal in record time. *1448 rue St-Mathieu, downtown, tel. 514/933–8414. Reservations advised. Dress: casual but neat. AE, DC, MC, V. Closed Sun.*

$$ **Pizzaiole.** The wood-fired oven pizzas have had no respite since they started to appear in Montréal in the beginning of the 1980s. Pizzaiole, the pioneer in the field, is still by far the best. The two branches have somewhat adopted the same fresh decor emphasizing the brick oven, but the clientele and the ambience of the rue Crescent location are a bit younger. In both places, there are about 20 possible combinations, without counting the toppings and extras that personalize a pizza in no time at all. Whether you choose a simple tomato-cheese or a ratatouille on a whole-wheat crust, all the pizzas are made to order and brought immediately to the table. The calzone, a turnover filled with a variety of meats and cheeses, is worth the trip. Try the thirst-quenching Québec-brewed Boréale beer on tap, or the local St. Ambroise bottled beer. *Two locations: 1446-A rue Crescent, tel. 514/845–4158; 5100 rue Hutchison, tel. 514/274–9349. Dress: casual. AE, DC, MC, V.*

Japanese

$$$–$$$$ **Katsura.** This cool, elegant Japanese restaurant introduced sushi to Montréal and is the haunt of businesspeople who equate raw food with power. If you're with a group or just want privacy, you can re-

serve a tatami room closed off from the rest of the restaurant by rice-paper screens. The sushi chefs create an assortment of raw seafood delicacies, as well as their own delicious invention, the Canada roll (smoked salmon and salmon caviar) at the sushi bar at the rear. Sushi connoisseurs may find some offerings less than top quality. The service is excellent, but if you sample all the sushi, the tab can be exorbitant. *2170 rue de la Montagne, downtown between Peel and Guy métros, tel. 514/849–1172. Reservations required, but you might get a seat at the sushi bar without them. Dress: casual but neat. AE, DC, MC, V. Closed weekend lunch.*

Lebanese

$ **Basha.** The neon lights along gaudy rue Ste-Catherine and the ebb and flow of the crowd make this fast-food restaurant an entertaining spot for a quick evening bite. Bistro chairs and bare tables make up the utilitarian decor, and diners pick up plastic trays and choose their kebabs and falafels from the cafeteria-style counter. The menu, with prices as low as $2 and $3, includes beef and lamb shish-kebab sandwiches and platters, chicken brochettes, a daily falafel special, and a "Basha" grill platter. Open until 3 AM on weekends and until midnight during the week, this is one of the city's night-owl meccas; Montréalers stop by after a late movie for sticky, sweet Arab pastries and coffee. *930 rue Ste-Catherine O, level 2 (McGill or Peel Métro), tel. 514/866–4272. There is another downtown location at 2140 rue Guy, tel. 514/932–6682. Dress: casual. No credit cards.*

Sausages

$ **Chez Better.** The rustic fieldstone walls of historic Maison Sauvegarde create a fitting ambience for this North American branch of a popular European sausage house. Although the decor—exposed stone walls, casement windows, dimmed lighting—is upscale, the limited nature of the menu keeps prices down, to only $3.25 (excluding taxes) in the case of the "Better Special," a satisfying sandwich of one mild sausage on freshly baked bread. It's a convenient refueling stop for visitors touring Vieux-Montréal, only a few steps from Place Jacques-Cartier and the Info-Touriste center on rue Notre-Dame Est. This Notre-Dame restaurant is the most elegant of the five "Betters," although all serve the same wide variety of sausages, imported beers, and rich desserts. Service is politely efficient and the noontime crowd lively; dining is more subdued in the evenings. *160 rue Notre-Dame E (Champ-de-Mars Métro), 5400 chemin Côte-des-Neiges, 1310 boul. de Maisonneuve, 4382 boul. St-Laurent, and 1430 rue Stanley; tel. 514/861–2617. Dress: casual. AE, MC, V.*

Seafood

$$$ **Chez Delmo.** This stretch of rue Notre-Dame is halfway between the courts and the stock exchange, and at lunchtime Chez Delmo is filled with professionals gobbling oysters and fish. The first room as you enter is lined with two long, dark, wood bars, which are preferred by those wishing a fast lunch. Above one is a mural depicting a medieval feast. In the back is a more sedate and cheerful dining room. In either room the dining is excellent and the seafood fresh. A good first course, or perhaps a light lunch, is the seafood salad, a delicious mix of shrimp, lobster, crab, and artichoke hearts on a bed of Boston lettuce, sprinkled with a scalliony vinaigrette. The poached salmon with hollandaise is a nice slab of perfectly cooked fish with potatoes and broccoli. The lobsters and oysters are priced according to mar-

ket rates. Chez Delmo was founded at the same address in 1910. The service is efficient and low-key. *211–215 rue Notre-Dame O, Vieux-Montréal, tel. 514/849–4061. Dinner reservations advised. Dress: casual but neat. AE, DC, MC, V. Closed Sun., 2 wks in midsummer, and Christmas week.*

Steaks

$$$ **Moishe's.** A paradise for carnivores, Moishe's is the last place to receive dietetic advice. The meat portions are as large as a pound, which will no doubt wreak havoc with your cholesterol level. Rib steak, T-bone, and filet mignon are all grilled on wood and presented with dill-scented pickles, cole slaw, and french fries or baked potato. The meat, imported from the western United States, is juicy and tender, marbled and delectable, and aged 21 days in the restaurant's cold chambers. Moishe's grouchy service, its white aluminum-siding exterior and dark interior (reminiscent of an all-male private club), and its bland desserts don't seem to frighten away the real meat eaters. For those with a smaller appetite, the portions can be shared, but it will cost you an additional $4 and the waiter's reproachful look. *3961 boul. St-Laurent, tel. 514/845–3509. Reservations required for parties of 3 or more. Dress: casual. AE, DC, MC, V.*

$ **Le Tramway.** The cheery, fire-engine-red facade of this steak and burger restaurant draws diners off rue Ste-Catherine, especially in winter, when the lanterns inside glow a warm welcome. Once you're aboard, the Tramway is a trip back some 50 years to a time when streetcars, not the Métro, ferried people around downtown Montréal. Interior decorations are refashioned memorabilia: old lamp fixtures, former fare boxes that now hold plants, and overhead racks now used as shelves above the shiny, red banquettes. A reasonably priced menu concentrates on juicy hamburgers, although there is a "jumbo" smoked-meat sandwich with dill pickle and fries and a great thick Polish sausage garnished with sauerkraut and salad, all under $10. There are a few more expensive selections, such as the charbroiled prime-rib steak and filet mignon, so this streetcar is a desirable choice for family diners with varying tastes and appetites. *1122 rue Ste-Catherine O, tel. 514/875–6300. No reservations. Dress: casual. AE, DC, MC, V.*

Tearooms

$–$$ **La Chartreuse.** This tiny tearoom, in the Viennese tradition, has big surprises in store. Although it's best known for its scrumptious desserts, the tearoom serves quiches, salads, and soups as well. Mouthwatering and filling cakes including *rigo iancsi*, a Hungarian cake smothered in chocolate sauce, and the gâteau autrichien au café, a cake with nuts and whipped cream, are exhibited on the counter. The espresso and cappuccino complement the desserts, and the coffee is served with liqueurs, chocolate, cinnamon, or cream (whipped or not). Mozart is played discreetly in the background. *3439 rue St-Denis, tel. 514/842–0793. No reservations. Dress: casual. No credit cards. Closed Mon.*

Restaurants near Montréal

$$$$ **La Sucrerie de la Montagne.** On the road to Rigaud in the direction of Ottawa, maple syrup flows from carafes year-round and seasons the plates of pork and beans, *tourtière*, maple-glazed ham, omelet sou-

fflés, and crêpes cooked over wood fires at this old-fashioned sugar hut. Even the bread is baked on the premises in the old brick ovens fired with maple wood. Everything in this young maple grove is intended to re-create the atmosphere of the sugar season: from the sap flowing in the snow (in season) to the workhorses to men collecting the sap bucket by bucket. Pierre Faucher, the owner of this immense sugar cabin, who looks more like a lumberjack than a restaurateur, greets the Sunday passersby as well as the buses overflowing with Japanese tourists in the middle of July. An old-fashioned general store sells Québec handcrafts and maple syrup. During the sugaring season (March–mid-April) a complete meal costs $28 adults, $14 children 8–12, $8 children 3–7; off-season it costs $30 for lunch and $40 for dinner for adults. Ask about reduced rates for children. *300 rang St-Georges, Rigaud (Rte. 40, exit 17), tel. 514/451–5204. Reservations required. Dress: casual. AE, MC, V.*

$$$$ ★ **Les Trois Tilleuls.** In Saint Marc sur Richelieu, 30 minutes southeast of town, you can lunch or dine on delectable food right on the Râivière Richelieu. This small romantic inn, one of the Relais et Châteaux chain, has a terrace on the river and a large, airy dining room. Chef Roger Robin specializes in cream of onion soup, sweetbreads, and game dishes made with rabbit, quail, and venison. You can stay overnight in one of the two dozen rooms, or splurge for the palatial royal suite. *290 rue Richelieu, Saint Marc sur Richelieu, tel. 514/584–2231, fax 514/584–3146. Reservations required. Dress: casual but neat. AE, DC, MC, V.*

$$$ **Le Mitoyen.** North of the city, in the small village of Ste-Dorothée (today part of the city of Laval), is this great French restaurant that leans resolutely in favor of nouvelle cuisine. People come mainly from Montréal to taste the inventions of the self-taught chef. The meticulously decorated old house with the red roof is a haven for gourmands. Although it changes along with the seasons, the menu will always include such delicious creations as galette of smoked salmon, sweetbreads ragout with artichoke hearts, guinea hen with sherry wine vinegar, and quail with juniper berries in puff pastry. All are heavenly. For dessert, the maple nougat glacé or the poached pears in red wine and pepper end the meal elegantly. *652 Pl. Publique Ste-Dorothée, Laval (Rte. 13 N), tel. 514/689–2977. Reservations required. Dress: casual but neat. AE, MC, V. Closed Mon. and lunch Tues.–Sat.*

Lodging

On the island of Montréal alone there are 22,000 rooms available in every type of accommodation, from world-class luxury hotels to youth hostels, from student dormitories to budget executive motels. Keep in mind that during peak season (May–August) it may be difficult to find a bed without reserving, and most, but not all, hotels raise their prices. Rates often drop from mid-November to early April. Throughout the year a number of the better hotels have two-night, three-day, double-occupancy packages that offer substantial discounts.

If you arrive in Montréal without a hotel reservation, the tourism information booths at either airport can provide you with a list of hotels and room availability. You must, however, make the reservation yourself. There are no information booths at the Voyageur bus terminal, but the Gare Centrale is directly behind Le Reine

The following list is composed of recommended lodgings in Montréal for various budgets. The rates quoted are for a standard double room in May 1993; off-season rates are almost always lower.

Highly recommended hotels in each price category are indicated by a star ★.

Category	Cost*
$$$$	over $160
$$$	$120–$160
$$	$85–$120
$	under $85

**All prices are for a standard double room, excluding an optional service charge.*

Downtown

$$$$ **Bonaventure Hilton International.** This 393-room Hilton—situated atop a Métro station, the Place Bonaventure exhibition center, and a mall crowded with shops and restaurants—rises 17 stories. From the outside the massive building is uninviting, but the kind staff inside warms things up. When you exit the elevator, you find yourself in a spacious reception area flanked by an outdoor swimming pool (heated year-round) and 2½ acres of gardens, complete with ducks. Also on this floor is a complex of three restaurants and a nightclub that features well-known international entertainers. Le Castillon is the flagship restaurant, known for its three-course, 55-minute businessperson's lunch. On Sunday, there's a special theme menu. All rooms have fully stocked minibars and black-and-white TVs in the bathrooms. The furnishings are a bit dowdy, but comfortable. The Bonaventure has excellent access to the Métro station of the same name beneath it and to all the shops at Place Ville-Marie through the Underground City. *1 Pl. Bonaventure, H5A 1E4, tel. 514/878–2332 or 800/445–8667, fax 514/878–1442. 393 rooms. Facilities: 3 restaurants, nightclub, health club with sauna, pool, rooftop garden, gift shop, shopping mall, 24-hr room service. AE, D, DC, MC, V.*

$$$$ **Hôtel du Parc.** Half a block away from the acres of greenery in Parc du Mont-Royal is this perfectly located hotel, which caters mostly to a corporate clientele. Rooms are large, and the decor is modern and well maintained. From the lobby you can descend to a shopping mall with many stores and movie theaters. The nightlife of rue Prince Arthur is six blocks away. *3625 av. du Parc, H2X 3P8, tel. 514/288–6666, in Canada, 800/363–0735; in U.S., 800/448–8355; fax 514/288–2469. 358 rooms, 20 suites. Facilities: restaurant, café-bar, health club, squash courts, 2 pools, tennis court, no-smoking floors, gift shop. AE, D, DC, MC, V.*

$$$$ **Hotel Inter-Continental Montréal.** This first Inter-Continental property in Montréal, built in 1991, brings hotel luxury to Vieux-Montréal. The 24-story hotel is linked to the World Trade Centre, the block-long retail and office development that combines old and new in the former financial heart of the city, close to Vieux-Montréal attractions and the Palais des Congrès convention center. Le Continent, the elegant restaurant located in the main lobby, serves international cuisine, and there are also two bars, including Chez Plume, at ground level. The rooms are done in soft pastel colors, and match the Victorian flavor of the banquet center in the Nordheimer Build-

ing next door. The interior of the hotel makes rich use of granite and wood paneling. Other facilities include minibars and refrigerators in rooms, 12 meeting rooms, twice-daily maid service, complimentary shoe shine, a daily newspaper, and a ballroom once frequented by actress Sarah Bernhardt. *360 rue St-Antoine O, H2Y 3X4, tel. 514/987–9900, in U.S., 800/327–0200; in Canada, 800/361–3600; fax 514/874–8550. 335 rooms, 22 suites. Facilities: restaurant, health club with sauna, indoor pool, cable TV, 24-hr room service. AE, DC, MC, V.*

$$$$ **Hôtel Vogue.** One of Montréal's newest and most elegant hotels, the Vogue opened in late 1990, happily surprising everyone who remembered this building as a drab office tower. Now beautifully transformed, with tall windows and a facade of polished rose granite and deep aqua trim, this hotel is chic, sophisticated, and in the heart of downtown, right across rue de la Montagne from Ogilvy department store. The lobby's focal point, the L'Opéra Bar, boasts an expansive bay window. Room furnishings are decorated in striped silk, and double-, queen-, and king-size beds are draped with satiny duvets. Fax machines and multiline telephones in rooms appeal to business travelers. Bathrooms come with Jacuzzis, televisions, and phones. The Société Café on the lobby level is a favorite among downtowners. *1425 rue de la Montagne, H3G 1Z3, tel. 514/285–5555 or 800/465–6654, fax 514/849–8903. 148 rooms, 6 suites. Facilities: restaurant, bar, exercise room. AE, D, DC, MC, V.*

$$$$ **Le Centre Sheraton.** In a huge 37-story complex well placed between the downtown business district and the restaurant streets of Crescent and Bishop, this Sheraton offers a wide variety of services to both the business and tourist crowds. It's also a favorite with international entertainment celebrities. There are two restaurants, two bars, an indoor pool, a health club, and indoor parking. The elite, five-story Towers section is geared toward business travelers. The Sheraton caters to conventions, so expect to encounter such groups when you stay here. Though the decor is beige and unremarkable (once inside you could be in any large, modern hotel in any North American metropolis), the location's the thing. *1201 boul. René-Lévesque O, H3B 2L7, tel. 514/878–2000 or 800/325–3535, fax 514/878–3958. 824 rooms, 40 suites. Facilities: 2 restaurants, 2 bars, health club with whirlpool and sauna, indoor pool, unisex beauty parlor, gift shop. AE, D, DC, MC, V.*

$$$$ **Le Meridien.** This Air France property rises 12 stories from the center of the Complexe Desjardins, a boutique-rich mall in the middle of the plushest stretch of the Underground City. The hotel caters to businesspeople and tourists who want ultramodern European style and convenience. Le Meridien is designed on a plan of circles of privilege within these already-exclusive surroundings. For instance, within Le Café Fleuri French restaurant there's a chicer, pricier enclave called Le Club. There are no-smoking floors and an indoor pool, sauna, and whirlpool facility. And if the atmosphere ever seems too confining, you can always burst out the door and go to Chinatown, a five-minute walk away. *4 Complexe Desjardins, C.P. 130, H5B 1E5, tel. 514/285–1450 or 800/543–4300, fax 514/285–1243. 572 rooms, 28 suites. Facilities: 3 restaurants, business center, piano bar, indoor pool, sauna, whirlpool, nearby YMCA and YWCA, baby-sitting services located in complex with shops and boutiques. AE, D, DC, MC, V.*

$$$$ ★ **Le Westin Mont-Royal.** Service and hospitality make this establishment stand out among Montréal's best hotels. The shiny brass entrance opens onto a small lobby with a usually busy concierge desk and a discreet reception counter. The clientele here is primarily corporate, and the large rooms are decorated to serve that market: flo-

Auberge de Jeunesse Internationale de Montréal, **14**
Bonaventure Hilton International, **21**
Château Versailles, **2**
Delta Montréal, **17**
Holiday Inn Crowne Plaza, **18**
Hotel Inter-Continental Montréal, **26**
Hôtel de la Montagne, **4**
Hôtel du Parc, **15**
Hôtel Radisson des Gouverneurs de Montréal, **22**
Hôtel Vogue, **5**
Howard Johnson Hôtel Plaza, **16**
La Citadelle, **19**
Le Centre Sheraton, **9**
Le Château Champlain, **10**
Le Meridien, **23**
Le Nouvel Hôtel, **3**
Le Reine Elizabeth (Queen Elizabeth), **20**
Le Royal Roussillon, **24**
Le Shangrila Best Western, **11**
Le Westin Mont-Royal, **12**
Lord Berri, **25**
McGill Student Apartments, **13**
Ritz-Carlton, **6**
Université de Montréal Residence, **1**
YMCA, **8**
YWCA, **7**

Montréal Lodging

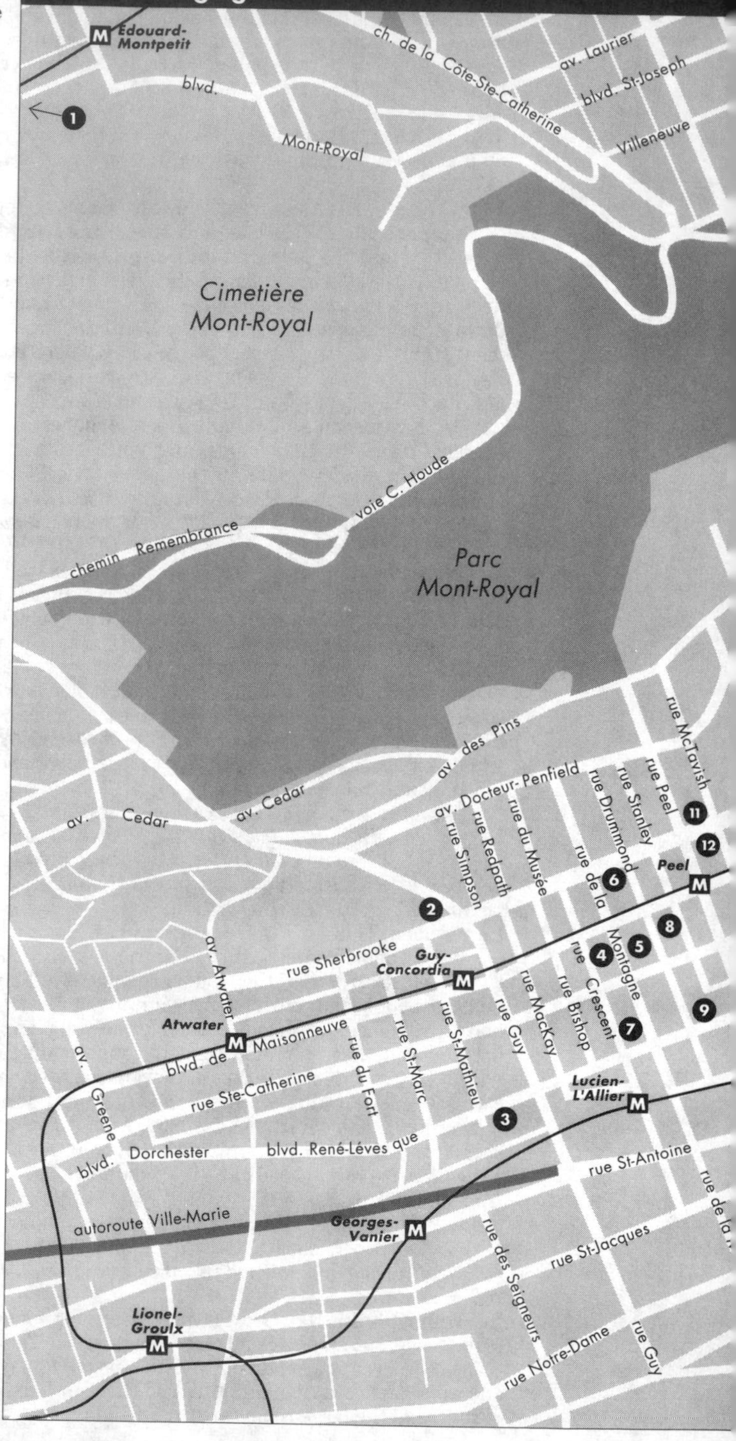

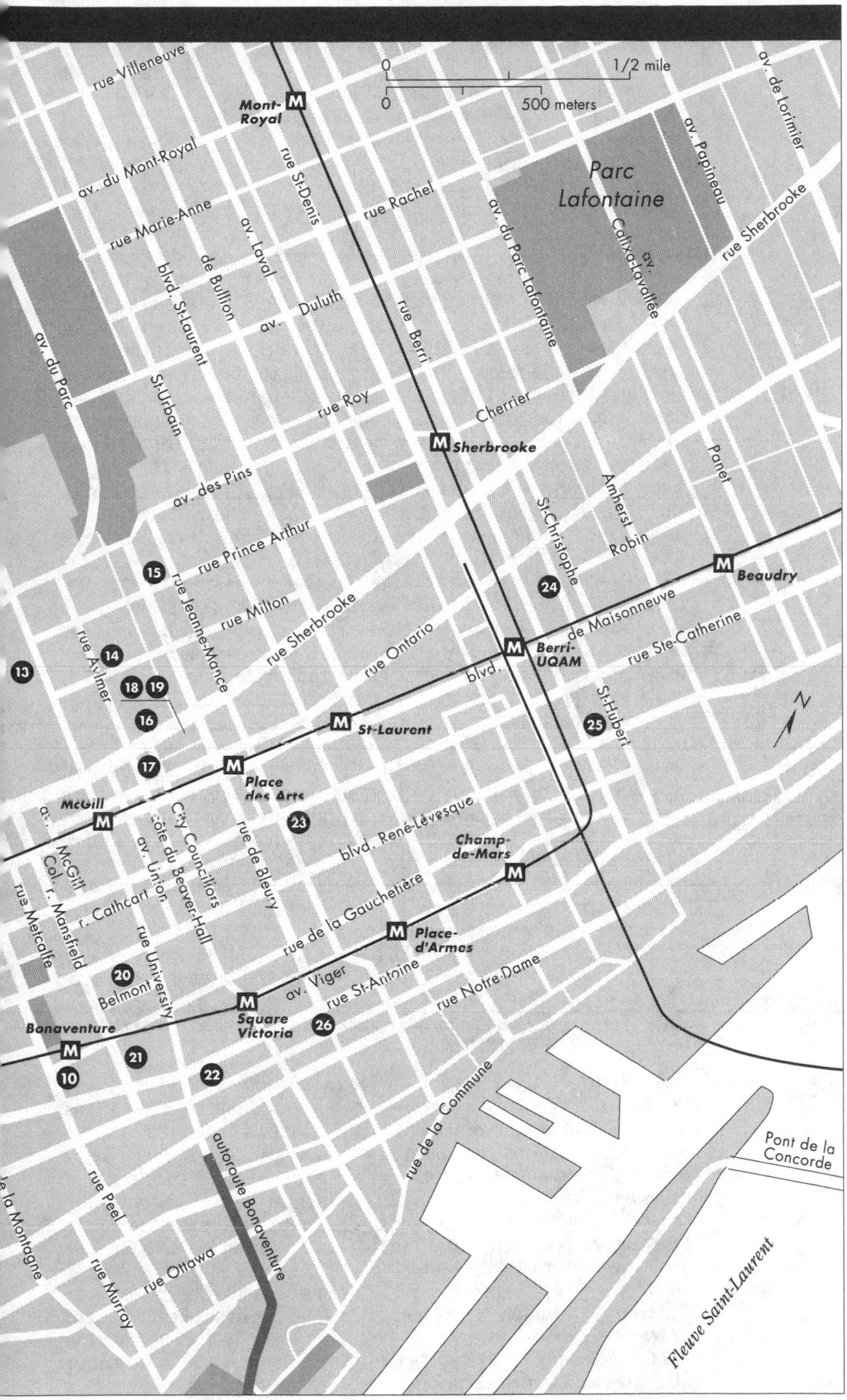
0
1/2 mile
0
500 meters
rue Villeneuve
Mont-Royal
av. du Mont-Royal
rue Marie-Anne
rue St-Denis
rue Rachel
Parc Lafontaine
av. Papineau
av. de Lorimier
av. Calixa-Lavallée
av. du Parc Lafontaine
rue Sherbrooke
blvd. St-Laurent
de Bullion
av. Laval
av. Duluth
rue Berri
av. du Parc
St-Urbain
rue Roy
Cherrier
Sherbrooke
Panet
Amherst
St-Christophe
av. des Pins
rue Prince Arthur
Robin
Beaudry
rue Jeanne-Mance
rue Milton
rue Sherbrooke
de Maisonneuve
rue Ontario
Berri-UQAM
rue Ste-Catherine
blvd.
rue Aylmer
St-Hubert
N
St-Laurent
Place des Arts
McGill
City Councillors
Côte du Beaver-Hall
av. Union
rue de Bleury
blvd. René-Lévesque
Champ-de-Mars
McGill Col.
r. Mansfield
r. Cathcart
rue Metcalfe
rue University
rue de la Gauchetière
Place-d'Armes
av. Viger
rue St-Antoine
rue Notre Dame
Belmont
Bonaventure
Square Victoria
rue de la Commune
Pont de la Concorde
autoroute Bonaventure
rue Peel
de la Montagne
rue Ottawa
rue Murray
Fleuve Saint-Laurent
10
13
14
15
16
17
18
19
20
21
22
23
24
25
26

ral chintzes, plush carpeting, and English traditional furnishings. Even the least expensive room has a bathroom telephone, minibar, hair dryer, and safe. For stress control, the hotel has a well-equipped health club, a heated outdoor swimming pool with a swimming tunnel connecting it to the building, a whirlpool, and two saunas. Two of the city's best restaurants are located here—Le Cercle and Zen. *1050 rue Sherbrooke O, H3A 2R6, tel. 514/284–1110 or 800/332–3442, fax 514/845–3025. 300 rooms, including 29 suites. Facilities: 2 restaurants, lounge, health club, heated outdoor pool, 24-hr room service.*

$$$$ ★ **Le Reine Elizabeth.** If the Ritz-Carlton is a stately old cruise ship, then Le Reine Elizabeth, also called the Queen Elizabeth, is a battleship. Massive and gray, this Canadian Pacific hotel sits on top of the Gare Centrale train station in the very heart of the city, beside Mary Queen of the World Catholic Cathedral and across the street from Place Ville-Marie. The lobby is a bit too much like a railway station—hordes march this way and that—to be attractive and personal, but upstairs the rooms are modern, spacious, and spotless, especially in the more expensive Entrée Gold section. All the latest gadgets and other trappings of luxury are present. The hotel is home to the Beaver Club (*see* Dining, *above*), a flagship restaurant that is considered an institution. There's a cheaper restaurant, too, as well as four lounges. Conventions are a specialty here. *900 boul. René-Lévesque O, H3B 4A5, tel. 514/861–3511 or 800/441–1414, fax 514/954–2256. 929 rooms, 81 suites. Facilities: 4 restaurants, 2 bars-lounges, beauty salon, boutiques, gift shops. AE, D, DC, MC, V.*

$$$$ ★ **Ritz-Carlton.** This property floats like a stately old luxury liner along rue Sherbrooke. It was opened in 1912 by a consortium of local investors who wanted a hotel where their rich European friends could stay and indulge their champagne-and-caviar tastes. Since then many earthshaking events have occurred here, including the marriage of Elizabeth Taylor and Richard Burton. Power breakfasts, lunches, and dinners are the rule at the elegant Café de Paris, and the prime minister and others in the national government are frequently sighted eating here. A less heady atmosphere prevails at the Ritz-Carlton's two other excellent restaurants. Guest rooms are a successful blend of Edwardian style—some suites have working fireplaces—with such modern accessories as electronic safes. Careful and personal attention are hallmarks of the Ritz-Carlton's service. Even if you're not a guest, stop by the Ritz's Hotel Courtyard during the summer for afternoon tea and to see the duck pond, a Ritz tradition since 1912. *1228 rue Sherbrooke O, H3G 1H6, tel. 514/842–4212 or 800/223–6800, fax 514/842–3383. 201 rooms, 39 suites. Facilities: restaurant, bar, piano bar, gift shop, barber shop, and 24-hr room service. AE, DC, MC, V.*

$$$ **Delta Montréal.** The French-style Delta is making a bid to break into the ranks of Montréal's world-class hotels. Many of the spacious guest rooms have balconies and excellent views of the city. The Le Bouquet restaurant and the piano lounge are designed like 19th-century Parisian establishments, with dark wood paneling and brass chandeliers. The cuisine is Continental and not above trendy touches like grilling over mesquite. The Delta has the most complete exercise and pool facility in Montréal. There are indoor and outdoor pools, two international squash courts, an exercise room, a sauna, and a whirlpool. The innovative Children's Creative Centre lets your children play (under supervision) while you gallivant around town. *475 av. President-Kennedy, H3A 2T4, tel. 514/286–1986 or 800/268–1133, fax 514/284–4306. 443 rooms, 10 suites. Facilities: restaurant; jazz bar (which also serves lunch weekdays); indoor and outdoor*

pools; health club with whirlpool, sauna, squash courts, aerobics classes; children's center; gift shop; pinball and video-game rooms. AE, DC, MC, V.

$$$ **Holiday Inn Crowne Plaza.** The flagship of the Holiday Inn chain's downtown Montréal hotels, the Crowne Plaza could just as well have been plopped down in Las Vegas or Atlanta. On the other hand, one doesn't stay in Holiday Inns for originality of design. This hotel *does* sparkle: It is constantly being upgraded, and has the largest indoor pool of the city's hotels, in addition to a health club, café-restaurant, and two bars. It has two suites, a penthouse, and two business floors. Popular for conventions, this hotel is near Métro McGill, rue Sherbrooke shopping, and downtown. *420 rue Sherbrooke O, H3A 1B4, tel. 514/842–6111 or 800/465–4329, fax 514/842–9381. 478 rooms, 6 suites. Facilities: café-restaurant, 2 bars, indoor pool, health club with sauna and whirlpool, unisex beauty parlor, gift shop. AE, D, DC, MC, V.*

$$$ ★ **Hôtel de la Montagne.** Upon entering the reception area you'll be greeted by a naked, butterfly-winged nymph who rises out of a fountain. An enormous crystal chandelier hangs from the ceiling and tinkles to the beat of disco music played a little too loudly. The decor resembles Versailles rebuilt with a dash of art nouveau and is reminiscent of a mid-'70s discothèque. The rooms are tamer, large, and comfortable. As for the food, it's excellent, especially in the main restaurant—Le Lutetia—known as one of the best and most innovative gourmet eateries in Montréal (*see* Dining, *above*). Tea and cocktails are served in the two lobby bars on each side of the hall, and a tunnel connects the hotel to Thursday's/Les Beaux Jeudis, a popular singles bar, restaurant, and dance club all rolled into one. Clientele is a truly bilingual mixture of French-speaking Montréalers stopping by for a drink and Torontonians in town on business. If you're staying elsewhere, the reception area is at least worth a visit. *1430 rue de la Montagne, H3G 1Z5, tel. 514/288–5656 or 800/361–6262, fax 514/288–9658. 135 rooms. Facilities: 2 restaurants, disco-bar, pool. AE, D, DC, MC, V.*

$$$ **La Citadelle.** There's a small pack of hotels on rue Sherbrooke, all of them convenient to Place des Arts, shopping, and the financial district; La Citadelle, a Clarion Hotel property, is one of them. This relatively small business hotel offers both four-star elegance in a low-key atmosphere and service, along with all the features of its better-known brethren: minibars, in-room movies, a small health club with an indoor pool, etc. There's also a passable French restaurant, C'est La Vie. *410 rue Sherbrooke O, H3A 1B3, tel. 514/844–8851 or 800/465–6654, fax 514/844–0912. 180 rooms. Facilities: restaurant; lounge; health club with Nautilus, sauna, and steam room; indoor pool; gift shop. AE, DC, MC, V.*

$$$ **Le Château Champlain.** In the heart of downtown Montréal, at the southern end of Place du Canada, is this 36-floor skyscraper with distinctive half moon–shape windows. The decor inside is formal, with only 20 rooms per floor. A number of floors are reserved for nonsmokers. Underground passageways connect the Champlain with the Bonaventure Métro station, the Bonaventure Hilton International, and Pl. Ville-Marie. *1 Pl. du Canada, H3B 4C9, tel. 514/878–9000 or 800/268–9411, fax 514/878–6761. 510 rooms, 46 suites. Facilities: 3 restaurants, lounge, health club with sauna and whirlpool, large indoor pool, gift shops. AE, DC, MC, V.*

$$$ **Le Shangrila Best Western.** If you're a frequent traveler to Montréal, you may want to try something different: an Oriental-style hotel. The hotel's decor from reception to restaurant to rooms is modern, with an amalgam of Korean, Chinese, Japanese, and Indian motifs and artwork. In addition to special corporate-class extras, such as a

lounge for buffet breakfasts and snacks, there are also pluses for the fitness fanatic: more than 10 health rooms—private rooms with exercise facilities. For your hunger pangs, there's a large Szechuan-style restaurant, Dynastie de Ming, on the lobby level. During the week the clientele is corporate; on weekends most of the guests are tourists from the United States and Ontario. Le Shangrila is situated across the street from Le Westin Mont-Royal on rue Sherbrooke, one block from Métro Peel. *3407 rue Peel, H3A 1W7, tel. 514/288–4141 or 800/361–7791, fax 514/288–3021. 146 rooms, 17 suites. Facilities: café, restaurant, bar, business lounge, gift shop, salon. AE, D, DC, MC, V.*

$$ ★ **Château Versailles.** The excellently situated, small, charming hotel occupies a row of four converted mansions on rue Sherbrooke Ouest. The owners have decorated it with many antique paintings, tapestries, and furnishings; some rooms have ornate moldings and plaster decorations on the walls and ceilings. Each room also has a full bath, TV, and air-conditioning. The reception area is designed to look like a European pension. Across the street, at 1808 rue Sherbrooke, the Villeneuve family has added a former apartment hotel as an annex to the original town houses. Called La Tour Versailles, it offers 107 larger, more Spartan rooms—at the same reasonable price—and a restaurant run by Christien Lévêque, former chef at the Ritz. It's aptly called the Champs-Élysées. The staff is extremely helpful and friendly. The Versailles is unassuming, not too expensive, and classy. *1659 rue Sherbrooke O (near Métro Guy-Concordia), H3H 1E3, tel. 514/933–3611 or 800/361–3664, fax 514/933–7102. 70 rooms in Château, 105 rooms and 2 suites in La Tour. Facilities: breakfast room in the Château, restaurant in La Tour. AE, DC, MC, V.*

$$ ★ **Hôtel Radisson des Gouverneurs de Montréal.** Abutting the stock exchange, this property rises above a stunning three-story atrium-reception area and is especially attractive to the convention crowds. It's centrally located and is near the Place Bonaventure, the western fringe of Vieux-Montréal, and the Métro Square Victoria (accessible via an underground passage). Amenities include the usual health club and pool facilities, a more exclusive floor for higher-paying guests, and a shopping arcade on the underground level. Most outstanding, however, are the restaurants. The Tour de Ville on the top floor is the city's only revolving restaurant, and its bar has live jazz nightly. Chez Antoine, an art nouveau–style bistro, serves gourmet salads and sandwiches. *777 rue University, H3C 3Z7, tel. 514/879–1370 or 800/361–8155, fax 514/879–1761. 692 rooms, 23 suites. Facilities: 2 restaurants, bar, health club with spa and steam room, indoor pool, gift shop. AE, DC, MC, V.*

$$ **Howard Johnson Hôtel Plaza.** This medium-size, medium-price hotel, next to the McGill campus, caters to the business trade and families. Exercise machines and a spa with sauna have been added, and the lobby was redone. The decor of the restaurant is Italianate, with lots of brass and marble and with bay windows overlooking the street. There's also a terrace for summer dining outdoors. The Hôtel Plaza is handy to downtown business and shopping areas. *475 rue Sherbrooke O, H3A 2L9, tel. 514/842–3961 or 800/446–4656, fax 514/842–0945. 200 rooms. Facilities: restaurant, café. AE, DC, MC, V.*

$$ **Le Nouvel Hôtel.** The Nouvel Hôtel is what hotel managers like to call a "new concept"—in its four towers it has studios and 2½-room apartments. It's not very classy, but it's brightly colored and functional. Le Nouvel Hôtel is near the restaurant district, five or six blocks from the heart of downtown and two blocks from the Guy-Concordia Métro station. *1740 boul. René-Lévesque O, H3H 1R3, tel. 514/931–8841 or 800/363–6063, fax 514/931–3233. 126 rooms, 60*

2½-room units. Facilities: restaurant, bar, gift shop, pool. AE, DC, MC, V.

$$ **Lord Berri.** Next to the Université du Québec à Montréal, the Lord Berri is a new, moderately priced hotel convenient to the restaurants and nightlife of rue St-Denis. It offers some of the services of its more expensive competition: minibars, in-room movies, and no-smoking floors. The Il Cavaliere restaurant serves Italian food and is popular with a local clientele. The Berri-UQAM Métro stop is a block away. *1199 rue Berri, H2L 4C6, tel. 514/845–9236 or 800/363–0363, fax 514/849–9855. 154 rooms. Facilities: restaurant, gift shop. AE, DC, MC, V.*

$ **Le Royal Roussillon.** This hotel is adjacent to the Terminus Voyageur bus station (buses park directly beneath one wing of the hotel), and some of the bus station aura seems to rub off on the Roussillon: It's a little dingy. But if you're stumbling after a long bus ride and want somewhere to stay *now,* the Rousillon's rooms are large and clean, the service is friendly, and the price is right. It's also handy to the Berri-UQAM Métro station. *1600 rue St-Hubert, H2L 3Z3, tel. 514/849–3214, fax 514/849–9812. 147 rooms. Facilities: restaurant. AE, DC, MC, V.*

$ **YMCA.** This clean Y is downtown, next to Peel Métro station. Book at least two days in advance. Women should book seven days ahead because there are fewer rooms with showers for them. Anyone staying summer weekends must book a week ahead, as well. *1450 rue Stanley, H3A 2W6, tel. 514/849–8393, fax 514/849–7821. 331 rooms, 429 beds. AE, MC, V.*

$ **YWCA.** Very close to dozens of restaurants, the Y is right downtown, one block from rue Ste-Catherine. Although men can eat at the café, the overnight facilities and health club are for women only. If you want a room with any amenities you must book in advance. *1355 boul. René-Lévesque, H3G 1P3, tel. 514/866–9941, fax 514/861–1603. 107 rooms, some with sink and bath. Facilities: café, gym, pool, sauna, whirlpool, weight room, fitness classes. MC, V.*

McGill University Area

$ **Auberge de Jeunesse Internationale de Montréal.** The youth hostel near the McGill campus in the student ghetto charges $15 for members, $19 for non-Canadian nonmembers, and $17 for Canadian nonmembers, per night per person. Reserve early during the summer tourist season. *3541 rue Aylmer, H2X 2B9, tel. 514/843–3317. 112 beds. Facilities: rooms for 4–12 people (same sex); a few rooms available for couples and families. MC, V.*

$ **McGill Student Apartments.** From mid-May to mid-August, when McGill is on summer recess, you can stay in its dorms on the grassy, quiet campus in the heart of the city. Nightly rates: $27.50 students; $36.50 nonstudents (single rooms only). *3935 rue University, H3A 2B4, tel. 514/398–6367. 1,000 rooms. Facilities: campus swimming pool and health facilities (visitors must pay to use them).*

Université de Montréal Area

$ **Université de Montréal Residence.** The university's student housing accepts visitors from May 9 to August 22. It's on the other side of Mont Royal, a long walk from downtown and Vieux-Montréal, but there's the new Université de Montréal Métro stop right next to the campus. Nightly rates: $21 students per night, $100 students per week, $31 nonstudents per night. *2350 boul. Édouard-Montpetit,*

H3C 3J7, tel. 514/343–6531. 1,171 rooms. Facilities: campus sports center with pool and gym (visitors must pay to use it). AE, MC, V.

Bed-and-Breakfasts

Bed and Breakfast à Montréal. Most of the more than 50 homes are downtown or in the elegant neighborhoods of Westmount and Outremont. Some of them can be quite ritzy. Others are less expensive, but all provide breakfast and a wealth of information about the city. *Contact: Marian Kahn, Box 575, Snowdon Station, Montréal H3X 3T8, tel. 514/738–9410. Single $35–$55, double $55–$105. AE, MC, V accepted for deposits only; the balance must be paid with cash or traveler's checks.*
Downtown B&B Network. This organization will put you in touch with 75 homes and apartments, mostly around the downtown core and along rue Sherbrooke, that have one or more rooms available for visitors. These homes generally are clean, lovingly kept up, and filled with antiques. Even during the height of the tourist season, this organization has rooms open. *Contact: Bob Finkelstein, 3458 av. Laval (at rue Sherbrooke), Montréal H2X 3C8, tel. 514/289–9749. Single $25–$40, double $35–$55. AE, MC, V.*

The Arts and Nightlife

The entertainment section of the *Gazette*, the English-language daily paper, is a good place to find out about upcoming events in Montréal. The Friday weekend guide has an especially good list of all events at the city's concert halls, theaters, clubs, dance spaces, and movie houses. Other publications listing what's on include *The Mirror*, *Hour*, *Scope*, and *Voir* (in French), distributed free at restaurants and other public places.

For tickets to major pop and rock concerts, shows, festivals, and hockey and baseball games, go to the individual box offices or call Admission (tel. 514/790–1245). Ticketron outlets are located in La Baie department store and in all Provigo supermarkets. Place des Arts tickets may be purchased at its box office underneath the Salle Wilfrid-Pelletier, next to the Métro station.

The Arts

Music The **Orchestre Symphonique de Montréal** has gained world renown under the baton of Charles Dutoit. When not on tour its regular venue is the Salle Wilfrid-Pelletier at the Place des Arts. The orchestra also gives Christmas and summer concerts in the Notre-Dame Basilica and pop concerts at the Arena Maurice Richard in the Olympic Park. For tickets and program information, call 514/842–9951. Also check the *Gazette* listings for its free summertime concerts in Montréal's city parks. Montréal's other orchestra, the **Orchestre Métropolitain de Montréal** (tel. 514/598–0870), also stars at Place des Arts most weeks during the October–May season. McGill University, at Pollack Concert Hall (tel. 514/398–4547) and Redpath Hall (tel. 514/398–8993), is also the site of many classical concerts. The most notable are given by the **McGill Chamber Orchestra,** which also occasionally plays at Place des Arts with guest artists. **L'Opéra de Montréal,** founded in 1980, stages four productions a year at Place des Arts (tel. 514/985–2222).

The 20,000-seat **Montréal Forum** (tel. 514/932–6131) and the much larger Olympic Stadium are where rock and pop concerts are staged. More intimate concert halls include the **Théâtre St-Denis** (1594 rue St-Denis, tel. 514/849–4211) and the **Spectrum** (318 rue Ste-Catherine O, tel. 514/861–5851).

Theater French-speaking theater lovers will find a wealth of dramatic productions. There are at least 10 major companies in town, some of which have an international reputation. Best bets are productions at **Théâtre d'Aujourd'hui** (3900 rue St. Denis, tel. 514/282–3900), **Théâtre du Nouveau Monde** (84 rue Ste-Catherine O, tel. 514/861–0563), and **Théâtre du Rideau Vert** (4664 rue St-Denis, tel. 514/844–1793). Anglophones have less to choose from, unless they want to chance the language barrier. **Centaur Theatre,** the best-known English theatrical company, stages productions in the Beaux Arts–style former stock exchange building at 453 rue St-François-Xavier in Vieux-Montréal (tel. 514/288–3161). English-language plays can also be seen at the **Saidye Bronfman Centre** at 5170 chemin de la Côte Ste-Catherine (tel. 514/739–7944). Michel Tremblay is Montréal's premier playwright, and all of his plays are worth seeing, even if in the English translation. Touring companies of Broadway productions can often be seen at the completely renovated and expanded **Théâtre St-Denis** on rue St-Denis (tel. 514/849–4211), as well as at Place des Arts (tel. 514/842- 2112)—especially during the summer months.

Dance Traditional and contemporary dance companies thrive in Montréal, though many take to the road or are on hiatus in the summer. Among the best known are **Ballets Classiques de Montréal** (tel. 514/866–1771); **Les Grands Ballets Canadiens,** the leading Québec company (tel. 514/849–8681); **O Vertigo Danse** (tel. 514/251–9177); **Montréal Danse** (tel. 514/845–2031); **LaLaLa Human Steps** (tel. 514/288–8266); **Les Ballets Jazz de Montréal** (tel. 514/982–6771); **Margie Gillis Fondation de Danse** (tel. 514/845–3115); and **Tangente** (tel. 514/525-5584)—a nucleus for many of the more avant-garde dance troupes. When not on tour, many of these artists can be seen at Place des Arts or at any of the Maisons de la Culture (tel. 514/872–6211) performance spaces around town. Montréal's dancers have a brand-new downtown performance and rehearsal space, the Agora Dance Theatre, affiliated with the Université de Montréal dance faculty (840 rue Cherrier E, tel. 514/525–1500). Check newspaper listings for details. Every other September (that is, in the odd-numbered years, such as 1995), the **Festival International de Nouvelle Danse** brings "new" dance to various venues around town. Tickets for this event always sell quickly.

Nightlife

Bars and Clubs Elegant dinner-theater productions have revitalized Montréal's English theater. Prices range from about $12 for the show alone to more than $50 for the show and dinner (not including drinks—which can run up to about $6.50 each—tips, or tax). **La Diligence** (tel. 514/731–7771) has two dinner theaters and a solid reputation for presenting polished performances of popular productions—usually Broadway hits, as well as light musical comedies and plays in English. **Le Festin du Gouverneur,** at the old fort on Ile Ste-Hélène (tel. 514/879–1141), offers a unique dinner-theater experience. Light operatic airs, beautifully rendered as a merry 17th-century frolic in the military barracks mess hall, are served up with copious amounts of food and drinks. Great for group outings.

Classical For classical music, drop by the Bar de Vieux Montréal (tel. 514/499–9403), at 408 rue St. Francois-Xavier.

Jazz Montréal has a very active local jazz scene. The best-known club is Vieux-Montréal's **L'Air du Temps** (191 rue St-Paul O, tel. 514/842–2003). This small, smoky club presents 90% local talent and 10% international acts from 5 PM on into the night. There's a cover charge Thursday through Saturday. Downtown, duck into **Biddle's** (tel. 514/842–8656), at 2060 rue Aylmer, where bassist Charles Biddle holds forth most evenings when he's not appearing at a local hotel. Bernard Primeau's Trio is an upscale club that is also a restaurant serving ribs and chicken. There's a cover charge for the big acts. You also might try **Le Grand Café** (tel. 514/849–6955) at 1720 rue St-Denis, and **Quai des Brumes Dancing** (tel. 514/499–0467) at 4481 rue St-Denis.

Rock Rock clubs seem to spring up, flourish, then fizzle out overnight. **Club Soda** (tel. 514/270–7848), at 5240 avenue du Parc, the granddaddy of them all, sports a neon martini glass complete with neon effervescence outside. Inside it's a small hall with a stage, three bars, and room for about 400 people. International rock acts play here, as does local talent. It's also a venue for the comedy and jazz festivals. Open seven nights from 8 PM to 3 AM; admission ranges from nothing up to $20, depending. **Foufounes Électriques** (tel. 514/845–5484)—which translates as "electric buttocks"—at 97 rue Ste-Catherine Est in the Latin Quarter is the downscale, more avant-garde competitor of Club Soda. Foufounes is the center for the local band scene and also attracts up-and-coming acts from the United States. There's a "quiet" section for conversation and a "loud" section for music and dancing. Open weekdays 1 PM–3 AM, weekends 7 PM–3 AM; admission varies. Other clubs include **Déjà Vu** (1224 rue Bishop, tel. 514/866–0512), **Station 10** (2071 rue Ste-Catherine O, tel. 514/934–0484), **Back Street Rock Bar** (382 rue Mayor, tel. 514/987–7671), and **L'Ours Qui Fume**—The Smoking Bear (2019 rue St-Denis, tel. 514/845–6998).

Discos Montréalers are as into discos as you could imagine. The newest and the glitziest is **Metropolis** (59 rue Ste-Catherine Est, tel. 514/288–2020). The crowd is young, primarily French-speaking, and clad in black. It's open on weekends only, and costs $5 on Friday, $8 on Saturday. If a band is appearing, the admission fee is more. **Bowling Bar** (4428 boul. St-Laurent, tel. 514/285–8869) is particularly popular with the thirty-something crowd, and any kind of music goes—funk, rave, heavy metal. **L'Opera** (3523A boul. St-Laurent, tel. 514/284–7793) is *the* place to people-watch and to be seen, wearing the appropriate gear, of course—leather, plunging necklines, and minis. Other popular discothèques include the **Hard Rock Café** (1458 rue Crescent, tel. 514/987–1420) and the **Crocodile** (636 rue Cathcart, tel. 514/866–4979).

4 Excursions from Montréal

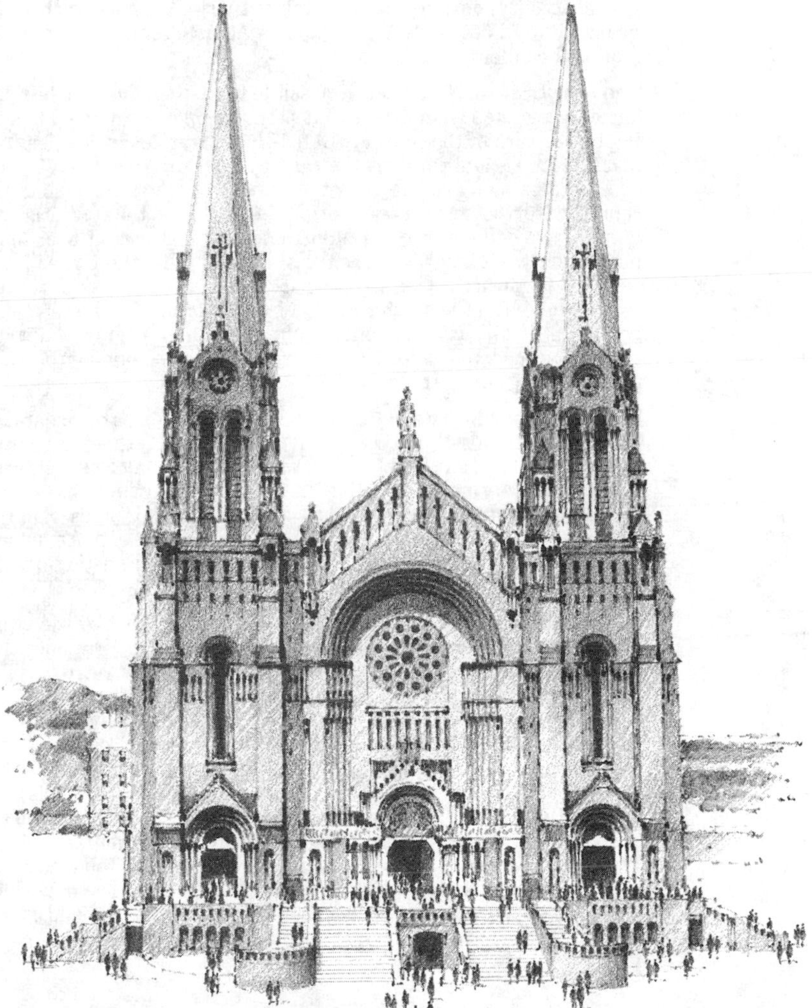

By Dorothy Guinan

Dorothy Guinan is a political researcher for the Montréal Gazette *and is a freelance writer.*

There are two major attractions beyond the city limits of Montréal: l'Estrie (formerly the Eastern Townships), where city folk retreat in summer, and Les Laurentides (the Laurentians), where they escape in winter. Les Laurentides are characterized by thousands of miles of unspoiled wilderness and world-famous ski resorts, while l'Estrie has rolling hills and farmland. As major vacation areas in both winter and summer, they offer outdoor activities on ski slopes and lakes and in their provincial parks.

Les Laurentides

Avid skiers might call Montréal a bedroom community for the Laurentians; just 56 kilometers (35 miles) to the north, they are home to some of North America's best-known ski resorts. The Laurentian range is ancient, dating to the Precambrian era (more than 600 million years ago). These rocky hills are relatively low, worn down by glacial activity, but they include eminently skiable hills, with a few peaks above 2,500 feet. World-famous Mont Tremblant, at 3,150 feet, is the tallest.

The **P'tit Train du Nord** made it possible to easily transport settlers and cargo to the Upper Laurentians. It also opened them up to skiing by the turn of the century. Before long, trainloads of skiers replaced settlers and cargo as the railway's major trade. The Upper Laurentians soon became known worldwide as the number-one ski center in North America—a position they still hold today. Initially a winter weekend getaway for Montréalers who stayed at boardinghouses and fledgling resorts while skiing its hills, the Upper Laurentians began attracting an international clientele, especially with the advent of the Canadian National Railway's special skiers' train, begun in 1928. (Its competitor, the Canadian Pacific Railway, jumped on the bandwagon soon after, doubling the number of train runs bringing skiers to the area.)

Soon, points north of Saint-Jérôme began to develop as resort areas: Saint-Sauveur-des-Monts, Saint-Jovite, Sainte-Agathe-des-Monts, Mont Tremblant, and points in between became major ski centers. The Upper Laurentians also began to grow as a winter haven for prominent Montréalers, who traveled as far north as Sainte-Agathe-des-Monts to establish private family ski lodges. A number of these properties continue to be preserved in their rustic turn-of-the-century wilderness settings.

Accessible only by train until the 1930s, when the highway was built, these were used primarily as winter ski lodges. But once the road opened up, cottages became year-round family retreats. Today, there is an uneasy alliance between the longtime cottagers and resort-driven entrepreneurs. Both recognize the other's historic role in developing the Upper Laurentians, but neither espouses the other's cause. At the moment, commercial development seems to be winning out. A number of large hotels have added indoor pools and spa facilities, and efficient highways have brought the country closer to the city—45 minutes to Saint-Saveur, 1½–2 hours to Mont Tremblant. Montréalers can drive up to enjoy the fall foliage or engage in spring skiing and still get home before dark. The only slow periods are early October, when there is not much to do, and June, when there is plenty to do but the area is beset by blackflies.

Important Addresses and Numbers

The major tourist office is the **Maison du Tourisme des Laurentides** at Saint-Jérôme, just off the Autoroute des Laurentides 15 at exit 39. *14142 rue de Lachapelle, RR 1, St-Jérôme J7Z 5T4, tel. 514/436-8532. Open mid-June–Aug., daily 8:30–8; Sept.–mid-June, Sat.–Thurs 9–5, Fri. 9–7.*

You can also get information in person at **Infotouriste** (1001 Sq. Dorchester, Montréal). Year-round regional tourist offices are located in the towns of Labelle, Mont Laurier, Mont Tremblant, Saint-Antoine, Saint-Sauveur-des-Monts, Saint-Jovite, Sainte-Adèle, and Sainte-Agathe-des-Monts. Seasonal tourist offices (mid-June–Labor Day) are also located in Bois Briand, Grenville, Lachute, L'Annociation, Sainte-Marguerite-du-Lac-Masson, Notre-Dame-du-Laus, Piedmont, Saint-Adolphe-Howard, and Val David. For information about ski conditions, telephone the Maison du Tourisme des Laurentides (*see above*) and ask for the ski info-line number.

Getting Around

By Car Autoroute des Laurentides 15, a six-lane highway, and the slower but more scenic secondary road, Route 117, lead to this resort country. Try to avoid traveling to and from the region on Friday evening or Sunday afternoon, as you're likely to sit for hours in bumper-to-bumper traffic.

By Bus Frequent bus service is available from the Terminus Voyageur (505 boul. de Maisonneuve E, tel. 514/842–2281) in downtown Montréal. **Limocar Laurentides'** service (tel. 514/435–8899) departs regularly for L'Annociation, Mont Laurier, Sainte-Adèle, Sainte-Agathe-des-Monts, and Saint-Jovite, among other stops en route. Limocar also has a service to the Basses Laurentides (Lower Laurentians) region, departing from the Laval bus terminal at the Métro Henri-Bourassa stop in north Montréal, stopping in many towns, and ending in Saint-Jérôme.

Exploring

Les Basses Laurentides The Laurentians are actually divided into two major regions—les Basses Laurentides (the Lower Laurentians) and les Hautes Laurentides (the Upper Laurentians). But don't be fooled by the designations; they don't signify great driving distances.

The Lower Laurentians start almost immediately outside Montréal. Considered the birthplace of the Laurentians, this area is rich in historic and architectural landmarks. Beginning in the mid-17th century, the governors of New France, as Québec was then called, gave large concessions of land to its administrators, priests, and top-ranking military, who became known as *seigneurs*. In the Lower Laurentians, towns like Terrebonne, Saint-Eustache, Lac-des-Deux-Montagnes, and Oka are home to the manors, mills, churches, and public buildings these seigneurs had built for themselves and their *habitants*—the inhabitants of these quasi-feudal villages.

Numbers in the margin correspond to points of interest on the Laurentians map.

Two of the most famous seigneuries are within an hour of Montréal:
1 **La Seigneurie de Terrebonne,** on l'Île-des-Moulins, is about 20 minutes from Montréal; La Seigneurie du Lac-des-Deux-Montagnes, in

The Laurentians

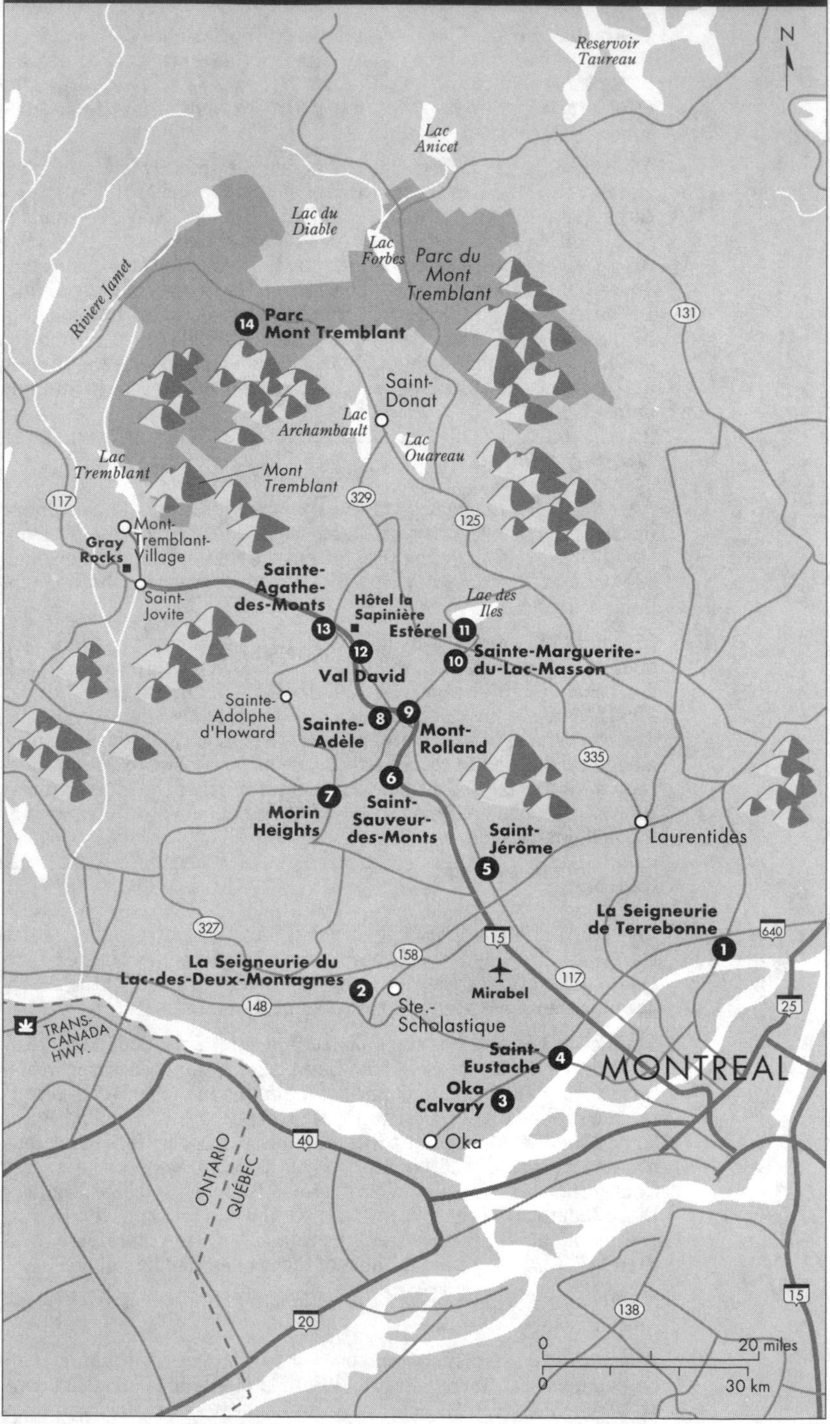

N
Reservoir Taureau
Lac Anicet
Lac du Diable
Lac Forbes
Parc du Mont Tremblant
Riviere Jamet
131
14 Parc Mont Tremblant
Saint-Donat
Lac Archambault
Lac Ouareau
Lac Tremblant
Mont Tremblant
117
329
125
Mont-Tremblant-Village
Gray Rocks
Saint-Jovite
Sainte-Agathe-des-Monts
Hôtel la Sapinière
Lac des Iles
13
Estérel 11
12
10 Sainte-Marguerite-du-Lac-Masson
Val David
Sainte-Adolphe d'Howard
Sainte-Adèle 8
9 Mont-Rolland
335
6
7
Morin Heights
Saint-Sauveur-des-Monts
Saint-Jérôme
5
Laurentides
La Seigneurie de Terrebonne
640
1
327
15
158
La Seigneurie du Lac-des-Deux-Montagnes
2
Ste.-Scholastique
Mirabel
117
148
25
TRANS-CANADA HWY.
Saint-Eustache 4
MONTREAL
Oka Calvary 3
Oka
40
ONTARIO
QUÉBEC
15
138
20
0
20 miles
0
30 km

St-Scholastique, is 40 minutes from Montréal. You reach Terrebonne by taking boulevard Pie-IX in Montréal to the bridge of the same name. From the bridge take Highway 25 North. Exit at Terrebonne to Highway 440.

Governor Frontenac gave the land to Sieur André Daulier in 1673. Terrebonne was maintained by a succession of seigneurs until 1832, when Joseph Masson, the first French Canadian millionaire, bought it. He and his family were the last seigneurs de Terrebonne; their reign ended in 1883.

Today, Terrebonne offers visitors a bona fide glimpse of the past. Now run by the Corporation de l'Ile-des-Moulins rather than a French aristocrat, the seigneurie's mansions, manors, and buildings have all been restored. Take a walk through Terrebonne's historical center and then stop at the **Centre d'Interprétation Historique de Terrebonne Museum.** It features three exhibits: the Seigneurial Regime; the water, saw, flour, and wool mills of the region that gave the island its name; and the beginning of the Industrial Revolution in Terrebonne. The Ile-des-Moulins art gallery hosts exhibitions of works by local artists, and a theater presents plays in French as well as musical matinees and outdoor summer shows ($7 for theater; most other activities free). *Cnr. boul. des Braves and rue St-Pierre, tel. 514/471–0619. Admission free. Open mid-May–late June, Tues.–Sun. 1–5; late June–early Sept., Tues.–Sun. 10–8.*

2 **La Seigneurie du Lac-des-Deux-Montagnes** was allotted to the Sulpician priests in 1717. Already appointed the seigneurs of the entire island of Montréal, the priests used this as the base from which to establish an Amerindian mission. To reach this mission, take Highway 13 or 15 North out of Montréal to Highway 640 West. Exit from Highway 640 West at Highway 148. Take this road into the town of Saint-Scholastique. A highlight of the seigneurie is the Sulpicians' seignorial manor on rue Belle-Rivière, erected between 1802 and 1808 in the village of Saint-Scholastique. The manor was used as part of the set for the late Claude Jutra's acclaimed film, *Kamouraska*, based on the novel by Québec's prize-winning author Anne Hébert.

To promote piety among the Amerindians, the Sulpicians erected
3 the **Oka Calvary (Stations of the Cross)** between 1740 and 1742. Three of the seven chapels are still maintained, and every September 14 since 1870, Québecois pilgrims have congregated here from across the province to participate in the half-hour ceremony that proceeds on foot to the Calvary's summit. A sense of the divine is inspired as much by the magnificent view of Lac-des-Deux-Montagnes as by religious fervor.

In 1887, the Sulpicians gave about 865 acres of their property located near the Oka Calvary to the Trappist monks, who had arrived in New France in 1880 from the Bellefontaine Abbey in France. Within 10 years they had built their monastery, the **Abbaye Cistercienne d'Oka,** and they transformed this land into one of the most beautiful domains in Québec. The abbey is one of the oldest in North America. Famous for creating Oka cheese, the Trappists established the Oka School of Agriculture, which operated until 1960. Today, the monastery is a noted prayer retreat. The gardens and chapel are open to visitors. *1600 chemin d'Oka, tel. 514/479–8361. Admission free. Chapel open daily 8– 12:15 and 1–8; gardens and boutique open weekdays 9:30–11:30 and 1–4:30, Sat. 9–4.*

Close by is the **Ferme Avicole d'Oka,** one of Québec's largest poultry farms, also developed by the Trappists. Tours of the breeding grounds for exotic pheasant, partridge, and guinea-hen fowl, as well as for the ordinary variety, are given, and there is a slide show of the transition from farm to table—an interesting encounter for city children. Fresh eggs and fowl can be bought on site. *1525 chemin d'Oka, tel. 514/479–8394. Store open weekdays 9–noon and 1–5, Sat. 9–5, Sun. 1–5.*

Kanestake, a Mohawk Indian reserve near Oka, made the headlines during the summer of 1990 when a 78-day armed standoff between Mohawk Warriors (the reserve's self-proclaimed peacekeeping force) and Canadian and provincial authorities took place. The Mohawks of Kanestake opposed the expansion of the Oka golf course, claiming the land was stolen from them 273 years before. When the standoff ended, the golf course was not expanded.

4 Nearby **Saint-Eustache** is another must for history buffs. One of the most important and tragic scenes in Canadian history took place here: the 1837 Rebellion. Since the British conquest of 1760, French Canadians had been confined to preexisting territories while the new townships were allotted exclusively to the English. Adding to this insult was the government's decision to tax all imported products from England, which made them prohibitively expensive. The result? In 1834, the French Canadian Patriot party defeated the British party locally. Lower Canada, as it was then known, became a hotbed of tension between the French and English, with French resistance to the British government reaching an all-time high. Rumors of rebellion were rife, and in December 1837, some 2,000 English soldiers led by General Colborne were sent in to put down the "army" of North Shore patriots by surrounding the village of Saint-Eustache. Jean-Olivier Chénier and his 200 patriots took refuge in the local church, which Colborne's cannons bombed and set afire. Chénier and 80 of his comrades were killed during the battle, and more than 100 of the town's houses and buildings erected during the seignorial regime were looted and burned down by Colborne's soldiers. Even today, traces of the bullets fired by the English army cannons are visible on the facade of Saint-Eustache's church at 123 rue St-Louis. Most of the town's period buildings are open to the public. Note especially **Manoir Globenski** and **Moulin Légaré,** the only water mill still in operation in Canada. For a guided tour or for a free brochure that gives a good walking-tour guide, visit the town's Arts and Cultural Services Center (235 rue St-Eustache, tel. 514/472–4440, ext. 282). Tours are offered from April until December.

Time Out Before heading north, stop at **Pâtisserie Grande-Côte** (367A chemin de la Grande-Côte, tel. 514/473–7307) to sample the wares of St-Eustache's most famous bakery and pastry shop.

Les Hautes Laurentides

5 Rivaling Saint-Eustache in Québec's historic folklore is **Saint-Jérôme,** founded in 1830. Today a thriving economic center and cultural hub off Route 117, it first gained prominence in 1868 when Curé Antoine Labelle became pastor of this parish on the shores of Rivière du Nord. Curé Labelle devoted himself to opening up northern Québec to French Canadians. Between 1868 and 1890, he founded 20 parish towns—an impressive achievement given the harsh conditions of this vast wilderness. But his most important legacy was the famous P'tit Train du Nord railway line, which he persuaded the government to build in order to open Saint-Jérôme to travel and trade.

Follow Saint-Jérôme's **promenade,** a 4-kilometer-long (2½-mile) boardwalk alongside the Rivière du Nord from rue de Martigny bridge to rue St-Joseph bridge for a walk through the town's history. Descriptive plaques en route highlight episodes of the Battle of 1837. The **Centre d'Exposition du Vieux-Palais** housed in St-Jérôme's old courthouse has temporary exhibits of contemporary art, featuring mostly Québec artists. A music hall next door sometimes hosts concerts. *185 rue du Palais, tel. 514/432–7171. Admission free. Open Tues.–Fri. noon–5, weekends 1–5.*

Saint-Jérôme's **Parc Régional de la Rivière-du-Nord** (1051 boul. International, tel. 514/431–1676) was created as a nature retreat. Paths throughout the park lead to the spectacular Wilson Falls (*chutes*, in French). Rain or shine, the Pavillon Marie-Victorin is open daily, with summer weekend displays and workshops devoted to nature, culture, and history.

The resort vacation area truly begins at Saint-Sauveur-des-Monts (Exit 60) and extends as far north as Mont Tremblant, where it turns into a wilderness of lakes and forests best visited with an outfitter. Laurentian guides planning fishing and hunting trips are concentrated around Saint-Donat near Parc Mont Tremblant.

To the first-time visitor, the hills and resorts around Saint-Sauveur, Sainte-Marguerite Station, Morin Heights, Val Morin, and Val David, up to Sainte-Agathe, form a pleasant hodgepodge of villages, hotels, and inns that seem to blend one into another.

6 **Saint-Sauveur-des-Monts,** exit 60 off the Autoroute, is the focal point for area resorts. It has gone from a 1970s sleepy Laurentian village of 4,000 residents that didn't even have a traffic light to a thriving year-round town attracting some 30,000 cottagers and visitors on weekends. Its main street, rue Principale, once dotted with quaint French restaurants, now boasts *brochetteries* and sushi bars, and the narrow strip is so choked in summertime by cars and tourists that it has earned the sobriquet "Crescent Street of the North," borrowing its name from the well-known, action-filled street in Montréal. Residents here once won the battle against a McDonald's opening. Now the parking lots of major franchise fast-food eateries are always packed. Despite all this development, Saint-Sauveur has managed to maintain some of its charming, rural character.

The gleaming white spires of **Saint-Sauveur Church** still dominate rue Principale, but **Saint Francis of the Birds** has not been so lucky. Built in 1951 with support from Montréal's Molson family, this sturdy, rustic log church with its fine stained-glass-window portraits of the Laurentian countryside no longer offers the worshiper or visitor a secluded and peaceful spiritual retreat. Where only a few years ago its immediate neighbors were modest chalets dotting the forest, today the empty, bankrupt Delta Hotel complex sits in the church's backyard. However, classical concerts can still be heard in the church every second Saturday evening during September and October (tel. 514/227–2423).

But for those who like their vacations—winter or summer—lively and activity-filled, Saint-Sauveur is *the* place where the action rolls nonstop. In winter, skiing is the main thing. (Mont-Saint-Sauveur, Mont Avila, Mont Gabriel, and Mont Olympia all offer special season passes and programs, and some ski-center passes can be used at more than one center in the region.) From Mont-Saint-Sauveur to Mont Tremblant, the area's ski centers (most situated in or near Saint-Sauveur, Sainte-Adèle, Sainte-Agathe, and Saint-Jovite) offer night skiing. All have ski instructors—many are members of the Canadian Ski Patrol Association.

Just outside Saint-Sauveur, the $7 million Mont Saint-Sauveur **Water Park** and tourist center (exit 58 or 60) will keep children occupied with slides, wave pools, snack bars, and more. The "Children's Island" is the park's latest attraction, with calm, shallow wading ponds designed for youngsters one to six years old. The man-made "Colorado" rafting river attracts the older, braver crowd; the nine-minute ride follows the natural contours of steep hills and requires about 12,000 gallons of water to be pumped per minute. *350 rue Saint-Denis, Saint-Sauveur-des-Monts, tel. 514/871–0101 or 800/363–2426. Admission: full day—$20 adults, $14 children 3 and over; half day (after 3 PM)—$16 adults, $12 children 3 and over; evening (after 5 PM)—$12 adults, $9 children 3 and over. Open mid-June–Aug., daily 10–7.*

7 Nearby in **Morin Heights,** there's a new spin on an old sport at **Ski Morin Heights** (exit 60, Autoroute 15 N, tel. 514/227–2020 or 800/661–3535), where snowboarding is the latest craze. Although it doesn't have overnight accommodations, Ski Morin Heights boasts a 44,000-square-foot chalet with a full range of hospitality services and sports-related facilities, eateries, après-ski activities, pubs, a health club, and a day-care center. There's also a large nursery on-site and special ski-lesson programs for children ages 2 and up.

The town's architecture and population reflect its English settlers' origins. Most residents are English-speaking. Morin Heights has escaped the overdevelopment of Saint-Sauveur but still offers the visitor a good range of restaurants, bookstores, boutiques, and crafts shops to explore. During the summer months, windsurfing, swimming, and canoeing on the area's two lakes are popular pastimes. Another popular attraction is **Théâtre Morin Heights** (tel. 514/226–1944), whose "professional amateur" productions are presented at a local elementary school during the summer months. Popular musicals, lighthearted comedies, mysteries, and children's plays are in the repertoire. Reservations are a must.

In the summer, holiday goers head for the region's golf courses (two of the more pleasant are 18-hole links at Sainte-Adèle and Mont Gabriel), campgrounds at Val David, Lacs Claude and Lafontaine, and beaches; in the fall and winter, they come for the foliage as well as alpine and Nordic skiing.

8 The busy town of **Sainte-Adèle** is full of gift and Québec-crafts shops, boutiques, and restaurants. It also has an active nightlife, including a few discos.

Just as much of a rave with adults as with children are the **Super Splash** waterslides. *1791 boul. Ste-Adèle, tel. 514/229–2925. 3 giant slides for adults, 3 for children. Admission: $15 adults, $10 children under 12, $40 families. Open June–Aug., daily 10–7.*

A couple of miles north on Highway 117, the reconstructed **Village de Seraphin**'s 20 small homes, grand country house, general store, and church recall the settlers who came to Sainte-Adèle in the 1840s. This award-winning historic town also features a train tour through the woods. *Tel. 514/229–4777. Admission: $8.75 adults, $6.75 children 12–17, $5.75 children 5–11. Open late May–late June and early Sept.–mid-Oct., weekends 10–5; late June–early Sept., daily 10–5.*

9 In **Mont Rolland, Station Touristique de Mont Gabriel** offers superb skiing, primarily for intermediate and advanced skiers. The on-site

lodge, **Auberge Mont Gabriel** (*see* Lodging, *below*), has week-long and weekend packages. *Autoroute 15, exit 64, Mont Rolland J0R 1G0, tel. 514/229-3547.*

10 Neighboring community **Sainte-Marguerite-du-Lac-Masson** celebrated its 125th anniversary in 1990. The town's Service des Loisirs (tel. 514/228-2545) is the place to call for details about events, as well as cruises and skating on Lac-Masson.

11 The permanent population of the town of **Estérel** is a mere 80 souls. But visitors to **Hotel d'Estérel,** a 135-room resort at Autoroute 69, near Sainte-Marguerite Station, swell that number into the thousands. Founded in 1959 on the shores of Lac Dupuis, this 5,000-acre domain was bought by Fridolin Simard from Baron Louis Empain. Named Estérel by the baron because it evoked memories of his native village in Provence, Ville d'Estérel soon became a household word for holiday vacationers in search of a first-class resort area. (For more details, *see* Lodging, *below.*)

12 Children know **Val David** for its **Santa Claus Village.** This is Santa Claus's summer residence, where children can sit upon Santa's knee and speak to him. (He's bilingual, too: French and English.) On the grounds is a petting zoo, with goats, sheep, horses, and colorful birds. Bumper boats and games are run here, as well. *987 rue Morin, Val David, tel. 819/322-2146. Admission: $7 adults, $5.50 children 2-12. Open late May-early June, weekends 10-6; early June-late Aug., daily 10-6.*

Val David is a rendezvous for mountain climbers, ice scalers, dogsledders, hikers, and summer or winter campers. For equipment rentals and other information, contact the Maison du Tourisme des Laurentides (tel. 514/436-8532).

Val David is also a haven for artists, many of whose studios are open to the public. Most of their work is for sale. The **Atelier Bernard Chaudron, Inc.** (2449 chemin de l'Ile, tel. 819/322-3944), sells hand-shaped and hammered lead-free pewter objets d'art.

About 96 kilometers (60 miles) from Montréal, overlooking Lac des
13 Sables, is **Sainte-Agathe-des-Monts,** the largest commercial center for ski communities farther north. This lively resort area attracts campers to its spacious **Au Parc des Campeurs** (Rte. 329, 50 rue St. Joseph, Sainte-Agathe-des-Monts J8C 1M9, tel. 819/324-0482 or 800/324-0482), bathers to its municipal beach, and sailors to its lake cruises on the ***Alouette*** (tel. 819/326-3656) touring launch. Sailing is the favorite summer sport, especially during the "24 Heures de la Voile," a weekend sailing competition (tel. 819/326-0457) that takes place each year in June.

Scuba diving is also popular here. The **Service Ambulance Gilles Thibault Inc.** (124 rue Principale, tel. 819/326-4464) will refill air tanks and provide information about equipment rentals.

Perhaps the best way to view the scenery of the Upper Laurentians is to mountain climb. The **Fédération Québécoise de la Montagne** (4545 rue Pierre-de-Coubertin, C.P. 1000, Succursale M, Montréal H1V 3R2, tel. 514/252-3004) can give you information about this sport, as can the region's tourist offices.

About 1 kilometer (½ mile) north of Sainte-Agathe-des-Monts is the **Village du Mont-Castor,** an attractive re-creation of a turn-of-the-century Québecois village; more than 100 new homes have been built here in the traditional fashion of full-length logs set *pièce sur pièce* (one upon the other).

Farther north lie two of Québec's best-known ski resorts—Gray Rocks and Station Mont Tremblant Resort (*see* Lodging, *below*). Mont Tremblant is also car-racing country. Racing champion Jackie Stewart has called Mont Tremblant "the most beautiful racetrack in the world." The **Formula 2000 "Jim Russell Championships"** of the Canadian Car Championships (tel. 819/425–2739) take place here on weekends in June, July, August, and September.

The mountain and the hundreds of square miles of wilderness be-
14 yond it constitute **Parc Mont Tremblant.** Created in 1894, this was once the home of the Algonquin Indians, who called this area Manitonga Soutana, meaning "mountain of the spirits." Today it is a vast wildlife sanctuary of more than 500 lakes and rivers protecting about 230 species of birds and animals, including moose, deer, bear, and beaver. In the winter, its trails are used by cross-country skiers, snowshoers, and snowmobile enthusiasts. Moose hunting is allowed in season, and camping and canoeing are the main summer activities.

What to See and Do with Children

Mont Saint-Sauveur Water Park
Santa Claus Village

L'Estrie

L'Estrie (also known as the Eastern Townships) refers to the area in the southeast corner of the province of Québec, bordering Vermont and New York State. Its northern Appalachian hills, rolling down to placid lakeshores, were first home to the Abenaki natives, long before "summer people" built their cottages and horse paddocks here. The Abenaki are gone, but the names they gave to the region's recreational lakes remain— Memphremagog, Massawippi, Mégantic.

L'Estrie was initially populated by United Empire Loyalists fleeing the American War of Independence and, later, the newly created United States of America, to continue living under the English king in British North America. It's not surprising that l'Estrie is reminiscent of New England with its covered bridges, village greens, white church steeples, and country inns. The Loyalists were followed, around 1820, by the first wave of Irish immigrants—ironically, Catholics fleeing their country's union with Protestant England. Some 20 years later the potato famine sent more Irish pioneers to the townships.

The area became more Gallic after 1850, as French Canadians moved in to work on the railroad and in the lumber industry, and later to mine asbestos at Thetford. Around the turn of the century, English families from Montréal and Americans from the border states discovered the region and began summering at cottages along the lakes. During the Prohibition era, the area attracted even more cottagers from the United States. Lac Massawippi became a favorite summer resort of wealthy families whose homes have since been converted into gracious inns, including the Manoir Hovey and the Hatley Inn.

Today the summer communities fill up with equal parts French and English visitors, though the year-round residents are primarily French. Nevertheless, the locals are proud of both their Loyalist heritage and Québec roots. They boast of "Loyalist tours" and Victorian gingerbread homes and in the next breath direct visitors to the snowmobile museum in Valcourt, where, in 1937, native son Joseph-Armand Bombardier built the first *moto-neige* (snowmobile) in his garage. (Bombardier's inventions were the basis of one of Canada's biggest industries, supplying New York City and Mexico City with subway cars and other rolling stock.)

Over the past two decades, l'Estrie has developed from a series of quiet farm communities and wood-frame summer homes to a thriving all-season resort area. In winter, skiers flock to eight downhill centers and some 20 cross-country trails. By early spring, the sugar huts are busy with the new maple syrup. L'Estrie's southerly location makes this the balmiest corner of Québec, notable for its spring skiing. In summer, boating, swimming, sailing, golfing, and bicycling take over. And every fall the inns are booked solid with "leaf peepers" eager to take in the brilliant foliage.

Important Addresses and Numbers

In Montréal, information about l'Estrie is available at **Infotouriste** (*see above*). Year-round regional provincial tourist offices are located in the towns of Bromont, Danville, Granby, Magog, Sherbrooke, and Sutton. Seasonal tourist offices (June–Labor Day) are also located in Ayer's Cliff, Coaticook, Knowlton, La Patrie, Lac-Mégantic, Lennoxville, Masonville, North Hatley, and Pike River. Seasonal bureaus' schedules are irregular, so contact the **Association Touristique de l'Estrie** (25 Brocage, Sherbrooke, J1L 2J4, tel. 819/820–2020) before visiting. The association also provides lodging information.

Getting Around

By Car Take Autoroute 10 East from Montréal; from New England take U.S. 91, which becomes Autoroute 55 as it crosses the border at Rock Island.

By Bus Buses depart daily from the Terminus Voyageur in Montréal (505 boul. de Maisonneuve E, tel. 514/842–2281), to Granby, Lac-Mégantic, Magog, Sherbrooke, and Thetford Mines.

Exploring

Numbers in the margin correspond to points of interest on the L'Estrie (Eastern Townships) and Montérégie map.

15 **Granby,** about 80 kilometers (50 miles) from Montréal, is considered to be the gateway to l'Estrie. This town is best known for its zoo, the **Jardin Zoologique de Granby.** It houses some 800 animals from 225 species. Two rare snow leopards on loan from Chicago's Lincoln Park Zoo and New York's Bronx Zoo have won the zoo recognition from the International Union for the Conservation of Nature. The complex includes amusement park rides and souvenir shops as well as a playground and picnic area. *347 rue Bourget, tel. 514/372–9113. Admission: $15 adults, $13 senior citizens, $8 children 5–17 and people with disabilities, $4 children 1–4. Open late May–early Sept., daily 9:30–5; Sept., weekends 9–5.*

Granby is also gaining repute as the townships' gastronomic capital. Each October, the month-long Festival Gastronomique attracts more than 10,000 *gastronomes* who use the festival's "gastronomic passport" to sample the cuisines at several dining rooms. To reserve a passport, contact: Festival Gastronomique de Granby et Région, 650 rue Principle, Granby J2G 8L4. *Tel. 514/378–7272.*

L'Estrie (Eastern Townships) and Montérégie

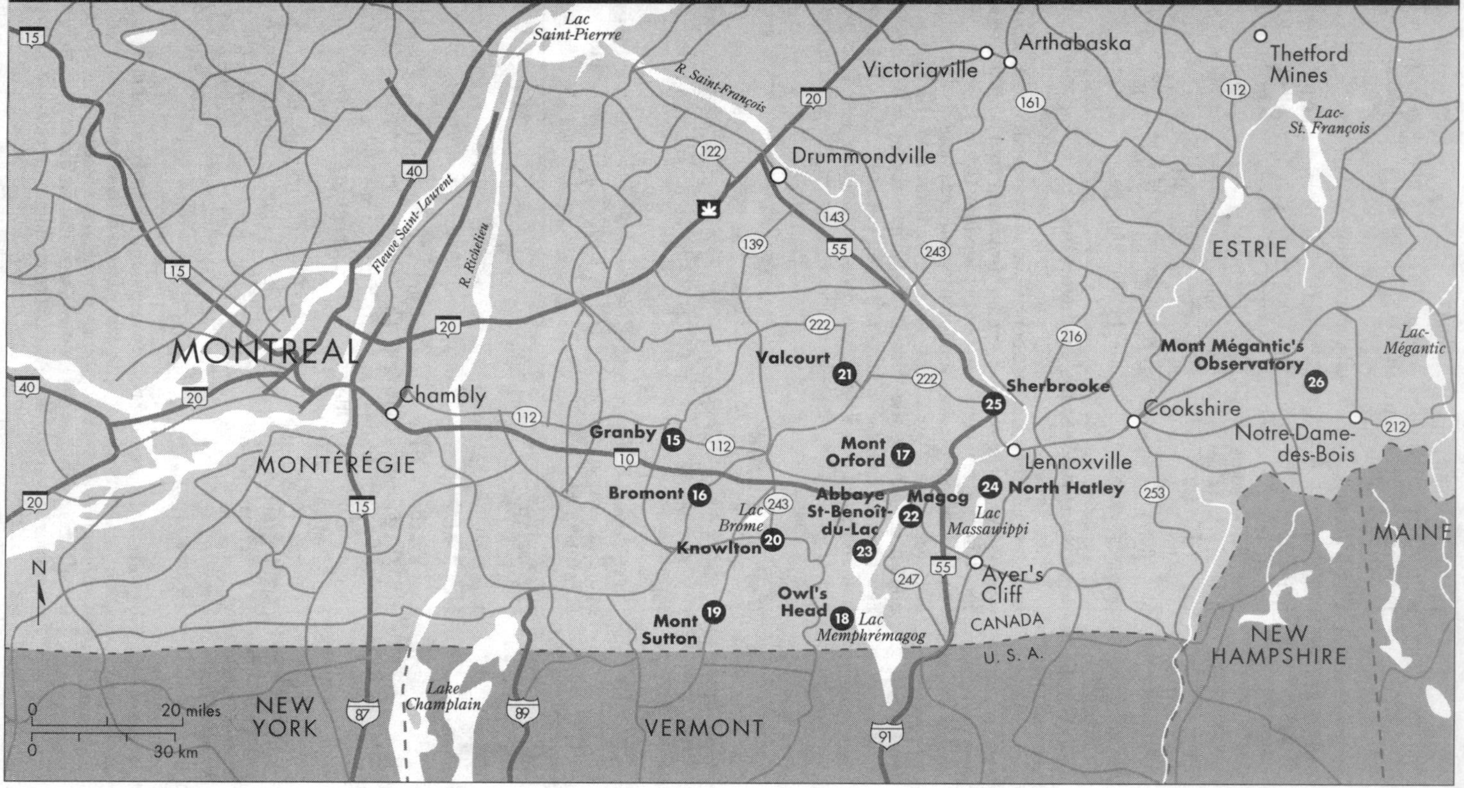

The **Yamaska** recreation center on the outskirts of town features sailboarding, swimming, and picnicking all summer, and cross-country skiing and snowshoeing in winter.

In the past two decades, l'Estrie has developed into a scenic and increasingly popular ski center. Although it is still less crowded and commercialized than the Laurentians, it boasts ski hills on four mountains that dwarf anything the Laurentians have to offer, with the exception of lofty Mont Tremblant. And, compared with those in Vermont, ski-pass rates are still a bargain.

16 **Bromont**, closest to Montréal, is as lively at night as during the day.
It offers the only night skiing in l'Estrie and a slope-side disco, **Le**
17 **Débarque,** where the action continues into the night après-ski. **Mont**
Orford, located at the center of a provincial park, offers plenty of
challenges for alpine and cross-country skiers, from novices to vet-
18 erans. **Owl's Head** has become a mecca for skiers looking for fewer
crowds on the hills. It also boasts a 4-kilometer (2.4-mile) intermediate run, the longest in l'Estrie. Aside from superb skiing, Owl's
Head offers tremendous scenery. From the trails you can see nearby
Vermont and Lac Memphrémagog. (You might even see the lake's
legendary sea dragon, said to have been sighted around 90 times
19 since 1816.) As it has for decades, **Mont Sutton** attracts the same die-
hard crowd of mostly Anglophone skiers from Québec. It's also one
of the area's largest resorts, with trails that plunge and wander
through pine, maple, and birch trees slope-side. **Sutton** itself is a
well-established community with crafts shops, cozy eateries, and
bars (La Paimpolaise is a favorite among skiers).

Bromont and Orford are *stations touristiques* (tourist centers), meaning that they offer a wide range of activities in all seasons—boating, camping, golf, horseback riding, swimming, tennis, water parks, trail biking, canoeing, fishing, hiking, cross-country and downhill skiing, and snowshoeing. A water-slide park (tel. 514/534–2200)—take exit 78 off Autoroute 10—and a large flea market (weekends from May to mid-November) offer pleasant additions to horseback riding. The same exit will bring you to Bromont's factory outlet shopping malls (50 rue Gaspé). There are about 30 shops that carry Canadian, American, and European designer goods at discount prices.

20 Along the shore of Lac Brome is the village of **Knowlton,** a pleasant
place to shop for antiques and gifts. In summer check to see what's
playing at Knowlton's popular **Théâtre Lac Brome** (*see* The Arts, *below*). In winter many Montréalers come here to ski at **Glen Mountain**
(off Route 243, tel. 514/243–6142).

21 **Valcourt** is the birthplace of the inventor of the snowmobile, so it follows that this is a world center for the sport, with more than 1,500
kilometers (1,000-plus miles) of paths cutting through the woods and
meadows. The **Musée Joseph-Armand Bombardier** displays this inno-
vator's many inventions year-round. *1001 av. Joseph-Armand Bombardier, tel. 514/532– 5300. Admission: $5 adults, $3 students and
senior citizens, children under 5 free, $13 families. Open late June–
Aug., daily 10–5:30; Sept.–late June, Tues.–Sun. 10–5.*

South of Mont Orford at the northern tip of Lac Memphrémagog, a
large body of water reaching into northern Vermont, lies the bus-
22 tling resort town of **Magog,** which celebrated its centenary in 1988.
A once sleepy village, the town has grown into a four-season resort
destination. Two sandy beaches, great bed-and-breakfasts, hotels
and restaurants, boating, ferry rides, bird-watching, sailboarding,

aerobics, horseback riding, and snowmobiling are just some of the activities offered.

Stroll along Magog's **rue Principale** for a look at boutiques, art galleries, and crafts shops with local artisans' work. Other shops are spread throughout downtown, where the streets are lined with century-old homes and churches, some of which have been converted into storefronts, galleries, and theaters.

Magog is lively after dark, with a variety of bars, cafés, bistros, and great restaurants to suit every taste and pocketbook. **La Lanterne** (tel. 819/843–7205) is a popular hangout. The more sedentary may find **La Source's** (tel. 819/843–0319) array of cheeses, pâtés, and Swiss chocolates irresistible.

23 Near Magog is the **Abbaye St-Benoît-du-Lac.** To reach St-Benoît from Magog, take the road to Austin and then follow the signs for the side road to the abbey. This abbey's slender bell tower juts up above the trees like a fairy-tale castle. Built on a wooded peninsula in 1912 by the Benedictines, the abbey is home to some 60 monks, who sell apples and apple cider from their orchards as well as distinctive cheeses: Ermite, St-Benoît, and ricotta. Gregorian masses are held daily. Check for those open to the public (tel. 819/843–4080). The abbey was once known as a favorite retreat for some of Québec's best-known politicians; they abandoned the thrust-and-cut of their secular concerns for spiritual rejuvenation.

24 **North Hatley**,the town on the tip of Lac Massawippi, is home to **The Pilsen,** Québec's earliest microbrewery. Although the beer is no longer brewed on-site, the Pilsen (tel. 819/842–2971) still serves Massawippi pale ale on tap. For those who ask, proprietor Gilles Peloquin will arrange a visit to the famous brewery, now located in nearby Lennoxville. The pub also has great food, loads of atmosphere, and a convivial crowd year-round. The avant-garde **Piggery** theater is based in North Hatley (*see* the Arts, *below*).

25 The region's unofficial capital and largest city is **Sherbrooke,** named in 1818 for Canadian Governor General Sir John Coape Sherbrooke. Founded by Loyalists in the 1790s, and located along the St-François River, it boasts a number of art galleries, including the **Musée des Beaux-Arts de Sherbrooke** (174 rue du Palais, tel. 819/821–2115; admission: $2 adults, $1 students and senior citizens, Wed. evenings free; open Tues., Thurs–Sun. 1–5, Wed. 1–9). The Sherbrooke Tourist Information Center conducts city tours from late June through August. Call for reservations. (48 rue Dépôt, tel. 819/564–8331).

For a more cosmic experience, continue from Sherbrooke along
26 Route 212 to **Mont Mégantic's Observatory.** Both amateur stargazers and serious astronomers are drawn to this site, located in a beautifully wild and mountainous part of l'Estrie. The observatory is at the summit of l'Estrie's second-highest mountain (3,601 feet), whose northern face records annual snowfalls rivaling any in North America. The observatory is a joint venture by l'Université de Montréal and l'Université Laval. Its powerful telescope allows resident scientists to observe celestial bodies 10 million times smaller than the human eye can detect. There's a welcome center on the mountain's base, where amateur stargazers can get information about the evening celestial sweep sessions, Thursday through Saturday. *Notre-Dame-des-Bois, tel. 819/888–2822. Open late June–Labor Day, daily 10–5.*

What to See and Do with Children

Jardin Zoologique de Granby,

Shopping

When in the Laurentians, consider strolling along Saint-Sauveur-des-Monts' rue Principale with its shops, fashion boutiques, and outdoor café terraces decorated with bright awnings and flowers. Housed in a former bank, **La Voute Boutique** (239B rue Principale, tel. 514/227–1234) carries such international labels as Byblos and an up-to-the-minute all-season selection of coordinates in cotton, knits, suede, and leather, plus sequined dresses, sweaters, pants, jackets, and suits from France, Italy, and Spain. If you feel like shopping for your stomach, have a bite at **Jardin des Oliviers** (239 rue Principale, tel. 514/227–2110), a popular, moderately priced French restaurant in the middle of town.

Saint-Sauveur-des-Monts is also home to **Les Factoreries Saint-Sauveur** (100 rue Guindon, Exit 60 from Hwy. 15, tel. 514/227–1074), a factory outlet mall with 12 boutiques. Canadian, American, and European manufacturers sell a variety of goods at reduced prices, from designer clothing to exclusive household items.

Magog's rue Principale, in l'Estrie, is another interesting place to browse. The street is dotted with boutiques, art galleries, and crafts shops with local artisan's work. **Amandine** (499 rue Principale O, tel. 819/847–1346) is a lovely gift shop with unusual dishes, stemware, luxury bath items, and Belgian chocolates. When you want a rest, drop by **La Source** (420 rue Principale O, tel. 819/843–0319), a small tea room with an array of cheeses, pâtés, and Swiss chocolates. Other shops are spread throughout the town's downtown, where the streets are lined with century-old homes and churches, some of which have been converted into storefronts, galleries, and theaters.

Factory outlet shopping is gaining popularity in l'Estrie also—especially in Bromont, where **Les Versants de Bromont** (120 boul. Bromont, Exit 78 from Hwy. 10, tel. 819/843–8300) houses 27 boutiques. Shoppers can save between 30% and 70% on items carrying such national and international labels as Liz Claiborne, Vuarnet, and Oneida.

Sports and Fitness

Bicycling **Base de Plein Air Davignon** (319 chemin Gale, Bromont, tel. 514/534–2277 or 800/363–8952) rents bicycles, as does **Vélo Sutton** (33 rue Principale N, Sutton, tel. 819/538–2561).

Deltaplaning If white-water rafting isn't adventure enough, there is always deltaplaning, in which human and machine become one. The **Vélidelta Free-Flying School** (C.P. 631, Mont Rolland J0R 1G0, tel. 514/229–6887) offers lessons on free-flying, flight simulation, and the more advanced tricks of the trade you'll need to earn the required deltaplane pilot's license, including flight maneuvers, speed, and turns. Equipment is provided. You can choose a one-day initiation flying lesson, or four-day course.

Fishing There are more than 60 outfitters (a.k.a. innkeepers) in the northern Laurentians area, where provincial parks and game sanctuaries abound. Pike, walleye, and lake and speckled trout are plentiful just a three-hour drive north of Montréal. Outfitters provide the dedicated angler with accommodations and every service wildlife and wilderness enthusiasts could possibly require. Open year-round in most cases, their lodging facilities range from the most luxurious first-class resort to the log-camp type "back of beyond." As well as supplying trained guides, all offer services and equipment to allow neophytes or experts the best possible fishing in addition to boating, swimming, river rafting, windsurfing, ice fishing, cross-country skiing, hiking, or just relaxing amid the splendor of this still spectacularly unspoiled region.

Outfitters recommended by the Laurentian tourist association include **Pourvoirie des 100 Lacs Nords** (tel. 514/444–4441), run by Claude Lavigne; **Club de Chasse et Pêche du Lac Beauregard** (tel. 819/425–7722) in Saint-Jovite; and **Pourvoirie Boismenu** (tel. 819/597–2619) at Lac-du-Cerf, run by Adrien Boismenu. Before setting off into the wilds, consult the Fédération des Pourvoyeurs du Québec (Québec Outfitters Federation, 2485 boul. Hamel, Québec G1P 2H9, tel. 418/527–5191) or ask for its list of outfitters available through tourist offices.

Don't forget: Fishing requires a permit, available from the regional offices of the Ministère du Loisir, de la Chasse et de la Pêche (6255 13ième av., Montréal H1X 3E6, tel. 514/374–2417), or inquire at any Laurentians sporting-goods store displaying an "authorized agent" sticker.

Golf Club de Golf Chantecler Sainte-Adèle is an 18-hole golf course in the Laurentians. *Exit 67, 2520 chemin du Golf, Ste-Adèle, tel. 514/229–3742.*

Les Rochers Bleus is an 18-hole golf course in Sutton, located in Estrie. Reservations must be made in advance. *550 Rte. 139, Sutton, tel. 514/538–2324.*

When in the Charlevoix region, you may want to try the 18-hole course in Pointe-au-Pic, **Club de Golf de Manoir Richelieu.** *181 av. Richelieu, Pointe-au-Pic, tel. 418/665–3703 or 800/463–2613.*

Horseback Riding As the former Olympic equestrian site, **Bromont** is horse country, and every year in late June and early July it holds a riding festival (tel. 514/534–3255).

Mountain Climbing Mountain climbing is one of the best ways to view the scenery of the Upper Laurentians. For information, contact the **Fédération Québecoise de la Montagne.** *4545 rue Pierre-de-Coubertin, C.P. 1000, Succ. M, Montréal H1V 3R2, tel. 514/252–3004.*

River Rafting According to expert river rafters, the Rivière Rouge in the Laurentians rates among the best in North America, so it's not surprising that this river has spawned a miniboom in the sport. Just an hour's drive north of Montréal, the Rouge cuts across the rugged Laurentians through rapids, canyons, and alongside beaches. From April through October, the adventurous can experience what traversing the region must have meant in the days of the voyageurs and *coureurs du bois*, though today's trip, by comparison, is much safer and more comfortable.

Four companies specializing in white-water rafting are on-site at the trip's departure point near Calumet. (Take Rte. 148 past Calumet; turn onto chemin de la Rivière Rouge until you see the signs for the access road to each rafter's headquarters.) **Aventures en Eau Vive** (tel. 819/242–6084), **Nouveau Monde** (tel. 819/242–7238), **Propulsion** (tel. 514/953–3300), and **W-3 Rafting** (tel. 514/334–0889) all offer four- to five-hour rafting trips. All provide transportation to and from the river site, as well as guides, helmets, life jackets, and, at the end of the trip, a much-anticipated meal. Most have facilities on-site or nearby for dining, drinking, camping, bathing, swimming, hiking, and horseback riding.

Skiing *Les Laurentides* With the longest vertical drop (2,131 feet) in eastern Canada, **Mont Tremblant** (tel. 819/425–8711) offers a wide range of ski trails. Beginners favor the 5-kilometer (3-mile) Nansen trail; intermediate skiers head for the steeply sloped Flying Mile and Beauchemin runs. Experts choose the challenging Duncan and Expo runs on the mountain's north side. The Vancouver-based developers who bought the resort in 1991 promised to invest $47 million over five years in order to turn Mont Tremblant into a world-class ski and four-season resort. The speedy Duncan Express, a quadruple chair lift, is only a beginning.

Ski Mont Gabriel (tel. 514/229–3547) in Mont Rolland has 16 downhill trails primarily for intermediate and advanced skiers. The most popular runs are the Tamarack and the O'Connell trails for advanced skiers and Obergurgl for intermediates.

For something different, try **Ski Morin Heights** (*see* Les Laurentides, *above*), where snowboarding is the latest craze.

L'Estrie In l'Estrie the larger downhill slopes include **Mont Bromé** (tel. 514/534–2200) in Bromont (site of the 1986 World Cup) with 22 trails, **Mont Orford** (tel. 819/843–6548) with 39, **Owl's Head** (tel. 514/292–3342) with 27, and **Mont Sutton** (tel. 514/538–2339), where you pay to ski by the hour, with 53. The steepest drop, one of 853 meters (2,800 feet), is at Orford. All four resorts feature interchangeable lift tickets so skiers can test out all the major runs in the area. Call Ski East, tel. 819/820–2020.

With more than 20 cross-country sites, l'Estrie is a peaceful getaway. Trails at Bromont crisscross the site of the 1976 Olympic equestrian center. Three inns—Le Manoir Hovey, Auberge Hatley, and the Ripplecove Inn (*see* Dining *and* Lodging, *below*)—offer the **Skiwippi**, a week-long package of cross-country treks from one inn to another. The network covers some 32 kilometers (20 miles) of l'Estrie.

Snowmobiling **Point de Vue Canada** offers snowmobilers tours in the Laurentians, in Charlevoix, and as far north as the James Bay region. The group also has such adventure packages as "The Magic of the Nunavik Arctic," a week-long adventure in Québec's Grand Nord, where participants spend one night in an igloo, travel on dogsleds, and ice fish. *1227 av. St-Hubert, Suite 200, Montréal H2L 3Y8, tel. 514/843–8161.*

Dining

Whether you enjoy a croissant and espresso at a sidewalk café or order *poutine* (a streetwise mix of homemade french fries—*frites*—and curd cheese and gravy) from a fast-food emporium, you won't soon forget your meals in Québec. There is no such thing as simply "eating out" in the province; restaurants are an integral slice of Québec life.

Outside Montréal and Québec City, you can find both good value and classic cuisine. Cooking in the province tends to be hearty, with such fare as cassoulet, *tourtières* (meat pies), onion soup, and apple pie heading up menus. In the Laurentians, chefs at some of the finer inns have attracted international followings. Local blueberries and maple syrup find their way into a surprising number of dishes.

Early reservations are essential. Monday or Tuesday is not too soon to book weekend tables at the best provincial restaurants. If you have any doubt about acceptable dress at a restaurant, call ahead. Jacket and tie are still the rule at many first-rate restaurants, even in summer.

Granby and its environs is one of Québec's foremost regions for traditional Québecois cuisine, here called *la fine cuisine estrienne*. Specialties include such mixed-game meat pies as *cipaille* and sweet, salty dishes like ham and maple syrup. Actually, maple syrup—on everything and in all its forms—is a mainstay of Québecois dishes. L'Estrie is one of Québec's main maple-sugaring regions.

In addition to maple sugar, the flavorings cloves, nutmeg, cinnamon, and pepper—spices used by the first settlers—have never gone out of style here, and local restaurants make good use of them in their distinctive dishes. The full country experience of l'Estrie includes warm hospitality at area lodges and inns.

Highly recommended restaurants in each price category are indicated by a star ★.

Category	Cost*
$$$$	over $35
$$$	$25–$35
$$	$15–$25
$	under $15

**per person, excluding drinks, service, 7% federal tax, and 4% provincial tax*

Les Laurentides

Ste-Adèle **La Clef des Champs.** This family-owned hillside restaurant, well known for its gourmet French cuisine, is a charming alternative to even the most superbly prepared hotel fare. It is tucked away among trees and faces a mountain, and it serves elegant dishes in a cozy, romantic atmosphere. Try the *noisette d'agneau en feuilleté* (lamb in pastry) or fresh poached salmon in red wine sauce. Top off your meal with the *gâteau aux deux chocolats* (two-chocolate cake). *875 chemin Ste-Marguerite, tel. 514/229–2857. Reservations advised. Dress: casual. AE, DC, MC, V. Closed Mon. Oct.–May, except on holidays. $$$$*

★ **L'Eau à la Bouche.** A consistent award winner in gastronomic circles, the restaurant has received top laurels among the Laurentians region's auberge–restaurants for its superb marriage of nouvelle cuisine and traditional Québec dishes. The care and inventiveness of chef-proprietor Anne Desjardins, who opened the Bavarian-style property a decade ago with her husband, Pierre Audette, is extraordinary. Such dishes as goat cheese tart, saddle of rabbit with onions, *baluchon* of lobster and scallops, roast partridge stuffed with oyster mushrooms and cream sauce and *pavé* of dark chocolate with English cream leave dinner guests clamoring for more. *3041 boul. Ste-Adèle, Rte. 117, tel. 514/229–2991. Reservations required. Dress: casual but neat. AE, DC, MC, V. $$$$*

Ste-Agathe ★ **Chatel Vienna.** Run by Eberhards Rado and his wife, who is also the chef, this Austrian restaurant presents Viennese and other Continental dishes and serves them up in a lakeside setting. You may want to try the prize-winning home-smoked trout, served with an herb and spice butter, and garden fresh vegetables. Opt for a variety of schnitzels (veal dishes), a sauerkraut plate, or venison. Meals are accompanied by hot spiced wine, Czech pilsner beer, or dry Austrian and other international white wines. A Sunday buffet brunch tempts the palate with approximately 30 dishes, and is served from 11:30 until 2 for under $20. *6 rue Ste-Lucie, tel. 819/326–1485. Reservations advised. Dress: casual. MC, V. $$–$$$*

Chez Girard. Excellent French cuisine is the hallmark of this restaurant–auberge on the shores of Lac des Sables. The airy dining room has windows facing the lake and pastel colors that create a soft, romantic atmosphere. Some of the house specialties include *saumon au champagne* (salmon with champagne), lamb with cream of garlic sauce, caribou, and *feuilleté d'escargots et de pleurotes* (escargots and mushroom pastry). A Sunday brunch is offered for $16.95. *18 rue Principale O, tel. 819/326–0922. Reservations advised. Dress: casual. AE, DC, MC, V. $$–$$$*

St-Sauveur-des-Monts **Auberge Saint-Denis.** The distinction "Relais Gourmand" was earned by this classic Québec inn for its fine French cuisine. Specializing in game, the artfully presented dishes are served in one of three dining rooms with a huge stone fireplace. Try the *arrivage de gibier*, an assortment of wild game with an exotic fruit sauce. *61 St-Denis, tel. 514/227–4602. Reservations advised for dinner. Dress: casual but neat. AE, DC, MC, V. $$$*

l'Estrie

Ayer's Cliff **The Ripplecove Inn.** The Ripplecove vies with the Hatley and Hovey inns (*see* Lodging, *below*) for best in the region. Its accommodations and service are consistently excellent, and the dining room is an award winner. The English-pub style dining combines classical and French cuisine in such dishes as *mousseline de rouget et truite* (mullet and trout mousse served with lobster and dill sauce), followed by *rable de lapereau* (stuffed rabbit with paprika sauce), topped off with a sublime dessert, such as *nougat glacé au coulis framboise* (nougat with raspberry sauce). The menu changes seasonally. *700 chemin Ripplecove, C.P. 246, tel. 819/838–4296. Reservations advised on weekends. Dress: casual. AE, MC, V. $$$*

Magog **Auberge de l'Étoile.** This popular restaurant serves three meals a day in casual surroundings. Its somber interior, decorated in dark colors, is brightened by the windows facing Lac Memphé-Magog. House specialties include wild game and Swiss fondue. *1150 rue Principale O, tel. 819/843–6521. Reservations advised. Dress: casual. AE, DC, MC, V. $$*

Notre-Dame-des-Bois **Aux Berges de l'Aurore.** Although this tiny bed-and-breakfast has spectacular views, situated as it is at the foot of Mont Mégantic, the draw here is the inn's cuisine. The award-winning restaurant features a five-course meal with ingredients supplied from the inn's huge fruit, vegetable, and herb garden, as well as wild game from the surrounding area: boar, fish, hare, and quail. It has been attractively furnished by its owners, Michel Martin and Daniel Pepin, and is closed from January until May. *51 chemin de l'Observatoire, tel. 819/888–2715. Reservations advised. Dress: casual. MC, V. $$$*

Sherbrooke Restaurant au P'tit Sabot. On Sherbrooke's main drag, this restaurant offers a pleasant refuge from the hustle and bustle. With room for only 35 patrons, a piano in the corner, and pink decor, a romantic atmosphere prevails. This restaurant recently won an award for the best local-style eatery in the region. Among the many provincial dishes are wild boar, quail, and bison. *1410 rue King O, tel. 819/563–0262. Reservations accepted. Dress: casual. AE, DC, MC, V. $$*

Pointe-au-Pic **Auberge des 3 Canards.** This inn has made a name for itself in the region, not only for its accommodations but also for its award-winning restaurant. The menu, which changes with the seasons, may include *gratin d'escargots aux bluets* (snails with a blueberry and grapefruit sauce baked au gratin) as an appetizer, and stuffed pheasant—the breasts smothered in mustard sauce and the legs seasoned with spicy maple sauce—as a main course. Desserts are all homemade, including Pomme de l'Ile aux Coudres—cheese topped apples with a touch of honey. Meals are elegantly presented in a rustic setting. The warmth of the natural wood contrasts with the pale and deep blue touches throughout. *49 côte Bellevue, tel. 418/665–3761. Reservations advised. Dress: casual. AE, MC, V. $$$$*

Sugar Huts

Every March the combination of sunny days and cold nights causes the sap to run in the maple trees. Sugar huts (*cabanes à sucre*) go into operation boiling the sap collected from the trees in buckets (now, at some places, complicated tubing and vats do the job). The many commercial shacks scattered over the area host "sugaring offs" and tours of the operation, including the tapping of maple trees, the boiling vats, and *tire sur la neige*, when hot syrup is poured over cold snow to give it a taffy consistency just right for "pulling" and eating. A number of cabanes offer hearty meals of ham, baked beans, and pancakes, all drowned in maple syrup. It's best to call before visiting these cabanes: **Erablière Patoine** (1105 chemin Beauvoir, tel. 819/563–7455) in Fleurimont, near Sherbrooke, and **Bolduc** (525 chemin Lower, tel. 819/875–3022) in Cookshire.

Lodging

Weary travelers have a full spectrum of accommodation options in Québec: from large resort hotels in the Laurentians and Relais et Châteaux properties in l'Estrie to shared dormitory space in rustic youth hostels near the heart of Gaspé. For information on camping in the province's private trailer parks and campgrounds, write for the free publication "Québec Camping," available from **Tourisme Québec** (12 rue Ste Anne, Québec G1X 3X2, tel. 418/643–2280). Inquiries about camping in Québec's three national parks should be directed to **Parks Canada Information Services** (3 Buade St., Box 6060, Haute Ville, Québec City G1R 4V7, tel. 418/648–4177). **Agricotours** (4545 av. Pierre de Couberten, C.P. 1000, Succursale M, Montréal H1V 3R2, tel. 514/252–3138), the Québec farm-vacation association, can provide lists of guest farms in the province.

Highly recommended lodgings in each price category are indicated by a star ★.

Category	Cost*
$$$$	over $125
$$$	$90–$125

$$	$50–$90
$	under $50

**Prices are for a standard double room, excluding 10% service charge, 7% federal tax, and 4% provincial tax, unless Modified American Plan (MAP) is indicated. MAP charges apply to each guest and include all meals, service charges, and taxes.*

Les Laurentides

Estérel

Hôtel d'Estérel. If this all-inclusive resort were in the Caribbean, it would probably be run by Club Med, given the nonstop activities. The property includes a private 18-hole golf course, beach, marina, downhill-skiing facilities, 87 kilometers of cross-country ski trails, outdoor skating rink, and sports complex. Comfortable rooms offer a view of either the lake or the beautiful flower gardens. *39 boul. Fridolin Simard, J0T 1E0, tel. 514/228–2571 or 800/363–3623, fax 514/228–4977. 135 rooms. Facilities: restaurant, disco, indoor pool, tennis courts, and gym. MAP optional. AE, DC, MC, V. $$$$*

Mont Rolland

Auberge Mont Gabriel. At this deluxe resort located on a 1,200-acre estate, choose to relax in one of the spacious, modern rooms with a view of the valley, or be close to nature in one of the cozy log cabins with fireplaces to keep you warm. The dining is superb here. Tennis, golf, and ski-week and -weekend packages are available. *Autoroute 15, Exit 64, J0R 1G0, tel. 514/229–3547, fax 514/229–7034. 120 rooms, 10 suites. Facilities: restaurant, 18-hole golf course, indoor and outdoor pools, 6 tennis courts. MAP optional. AE, DC, MC, V. $$$*

Mont Tremblant
★

Station Mont Tremblant Lodge. Only 90 minutes from Montréal, on 14-kilometer-long (9-mile-long) Lac Tremblant, this is the northernmost resort that is easily accessible in the Upper Laurentians. Accommodations include modern condo units with kitchenettes, a rustic lodge, and individual cabins. The partying is lively in winter, with lots of après-ski bars in the hotel and the immediate area. In summer, guests swim, windsurf, and sail. *3005 chemin Principale, J0T 1Z0, tel. 819/425–8711 or 800/461–8711, fax 819/681–5590. Facilities: restaurant, bar, disco, golf course, tennis courts, horseback riding, private beach. MAP optional. AE, MC, V. $$$–$$$$*

Club Tremblant. Across the lake from Mont Tremblant Lodge, this hotel was built as a private retreat in the 1930s by a wealthy American. The original large, log-cabin lodge is furnished in colonial style, with wooden staircases and huge stone fireplaces. The rustic but comfortable main lodge has excellent facilities and a dining room serving four-star gourmet cuisine. Both the main lodge and the deluxe condominium complex—fireplaces, private balconies, kitchenettes, and split-level design de rigueur—built just up the hill from the lodge, offer magnificent views of Mont Tremblant and its ski hills. Warm-weather activities include swimming, fishing, boating, and tennis. There is a golf course nearby. *av. Cuttle, J0T 1Z0, tel. 819/425–2731, fax 819/425–9903. 150 rooms. Facilities: restaurant, indoor pool, exercise room. MAP optional. AE, DC, MC, V. $$$–$$$$*

Auberge Villa Bellevue. This equally venerable and less expensive alternative to Gray Rocks (*see below*) is on Lac Ouimet, and has been run by the Dubois family for more than three generations. Supporting its reputation as a family resort, the inn invites children under 18 who share a room with their parents to stay free and pay for meals only during the summer. In winter, weekend packages include transportation to nearby Mont Tremblant. The hotel has a list of local baby-sitters, and offers a full summer program of children's activities. Accommodations range from hotel rooms to chalets and condominiums. In summer, tennis lessons for adults and children are available. Sailing, windsurfing, waterskiing, and lounging about on the outdoor lakeside terrace are other possible pastimes at Villa Bellevue. The indoor swimming pool and fitness center offer nonskiers plenty of physical activity during the winter without having to step outdoors. *845 rue Principale, J0T 1Z0, tel. 819/425–2734 or 800/567–6763, fax 819/425–9360. 86 rooms, 14 suites. Facilities: restaurant, indoor pool, gym, tennis courts, private beach, marina. MAP optional. AE, DC, MC, V. $$$*

Auberge du Cog de Montagne. Owners Nino and Kay Faragalli have earned a favorable reputation for their auberge, situated on Lac Moore. The cozy, family-run inn, is touted for its friendly service, great hospitality, and modern accommodations. Kudos have also been garnered for the great Italian cuisine served up nightly, which also draws a local crowd: Reservations are a must. Year-round facilities and activities, on-site or nearby, include canoeing, kayaking, sailboarding, fishing, badminton, tennis, horseback riding, skating, and skiing. *2151 chemin Principale, C.P. 208, Lac Moore, J0T 1Z0, tel. 819/425–3380, fax 819/425–7846. 16 rooms. Facilities: restaurant, exercise room, sauna, private beach. MAP in winter, optional in summer. AE, MC, V. $$–$$$$*

Morin Heights

The Auberge Swiss Inn. Located within 4 kilometers (3 miles) of Ski Morin Heights, this moderately priced inn is a well-situated bargain. The authentic Swiss-style chalet exudes coziness, from the wood paneling and fireplace lounge to the individually decorated rooms. *796 Rte. St-Adolphe, J0R 1H0, tel. 514/226–2009, fax 514/226–5709. 10 rooms. Facilities: restaurant, canoeing, cross-country skiing, lounge. MC, V. $$*

Pointe-du-Lac

★ **L'Auberge du Lac Saint-Pierre.** Set on the lake near Trois Rivières, halfway between Montréal and Québec City, this modern small hotel was built in 1988 and has quickly gained the highest ratings for cuisine and accommodations. The luxurious rooms are done in soothing pastels, with television, telephones, and many whirlpool baths. Lake views from the dining room, the conservatory, and many of the guest rooms add to the tranquillity. It's an ideal stop on a tour of southern Québec. *1911 Notre-Dame (Rte. 138), Box 10, G0X 1Z0, tel. 819/377–5971, fax 819/377–5579. 30 rooms. Facilities: restaurant, heated outdoor pool, tennis court, meeting rooms for 40 and 15, business equipment rentals. MAP optional. AE, MC, V. $$$*

Ste-Adèle

Le Chantecler. This Montréaler favorite on Lac Rond is nestled at the base of a mountain with 22 downhill ski runs. Skiing is the obvious draw—trails begin almost at the hotel entrance. (It's been the official training site of the National Alpine Ski Teams.) The condominium units, hotel rooms, and chalets all have a rustic appeal, furnished with Canadian pine. Summer activities include tennis, golf, and boating. An indoor pool and spa, as well as a beach, make swimming a year-round possibility. *1474 chemin Chantecler, C.P. 1048, J0R 1L0, tel. 514/229–3555; elsewhere in Québec, 800/363–2420; fax 514/229–5593. 300 rooms, 20 suites. Facilities: restaurant, indoor pool, spa, private beach, golf course. MAP optional. AE, DC, MC, V. $$$$*

L'Eau à la Bouche. This 25-room auberge has received commendations for superb service and luxurious appointments, and is perfect for weekend getaways or business retreats. Its restaurant is a draw in itself (*see* Dining, *above*). The auberge faces Le Chantecler's ski slopes, so skiing is literally at the door. Tennis, sailing, horseback riding, and a golf course are nearby. Package rates are available. *3003 boul. Ste-Adèle, J0R 1L0, tel. 514/229–2991, fax 514/229–7573. 25 rooms. Facilities: restaurant, pool, flower garden terrace, wine cellar, facilities for people with disabilities. MAP optional. AE, MC, V. $$$–$$$$*

Auberge aux Croissants. Situated at the foot of the Laurentian Mountains, this inn is only a five-minute drive from Mont-Saint-Sauveur. Although most rooms have no TV or telephone, such conveniences are found in one of the two cozy lounges, and an impressive buffet-breakfast is included with the price of the room. *750 chemin Ste-Marguerite, J0R 1L0, tel. 514/229–3838. 12 rooms with private bath, 1 with whirlpool bath, 1 suite. MC, V. $$*

Ste-Agathe **Auberge du Lac des Sables.** A favorite with couples, this inn offers a quiet, relaxed atmosphere in a country setting with a magnificent view of Lac des Sables. Enjoy the view from your balcony or from the dining room. All rooms have contemporary decor, with queen-size beds and color TVs. A complimentary breakfast is served. *230 St-Venant, J8C 3Z7, tel. 819/ 326–3994, fax 819/326–7556. 19 rooms. Facilities: whirlpool. MC, V. $$$*

Ste-Jovite **Gray Rocks.** This oldest ski resort in the Laurentians has its own private mountain ribboned by 20 ski runs; a sprawling wood hotel with modern chalets and condominium units overlooks Lac Ouimet. Winter ski packages, including cross-country, are good value for the money, as are the summer tennis packages. Gray Rocks also runs the more intimate Auberge le Château with 24 rooms farther along Route 327 North. *Rte. 327 N, J0T 2H0, tel. 819/425–2771 or 800/ 567–6767, fax 819/425–3474. 306 rooms, 13 with shared bath. Facilities: restaurant, 22 clay tennis courts, tennis school, riding stables, marina, La Spa fitness center with hot tubs, indoor swimming pool, children's activity programs, private airstrip and seaplane anchorage. MAP optional. Ski packages available. AE, MC, V. $$–$$$$*

Val David **Hôtel La Sapinière.** Comfortable accommodations are offered in this homey, dark-brown frame hotel with its bright country flowers. Each room—with country-style furnishings and pastel floral accents—has its own personality, yet all rooms come with such luxurious little extras as thick terry-cloth bathrobes and hair dryers. Relax in one of several cozy lounges scattered throughout the hotel, in front of a blazing fire. The property is best known for its fine dining room and wine cellar. *1244 chemin de la Sapinière, J0T 2N0, tel. 819/322–2020 or 800/567–6635, fax 819/322–6510. 70 rooms. MAP. AE, DC, MC, V. $$$$*

L'Estrie

Bromont **Le Château Bromont Resort Spa.** Massages, algotherapy, electropuncture, algae wraps, facials, and aroma therapy are just a few of the pampering services at this European-style resort spa. The Atrium houses an indoor pool, hot tubs, and a sauna, and there are also outdoor hot tubs, squash, racquetball, and badminton courts. Rooms are large and comfortable, with contemporary furniture, but those facing the Atrium are a little somber. Chef Daniel Guay creates "cuisine sauvage" at the château's dining room, Les Quatres Canards. (There is also a special spa menu offered.) L'Equestre Bar, named for Bromont's equestrian interests, has a cocktail hour and live entertainment. *90 rue Stanstead, J0E 1L0, tel. 514/534–3433, fax 514/534–0514. 147 rooms. Facilities: restaurant, bar, spa, indoor pool, sauna. MAP optional. AE, DC, MC, V. $$$–$$$$*

Eastman **Centre de Santé Eastman.** This four-season resort offers respite to the bone-weary and bruised skier. The 20 country-style rooms are located in three separate houses: the rustic Maison Canadienne, the country-style Volet Bleu, and the modern Pavillon Kaufman. Holistic spa treatments include massage (Swedish and shiatsu) and gentle body conditioning and stretch workouts. There's also horseback riding and cross-country skiing. Top off an already healthy day with fine vegetarian cuisine offered in the dining room. *895 chemin Diligence, J0E 1P0, tel. 514/297–3009, fax 514/297–3370. 20 rooms. Facilities: dining room. MAP. AE, MC, V. $$$–$$$$*

Lennoxville **Bishop's University.** If you are on a budget, this is a great place to stay. The prices can't be beat, and the location near Sherbrooke is good for touring. The university's grounds are lovely, with a river cutting through the campus and its golf course. Much of the architecture is reminiscent of stately New England campuses. Visit the university's 136-year-old chapel, and also look for the butternut tree, an endangered species in l'Estrie. Reservations for summer guests are accepted as early as September, so it's a good idea to book in advance. *Rue College, J1M 1Z7, tel. 819/822–9651, fax 819/822–9615. 559 beds. Facilities: sports complex with Olympic-size indoor pool, tennis courts. MC, V. Closed Sept.–early May. $*

Magog **O'Berge du Village.** Half of this condo complex is on a time-share basis and half is run like a hotel. Rustic Canadian pine furniture and fireplaces adorn the condos, which accommodate from two to eight people. All units have a balcony facing the lake and a fully equipped kitchenette. If you don't feel like cooking, you can try the bistro; for those with something more elaborate in mind, enjoy dinner in the formal dining room. *261 rue Merry S, J1X 3L2, tel. 819/843–6566 or 800/567–6089, fax 819/843–2924. 117 rooms. Facilities: restaurant, bistro, wine bar, indoor and outdoor pools, games room, marina, aquatic sports, day-care service, daily activities in the summer. AE, MC, V. $$$*

North Hatley **Auberge Hatley.** Gourmet cuisine is the main attraction at this country inn, whose dining room was once named the top restaurant in Québec in the annual Ordre du Mérite de la Restauration awards. After savoring chef Alain Labrie's fine cuisine, guests sleep it off in one of the 25 charmingly decorated rooms in this 1903 country manor, a member of Relais & Châteaux. *325 Virgin Rd., C.P. 330, J0B 2C0, tel. 819/842–2451, fax 819/842–2907. 25 rooms, some with Jacuzzi and fireplace. Facilities: restaurant. MAP. AE, MC, V. Closed last 2 wks in Nov. $$$$*

★ **Manoir Hovey.** Overlooking the perfectly pristine Lac Massawippi, this retreat has the ambience of a private estate, while offering the activities of a resort—boating, water skiing, mountain biking, cross-country skiing, tennis, and more. Built in 1900 as a summer home for Henry Atkinson, then owner of Georgia Power in Atlanta, Hovey Manor resembles George Washington's home at Mount Vernon, Virginia. Each wallpapered room has personality, with a mix of antiques and newer wood furniture, richly printed fabrics, and lace trimmings. Many rooms have working fireplaces and private balconies. The dining room serves exquisite Continental and French cuisine; the changing dinner menu might include warm roulades of Swiss chard with spring lamb, preserved apricots, and roasted hazelnuts; swordfish with a sabayon of leeks and pink peppercorns au gratin; or grilled tenderloin of beef marinated with juniper berries and a sauce of tarragon and horseradish. Dinner, breakfast, and most sports facilities are included in room rates. *C.P. 60, J0B 2C0, tel. 819/842–2421, fax 819/842–2248. 40 rooms and 4-bedroom cot-*

tage. Facilities: dining room, library, 2 bars, heated outdoor pool, tennis courts, 2 beaches, 2 conference rooms, water sports, mountain bikes, ice fishing, ski trails. MAP. AE, DC, MC, V. $$$$

Orford **Auberge Estrimont.** An exclusive complex in cedar combining hotel rooms, condos, and larger chalets, Auberge Estrimont is close to ski hills, riding stables, and golf courses. Every room, whether in the hotel or in an adjoining condo unit, has a fireplace and a private balcony. *44 av. de l'Auberge, C.P. 98, Orford-Magog, J1X 3W7, tel. 819/843–1616 or 800/567–7320, fax 819/843–4909. 76 rooms, 7 suites. Facilities: restaurant; bar; indoor and outdoor pools; tennis, squash, racquetball courts; exercise room; sauna; Jacuzzi; cross-country ski trails. AE, DC, MC, V. $$$*

Sutton **Auberge la Paimpolaise.** This auberge is located right on Mont Sutton, 50 feet from the ski trails. Nothing fancy is offered, but the location is hard to beat. Rooms are simple, comfortable, and clean, with a woodsy appeal. All-inclusive weekend ski packages are available. A complimentary breakfast is served. *615 rue Maple, J0E 2K0, tel. 514/538–3213, fax 514/538–3970. 29 rooms. MAP optional. AE, MC, V. $$–$$$*

Auberge Schweizer. No matter what the season, this lodge is the perfect place to relax. It has its own farm, and guests feast on home-cooked meals with vegetables straight from the garden. Nearby is a pond for swimming, as well as some hiking trails and ski trails. In addition to the standard accommodations, the auberge has a two-bedroom chalet, each bedroom with private bath and powder room; a three-bedroom chalet with one bath and a playroom; and another three-bedroom/three-bathroom chalet. All the chalets have kitchens, and two have washers and dryers. *357 chemin Schweizer, J0E 2K0, tel. 514/538–2129. 11 rooms, 3 chalets with fireplace. V. $–$$*

The Arts and Nightlife

The Arts

Lac Brome Théâtre Lac Brome (tel. 514/243–0361) is an English-language theater company that stages productions of classic Broadway and West End hits. The 175-seat, air-conditioned theater is located behind Knowlton's popular pub of the same name.

Lac Massawippi **L'Association du Festival du Lac Massawippi** presents an annual antiques and folk-arts show (tel. 819/563–4141) each July. The association also sponsors a series of classical music concerts performed at the L'Eglise Sainte Catherine in North Hatley, on Sundays starting in late April and continuing until the end of June.

Lennoxville Lennoxville's **Centennial Theatre** at Bishop's University (tel. 819/822–9692) presents a roster of international, Canadian, and Québecois jazz, classical, and rock concerts, as well as dance, mime, and children's theater. Jazz greats Gary Burton, Carla Bley, and Larry Coryell have appeared here, as have such classical artists as the Amsterdam Guitar Trio and the Allegri String Quartet.

Magog **Théâtre le Vieux Clocher** (64 rue Merry N, tel. 819/847–0470) presents pop and rock concerts, and occasionally French plays.

North Hatley **The Piggery,** housed in a former pig barn in North Hatley on the shores of Lac Massawippi, reigns supreme in l'Estrie cultural life. The venue is renowned for its risk taking, often presenting new plays by Canadian playwrights and even experimenting with bilingual productions. *Box 390, North Hatley J0B 2C0, tel. 819/842–2432 or 819/842–2431. Reservations required. Season runs June–Aug.*

Orford Orford's regional park is the site of an annual arts festival highlighting classical music, pops, and chamber orchestra concerts. Since 1951, thousands of students have come to the **Orford Arts Center** to study and perform classical music in the summer. Canada's internationally celebrated Orford String Quartet originated here. Festival Orford has recently expanded to include jazz and folk music. *Orford Arts Center, Box 280, Magog J1X 3W8, tel. 819/843–3981; in Canada from May to Aug., 800/567–6155.*

Sutton Sutton is also home to the visual and performing arts. **Arts Sutton** (7 rue Academy, tel. 514/538–2563) is a long-established mecca for the visual arts.

Nightlife

The Laurentians and l'Estrie are your best bets when looking for nightlife in Québec's outlying regions. Après-ski bars, bistros, and cafés are spread throughout the Laurentians. In Piedmont, **La Nuit Blanche** (762 rue Principale, tel. 514/227–5419) is a popular dancing spot. If live music is what you want, head to **Bourbon Street** (2045 Rte. 117, tel. 514/229–2905) in Mont Rolland. **Les Vieilles Portes** (185 rue Principale, tel. 514/227–2662) in Saint-Sauveur is a popular pub where you can relax, order your favorite beer, and have a bite to eat.

If you are looking for action in l'Estrie, visit Magog, a village that comes to life after dark. **La Lanterne** (70 rue du Lac, tel. 819/843–7205) is a popular restaurant-bar that often hosts theme nights. For information, tune in to the local radio station. **La Grosse Pomme** (270 rue Principale O, tel. 819/843–9365) is also a popular place. This multilevel complex considers itself a cinema-bar, with huge video screens, dance floors, and restaurant service. An outdoor summer terrace has live entertainment. **The Auberge Orford** (20 rue Merry S, tel. 819/843–9361) is another outdoor summer terrace that doesn't stop. Here you can enjoy live entertainment.

5 Québec City

By Alice H. Oshins

Updated by Dorothy Guinan

An excursion to French-speaking Canada is incomplete without a visit to Québec City, located in one of the most beautiful natural settings in North America. The Vieille Ville (Old City) measures 11 square kilometers (7 square miles) and is a lot of ground to cover. This well-preserved part of town is a small and dense place, steeped in four centuries of history and French tradition. Once you begin to explore firsthand the 17th- and 18th-century buildings, the ramparts that once protected the city, and the numerous parks and monuments, you will soon realize how much there is to see.

The oldest municipality in Québec province, Québec City was the first settlement of French explorers, fur trappers, and missionaries in the 17th century, who came here to establish the colony of New France. Today it still resembles a French provincial town in many ways, with its family-oriented residents with strong ties to their past. More than 95% of its metropolitan population of 650,000 are French-speaking. Québec City is also a fortified city, the only one in North America, an attribute that led UNESCO to declare it a World Heritage treasure.

Québec City is huddled on a cliff above the St. Lawrence River, at a point where the body of water narrows; this strategic location forged its historic destiny as a military stronghold. When Winston Churchill visited Québec City in the early 1940s, he named it "Gibraltar of North America" because of its position at the gateway to the continent. The city's military prominence paved the way for its leading political role, first as the French colony's administrative center and eventually as the capital of Québec province.

In 1535, French explorer Jacques Cartier first came upon what the Algonquin Indians called "Kebec," meaning "where the river narrows." New France, however, was not actually founded in the area of what is now Québec City until 1608, when another French explorer, Samuel de Champlain, recognized the military advantages of the location and set up a fort. Along the banks of the St. Lawrence, on the spot now called Place Royale, this fort developed into an economic center for fur trade and shipbuilding. Twelve years later, de Champlain realized the French colony's vulnerability to attacks from above and expanded its boundaries to the top of the cliff, where he built the fort Château St-Louis on the site of the present-day Château Frontenac.

During the early days of New France, the French and British fought for control of the area. In 1690, when an expedition led by Admiral Sir William Phipps arrived from England, Comte de Frontenac, New France's most illustrious governor, issued his famous statement, "Tell your lord that I will reply with the mouth of my cannons."

England was determined to conquer New France. The French constructed walls and other military structures and had the advantage of the defensive position on top of the cliff, but they still had to contend with Britain's naval supremacy. On September 13, 1759, the British army, led by General James Wolfe, scaled the colony's cliff and took the French troops led by Général Louis-Joseph Montcalm by surprise. The British defeated the French in a 20-minute battle on the Plains of Abraham, and New France came under English rule.

The British brought their mastery of trade to the region. During the 18th century, Québec City's economy prospered because of the success of the fishing, fur trading, shipbuilding, and timber industries. In order to further protect the city from invasion, the British continued to expand upon the fortifications left by the French. Defensive structures that were built included a wall encircling the city and a star-shape citadel, both of which still enhance the city's urban landscape. The city remained under British rule until 1867, when the Act of Confederation united several Canadian provinces (Québec, Ontario, New Brunswick, and Nova Scotia) and designated Québec City the capital of the province of Québec.

During the mid-19th century, the economic center of eastern Canada shifted west from Québec City to Montréal and Toronto. Today government is Québec City's main business: About 30,000 civil-service employees work and live in the area. Office complexes continue to appear outside the older portion of town; modern malls, convention centers, and imposing hotels now cater to an established business clientele.

Despite the period of British rule, Québec City has remained a center of French Canadian culture. It is home to Université Laval (Laval University), a large Catholic institution that grew out of Séminaire de Québec (Québec Seminary), founded in 1663 by French bishop François de Montmorency Laval; today Laval has a sprawling campus in the suburb of Sainte-Foy. Québec City also has several theaters, including the Grand Théâtre de Québec, where local artists perform plays that deal directly with French Canadian culture. The Québec government has completely restored many of the centuries-old buildings of Place Royale, one of the oldest districts on the continent. The city's ancient stone churches and homes, as well as its cultural institutions, such as Musée de Québec and Musée de la Civilisation, are firmly rooted in French Canadian society.

Québec City is a wonderful place in which to wander on foot. Its natural beauty is world renowned. You're bound to enjoy the view from Parc Montmorency (Montmorency Park), where the Laurentian Mountains jut majestically over the St. Lawrence River. Even more impressive vistas are revealed if you walk along the walls or climb to the city's highest point, Cap Diamant (Cape Diamond). Several blissful days may be spent investigating the narrow cobblestone streets of the historic Old City, browsing for local arts and crafts in the boutiques of quartier Petit-Champlain, or strolling the Terrasse Dufferin promenade along the river. When you've worked up an appetite, you can stop to indulge in one of the many reliable cafés and restaurants, with a choice of French, Québecois, and international fare. If you've had enough of the past, another vibrant, modern part of town beckons beyond the city gates. And if you're tired of walking you can always board a calèche (horse-drawn carriage) near the city gates or hop on the ferry across the St. Lawrence River to Lévis for a thrilling view of the Québec City skyline. What follows will help you uncover some of the secrets of this exuberant, romantic place.

Essential Information

Arriving and Departing by Plane

Airports/ Airlines Québec City has one airport, **Québec City International Airport,** located in the suburb of Sainte-Foy, approximately 19 kilometers (12 miles) from downtown. Few U.S. airlines fly directly to Québec City. You usually have to stop in Montréal or Toronto and take one of the regional and commuter airlines, such as Air Canada's **Air Alliance** (tel. 418/692–0770) or **Canadian Airlines International** (tel. 418/

Metropolitan Québec City Exploring *(Boxes Refer to Detail Maps)*

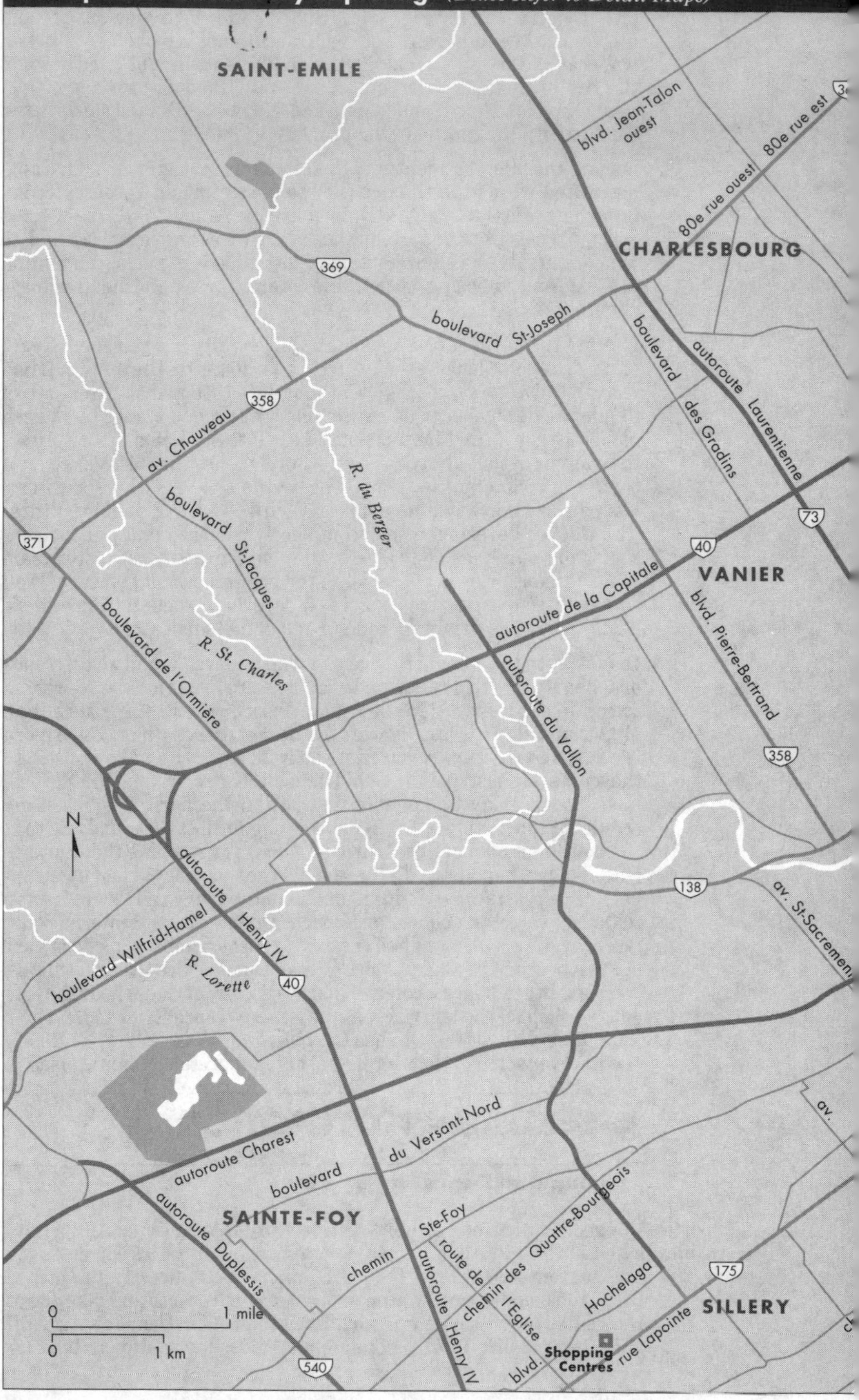
SAINT-EMILE
CHARLESBOURG
VANIER
SAINTE-FOY
SILLERY
blvd. Jean-Talon ouest
80e rue ouest
80e rue est
369
boulevard St-Joseph
boulevard des Gradins
autoroute Laurentienne
73
40
358
av. Chauveau
R. du Berger
boulevard St-Jacques
371
autoroute de la Capitale
blvd. Pierre-Bertrand
boulevard de l'Ormière
R. St. Charles
autoroute du Vallon
N
autoroute Henry IV
138
av. St-Sacrement
boulevard Wilfrid-Hamel
R. Lorette
autoroute Charest
boulevard du Versant-Nord
av.
autoroute Duplessis
chemin Ste-Foy
route de l'Eglise
chemin des Quatre-Bourgeois
Hochelaga
175
0
1 mile
0
1 km
540
blvd.
Shopping Centres
rue Lapointe

GIFFARD
BEAUPORT
320
rue Seigneurial
avenue Royale
avenue Bourg-Royal
TO
ÎIE D'ORLEANS,
COTE DE BEAUPRÉ
avenue
chemin Royal
blvd. Ste-Anne
Baie de Beauport
blvd. d'Estimauville
440
blvd. Henri-Bourassa
1re Avenue
av. du Colisée
autoroute Dufferin-Montmorency
chemin de la Canardière
avenue Lamontagne
360
Estuaire de la
Rivière St-Charles
QUEBEC
Rivière St-Charles
3e Avenue
Tours 1 & 2
LOWER
TOWN
LEVIS
UPPER
TOWN
autoroute Charest
Grande Allée
440
chemin Ste-Foy
Tour 3
132
boulevard Réné Levesque
175
chemin St-Louis
Champlain
blvd.
Fleuve Saint-Laurent
Maguire
min Saint-Louis
ST-DAVID-
DE-L'AUBERIVIERE
20

692–1031). Air Alliance offers a direct flight between Newark, New Jersey, and Québec City seven days a week.

Between the Airport and Québec City The ride from the airport into town should be no longer than 30 minutes. Most hotels do not have an airport shuttle, but they will make a reservation for you with a bus company. If you're not in a rush, a shuttle bus offered by Maple Leaf Tours (*see below*) is convenient and half the price of a taxi.

By Bus **Maple Leaf Tours** (240 3ième rue, tel. 418/649–9226) has a shuttle bus that runs from the airport to hotels and costs under $10 one way. The shuttle makes several trips to and from the airport every day. A schedule is posted at the airport. Stops include the major hotels in town, and any other hotel upon request. Reservations for the shuttle bus are necessary when traveling to the airport.

By Taxi Taxis are always available immediately outside the airport exit near the baggage claim area. Some local taxi companies are **Taxi Québec** (975 8ième av., tel. 418/522–2001) and **Taxi Coop de Québec** (496 2ième av., tel. 418/525–5191), the largest company in the city. A ride into the city costs approximately $25.

By Limousine Private limo service is expensive, starting at $50 for the ride from the airport into Québec City. Try **Groupe Limousine A-1** (30 chemin de la Cornière, Lac Beauport, tel. 418/849–7473). **Maple Leaf Tours** (240 3ième rue, tel. 418/649–9226) acts as a referral service for local companies offering car service.

By Car If you're driving from the airport, take Route 540 (Autoroute Duplessis) to Route 175 (boul. Laurier), which becomes Grande Allée and leads right to the Old City. The ride is about 30 minutes and may be only slightly longer (45 minutes or so) during rush hours (7:30–8:30 AM into town, and 4–5:30 PM leaving town).

Arriving and Departing by Car, Train, and Bus

By Car Montréal and Québec City are connected by Autoroute 20 on the south shore of the St. Lawrence River and by Autoroute 40 on the north shore. On both highways, the ride between the two cities is about 240 kilometers (150 miles) and takes approximately three hours. U.S. I–87 in New York, U.S. I–89 in Vermont, and U.S. I–91 in New Hampshire connect with Autoroute 20. Highway 401 from Toronto also connects with Autoroute 20.

Driving northeast from Montréal on Autoroute 20, follow signs for Pont Pierre-Laporte (Pierre-Laporte Bridge) as you approach Québec City. After you've crossed the bridge, turn right onto boulevard Laurier (Route 175), which becomes the Grande Allée leading into Québec City.

It is necessary to have a car only if you are planning to visit outlying areas. The narrow streets of the Old City leave few two-hour metered parking spaces available. However, there are several parking garages at central locations in town, with rates running approximately $10 a day. Main garages are located at City Hall, Place d'Youville, Complex G, Place Québec, Château Frontenac, Québec Seminary, rue St-Paul, and the Old Port.

Rental Cars *See* Car Rentals in Chapter 1.

By Train **VIA Rail,** Canada's passenger rail service, travels from Montréal to Québec City four times daily on weekdays, three times a day on Saturday, and twice on Sunday. The trip follows the south shore of the St. Lawrence River, and takes less than three hours. The train makes a stop in Sainte-Foy and has first-class service available. Tickets must be purchased in advance at any VIA Rail office or travel agent. The basic one-way rate is about $40. At certain periods throughout the year, that price is reduced to $23. Reservations must be made at least five days in advance. The discount is not offered on Friday, Sunday, or holidays. First-class service costs about $65 each way. *Tel. 418/692–3940; in Québec City and in Sainte-Foy, 800/361–5390; in Québec province, tel. 800/361–5390.*

The train arrives in Québec City at the 19th-century **Gare du Palais** (450 rue de la Gare du Palais, tel. 418/524–6452), in the heart of the Old City.

By Bus **Voyageur Inc.** provides regular service from Montréal to Québec City daily, departing hourly 6 AM–9 PM, with an additional bus at 11 PM. The cost of the three-hour ride is $35 one way. A round-trip costs $50, if you return within 10 days and do not travel on Friday. Senior citizens travel for $25 each way. You can only purchase tickets at the terminal; tickets are not sold on the bus.

Bus Terminals **Montréal:** Voyageur Terminal (505 boul. de Maisonneuve E, tel. 514/842–2281).

Québec: Downtown Terminal (225 boul. Charest E, tel. 418/524–4692); Sainte-Foy Terminal (2700 boul. Laurier, tel. 418/651–7015).

Getting Around

Walking is the best way to explore Québec City. The Old City measures 11 square kilometers (7 square miles), and most historic sites, hotels, and restaurants are located within the walls or a short distance outside. City maps are available at tourist information offices.

By Bus The public transportation system in Québec City is dependable, and buses run frequently. You can get to anywhere in Québec City and the outlying areas, although you may be required to transfer. The city's transit system, **Commission de Transport de la Communauté Urbaine de Québec (CTCUQ)** (tel. 418/627–2511) runs buses approximately every 15 or 20 minutes that stop at major points around town. The cost is $1.80, children under 5 free; you'll need exact change. All buses stop in Lower Town at Place Jacques-Cartier or outside St-Jean Gate at Place d'Youville in Upper Town. Transportation maps are available at tourist information offices.

By Taxi Taxis are stationed in front of major hotels, including the Château Frontenac, Hilton International, Loews Le Concorde, and Hôtel des Gouverneurs, as well as in front of Hôtel de Ville (City Hall) along rue des Jardins and Place d'Youville outside St-Jean Gate. For radio-dispatched cars, try **Taxi Coop de Québec** (tel. 418/525–5191) and **Taxi Québec** (tel. 418/522–2001). Passengers are charged an initial $2.25, plus $1 for each kilometer.

By Limousine Groupe Limousine A-1 (30 chemin de la Cornière, Lac Beauport, tel. 418/849–7473) has 24-hour service.

Important Addresses and Numbers

Tourist Information **Québec City Region Tourism and Convention Bureau** has two tourist information centers:

Québec City: 60 rue d'Auteuil, tel. 418/692–2471. Open June–early September, daily 8:30–8; early September–mid-October, daily 8:30–5:30; mid-October–mid-April, weekdays 9–5; mid-April–May, weekdays 8:30–5:30.

Sainte-Foy: 3005 boul. Laurier (near the Québec and Pierre-Laporte bridges), tel. 418/651–2882. Open June–August, daily 8:30–8; September–mid-October, daily 8:30–6; mid-October–mid-April, daily 9–5; mid-April–May, daily 8:30–6.

Québec Government Tourism Department: 12 rue Ste-Anne (Place d'Armes), tel. 418/643–2280 or 800/363–7777. Open fall–winter, daily 9–5; summer, daily 8:30–7:30.

U.S. Consulate The consulate (2 Place Terrasse Dufferin, tel. 418/692–2095) faces the Governors Park near the Château Frontenac.

Emergencies **Police and fire,** tel. 418/691–6911; **provincial police,** tel. 418/623–6262.

Medical Care **Hôtel-Dieu Hospital** (11 côte du Palais, tel. 418/691–5042) is the main hospital inside the Old City; **Jeffrey Hale Hospital** (1250 chemin Sainte-Foy, tel. 418/683–4471) is opposite St. Sacrament Church.

24-hour Medical Service (tel. 418/687–9915).

Distress Center (tel. 418/683–2153).

24-hour Poison Center (tel. 418/656–8090).

Dental Service 1175 rue Lavigerie, Room 100, Sainte-Foy, tel. 418/653–5412; weekends, tel. 418/656–6060. Open Monday and Tuesday 8–8, Wednesday and Thursday 8–5, Friday 8–4.

Pharmacy **Pharmacie Brunet** (Les Galeries Charlesbourg, 4266 1ière av., north of Québec City in Charlesbourg, tel. 418/623–1571) is open daily, 24 hours a day.

Traffic Tel. 418/643–6830.

Weather Tel. 418/648–7766.

English-language Bookstore **La Maison Anglaise** (Place de la Cité, Sainte-Foy, tel. 418/654–9523).

Travel Agencies **Inter-Voyage** (1095 rue de l'Amérique française, tel. 418/524–1414) is located on the first floor of the Édifice Bon Pasteur (Bon Pasteur Building), on the corner of rue St-Amable and rue de l'Amérique française, near the Parliament. It's open weekdays 8:30–5:30.

Opening and Closing Times

Most banks are open Monday through Wednesday 10–3 and close later on Thursday and Friday. **Bank of Montreal** (Place Laurier, 2700 boul. Laurier, Sainte-Foy, tel. 418/525–3786) is open on Saturday 10–3. For currency exchange, **Banque d'Amérique** (24 côte de la Fabrique, tel. 418/694–1937) is open late June–August, weekdays 9–6, weekends 9–5; September–late June, weekdays 9–5, weekends 10–4.

Museum hours are typically 10–5, with longer evening hours during summer months. Most are closed on Monday.

Shopping hours are Monday through Wednesday 9:30–5:30, Thursday and Friday 9:30–9, and Saturday 9:30–5. Stores tend to stay open later during summer months.

During the winter, many attractions and shops change their hours; visitors are advised to call ahead.

Guided Tours

Orientation Tours

By Bus

The three major touring companies—Gray Line, Maple Leaf, and Visite Touristique de Québec—offer similar full- and half-day guided bus tours in English. Tours cover such sights as Québec City, Montmorency Falls, and Sainte-Anne-de-Beaupré; combination city and harbor cruise tours are also available. Québec City tours operate year-round; other excursions to outlying areas may operate only in the summer.

Tickets for **Gray Line** (720 rue des Rocailles; departure from Château Frontenac terrace, tel. 418/622–7420) bus tours can be purchased at most major hotels or at the kiosk at Terrasse Dufferin at Place d'Armes. Tours run year-round and cost $13–$70 adults, half-price children 5–12.

Maple Leaf Sightseeing Tours (240 3ième rue, tel. 418/649–9226) offers guided tours in a minibus. Call for a reservation, and the company will pick you up at your hotel. Prices are $20–$91, with reduced rates for children under 12.

Visite Touristique de Québec (C.P. 246, Québec, tel. 418/653–9722) gives tours (in English or French) in a panoramic bus, and charges $20–$39, children 6–14 half-price, children under 6 free.

Smaller companies offering tours include **La Tournée du Québec Inc.** (tel. 418/831–1385) and **Fleur de Lys** (418/831–0188).

By Ferry

The Québec–Lévis ferry makes a 15-minute crossing of the St. Lawrence River to the town of Lévis. The first ferry leaves daily at 6:30 AM from the pier at rue Dalhousie, across from Place Royale. Crossings run every half hour from 7:30 AM until 6:30 PM, then hourly until 2:30 AM, with a final crossing at 3:45 AM. *Tel. 418/644–3704. Cost: $1.25 adults, 75¢ children 5–11 and senior citizens.*

By Horse-drawn Carriage

Hire a calèche on rue d'Auteuil between the St-Louis and Kent gates from **André Beaurivage** (tel. 418/687–9797). The cost is about $50 without tax or tip for a 45-minute tour of the Old City. Some drivers talk about Québec's history and others don't. So if you want a storyteller, ask in advance.

Special-Interest Tours

Boat Trips

Beau Temps, Mauvais Temps (22 rue du Quai, Suite 101, Sainte-Pétronille, Île d'Orléans, tel. 418/828–2275) offers two river cruises that stop to tour neighboring islands. Boats depart from piers at Saint-Laurent on Île d'Orléans, and Pier 19 at Vieux-Port, in Québec. The boat trip to Île-aux-Grues costs $72 for adults, with reduced rates for children. The trip to Grosse-Île costs $65 for adults; children under 12 are not accepted. Both trips include a light lunch.

Croisières AML Inc. (Pier Chouinard, 10 rue Dalhousie, across the street from the funicular, tel. 418/692–1159) runs cruises on the St. Lawrence River aboard the MV *Louis-Jolliet*. One- to three-hour cruises from May through mid-October cost $13–$24 for adults, half-price for children 5 and over, 10% discount for senior citizens.

Île d'Orléans

Beau Temps, Mauvais Temps (*see above*) has guided tours of Île d'Orléans by bus, walking tours of the island's historic manors and churches, and trips to a maple-sugar hut.

Walking Tours

Baillairgé Cultural Tours, Inc. (2216 chemin du Foulon, Sillery, tel. 418/658–4799; 51 rue des Jardins, 2nd Floor, tel. 418/692–5234) has a 2½-hour walking tour, "Québec on Foot," from late June through September at 9:30 AM and 2 PM daily. The tour leaves from 2 côte de la Fabrique and includes sights in both the Upper and Lower towns. The cost is about $12 adults, children under 12 free.

Exploring Québec City

Québec City's split-level landscape divides the Upper Town on the cape from the Lower Town, along the shores of the St. Lawrence. If you look out from the Terrasse Dufferin boardwalk in Upper Town, you will see the rooftops of Lower Town buildings directly below. Separating these two sections of the city is steep and precipitous rock, against which were built the city's more than 25 *escaliers* (staircases). Today you can also take the *funiculaire* (funicular), a cable car that climbs and descends the cliff between Terrasse Dufferin and the Maison Jolliet in Lower Town.

With the exception of some of the outlying suburbs, most of Québec City's historic area will interest tourists. The first two tours offered here focus primarily on the oldest sections of town, while the third tour strays off the beaten path to provide a glimpse of the modern part of the city.

Tour 1: Upper Town

Numbers in the margin correspond to points of interest on the Tours 1 and 2: Upper and Lower Towns map.

This tour visits the most prominent buildings of Québec City's earliest inhabitants, who came from Europe in the 17th century to set up political, educational, and religious institutions. Upper Town became the political capital of the colony of New France and, later, of British North America. It was also the place where the religious orders first set down their roots: The Jesuits founded the first school for priests in 1635; the Ursuline nuns, a school for girls in 1639; and the Augustine nuns, the first hospital in 1639. Historic buildings, with thick stone walls, large wood doors, glimmering copper roofs, and majestic steeples, compose the heart of the city.

1 Begin this tour where rue St-Louis meets rue du Fort at Upper Town's most central location, **Place d'Armes.** For centuries, this square seated on a cliff has been a meeting place for parades and military events. It is bordered by government buildings; at its west side, the majestic **Ancien Palais de Justice** (Old Courthouse), a Renaissance building from 1887, replaced the original 1650 courthouse, which was smaller and situated farther from the square. The present courthouse stands on land that was occupied by a church and convent of the Recollet missionaries (Franciscan monks), who in 1615 were the first order of priests to arrive in New France. The Gothic fountain at the center of Place d'Armes pays tribute to their arrival.

The colony's former treasury building, **Maison Maillou,** at 17 rue St-Louis, possesses architectural traits typical of New France: a sharply slanted roof, dormer windows, concrete chimneys, shutters with iron hinges, and limestone walls. Built between 1736 and 1753, it marks the end of rue du Trésor, the road colonists took on their way to pay rent to the king's officials. Maison Maillou is not open to tourists and is now used as the location for the Québec City Chamber of Commerce offices.

2 You are now within a few steps east of Québec City's most celebrated landmark, **Château Frontenac** (1 rue des Carrières, tel. 418/692–3861), once the administrative and military headquarters of New France. The imposing green-turreted castle with its slanting copper roof owes its name to the Comte de Frontenac, governor of the French colony between 1672 and 1698. Looking at the magnificence

of the château, you can see why Frontenac said, "For me, there is no site more beautiful nor more grandiose than that of Québec City."

Samuel de Champlain, who founded Québec City in 1608, was responsible for Château St-Louis, the first structure to appear on the site of the Frontenac; it was built between 1620 and 1624 as a residence for colonial governors. In 1784, Château Haldimand was constructed here, but it was demolished in 1892 to make way for Château Frontenac. The latter was built as a hotel in 1893, and it was considered to be remarkably luxurious at that time: Guest rooms contained fireplaces, private bathrooms, and marble fixtures, and a special commissioner traveled to England and France in search of antiques for the establishment. The hotel was designed by New York architect Bruce Price, who also worked on Québec City's **Gare du Palais** (Rail Station) and other Canadian landmarks, such as Montréal's Windsor Station. The Frontenac was completed in 1925 with the addition of a 20-story central tower. Owned by Canadian Pacific Hotels, it has accumulated a star-studded guest roster, including Queen Elizabeth, Madame Chiang Kai-shek, Ronald Reagan, and François Mitterrand, as well as Franklin Roosevelt and Winston Churchill, who convened here in 1943 and 1944 for two wartime conferences. As you head to the boardwalk behind the Frontenac, notice the glorious bronze statue of Samuel de Champlain, situated where he built his residence. The statue's steps are made of des Vosges granite, and the pedestal consists of Château-Landon stone, the same material used for the Arc de Triomphe in Paris.

3 Walk south along the boardwalk called the **Terrasse Dufferin** for a panoramic view of the St. Lawrence River, the town of Lévis on the opposite shore, Île d'Orléans, and the Laurentian Mountains. The wide boardwalk, with an intricate wrought-iron guardrail, was named after Lord Dufferin, who was governor of Canada between 1872 and 1878 and who had this walkway constructed in 1878. At its western tip begins the **Promenade des Gouverneurs,** which skirts along the cliff and leads up to Québec's highest point, Cap Diamant (Cape Diamond), and also to the Citadel.

As you pass to the southern side of the Frontenac, you will come to a
4 small park called **Jardin des Gouverneurs** (Governors' Park), which is bordered by three streets of old manors. During the French regime, the public area served as a garden for the governors who resided in Château St-Louis. The park's Wolfe-Montcalm Monument, a 50-foot obelisk, is unique in that it pays tribute to both a winning (English) and a losing (French) general. The monument recalls the 1759 battle on the Plains of Abraham, which ended French rule of New France. British General James Wolfe lived only long enough to hear of his victory; French Général Louis-Joseph Montcalm died shortly after Wolfe with the knowledge that the city was lost. *Admission free. Open daily.*

On the southeast corner of the park is the **U.S. Consulate** (2 Place Terrasse Dufferin). On the south side of the park is **avenue Ste-Geneviève,** lined with well-preserved Victorian homes dating from 1850 to 1900 that have been converted to quaint old-fashioned inns.

Make your way to the north side of the park and follow rue Mont Carmel until you come to another small park landscaped with foot-
5 paths and flower beds, **Cavalier du Moulin.** The former stone windmill, which became part of the French fortifications, was considered during the 17th century to be located on the outskirts of town because most of the city was situated below the cliff. The windmill was strategically placed so that its cannons could destroy the Cap-

Tours 1 and 2: Upper and Lower Towns

- Antiques District, **28**
- Basilique Notre-Dame-de-Québec, **11**
- Cavalier du Moulin, **5**
- Château Frontenac, **2**
- Couvent des Ursulines, **6**
- Edifice Price, **9**
- Eglise Notre-Dame-des-Victoires, **20**
- Explore, **24**
- Holy Trinity Anglican Cathedral, **7**
- Hôtel Clarendon, **8**
- Jardin des Gouverneurs, **4**
- Lévis-Québec Ferry, **23**
- Maison Chevalier, **18**
- Maison Louis-Jolliet, **16**
- Maison Montcalm, **29**
- Maison des Vins, **21**
- Monastère des Augustines de l'Hôtel-Dieu de Québec, **12**
- Musée de la Civilisation, **25**
- Musée du Fort, **15**
- Naturalium, **26**
- Parc de l'Artillerie, **30**
- Parc Montmorency, **14**
- Place d'Armes, **1**
- Place de Paris, **22**
- Place Royale, **19**
- Rue du Petit-Champlain, **17**
- Rue du Trésor, **10**
- Séminaire de Québec, **13**
- Terrasse Dufferin, **3**
- Vieux-Port de Québec, **27**

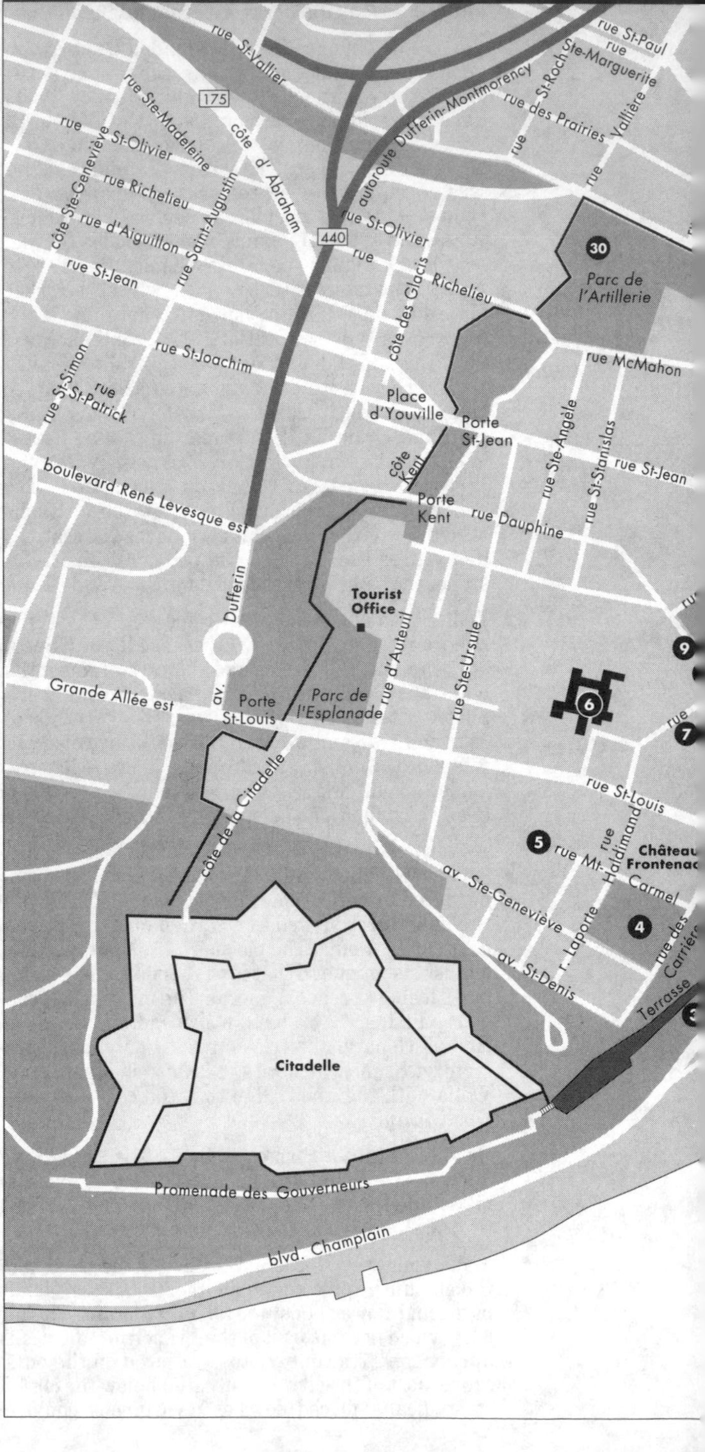

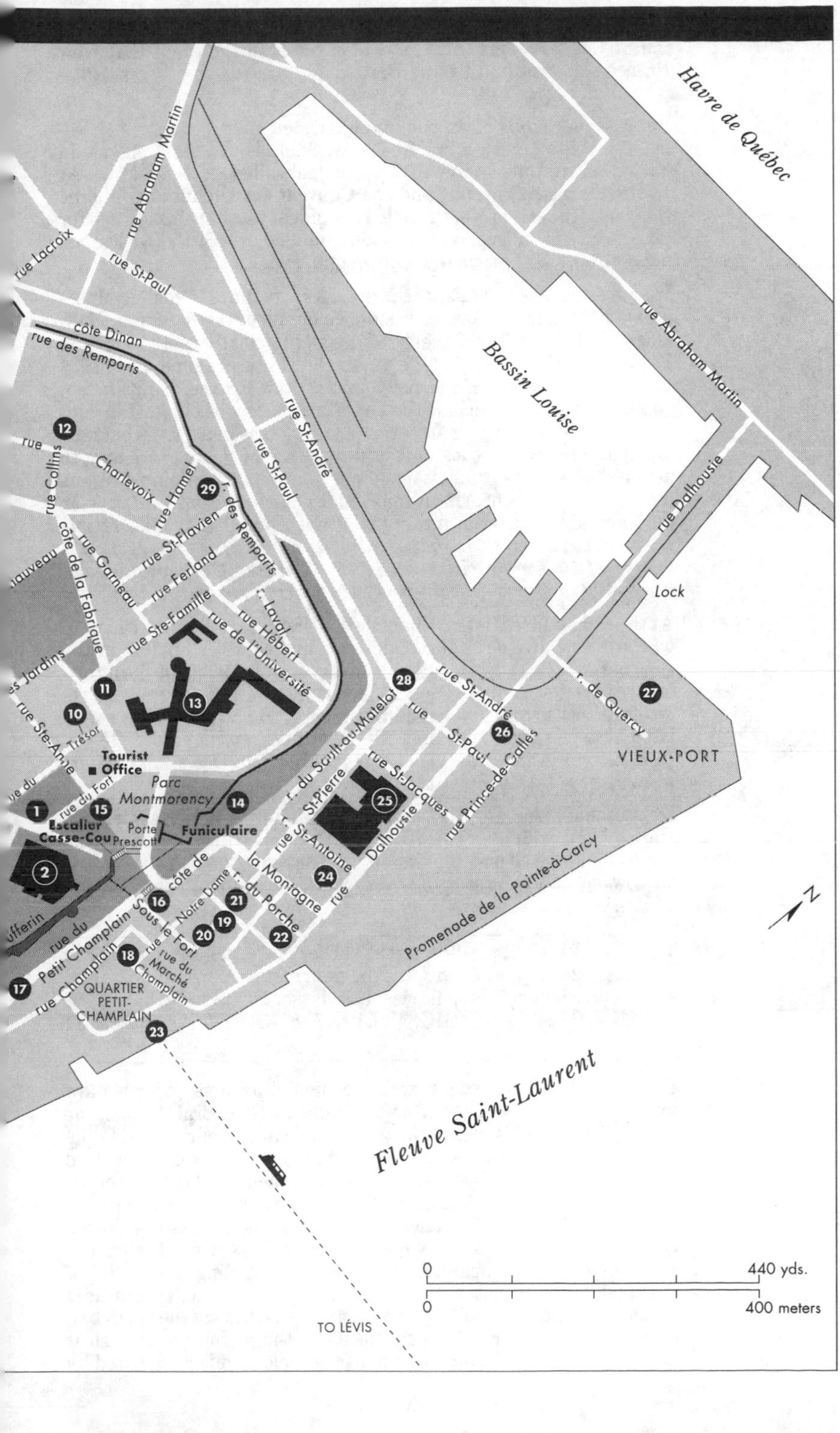
Havre de Québec
Bassin Louise
rue Abraham Martin
rue Abraham Martin
rue Lacroix
rue St-Paul
côte Dinan
rue des Remparts
rue St-André
rue St-Paul
rue Dalhousie
Lock
rue Collins
rue Charlevoix
rue Hamel
r. des Remparts
rue St-Flavien
rue Ferland
rue Garneau
côte de la Fabrique
rue Ste-Famille
rue Hébert
r. Laval
rue de l'Université
des Jardins
rue Ste-Anne
Trésor
Tourist Office
rue du Fort
Parc Montmorency
Escalier Casse-Cou
Porte Prescott
Funiculaire
côte de
rue Sous le Fort
rue du Petit Champlain
rue Champlain
rue du Marché Champlain
QUARTIER PETIT-CHAMPLAIN
Notre-Dame
r. du Porche
la Montagne
r. St-Antoine
r. St-Pierre
r. du Sault-au-Matelot
rue St-Jacques
rue Dalhousie
rue St-Paul
rue St-André
rue Prince-de-Galles
r. de Quercy
VIEUX-PORT
Promenade de la Pointe-à-Carcy
Fleuve Saint-Laurent
N
TO LÉVIS
440 yds.
400 meters
1
2
10
11
12
13
14
15
16
17
18
19
20
21
22
23
24
25
26
27
28
29

Diamant Redoubt (situated near Promenade des Gouverneurs) and the St-Louis Bastion (near St-Louis Gate) in the event that New France was captured by the British. *Admission free. Open May–Nov., daily 7 AM–9 PM.*

Retrace your steps down rue Mont Carmel, turn left on rue Haldimand and left again on rue St-Louis; then make a right on rue du Parloir until it intersects with a tiny street called rue Donnacona. At 6 12 rue Donnacona, you'll find the **Couvent des Ursulines** (Ursuline Convent), the site of North America's oldest teaching institution for girls, which is still a private school. Founded in 1639 by two French nuns, the convent has many of its original walls still intact.

Within the convent walls, the **Musée des Ursulines** (Ursuline Museum) is housed in the former residence of one of the founders, Madame de la Peltrie. The museum offers an informative perspective on 120 years of the Ursulines' life under the French regime, from 1639 to 1759. Exhibits tell of the early days of New France. For instance, you'll discover that because the Ursulines were without heat in winter, their heavy clothing sometimes weighed as much as 20 pounds. You'll also see why it took an Ursuline nun nine years of training to attain the level of a professional embroiderer; the museum contains magnificent pieces of ornate embroidery, such as altar frontals with gold and silver threads intertwined with precious jewels. *12 rue Donnacona, tel. 418/694–0694. Admission: $2.50 adults, $1.25 students, $1.50 senior citizens, $5.75 families. Open Jan.–Nov., Tues.–Sat. 9:30–noon and 1:30–4:40, Sun. 12:30–5:15.*

At the same address is the **Chapelle des Ursulines** (Ursuline Chapel), where French Général Montcalm was buried after he died in the 1759 battle. The chapel's exterior was rebuilt in 1902, but the interior contains the original chapel, which is the work of sculptor Pierre-Noël Levasseur, accomplished between 1726 and 1736. The votive lamp here was lit in 1717 and has never been extinguished. *12 rue Donnacona. Admission free. Open May–Oct., Tues.–Sat. 9:30–noon and 1:30–4:40, Sun. 12:30–5:15.*

Next to the museum at the **Centre Marie-de-l'Incarnation** are a bookstore and an exhibit on the life of the Ursulines' first superior, who came from France and cofounded the convent. *10 rue Donnacona, tel. 418/692–1569. Admission free. Open Feb.–Nov., Tues.–Sat. 10–11:30 and 2–4:30, Sun. 2–4:30.*

Time Out The neon-lit **Café Taste-Vin,** on the corner of rue des Jardins and rue St-Louis, shares a kitchen with the gourmet restaurant next door; sample delicious salads, pastries, and desserts. *32 rue St-Louis, tel. 418/692–4191. AE, DC, MC, V. Open Feb.–Oct., daily 7:30 AM–11 PM.*

From rue Donnacona, walk north to rue des Jardins. Within a few 7 yards you'll see the **Holy Trinity Anglican Cathedral.** This stone church dates to 1804 and is the first Anglican cathedral outside the British Isles. Its simple and dignified facade is reminiscent of London's St. Martin-in-the-Fields. The cathedral's land was originally given to the Recollet fathers (Franciscan monks from France) in 1681 by the king of France for a church and monastery. When Québec came under British rule, the Recollets made the church available to the Anglicans for services. Later, King George III of England ordered construction of the present cathedral, with an area set aside for members of the royal family. A portion of the north balcony still remains exclusively for the use of the reigning sovereign or her representative. The church houses precious objects donated by

George III. The oak benches were imported from the Royal Forest at Windsor. The cathedral's impressive rear organ has more than 2,500 pipes. *31 rue des Jardins, tel. 418/692–2193. Admission free. Open June–Aug., daily 9–9; Sept.–mid-Oct., weekdays 9–3.*

The building on the corner of rue des Jardins and rue Ste-Anne is one of Québec City's finest Art Deco structures. Geometric patterns
8 of stone and wrought iron decorate the interior of the **Hôtel Clarendon** (57 rue Ste-Anne, tel. 418/692–2480). Although the Clarendon dates back to 1866, it was reconstructed with its current Art Deco decor in 1930.

More Art Deco can be found next door at 65 rue Ste-Anne, the 15-
9 story **Edifice Price** (Price Building). The city's first skyscraper was built in 1929 and served as the headquarters of the Price Brothers Company, the lumber company founded in Canada by Sir William Price. Today it is owned by the provincial government and houses the offices of Québec City's mayor. Don't miss the interior: Exquisite copper plaques depict scenes of the company's early pulp and paper activities, while the two artfully carved maple-wood elevators are '30s classics.

Head back on rue Ste-Anne past the Holy Trinity Anglican Cathedral and continue straight on this street until it becomes a narrow, cobblestone thoroughfare lined with boutiques and restaurants. During the summer, the activity here starts buzzing early in the morning and continues until late at night. Stores stay open, artists paint, and street musicians perform as long as there is an audience, even if it's one o'clock in the morning.

10 Turn left into a narrow alley called **rue du Trésor,** where hundreds of colorful prints, paintings, and other artworks are on display. You won't necessarily find masterpieces here, but this walkway is a good stop for a souvenir sketch or two. During the French regime people came to this street to pay rent to the crown; the royal treasury stood at the end of the street, at Maison Maillou.

At the bottom of rue du Trésor, turn left on rue Buade. When you
11 reach the corner of côte de la Fabrique, you'll see the **Basilique Notre-Dame-de-Québec** (Our Lady of Québec Basilica), with the oldest parish in North America, dating to 1647. The basilica has been rebuilt on three separate occasions: in the early 1700s, when François de Montmorency Laval was the first bishop; in 1759, after cannons at Lévis fired upon it during the siege of Québec, and in 1922, after a fire. This basilica has a somber ambience despite its ornate interior, which includes a canopy dais over the episcopal throne, a ceiling of clouds decorated with gold leaf, richly colored stained-glass windows, and a chancel lamp that was a gift of Louis XIV. Perhaps the solemn mood here may be attributed to the basilica's large and famous crypt, which was Québec City's first cemetery; more than 900 people are interred here, including 20 bishops and four governors of New France. The founder of Québec City, Samuel de Champlain, is believed to be buried somewhere near the basilica. Archaeologists have been searching for his tomb for more than 40 years. *16 rue Buade, tel. 418/692–2533. Admission free. Open daily 8–6.*

The basilica marks the beginning of Québec City's Latin Quarter, which extends to the streets northwest of Québec Seminary (rue Buade, rue des Remparts, côte de la Fabrique, and côte du Palais) as far as rue St-Jean. This district was deemed the Latin Quarter because Latin was once a required language course at the seminary and was spoken among the students. Although Latin is no longer compulsory and Québec Seminary–Laval University has moved out to a larger campus in Sainte-Foy, students still cling to this neighborhood.

Head down côte de la Fabrique and turn right when it meets rue Collins. The cluster of old stone buildings sequestered at the end of the
12 street is the **Monastère des Augustines de l'Hôtel-Dieu de Québec** (Augustine Monastery). Augustine nuns arrived from Dieppe, France, in 1639 with a mission to care for the sick in the new colony, and they established the first hospital north of Mexico, the **Hôtel-Dieu Hospital,** which is the large building west of the monastery. The **Musée des Augustines** (Augustine Museum) is housed in hospital-like quarters with large sterile corridors leading into a ward that features a small exhibit of antique medical instruments used by the Augustines, such as an 1850 microscope and a pill-making device from the 17th century.

Upon request, the Augustines also offer guided tours of the chapel (1800) and the cellars used by the nuns as a hiding place beginning in 1659, during bombardments by the British. *32 rue Charlevoix, tel. 418/692–2492. Admission free. Open Tues.–Sat. 9:30–11:30 and 1:30–5, Sun. 1:30–5.*

Time Out For a crusty white or whole-wheat croissant, try **Croissant Plus** (50 rue Garneau, tel. 418/692–4215).

Retrace your steps on Collins Street and côte de la Fabrique. When you reach rue Ste-Famille on the left, you will find the wrought-iron
13 entrance gates of the **Séminaire de Québec** (Québec Seminary). Behind these gates lies a tranquil courtyard surrounded by austere stone buildings with rising steeples; these structures have housed classrooms and student residences since 1663. The seminary was founded by François de Montmorency Laval, the first bishop of New France, to train priests of the new colony. In 1852 the seminary became Université Laval (Laval University), the first Catholic university in North America. The university eventually outgrew these cramped quarters; in 1946, Laval moved to a larger, modern campus in the suburb of Sainte-Foy. The Musée du Séminaire (*see below*) offers guided tours of the seminary during the summer. *1 côte de la Fabrique.*

Head north across the courtyard to the **Musée du Séminaire** (Seminary Museum). Housed in a former student residence, the museum focuses on the three centuries of the seminary's existence, until 1940. It emphasizes European secular and religious works of art; there are more than 400 landscape and still-life paintings dating as far back as the 15th century. The museum also houses a showcase of scientific instruments that were acquired through the centuries for the purposes of research and teaching. A former chapel has been renovated and now holds an exhibit of elegant religious and secular antique silver. The museum also has a rare collection of Canadian money that was used in colonial times. *9 rue de l'Université, tel. 418/692–2843. Admission: $3 adults, $1.50 students, $1 children under 16, $2 senior citizens, $6 families; Tues. free. Open June–Sept., daily 10–5:30; Oct.–May, Tues.–Sun. 10–5.*

Then visit the Québec Seminary's **Chapelle Extérieure** (Outer Chapel), at the seminary's west entrance. The small Roman-style chapel was built in 1888, after the fire destroyed the first chapel, built in 1750. In 1950 a memorial crypt of Laval was added here. The chapel is open in the summer only, and follows the same schedule as the museum (*see above*).

Now exit the seminary from the east at rue de l'Université and head
14 south to côte de la Montagne, where **Parc Montmorency** (Montmorency Park) straddles the hill between Upper Town and Lower Town. This park marks the spot where Canada's first wheat was grown in 1618 and where the nation's first legislation was passed in 1694. A monument stands in tribute to Louis Herbert, a former apothecary and the first Canadian farmer, who cleared and tilled this area's land.

In 1688, Monseigneur de Saint-Vallier, the second bishop of New France, had his residence, the first episcopal palace, built here. In 1792 the palace's chapel became the seat of the first parliament of Lower Canada. The chapel was demolished in 1833, and a new legislative building was constructed that served as Québec's parliament until 1883, when it was destroyed by fire. A park monument commemorates Georges-Étienne Cartier, a French Canadian political leader and a father of the 1867 Confederation.

Take the **Escalier Frontenac** (Frontenac Stairway) up to the north end of the Terrasse Dufferin. You may be out of breath, but the climb is worth it for the 30-minute recap on the six sieges of Québec
15 City at the **Musée du Fort** (Fort Museum). This museum's sole exhibit is a sound-and-light show with a model of 18th-century Québec that reenacts the region's most important battles, including the Battle of the Plains of Abraham and the 1775 attack by American generals Arnold and Montgomery. *10 rue Ste-Anne, tel. 418/692–2175. Admission: $4.75 adults, $3.75 senior citizens, $2.75 students. Open June–Aug., daily 10–6; Apr.–May, Sept.–Oct., daily 10–5; Nov.–Mar., weekdays 11–3, weekends 11–5.*

As you exit from the museum, head southeast to the funicular booth along Terrasse Dufferin. Ride the funicular ($1.10) to Lower Town to begin Tour 2.

Tour 2: Lower Town

New France began to flourish in the streets of Lower Town along the banks of the St. Lawrence River. These streets became the colony's economic crossroads, where furs were traded, ships came in, and merchants established their residences.

Despite the status of Lower Town as the oldest neighborhood in North America, its narrow and time-worn thoroughfares have a new and polished look. In the '60s, after a century of decay as the commercial boom moved west and left Lower Town an abandoned district, the Québec government committed millions of dollars to restore the area to the way it had been during the days of New France. Today modern boutiques, restaurants, galleries, and shops catering to tourists occupy the former warehouses and residences.

Begin this tour on the northern tip of rue du Petit-Champlain at
16 **Maison Louis-Jolliet** (16 rue du Petit-Champlain, tel. 418/692–1132), which houses the lower station of the funicular and a souvenir shop. Built in 1683, this home was used by the first settlers of New France as a base for further westward explorations. It was in 1672, however, that Louis Jolliet—the first Canadian born in Québec to make history—discovered the Mississippi River. A monument commemorating this discovery stands in the park next to the house. At the north side of the house is **Escalier Casse-Cou** (Breakneck Steps), the city's first iron stairway. Its steepness is ample evidence of how it got its name. Its ambitious 1893 design was by Charles Baillairgé, a city architect and engineer, and it was built on the site of the original

17th-century stairway that linked Upper Town and Lower Town during the French regime. Today tourist shops, quaint boutiques, and restaurants are situated at various levels.

17 Heading south on **rue du Petit-Champlain,** the city's oldest street, you'll notice the cliff on the right that borders this narrow thoroughfare, with Upper Town situated on the heights above. Rue du Petit-Champlain retains its size from when it was the main street of a harbor village, replete with trading posts and the homes of rich merchants. In 1977 artists, craftspeople, and private investors decided to initiate a revival of the street; today it consists of pleasant boutiques and cafés. The best buys here are the ceramics, wood carvings, and jewelry done by local artists. Natural-fiber weaving, Inuit carvings, hand-painted silks, and enameled copper crafts are some of the local specialties for sale.

At the point where rue du Petit-Champlain intersects with boulevard Champlain, make a U-turn to head back north on rue Champlain. One block farther, at the corner of rue du Marché-Champlain,
18 you'll find **Maison Chevalier,** an annex of the ethnographic Civilization Museum. This old stone house was built in 1752 for shipowner Jean-Baptiste Chevalier. It was restored in 1959, adding two 17th-century buildings to the original structure. Inside you will find the original wood beams and stone fireplaces, and an exhibit of 18th-century furniture. *50 rue du Marché-Champlain, tel. 418/643–2158. Admission free. Open late May–late June, Tues.–Sun. 10–5; late June–early Sept., daily 10–5; early Sept.–early Oct., Tues.–Sun. 10–5.*

East of Maison Chevalier, take rue Notre-Dame, which leads direct-
19 ly to **Place Royale,** formerly the heart of New France. This cobblestone square is encircled by buildings with steep Normandy-style roofs, dormer windows, and several chimneys. These were once the homes of wealthy merchants. Until 1686 the area was called Place du Marché, but its name was changed when a bust of Louis XIV, "*le Roi Soleil*" (the Sun King), was erected at its center.

During the late 1600s and early 1700s, when Place Royale was continually under threat of attacks from the British, the colonists progressively moved to higher and safer quarters atop the cliff in Upper Town. Yet after the French colony fell to British rule in 1759, Place Royale flourished again with shipbuilding, logging, fishing, and fur trading.

The small stone church at the south side of the Place Royale is the
20 **Église Notre-Dame-des-Victoires** (Our Lady of Victory Church), the oldest church in Québec, dating to 1688. It was built on the site of Samuel de Champlain's first residence, which also served as a fort and trading post. However, the church had to be completely restored on two occasions: after a fire in 1759 and more recently in 1969. It got its name from two French victories against the British: one in 1690 against Admiral William Phipps and another in 1711 against Sir Hovendon Walker. The interior contains copies of such European masters as Van Dyck, Rubens, and Boyermans; its altar resembles the shape of a fort. A scale model suspended from the ceiling represents *Le Brezé*, the boat that transported French soldiers to New France in 1664. The side chapel is dedicated to Sainte-Geneviève, the guardian saint of Paris. *Place Royale, tel. 418/692–1650. Admission free. Open mid-May–Sept., daily 9–4, except during Mass (Sun. 9:30, 11, and noon; May–Oct., Sat. 7 PM), marriages, and funerals; Oct.–mid-May, Tues.–Sat. 8:30–noon.*

21 Turn to the northwest corner of the square to the cool, dark, and musty cellars of the **Maison des Vins,** a former warehouse dating to 1689; here the Québec Société des Alcools sells more than 1,000 kinds of rare and vintage wines, which range in price from $10 to $1,000. *1 Pl. Royale, tel. 418/643–1214. Admission free. Open Tues. and Wed. 9:30–5:30, Thurs. and Fri. 9:30–9, Sat. 9:30–5.*

22 On the east side of Place Royale, take rue de la Place, which leads to an open square, **Place de Paris,** a newcomer to these historic quarters. Looming at its center is a black-and-white geometric sculpture, Dialogue avec l'Histoire (Dialogue with History), a gift from France positioned on the site where the first French settlers landed. Paris Mayor Jacques Chirac inaugurated the square in August 1987 with Québec City's Mayor Jean Pelletier. Its French counterpart is the Place du Québec, inaugurated in 1984 at St-Germain-des-Prés in Paris.

23 At this point of the tour you may conveniently catch the 15-minute **Lévis–Québec ferry** to the opposite shore of the St. Lawrence River. The boat docks a block south on rue Dalhousie; we recommend that you take the ferry for the opportunity of an unprecedented view of Québec City's skyline, with the Château Frontenac and the Québec Seminary high above the cliff. The view is even more impressive at night. *First ferry leaves at 6:30 AM. Crossings run every ½ hr between 7:30 AM and 6:30 PM, every hr between 7:30 PM and 2:30 AM, with a final crossing at 3:45 AM. Cost: $1.25 adults, 75¢ children and senior citizens.*

Time Out **Café Loft,** located in a converted garage on rue Dalhousie between Place de Paris and the Civilization Museum, offers delectable desserts, such as a pyramid-shape chocolate cake. Grab an inviting *baguette* sandwich and equally scrumptious quiches and salads. *49 rue Dalhousie, tel. 418/692–4864. AE, DC, MC, V. Open Mon.–Thurs. 11–11, Fri. 11 AM–1 AM, Sat. 9 AM–1 AM, Sun. 9 AM–11 PM.*

24 Next door to the Café Loft you will notice the new diorama, **Explore.** This 30-minute sound-and-light show works on the same principle as the one at the Musée du Fort (*see* Tour 1), except that it uses more modern diorama technology. The show tells the story of Québec and the age of exploration, opening with the native Indians and leading up to Cartier's entrance into the St. Lawrence River. *63 rue Dalhousie, tel. 418/692–2175. Admission: $4.75 adults, $3.75 senior citizens, $2.75 students. Open June–Aug., daily 10–6; Apr.–May, Sept., and Oct., daily 10–5; Nov.–Mar., weekdays 11–3, weekends 11–5.*

25 Continue north on the rue Dalhousie until you come to the **Musée de la Civilisation** (Civilization Museum). Wedged into the foot of the cliff, this spacious museum, with its striking limestone and glass facade, has been artfully designed to blend into the city landscape. Architect Moshe Safdie skillfully incorporated three historic buildings into the museum's modern structure: the house Estèbe, the site of the First Bank of Québec, and the Maison Pagé-Quercy. Many of the materials that were used to construct the newer portions of the museum are native to Québec province. The building's campanile echoes the shape of church steeples throughout the city.

The museum, which opened officially in 1988, houses innovative, entertaining, and sometimes playful exhibits devoted to aspects of Québec's culture and civilization. Several of the shows, with their imaginative use of artwork, video screens, computers, and sound, will appeal to both adults and children. An excellent permanent exhibition, "Memoires" ("Memories"), considers both Québec's history and French Canadian society today. In addition, there are dance, music, and theater performances and a good boutique for high-quality souvenirs. Guides are available in the exhibition rooms. *85 rue Dalhousie, tel. 418/643–2158. Admission: $5 adults, $4 senior citizens, $3 students; children under 16 free; Tues. free in winter. Open late June–early Sept., Thurs.–Tues. 10–7, Wed. 10–9; early Sept.–late June, Tues. and Thurs.–Sun. 10–5, Wed. 10–9.*

26 Across the street you'll find the **Naturalium**, Québec's new natural sciences museum. It features a fascinating showcase of 100,000 insects and arthropods; most are preserved, however some—like tarantulas and cockroaches—are very much alive. It houses over 800 preserved mammals, including some realistic portrayals of animals in nature. There are also 500 fossils and numerous minerals on display. The collection belongs to Georges Brossard, a self-taught entomologist and biologist.

One permanent exhibit, "Le Monde" ("The World"), is devoted to explaining the reproduction, nutrition, habitat, and social organization of living creatures. Another focuses on the Saint Lawrence River's fauna, and the constant struggle against its harsh environment. Also, visitors may drop by the laboratory to witness the procedure used to prepare the specimens for display. *84 rue Dalhousie, tel. 418/692–1515. Admission: $6.00 adults, $4.50 senior citizens over 60, $4 children 5–17, under 5 free. Open late June–early Sept., daily 10–9; early Sept.–late June, daily 10–5.*

27 From rue Dalhousie, head east toward the river to the **Vieux-Port de Québec** (Old Port of Québec). The breezes here from the St. Lawrence provide a cool reprieve on a hot summer's day. The old harbor dates to the 17th century, when ships first arrived from Europe bringing supplies and settlers to the new colony. At one time this port was among the busiest on the continent: Between 1797 and 1897, Québec shipyards turned out more than 2,500 ships, many of which passed the 1,000-ton mark. Yet Québec City's port saw a rapid decline after steel replaced wood and the channel to Montréal was deepened to allow larger boats to reach a good port upstream. In 1984, the 72-acre port was restored with a $100 million grant from the federal government; today it encompasses several parks. You can stroll along the riverside promenade, where merchant and cruise ships are docked. At its northern end, where the St. Charles meets the St. Lawrence, a lock protects the marina in the Louise basin from the generous tides of the St. Lawrence. Because Québec City is close to the Atlantic Ocean, it is susceptible to tides, which can range from 9 to 16 feet. At the northwest area of the port, an exhibition center, **Port de Québec in the 19th Century,** presents the history of the port in relation to the lumber trade and shipbuilding. *100 rue St-André, tel. 418/648–3300.*

The port's northwestern tip features the **Marché du Vieux-Port** (Farmer's Market), where farmers come from the countryside to sell their fresh produce. *Admission free. Open May–Oct., daily 8–8.*

28 You are now in the ideal spot to explore Québec City's **antiques district.** One block south from rue St-André, antiques boutiques cluster along rue St-Pierre and rue St-Paul (*see* Shopping, *below*). Rue St-Paul was formerly part of a business district where warehouses, stores, and businesses once abounded. After World War I, when shipping and commercial activities plummeted, the street consisted mainly of empty warehouses and offices. In 1964, the low rent and commercial nature of the area attracted several antiques dealers,

who set up shops along rue St-Paul. Today numerous cafés, restaurants, and art galleries have turned this area into one of the town's more fashionable sections.

Walk west along rue St-Paul and turn left onto a steep brick incline called côte Dambourges; when you reach côte de la Cantonerie, take the stairs back on the cliff to rue des Remparts. Continue approximately a block west along rue des Remparts until you come to the
29 last building in a row of purple houses. **Maison Montcalm** was the home of French Général Louis-Joseph Montcalm from 1758 until the capitulation of New France. A plaque dedicated to the general is situated on the right side of the house.

Continue west on rue des Remparts and turn left on rue de
30 l'Arsenal, which brings you to the **Parc de l'Artillerie** (Artillery Park). This National Historic Park is a complex of 20 military, industrial, and civilian buildings, so situated to guard the St. Charles River and the Old Port. Its earliest buildings served as headquarters for the French garrison and were taken over in 1759 by the British Royal Artillery soldiers. The defense complex was used as a fortress, barracks, and cartridge factory during the American siege of Québec in 1775 and 1776. The area was converted to an industrial complex providing ammunition for the Canadian army from 1879 until 1964, when it became a historic park. *2 rue d'Auteuil, tel. 418/648–4205. Admission: $3 adults, $1.50 children 6–16, senior citizens and children under 6 free, $6 families. Open late June–early Sept., daily 10–5.*

One of the three buildings you may visit is a former **powder house,** which in 1903 became a shell foundry. The building houses a detailed model of Québec City in 1808, rendered by two surveyors in the office of the Royal Engineers Corps, Jean-Baptiste Duberger of Québec and John By of England. The wood model was intended to show British officials (it was sent to England in 1813) the strategic importance of Québec so that more money would be provided to expand the city's fortifications. The model, which details the city's houses, buildings, streets, and military structures, is an accurate portrayal of Québec during the early 19th century. *Open early Sept.–early May, daily 1–5; early May–early Sept., daily 10–5.*

The **Dauphine Redoubt** (*dauphine* is "heir apparent" in English) was named after the son of Louis XIV and was constructed from 1712 to 1748. It served as a barracks for the French garrison until 1760, when it became an officers' mess for the Royal Artillery Regiment. When the British called their soldiers back to England in 1871, it became a residence for the Canadian Arsenal superintendent. *Open late June–early Sept., daily 10–5.*

The **Officers' Quarters** building, a dwelling for Royal Artillery officers until 1871 when the British army departed, is now a museum for children, with shows on military life during the British regime. *Open late June–early Sept., daily 10–5.*

Tour 3: Outside the City Walls

Numbers in the margin correspond to points of interest on the Tour 3: Outside the City Walls map.

In the 20th century, Québec City grew into a modern metropolis outside the city walls and its historic confines. In this tour, you will see a glimpse of modern-day Québec City and explore neighborhoods typically left off the tourist track.

31 Start close to St-Louis Gate at **Parc de l'Esplanade** (Esplanade Park), the site of a former military drill and parade ground. In the 19th century, this area was a clear and uncluttered space surrounded by a picket fence and poplar trees. Today you'll find the completely renovated **Poudrière de l'Esplanade** (Powder Magazine), which the British constructed in 1820; it houses a model depicting the evolution of the wall surrounding the Old City. *100 rue St-Louis, tel. 418/648–7016. Admission free. Open Apr., daily 1–5; May–Oct., daily 10–5.*

Esplanade Park is also the starting point to walk the city's 4.6 kilometers (3 miles) of walls; in the summer, guided tours begin here. The French began building ramparts along the city's natural cliff as early as 1690 to protect themselves from British invaders. But by 1759, when the British gained control of New France, the walls were still incomplete; the British took a century to finish them.

From the Powder Magazine, head south on Côte de la Citadelle,
32 which leads directly to the **Citadelle** (Citadel). Built at the city's highest point, the Citadel is the largest fortified base in North America still occupied by troops. The 25-building fortress was intended to protect the port, prevent the enemy from taking up a position on the Plains of Abraham, and provide a last refuge in case of an attack. The French had constructed previous structures on this site based on plans of Québec engineer Gaspard Chaussegros de Léry, who came to the region in 1716.

Having inherited incomplete fortifications, the British sought to complete the Citadel to protect themselves against retaliations from the French. As fate would have it, by the time the Citadel was completed in 1832, the invasions and attacks against Québec City had ended.

Since 1920 the Citadel has served as a base for the Royal 22nd Regiment. A collection of firearms, uniforms, and decorations from the 17th century is housed in the **Royal 22nd Regiment Museum,** located in the former powder house, built in 1750. If weather permits, you may witness the Changing of the Guard, an elaborate ceremony in which the troops parade before the Citadel in the customary red coats and black fur hats. *Côte de la Citadelle, tel. 418/648–3563. Guided tours only. Admission: $4 adults, $2 students under 18; free for people with disabilities. Open mid-Mar.–Apr., daily 10–3; May and June, daily 9–4; July–early Sept., daily 9–6; early Sept.–Oct., daily 9–4; Nov.–early Feb. and mid-Feb.–mid-March, groups only (reservations required); early Feb.–mid-Feb., daily 10–2. Changing of the Guard: mid-June–Labor Day, daily 10. Tattoo: July and Aug., Tues., Thurs., and weekends 7* PM *(for visitors on 6* PM *tour only).*

Retrace your steps back down côte de la Citadelle to Grande Allée.
33 Continue west until you come to the Renaissance-style **Parliament Buildings,** which mark the area known as **Parliament Hill,** headquarters of the provincial government. The constitution of 1791 designated Québec City the capital of Lower Canada until the 1840 Act of Union that united both Upper and Lower Canada and made Montréal the capital. In 1867, the Act of Confederation, uniting Québec, Ontario, New Brunswick, and Nova Scotia, made Québec City the capital of Québec province. Today the government is the biggest employer in Québec City, with about 30,000 civil servants working and living in the area.

The Parliament Buildings, erected between 1877 and 1884, are the seat of **L'Assemblée Nationale** (the National Assembly) of 125 pro-

Tour 3: Outside the City Walls

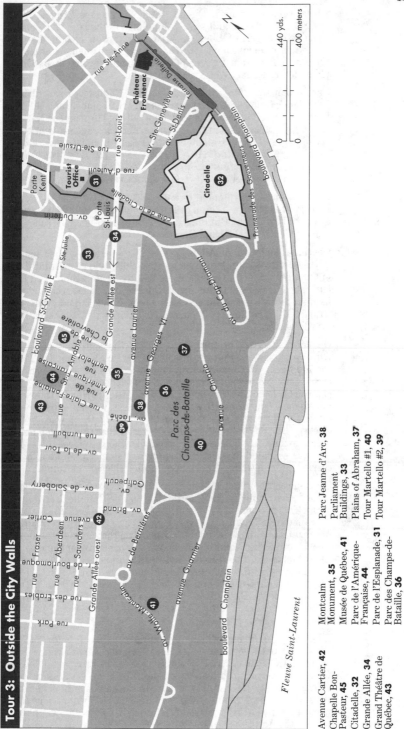

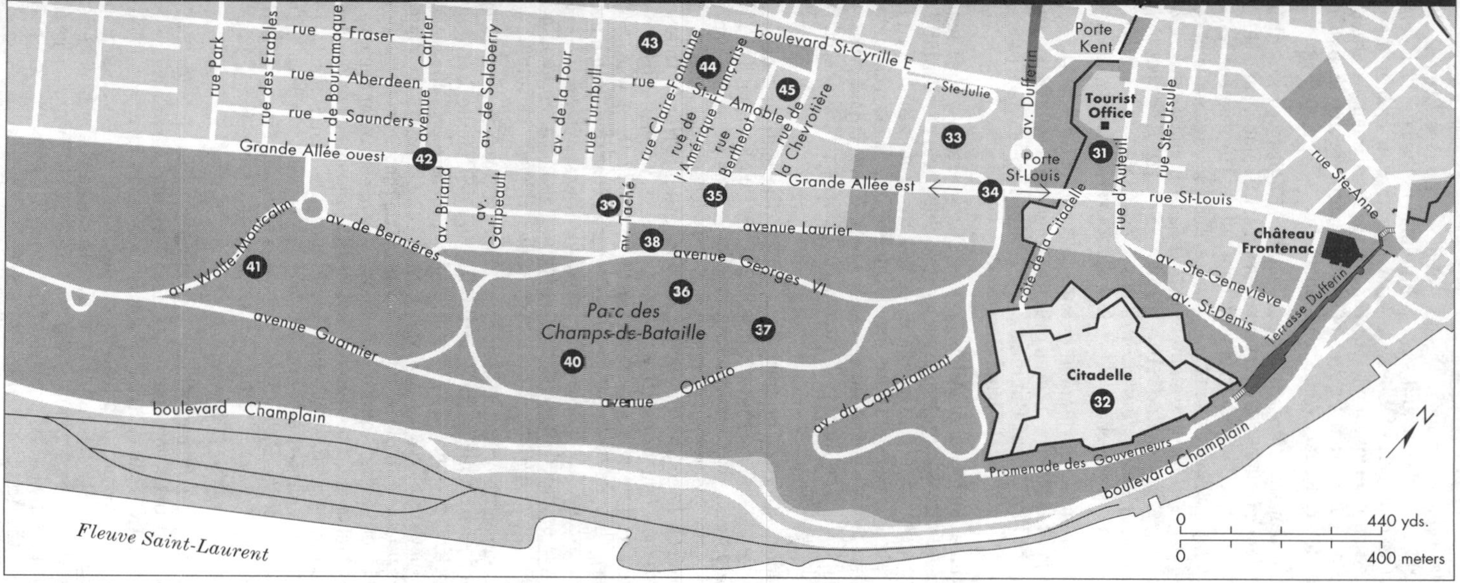

Avenue Cartier, **42**
Chapelle Bon-Pasteur, **45**
Citadelle, **32**
Grande Allée, **34**
Grand Théâtre de Québec, **43**
Montcalm Monument, **35**
Musée de Québec, **41**
Parc de l'Amérique-Française, **44**
Parc de l'Esplanade, **31**
Parc des Champs-de-Bataille, **36**
Parc Jeanne d'Arc, **38**
Parliament Buildings, **33**
Plains of Abraham, **37**
Tour Martello #1, **40**
Tour Martello #2, **39**

vincial representatives. Québec architect Eugène-Étienne Taché designed the classic and stately buildings in the late 17th-century Renaissance style of Louis XIV, with four wings set in a square around an interior court. In front of the Parliament, statues pay tribute to important figures of Québec history: Cartier, de Champlain, de Frontenac, Wolfe, and Montcalm.

The Parliament offers a 30-minute tour (in English or French) of the President's Gallery, the National Assembly Chamber, and the Legislative Council Chamber. The chamber of the 125-member National Assembly is decorated in green, white, and gold—colors that correspond to the House of Commons in both London and Ottawa. *Cnr. of av. Dufferin and Grande Allée E, door 3, tel. 418/643–7239. Admission free. Guided tours Jan.–May and Sept.–Nov., weekdays 9–4:30; late June–Aug., daily 9–4:30. Reservations required.*

Across from the Parliament on the south side of Grande Allée is the **Manège Militaire,** a turreted granite armory built in 1888, four years after the Parliament Buildings. It was also designed by Taché. It is still a drill hall for the 22nd Regiment.

34 Continue along **Grande Allée,** Québec City's version of the Champs-Elysées, with its array of trendy cafés, clubs, and restaurants. One of the oldest streets, Grande Allée was the route people took from outlying areas to sell their furs in Québec City. The street actually has four names: in the old city, it is rue St-Louis; outside the walls, Grande Allée; farther west, chemin St-Louis; and farther still, boulevard Laurier.

One block after the armory, on your left (the south side of Grande
Allée) you'll come to Place Montcalm. If you turn left, you'll be facing
35 the **Montcalm Monument.** France and Canada joined together to
erect this monument honoring Louis-Joseph Montcalm, who
claimed his fame by winning four major battles in North America—
but his most famous battle was the one he lost, when the British con-
quered New France on September 13, 1759. Montcalm was north of
Québec City at Beauport when he learned that the British attack
was imminent. He quickly assembled his troops to meet the enemy
and was wounded in battle in the leg and stomach. Montcalm was
carried into the walled city, where he died the next morning.

Continue south on Place Montcalm to one of North America's larg-
36 est and most scenic parks, **Parc des Champs-de-Bataille** (Battlefields
Park). This 250-acre area of gently rolling slopes offers unparalleled
37 views of the St. Lawrence River. West of the citadel are the **Plains of
Abraham,** the site of the famous 1759 battle that decided the fate of
New France. The Plains of Abraham were named after the river pilot Abraham Martin, who arrived in 1620 and owned several acres
here. *A free shuttle bus circles the Plains of Abraham, with 11 stops.
Also, a free guided bus tour of the Plains of Abraham is offered,
leaving from the Battlefield Park Interpretation Center (Pavillon
Baillargé, Musée de Québec, tel. 418/648–4071) mid-June–Aug. Telephone for departure times.*

Take avenue Laurier, which runs parallel to Battlefields Park, a
38 block west until you come to a neatly tended garden called **Parc
Jeanne d'Arc** (Joan of Arc Park); it is abundant with colorful flowers
and is centered on an equestrian statue of Jeanne d'Arc. A symbol of
courage, this statue stands in tribute to the heroes of 1759 near the
place where New France was lost to the British. The park also commemorates the Canadian national anthem *Oh Canada;* it was played
here for the first time on June 24, 1880.

If you continue west on avenue Laurier, you'll see a stone oval de-
39 fense tower, **Tour Martello #2** (Martello Tower), on the north corner of avenue Taché and avenue Laurier. This is the second of four Martello towers built in the early 19th century around Québec City to slow the enemy's approach to the city. At the left, toward the south
40 end of the park, stands **Tour Martello #1,** which was built between 1802 and 1810.

Of the 16 Martello towers in all of Canada, four were built in Québec City because the British government feared an invasion after the American Revolution. Tour #3 was located near Jeffery Hale Hospital in order to guard westward entry to the city, but it was demolished in 1904. Tour #4 is located on rue Lavigueur overlooking rivière St-Charles (St. Charles River). Towers 1 and 2 are open to the public; the first exhibits the history of the four structures, the second has an astrology display.

Continue a block west on rue de Bernières and then follow avenue George V along the outskirts of Battlefields Park until it intersects with avenue Wolfe-Montcalm. You'll come to the tall **Wolfe Monument,** which marks the place where the British general died. Wolfe landed his troops less than 2 miles (about 3 kilometers) from the city's walls; the 4,500 English soldiers scaled the cliff and opened fire on the Plains of Abraham. Wolfe was mortally wounded in battle and was carried behind the lines to this spot.

Turn left on avenue Wolfe-Montcalm for a leisurely stroll through
41 the **Musée de Québec** (Québec Museum). This neoclassical beaux-arts showcase houses the finest collection of Québec art. With one of the largest acquisition budgets of Canada's museums, it possesses more than 18,000 traditional and contemporary pieces. The portraits done by artists well known in the area, such as Ozias Leduc (1864–1955) and Horatio Walker (1858–1938), are particularly notable; some locals find paintings of their relatives on the walls here. The museum's very formal and dignified building in Battlefields Park was designed by Wilfrid Lacroix and erected in 1933 to commemorate the tricentennial anniversary of the founding of Québec. The museum recently received $22.4 million from the provincial government to renovate the original building, incorporating the space of a nearby, abandoned prison dating to 1867. A hallway of cells, with the iron bars and courtyard still intact, has been preserved as part of a permanent exhibition of the prison's history. *1 av. Wolfe-Montcalm, tel. 418/643–2150. Admission: $4.75 adults, $3.75 senior citizens, $2.75 students, children under 16 free. Open June–Aug., Thurs.–Tues. 10–5:45, Wed. 10–9:45; Sept.–May, Tues. and Thurs.–Sun. 10–5:45, Wed. 10–9:45.*

From the museum head north on avenue Wolfe-Montcalm, turning right on Grande Allée and walking a block until you reach avenue Cartier. At 115 Grande Allée Ouest is the **Krieghoff House.** This typical Québec home with its bell-shape roof and dormer windows is closed to tourists, but it's worth noting for its former owner, Cornelius Krieghoff, who lived there from 1858 to 1860. One of Canada's most famous landscape painters, Krieghoff was among the first to depict Québec scenery. Born in Amsterdam in 1815, he served in the American army, married a French Canadian in 1839, and settled in Québec in 1852.

42 Head north on **avenue Cartier** to indulge in the pleasures offered by the many good restaurants, clubs, and cafés lining the block. On the east side, stroll through the food mall, **Alimentation Petit-Cartier** (1191 avenue Cartier, tel. 418/524–3682). Here you'll find a super-

market and shops that sell French delicacies—cheeses, pastries, breads, and candies. Some of the better stores are **Boulangerie La Mère-Michele**, for breads and pastries such as petit fours, and **Le Vrac du Quartier**, where you can buy everything from spices to cookies in amounts you measure yourself. The mall also houses three restaurants: Café Rousseau, Le Piazetta, and Le Graffiti (*see* Dining, *below*).

Time Out On the east side of avenue Cartier is **Café Krieghoff**, named after the 19th-century painter who lived nearby. Grab a newspaper, play a game of chess, drink some of the best coffee in town, and complement it with quiche, a croissant, or dessert. *1089 av. Cartier, tel. 418/522-3711. MC, V. Open Sun.–Wed. 7 AM–midnight, Thurs.–Sat. 7 AM–1 AM.*

If you continue north along avenue Cartier, the first major intersection is boulevard St-Cyrille Est. Turn right and walk two blocks to
43 the concrete modern building of the **Grand Théâtre de Québec**, a center for the city's performing arts and home of the music school, La Conservatoire de Musique de Québec. Opened in 1971, the theater incorporates two main halls, both named after 19th-century Canadian poets. The "Grande Salle" of Louis-Frechette, named after the first Québec poet and writer to be honored by the French Academy, holds 1,800 seats and is used for concerts, opera, and theater. The "Petite Salle" of Octave-Crémazie, used for experimental theater and variety shows, derives its name from the poet who stirred the rise of Québec nationalism in the mid-19th century.

As the complex was being constructed, Montréal architect Victor Prus commissioned Jordi Bonet, a Québec sculptor, to work simultaneously on a three-wall mural. The themes depicted in the three sections are death, life, and liberty. Bonet wrote "La Liberté" on one wall to symbolize the Québecois' struggle for freedom and cultural distinction. The theater has a full repertoire in the winter, but no shows in the summer. *269 boul. St-Cyrille E, tel. 418/646-0609. Guided tours offered daily 9–5. Reservations required.*

High-waving flags east of the Grand Théâtre are displayed in the
44 **Parc de l'Amérique-Française**, dedicated to places in North America with a French-speaking population. Québec's own Fleur de Lys leads the way. The colors of blue and white, an emblem of Sun King Louis XIV, constitute a reminder of Québec's French origins, culture, and language. Inaugurated in 1985 by Québec Prime Minister Réne Lévesque, the park also flies flags from Acadia, British Columbia, Louisiana, Manitoba, Saskatchewan, and Ontario.

Take rue Claire-Fontaine a block south, turn left on rue St-Amable, and then left again on rue de la Chevrotière. On the west side of the
45 street you'll see the **Chapelle Bon-Pasteur** (Bon-Pasteur Chapel), which is surrounded by modern office complexes. This slender church with a steep sloping roof was designed by Charles Baillargé in 1868. Its ornate interior in a baroque style has carved wood designs painted elaborately in gold leaf. The chapel houses 32 religious paintings done by the nuns of the community from 1868 to 1910. Classical concerts are performed here between October and June. *1080 rue de la Chevrotière, tel. 418/641-1069 or 418/648-9710. Admission free. Open May–Sept., Tues.–Sun. 1–4; Oct.–Apr., by reservation only; musical artists' Mass Sun. at 10:45.*

Across rue de la Chevrotière is the entrance of a large, gray concrete modern office tower called **Anima G** (Complex G), Québec's tallest office building. The structure, 31 stories high, has by far the best view of the city and the environs. An express elevator ascends to the observation gallery on top. *1037 rue de la Chevrotière, tel. 418/644–9841. Admission free. Open late Jan.–early Dec., weekdays 10–4, weekends and holidays 1–5.*

What to See and Do with Children

Aquarium du Québec (Québec Aquarium). The aquarium, situated above the St. Lawrence River, houses more than 300 species of marine life, including reptiles, exotic fish, and seals from the lower St. Lawrence River. A wooded picnic area makes this spot ideal for a family outing. The Québec City transit system, Commission de Transport de la Communauté Urbaine de Québec (CTCUQ) (tel. 418/659–5264), runs buses here. *1675 av. des Hôtels, Sainte-Foy, tel. 418/659–5266. Admission: $5 adults, $1 children under 14, $4.25 senior citizens, $10 families. Open daily 9–5.*

Jardin Zoologique du Québec (Québec Zoological Gardens). Children usually enjoy going to zoos, but this one is especially scenic because of the DuBerger River, which traverses the grounds. About 250 animal species reside here, including bears, wildcats, primates, and birds of prey. Children will enjoy the farm and the horse-drawn carriage rides. The zoo is situated 11 kilometers (7 miles) west of Québec City on Route 73. Québec Urban Community Transit (tel. 418/627–2511) operates buses here. *8191 av. du Zoo, Charlesbourg, tel. 418/622–0312. Admission: (May–Oct.) $7 adults, $1 children under 14, $5 senior citizens, $14 families; (Nov.–Apr.) $4.25 adults, $1 children under 14, $3 senior citizens, $8 families. Open May–Oct., daily 9:30–6; Nov.–Apr., daily 9:30–5.*

Parc Cartier-Brébeuf. Stretched along the north bank of the St. Charles River, this national historic park commemorates the area where French explorer Jacques Cartier spent his first winter in Canada (1535–36); it also pays tribute to Father Jean de Brébeuf, founder of the Jesuit Order in New France. A replica of the *Grande Hermine*, the ship Cartier used on his second expedition to America, is stationed here. Playgrounds and 9 kilometers (5½ miles) of walking paths are available. *175 rue de l'Espinay, tel. 418/648–4038. Admission free. Call ahead for hrs.*

Parc de l'Artillerie (Artillery Park). This 20-building complex near St-Jean Gate has for centuries played an important part in the city's defense structures. The Officers' Quarters, barracks for Royal Artillery officers until 1871, has a special program for children designed to show how the military lived when Québec was a British colony, from 1759 to 1867. Children's toys and educational games are also available. *2 rue d'Auteil, tel. 418/648–4205. Admission: $3 adults, $1.50 children 6–16, $6 families, senior citizens and children under 6 free. Open late June–early Sept., daily 10–5.*

Parc du Porche. This playground has ladders and swings in a historic setting just outside Place Royale (between rue du Porche and rue de l'Union). *Admission free. Open daily.*

Shopping

Shopping is European-style along the fashionable streets of Québec City. The boutiques and specialty shops clustered along narrow streets (such as rue du Petit-Champlain, or rue Buade and rue St-Jean in the Latin Quarter) are located within one of the most striking historic settings on the continent.

Prices in Québec City tend to be on a par for the most part with those in Montréal and other North American cities, so you won't have much luck hunting for bargains. When sales occur, they are usually listed in the French daily newspaper, *Le Soleil*.

Stores are generally open Monday through Wednesday 9:30–5:30, Thursday and Friday until 9, and Saturday until 5. During the summer, shops may be open seven days a week, and most have later evening hours.

Shopping Centers

The mall situated closest to the Old City is **Place Québec** (5 Place Québec, tel. 418/529–0551), near the National Assembly. This multilevel shopping complex and convention center with 40 stores is connected to the Hilton International. **Alimentation Petit-Cartier** (1191 av. Cartier, tel. 418/524–3682), located off Grande Allée and a 15-minute walk from St-Louis Gate, is a food mall for gourmets, with everything from utensils to petits fours.

Other shopping centers are approximately a 15-minute drive west along Grande Allée. **Place Sainte-Foy** (2450 boul. Laurier, Sainte-Foy, tel. 418/653–4184) has 120 specialty stores. Next door is **Place de la Cité** (2600 boul. Laurier, Sainte-Foy, tel. 418/657–6920), with 120 boutiques. And finally there is the massive **Place Laurier** (2700 boul. Laurier, Sainte-Foy, tel. 418/653–9318), with more than 350 stores.

Quartier Petit-Champlain (tel. 418/692–2613) in Lower Town is a pedestrian mall with some 40 boutiques, local businesses, and restaurants. This popular district is the best area to find native Québec arts and crafts, such as wood sculptures, weaving, ceramics, and jewelry. Recommended stores in the area are **Poten-Ciel** (27 rue du Petit-Champlain, tel. 418/692–1743) for ceramics and **Pauline Pelletier** (38 rue du Petit-Champlain, tel. 418/692–4871) for porcelain.

Department Stores

Large department stores can be found in the malls of the suburb of Sainte-Foy, but some have outlets inside Québec City's walls.

Holt Renfrew & Co., Ltd. (Place Sainte-Foy, Sainte-Foy, tel. 418/656–6783), one of the city's more exclusive stores, carries furs, perfume, and tailored designer collections for men and women.

La Baie (Place Laurier, Sainte-Foy, tel. 418/627–5959) is Québec's version of the Canadian Hudson's Bay Company conglomerate, founded in 1670 by Montréal trappers Pierre Radisson and Medard de Groseillers; the company established the first network of stores in the Canadian frontier. Today, La Baie carries both men's and women's clothing and household wares.

Simons (20 côte de la Fabrique, tel. 418/692–3630), one of Québec City's oldest family stores, used to be the city's only source for fine British woolens and tweeds, and now the store has added a large selection of designer clothing, linens, and other household items.

Food and Flea Markets

Marché du Vieux-Port enables farmers from the Québec countryside to sell their fresh produce in the Old Port near rue St-André, from May through October, 8–8.

Rue du Trésor hosts a flea market near the Place d'Armes that features sketches, paintings, and etchings by local artists. Fine portraits of the Québec City landscape and region are plentiful. Good, inexpensive souvenirs also may be purchased here (*see* Tour 1, *above*).

Specialty Stores

Antiques Québec City's antiques district is located in the area of rue St-Paul and rue St-Pierre, across from the Old Port. French Canadian, Victorian, and art deco furniture, along with clocks, silverware, and porcelain, are some of the rare collectibles that can be found here. Authentic Québec pine furniture, characterized by simple forms and lines, is becoming increasingly rare and costly.

L'Héritage Antiquités (110 rue St-Paul, tel. 418/692–1681) specializes in precious Québecois furniture from the 18th century.
Antiquités Zaor (112 rue St-Paul, tel. 418/692–0581), the oldest store on rue St-Paul, is still the best place in the area to find excellent English, French, and Canadian antiques. The floor upstairs houses a fine collection of Québec wood furniture.

Art **Aux Multiples Collections** (43 rue Buade, tel. 418/692–4298) and **Galerie Brousseau et Brousseau** (Château Frontenac, 1 rue des Carrières, tel. 418/694–1828) feature a good selection of Inuit art done by Canada's native people, as well as such antique furniture and accessories as sculpted wood ducks.
Galerie Madeleine Lacerte (1 côte Dinan, tel. 418/692–1566), situated in Lower Town, sells contemporary art and sculpture.

Books English-language books are difficult to find in Québec. One of the city's first bookstores, **Librarie Garneau** (24 côte de la Fabrique, tel. 418/692–4262), is centrally located near City Hall and carries mostly volumes in French. Other popular bookstores in the city include **La Maison Anglaise** (Place de la Cité, Sainte-Foy, tel. 418/654–9523), with the best selection of English-language titles in the area, and **Classic Bookshop** (Place Laurier, boul. Laurier, tel. 418/653–8683).

Clothing **François Côté Collections** (35 rue Buade, tel. 418/692–6016) is a chic boutique with fashions for men.
La Maison Darlington (7 rue Buade, tel. 418/692–2268) carries well-made woolens, dresses, and suits for women by fine names in couture.
Louis Laflamme (Place Québec, tel. 418/523–6633) has a large selection of stylish men's clothes.

Crafts **Les Trois Colombes Inc.** (46 rue St-Louis, tel. 418/694–1114) sells hand-made items. You will find two floors filled with such goods as clothing made from hand-spun fabric, Indian and Inuit carvings, jewelry, pottery, and paintings.

Fur Fur trade has been an important industry for centuries in the area. Québec City is a good place to purchase high-quality furs at fairly reasonable prices. Since 1894, one of the best furriers in town has been **Jos Robitaille** (Place Sainte-Foy, Sainte-Foy, tel. 418/650–6185). The department store **J.B. Laliberté** (Mail Centre-Ville, tel. 418/525–4841) also carries furs.

Gifts **Collection Lazuli** (774 rue St-Jean, tel. 418/525–6528) features a tasteful selection of unusual art objects, gifts, and jewelry from around the world.

Jewelry **Bijouterie Louis Perrier** (48 rue du Petit-Champlain, tel. 418/692–4633) has Québec-made gold and silver jewelry. Exclusive jewelry can also be found at **Zimmermann** (46 côte de la Fabrique, tel. 418/692–2672).

Sports and Fitness

Two parks are central to Québec City: the 250-acre Battlefields Park, with its panoramic views of the St. Lawrence River, and Cartier-Brébeuf Park, which runs along the St. Charles River. Both are favorite spots for such outdoor sports as jogging, biking, and cross-country skiing. Scenic rivers and mountains close by (no more than 30 minutes by car) make this city ideal for the sporting life. For information about sports and fitness, contact **Québec City Region and Convention Bureau** (60 rue d'Auteuil, Québec G1R 4C4, tel. 418/692–2471) or **Québec City Bureau of Parks and Recreation** (65 rue Ste-Anne, 5th Floor, Québec, G1R 4S9, tel. 418/691–6278).

Participant Sports

Bicycling Short bike paths along rolling hills are found in Battlefields Park, located at the south side of the city. The best bet for a longer ride over flat terrain is the path north of the city skirting the St. Charles River; this route can be reached from Third Avenue near the Marie de l'Incarnation Bridge. Paths along the côte de Beaupré, beginning at the union of the St. Charles and St. Lawrence rivers, are especially scenic. They begin northeast of the city at rue de la Verandrye and boulevard Montmorency and continue 10 kilometers (6 miles) along the coast to Montmorency Falls.

Bicycles can be rented at **Location Petit Champlain** (94 rue du Petit-Champlain, tel. 418/692–2817).

Boating Lakes around the Québec City area have facilities for boating and canoeing. Take Route 73 north of the city to Saint-Dunstan de Lac Beauport, then take Exit 157, boulevard du Lac, to **Lac Beauport** (tel. 418/849–2821), one of the best nearby resorts. Boats and boards can be rented at **Campex** (8 chemin de l'Orrée, Lac Beauport, tel. 418/849–2236) for canoeing, kayaking, and windsurfing. You can also rent boats in **Lac St-Joseph,** 40 kilometers (25 miles) northwest of Québec City, at **La Vigie** (tel. 418/875–2727).

Fishing Permits are needed for hunting and fishing in Québec. They are available from the **Ministry of Recreation, Hunting, and Fishing** (Place de la Capitale, 150 boul. Réné Levesque E, tel. 418/643–3127). The ministry also publishes a pamphlet on fishing regulations that is available at tourist information offices.

Réserve Faunique des Laurentides (tel. 418/848–2422) is a wildlife reserve with good lakes for fishing, approximately 48 kilometers (30 miles) north of Québec City via Route 73.

Golf The Québec City region has 18 golf courses, and several are open to the public. Reservations during summer months are essential. **Club de Golf de Cap Rouge** (4600 rue St-Felix, tel. 418/653–9381) in Cap Rouge, with 18 holes, is one of the closest courses to Québec City. **Club de Golf de Beauport** (3533 rue Clemenceau, tel. 418/663–1578), a nine-hole course, is 20 minutes by car via Route 73 N. **Parc du Mont Sainte-Anne** (Rte. 360, C.P. 653 Beaupré, tel. 418/827–3778), a half-hour drive north of Québec, has one of the best 18-hole courses in the region.

Health and Fitness Clubs One of the city's most popular health clubs is **Club Entrain** (Place de la Cité, 2600 boul. Laurier, tel. 418/658–7771). Facilities include a weight room with Nautilus, a sauna, a whirlpool, aerobics classes, and racquetball and squash courts.

Nonguests at **Hôtel Radisson des Gouverneurs** (690 boul. Réné Levesque E, tel. 418/647–1717) can use the health club facilities, which include weights, a sauna, a whirlpool, and an outdoor heated pool, for a $5 fee.

Hilton International Québec (3 Place Québec, tel. 418/647–2411) has a smaller health club with weights, a sauna, and an outdoor pool available to nonguests for a $10 fee.

Pool facilities cost $2.25 at the **YMCA** (855 av. Holland, tel. 418/683–2155).

Hiking/Jogging The Parc Cartier-Brébeuf, north of the Old City along the banks of the St. Charles River, has about 13 kilometers (8 miles) of hiking trails. For more mountainous terrain, head 19 kilometers (12 miles) north via Route 73 to Lac Beauport. **Villages des Sports** (1860 boul. Valcartier, Val Cartier, tel. 418/844–3725), a man-made sports complex 24 kilometers (15 miles) from downtown on Route 371, has 16 kilometers (10 miles) of trails. For jogging, Battlefields Park and Parc Cartier-Brébeuf are the most popular places in the area.

Horseback Riding **Jacques Cartier Excursions** (978 av. Jacques Cartier N, Tewkesbury, tel. 418/848–7238), also known for rafting, offers summer and winter horseback riding. An excursion includes an hour of instruction and three hours of riding; the cost is $49 on weekends and $35 weekdays in spring and fall, and $55 on weekends and $39 on weekdays in winter.

Rafting Jacques Cartier River, about 48 kilometers (30 miles) northwest of Québec City, provides good rafting; the waterway flows south from Laurentian Park 56 kilometers (35 miles) from Québec City into the St. Lawrence River.

Jacques Cartier Excursions (978 av. Jacques Cartier N, Tewkesbury, G0A 4P0, tel. 418/848–7238) offers rafting trips on the Jacques Cartier River. Tours originate from Tewkesbury, a half-hour drive from Québec City, from May through September. A half-day tour costs $55 on weekends, $39 on weekdays. A full day costs $68 on weekends, $49 on weekdays. Wet suits cost $12 extra. In the winter, snow-rafting excursions are available, and include a two-hour sleigh ride and all-day mountain sliding in river rafts. The total cost is $49.

Nouveau Monde, Expeditions en Rivière (C.P. 100, chemin de la Rivière Rouge, Calumet, J0V 1B0, tel. 800/361–5033) has excursions on the Jacques Cartier River from mid-May through September. A 3-hour excursion costs $44. Reserve one month in advance for weekends, two weeks in advance for weekdays.

Skating The ice-skating season runs December through March. There is a 3.8-kilometer (2.4-mile) stretch for skating along the St. Charles River, between the Samson and Marie de l'Incarnation bridges, January through March, depending on the ice. Rentals and changing rooms are nearby. *Skating hours: weekdays noon–10, weekends 10–10.*

Place d'Youville, just outside St-Jean Gate, has an outdoor skating rink open from November to April. Nighttime skating can be done at **Villages des Sports** (1860 boul. Valcartier, Val Cartier, tel. 418/844–3725).

Skiing *Cross-country* Numerous trails exist for cross-country skiing enthusiasts. Battlefields Park on Québec City's south side, which you can access on Place Montcalm, has scenic marked trails. For information, call **Québec City Bureau of Parks and Recreation** (tel. 418/691–6278). Lac Beauport, 19 kilometers (12 miles) north of the city, has more than 20 marked trails (250 kilometers; 155 miles). Contact **Les Sentiers du Moulin** (99 chemin du Moulin, tel. 418/849–2778). **Parc du Mont Sainte-Anne** (Rte. 360, C.P. 400 Beaupré, G0A 1E0, tel. 418/827–4561), which is 40 kilometers (25 miles) northeast of Québec City, has 235 kilometers (141 miles) of cross-country trails. Contact **Rang Saint-Julien** (tel. 418/827–4561, ext. 408) for more information.

Downhill Four alpine ski resorts, all with night skiing, are located within a 30-minute drive of Québec City. **Parc du Mont Sainte-Anne** (Rte. 360, C.P. 400 Beaupré, G0A 1E0, tel. 418/827–4561) is the largest resort in eastern Canada, with 50 downhill trails, 12 lifts, and a gondola. **Stoneham** (1420 av. Hibou, Stoneham, Québec, G0A 4P0, tel. 418/848–2411) is known for its long, easy slopes with 25 downhill runs and 10 lifts. Two smaller alpine centers can be found at Lac Beauport: 14 trails at **Mont St-Castin** (82 chemin le Tour du Lac, Box 1129, Lac Beauport, Québec G0A 2C0, tel. 418/849–6776) and 24 trails at **Le Relais** (1084 boul. du Lac, Box 280, Lac Beauport, Québec G0A 2C0, tel. 418/849–1851). Upon request, most major hotels arrange skibus service for guests for a fee.

A municipal bus service, **Skibus** (tel. 418/627–2511), is offered on weekends. It leaves from Place Laurier (2700 boul. Laurier, Sainte-Foy) at 8 AM for Stoneham and Mont Sainte-Anne and returns once a day (at 4:05 from Stoneham, and at 4:15 from Mont Sainte-Anne). The cost each way is $3.50 for Stoneham and $4 for Mont Sainte-Anne.

Visite Touristique de Québec (tel. 418/653–9722) offers a bus service to Mont Sainte-Anne and Stoneham. For Mont Sainte-Anne, it leaves from major hotels in Québec daily between 7:30 AM and 8:30 AM and returns at 4:30 PM. For Stoneham, it leaves from major hotels daily between 7:45 AM and 8:45 AM, and returns at 4:30 PM. It costs $7 each way. Telephone for reservations.

Brochures about ski centers in Québec are available at Québec Tourism and Convention Bureaus or by phoning 800/363–7777.

Tennis At **Montcalm Tennis Club** (901 boul. Champlain, Sillery, tel. 418/687–1250), south of Québec City in Sillery, four indoor and seven outdoor courts are open daily from 8 AM to 10 PM. Twelve indoor courts are also available at **Tennisport** (6280 boul. Hammel, Ancienne Lorette, tel. 418/872–0111).

Spectator Sports

Tickets for sporting events can be purchased at **Colisée de Québec** (Québec Coliseum; 2205 av. du Colisée, tel. 418/523–3333 or 800/463–3333) or through Billetech, whose main outlet is at the **Grand Théâtre de Québec** (269 boul. René Levesque E, tel. 418/643–8131). Other outlets are at Bibliothèque Gabrielle-Roy, Palais Montcalm, La Baie department store (Place Laurier, Sainte-Foy, tel. 418/627–5959), and Provigo supermarkets. The outlet hours vary depending on the location.

Harness Racing Horse racing is on view at the racetrack **Hippodrome de Québec.** *C.P. 2053, Parc de l'Exposition, tel. 418/524–5283. Admission: $2.25 adults, $1.25 senior citizens, children under 12 free.*

Hockey A National Hockey League team, the Québec Nordiques, plays at the **Colisée de Québec** (Québec Coliseum). *2205 av. du Colisée, Parc de l'Exposition, tel. 418/523-3333 or 800/463-3333. Open Oct.–Mar., daily.*

Dining

Québec City reveals its French heritage most obviously in its cuisine. You'll discover a French touch in the city's numerous cafés and brasseries and in the artful presentation of dishes at local restaurants. Most dining establishments usually have a selection of dishes à la carte, but you'll often experience more creative specialties by opting for the table d'hôte, a two- to four-course meal chosen daily by the chef. At dinner, many restaurants will offer a *menu de dégustation*, a five- to seven-course dinner of the chef's finest creations.

Although many visitors will find a gourmet meal in their price range, budget-conscious diners may want to try out the more expensive establishments during lunchtime. Lunch usually costs about 30% less than dinner, and many of the same dishes are available. Lunch is usually served 11:30 through 2:30; dinner, 6:30 until about 11. You should tip about 15% of the bill.

Québec City is the best place in the province to sample French Canadian cuisine, composed of robust, uncomplicated dishes that make use of the region's bounty of foods, including fowl and wild game (caribou, quail, venison), maple syrup, and various berries and nuts. Because Québec has a cold climate for a good portion of the year, it has a traditionally heavy cuisine, with such specialties as *cretons* (pâtés), *tourtière* (meat pie), and *tarte au sucre* (maple-syrup pie).

Highly recommended restaurants in each price category are indicated by a star ★.

Category	Cost*
$$$$	over $30
$$$	$20–$30
$$	$10–$20
$	under $10

**per person, excluding drinks, service, 7% federal sales tax, and 4% provincial sales tax*

$$$$

★ **A la Table de Serge Bruyère.** This restaurant has put Québec on the map of great gastronomic cities. The city's most famous culinary institution serves classic French cuisine presented with plenty of crystal, silver, and fresh flowers and with relentless attention to detail. Only one sitting is offered each night. Chef Serge Bruyère came to Québec City from Lyons, France, and worked at various restaurants until he opened his own in 1980. The *menu gourmand* is a five-course meal for about $50. The extensive wine list starts at $26 and goes up to $800. Wine is also available by the glass. Specialties include scampi in puff pastry with fresh tomatoes, scallop stew with watercress, and duckling supreme with blueberry sauce. In 1984, Bruyère expanded inside the restaurant's old 1843 Livernois build-

Québec City Dining and Lodging

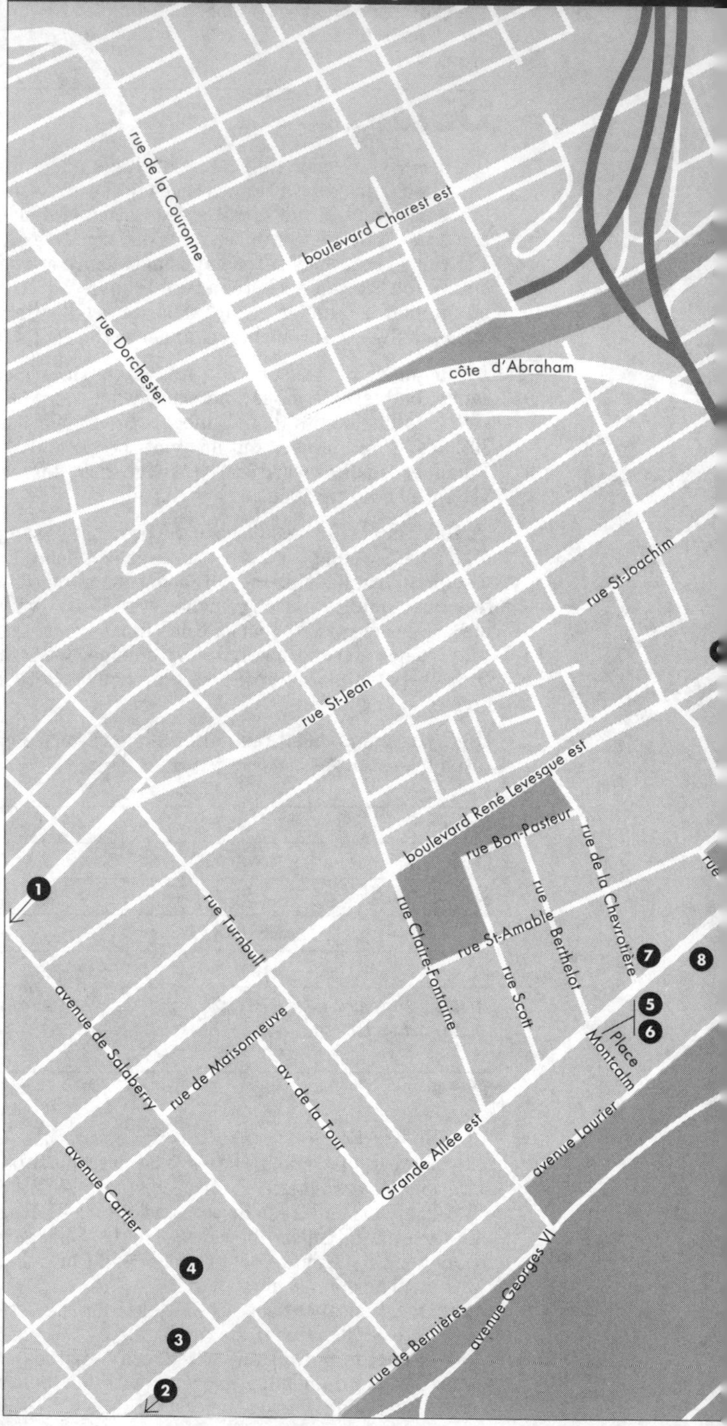

Dining

À la Table de Serge Bruyère, **19**
Aux Anciens Canadiens, **23**
Café de la Paix, **22**
Casse-Crepe Breton, **16**
Chalet Suisse, **21**
Chez Temporel, **20**
Gambrinus, **33**
L'Anse aux Barques, **31**
L'Apsara, **11**
L'Astral, **5**
Le Café de la Terrasse, **28**
Le Cochon Dingue, **30**
Le Graffiti, **4**
Le Marie Clarisse, **32**
Le Paris Brest, **7**
Le Saint-Amour, **12**
L'Echaudée, **34**
Les Frères de la Côte, **18**
Mille Feuille, **15**
Paparazzi, **2**

Lodging

Château Bonne Entente, **1**
Château Frontenac, **29**
Château de la Terrasse, **27**
Hilton International Québec, **10**
Hôtel du Théâtre, **14**
Hôtel Loews Le Concorde, **6**
Hôtel Radisson Gouverneurs Québec, **9**
L'Auberge du Quartier, **3**
L'Auberge Saint-Louis, **24**
Le Château de Pierre, **25**
L'Hôtel du Vieux Québec, **17**
Manoir d'Auteuil, **13**
Manoir des Remparts, **35**
Manoir Lafayette, **8**
Manoir Sainte-Geneviève, **26**

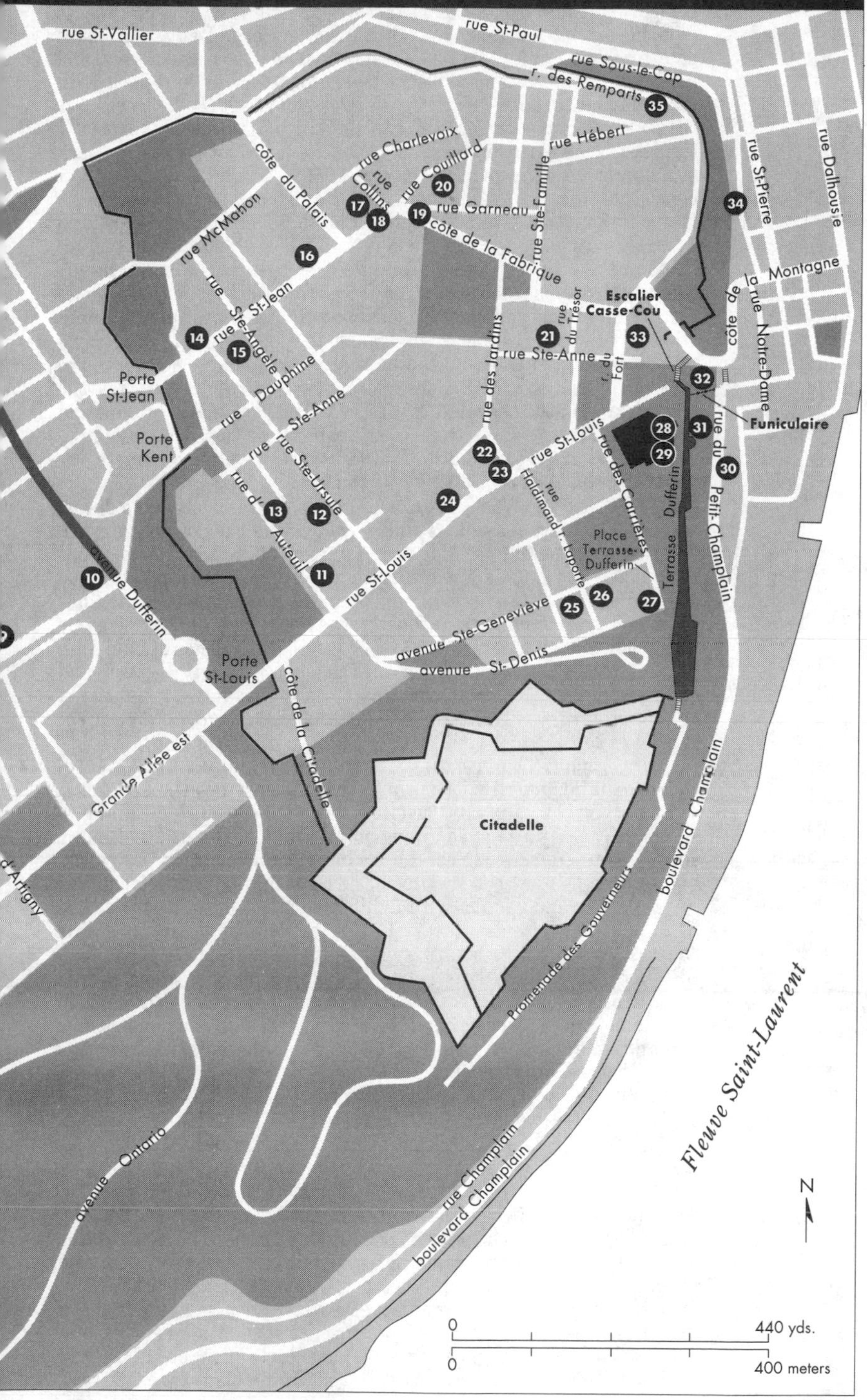
rue St-Vallier
rue St-Paul
rue Sous-le-Cap
r. des Remparts
rue Hébert
rue Charlevoix
rue Couillard
rue Collins
rue Garneau
côte du Palais
côte de la Fabrique
rue Ste-Famille
rue St-Pierre
rue Dalhousie
rue McMahon
rue St-Jean
rue Ste-Angèle
rue du Trésor
Escalier Casse-Cou
côte de la Montagne
rue Notre-Dame
rue des Jardins
rue Ste-Anne
r. du Fort
rue Dauphine
Porte St-Jean
Porte Kent
Funiculaire
rue St-Louis
rue des Carrières
rue Ste-Ursule
rue d'Auteuil
rue Haldimand
r. Laporte
Place Terrasse-Dufferin
Terrasse Dufferin
rue du Petit-Champlain
avenue Dufferin
avenue Ste-Geneviève
avenue St-Denis
Porte St-Louis
côte de la Citadelle
Grande Allée est
Citadelle
d'Artigny
boulevard Champlain
Promenade des Gouverneurs
Fleuve Saint-Laurent
avenue Ontario
rue Champlain
N
0
440 yds.
0
400 meters
10
11
12
13
14
15
16
17
18
19
20
21
22
23
24
25
26
27
28
29
30
31
32
33
34
35

ing and created a minimall with a European-style tearoom, a contemporary piano bar, and a food store—all serving gourmet treats from his celebrated kitchen. If A la Table de Serge Bruyère is out of your price range, **A la Petite Table** in the food mall is less formal and less expensive, with such dishes as seafood terrine and pork with tarragon sauce. *1200 rue St-Jean, tel. 418/694–0618. Reservations required. Jacket required. AE, DC, MC, V. No lunch weekends.*

Café de la Paix. An evening spent at this local favorite takes you back to a dining experience in Paris circa 1930. The tables could not get closer nor the lights dimmer amid the art deco extravagance of lamps in Venetian glass, wood sculpted in geometric patterns, and stained-glass windows. The food is on a par with other fine restaurants in the city, but there are hints that the chefs are relying on their reputations (the restaurant dates from 1952). The table d'hôte includes such tasty dishes as pheasant with peaches. Salmon comes with four sauces: raspberry vinegar, hollandaise, tarragon, or mustard. The meat entrées, including filet mignon and leg of lamb, are also recommended. You choose your dessert from a cart; try the fresh fruit and the chocolate truffle cake. The service is prompt and attentive. Private dining rooms are available on the second floor. *44 rue des Jardins, tel. 418/692–1430. Reservations advised. Dress: casual but neat. AE, DC, MC, V. No lunch Sun. in winter.*

Le Marie Clarisse. Wood-beam ceilings, stone walls, sea-blue decor, and a lit fireplace make this dining spot one of the coziest in town. Housed in an ancient building on the bottom of the Breakneck Steps near Place Royale, Le Marie Clarisse is well known for its unique seafood dishes, such as halibut with nuts and honey and scallops with port and paprika. Occasionally, the menu includes a good game dish, such as caribou with curry. The *menu du jour* has about seven entrées to choose from; dinner includes soup, salad, dessert, and coffee. Wines are served from the restaurant's cellar. *12 rue du Petit-Champlain, tel. 418/692–0857. Reservations required. Dress: casual but neat. AE, DC, MC, V. Closed Sun. and lunch Sat.*

★ **Le Saint-Amour.** This restaurant has all the makings of a true haute-cuisine establishment without having a pretentious atmosphere. A light and airy atrium, with a retractable roof for outdoor dining in summer, creates a relaxed dining ambience. Chef Jean-Luc Boulay continues to educate himself by taking various courses in France; his studies pay off in the creation of such specialties as stuffed quails in port sauce and salmon with light chive mousse. Sauces here are light, with no flour or butter. The *menu de dégustation* has nine courses, and the *menu gastronomique* has seven courses. If you plan to order one of these two menus, it's a good idea to mention this when making your reservation. Wines can be ordered by the glass to complement courses. The chef's true expertise shines when it comes to his diverse dessert menu. Try the nougat ice cream with fresh figs or the three-chocolate cake. Better yet, order the Saint-Amour assortment of desserts. *48 rue Ste-Ursule, tel. 418/694–0667. Reservations advised. Dress: casual but neat. AE, DC, MC, V.*

$$$

★ **Aux Anciens Canadiens.** This establishment is named after a book by Philippe-Aubert de Gaspé, who once resided here. The house dates back to 1675 and has four dining rooms with different themes. The *vaisselier* (dish room) is bright and cheerful, with colorful antique dishes, a fireplace, and an antique stove. Another room displays guns from the French regime. Come for the authentic French Canadian cooking; hearty specialties include duck in maple glaze and lamb with blueberry wine sauce. The restaurant also serves the best caribou drink in town. (Caribou is a local beverage made with sweet red wine and whiskey, and is known for its kick.) *34 rue St-Louis, tel. 418/692–1627. Reservations advised. Dress: casual. AE, DC, MC, V.*

L'Astral. This circular restaurant on the 29th floor of the Hôtel Loews Le Concorde revolves high above Battlefields Park and the Old City. The food is not the best in town, but the views are excellent. The modern and uninspired decor does not detract from the view, either; there's no room for anything besides the dining tables next to large windows and the vast buffet of salads, meat, and poultry dishes. Sunday brunch consists of more than 45 items ($21 adults, $9 children under 12). *1225 Pl. Montcalm, tel. 418/647–2222. Reservations advised. Dress: casual but neat. AE, DC, MC, V.*

Le Graffiti. A good alternative to Old City dining, this restaurant, housed in a modern gourmet food mall, serves the cuisine of Provence. It's a romantic setting, with dark mahogany-paneled walls and large bay windows that look out onto the passersby along avenue Cartier. The distinctive menu includes such dishes as scampi spiced with basil and red pepper, and chicken liver mousse with pistachios. The reasonably priced table d'hôte comes with soup, appetizer, entrée, dessert, and coffee. Desserts are made fresh each day. *1191 av. Cartier, tel. 418/529–4949. Reservations advised. Dress: casual but neat. AE, DC, MC, V.*

★ **Gambrinus.** This comfortable restaurant offers excellent Continental cuisine in two elegant, mahogany-paneled, plant-filled dining rooms with windows facing the street. The reliable menu includes a range of meat, fish, and pasta entrées, with such specialties as pheasant supreme with fruit, seafood in puff pastry with saffron, and rack of lamb with basil. The table d'hôte is a good bet and provides generous portions and delectable desserts. Service here is unrushed and thoroughly professional. Gambrinus is conveniently located near rue du Trésor and the Château Frontenac. *15 rue du Fort, tel. 418/692–5144. Reservations advised. Dress: casual but neat. AE, DC, MC, V. No lunch weekends.*

★ **Le Paris Brest.** This busy restaurant on Grande Allée serves a gregarious crowd attracted to its tastefully prepared French dishes. Its angular halogen lighting and soft yellow walls add a fresh, modern touch to this historic building. Traditional fare, such as *escargots au Pernod* (snails with Pernod) and steak tartare, are presented artistically. Popular dishes served here include lamb with herbs from Provence and beef Wellington. A la carte and main-course dishes are accompanied by a generous side platter of vegetables. Wine prices range from $22 to $250. *590 Grande Allée E, tel. 418/529–2243. Reservations advised. Dress: casual but neat. AE, DC, MC, V.*

$$

Chalet Suisse. This large chalet close to Place d'Armes serves Swiss cuisine. Fondues are a mainstay, and there are 25 different ones to choose from; the Gruyère and the chocolate fondues are two of the tastiest house specialties. Another popular dish is *raclette*, a Swiss dish with melted cheese, served with bread and potatoes as well as such diverse flavorings as onions, pickles, and ham. The spacious chalet looms three stories high with clichéd murals of alpine scenes. In the summer, there are umbrella-shaded café tables outside. *32 rue Ste-Anne, tel. 418/694–1320. Reservations accepted. Dress: casual. AE, DC, MC, V.*

L'Anse Aux Barques. Seafood is served on three floors of the Demers House, a building dating back to the late 17th century, just a stone's throw from the Québec–Lévis ferry terminal. The chef suggests the

Passerelle—filet mignon and jumbo shrimp—or any of his daily creations. A popular all-you-can-eat mussels and fries special is available between September and May; you choose among 17 imaginative sauces, from a hot pepper concoction to a smoked salmon and cream. Top off your meal with a homemade dessert. *28 rue du Petit Champlain, tel. 418/692–4674. Reservations advised. Dress: casual. AE, DC, MC, V.*

L'Apsara. The Cambodian family that owns this restaurant near the St-Louis Gate excels at using both subtle and tangy spices to create unique flavors that are ideal for those seeking a reprieve from French fare. Decor combines Western and Eastern motifs, with flowered wallpaper, Oriental art, and small fountains. Innovative dishes from Vietnam, Thailand, and Cambodia include such starters as *fleur de pailin* (a rice paste roll filled with fresh vegetables, meat, and shrimp) or *mou sati* (pork kebabs with peanut sauce and coconut milk). The assorted miniature Cambodian pastries are delicious with tea served from a little elephant container. *71 rue d'Auteuil, tel. 418/694–0232. Reservations accepted. Dress: casual. AE, MC, V.*

Le Café de la Terrasse. This restaurant, housed in the landmark Château Frontenac, does not share the hotel's opulence, but it does offer a view along Terrasse Dufferin and the St. Lawrence River. You can try the businessperson's breakfast buffet of fruits, omelets, and croissants and an à la carte lunch menu of salads and sandwiches. Standard but dependable Continental dishes are served during the lunch and dinner buffets. *Château Frontenac, 1 rue Carrières, tel. 418/692–3861. Reservations accepted. Dress: casual but neat. AE, DC, MC, V.*

★ **L'Echaudée** (Whitewash). This chic black-and-white bistro attracts a mix of business and tourist clientele because of its location between the financial and antiques districts in Lower Town. The modern decor features a stark dining area with a mirrored wall and a stainless-steel bar where you dine atop high stools. Lunch offerings include *cuisse de canard confit* (duck confit) with french fries and fresh seafood salad. The three-course brunch for Sunday antiques shoppers includes giant croissants and a tantalizing array of desserts. *73 Sault-au-Matelot, tel. 418/692–1299. Weekend reservations advised. Dress: casual. AE, DC, MC, V. Closed Sun. and Mon. dinners Sept.–May.*

Paparazzi. The story goes like this: two Québecers were dining in Napa Valley, California. They were so impressed by chef Suzanne Sylvester, they convinced her to pack up her Harley Davidson and move to Québec City. In 1993, after four months of study in southern Italy, the threesome opened the Paparazzi, an Italian restaurant located about a 15-minute drive west of the Old City. Its sleek, bistro ambiance—bare wooden tables, halogen lighting, wrought iron accents—competes with many of the finer dining establishments in town, but without the high prices. The menu is imaginative, and changes twice a year. Specialties include the pizza paparazzi, with wild mushrooms, fresh tomatoes, and a mix of cheeses. Choose from a list of interesting desserts. *1365 av. Maguire, Sillery, tel. 418/683–8111. Reservations advised. Dress: casual. AE, DC, MC, V.*

$

Casse-Crêpe Breton. Crêpes in generous proportions are served in this small, square, diner-style restaurant on rue St-Jean. From a menu of 15 ingredients, pick your own chocolate or fruit combinations, or design a larger meal with cheese, ham, and vegetables. The tables surround three round hot plates at which you watch your creations being made. Crêpes made with two to five ingredients cost under $5. *1136 rue St-Jean. tel. 418/692–0438. No reservations. Dress: casual. No credit cards. Open weekdays 7:30 AM–11 PM, weekends 7:30 AM–midnight.*

★ **Chez Temporel.** Tucked behind rue St-Jean and côte de la Fabrique, this homey café is an experience *très français*. The aroma of fresh coffee fills the air. The rustic decor incorporates wooden tables, chairs, and benches, and a tiny staircase winds to an upper level. Croissants are made in-house; the staff will fill them with Gruyère and ham or anything else you want. Try the equally delicious croque-monsieur and quiche Lorraine. *25 rue Couillard, tel. 418/694–1813. No reservations. Dress: casual. No credit cards. Open 7 AM–1 AM.*

Le Cochon Dingue. Across the street from the ferry in Lower Town is this cheerful café (whose name translates to "The Crazy Pig"), with sidewalk tables and indoor dining rooms, which artfully blend the chic and the antique. Black-and-white checkerboard floors contrast with ancient stone walls that are typical of the oldest sections of town. Café fare includes dependably tasty homemade quiches, thick soups, and such desserts as fresh raspberry tarte and maple-sugar pie. *46 boul. Champlain, tel. 418/692–2013. Reservations accepted. Dress: casual. AE, MC, V. Open weekdays 7 AM–11 PM, weekends 8 AM–midnight.*

Les Frères de la Côte. This pizza house, although located in the heart of the tourist district, is a favorite for many locals—including some provincial politicians. The friendly, boisterous atmosphere flows from its doors into the foyer, where you will find hundreds of snapshots documenting happy dining experiences. On the menu, you'll find 17 kinds of pizza, but there is also a full range of other dishes—like pasta with blue cheese, lamb with herbes de province, or grilled spicy Italian sausage with fries. For dessert, try the apple pie served with an orange, caramel glaze, and cream. And when it comes time to leave, don't overlook the tempting basket of homemade bread for sale. *1190 rue St-Jean, tel. 418/692–5445. Reservations advised. Dress: casual. AE, MC, V.*

Mille Feuille. In the heart of the Latin Quarter is this vegetarian restaurant situated in a well-preserved, historic building that dates to 1782. The daily menu offers three or four creative dishes, such as cabbage leaves stuffed with brown rice and vegetables and topped with rich tomato sauce and fresh Parmesan cheese, and Greek-style pizza with black olives. All dishes are served with soup and salad. On Saturday and Sunday a "health brunch" is served from 9 AM to 3 PM, and costs about $6. *32 rue Sainte-Angèle, tel. 418/692–2147. May close during winter months. Also at 1405 chemin Ste.-Foy (a 10-min drive west of the city), tel. 418/681–4520. Reservations accepted. Dress: casual. MC, V.*

Lodging

With more than 35 hotels within its walls, Québec City has a range of lodging options. Landmark hotels stand as prominent as the city's most historic sites; modern high rises outside the ramparts offer spectacular views of the Old City. Also, visitors can immerse themselves in the city's historic charm by staying in one of the many old-fashioned inns where no two rooms are alike.

Whichever kind of accommodations you choose, be sure to make a reservation during peak season, from May through September. If you are planning to visit during the summer or at the time of the Winter Carnival in February, you may have trouble finding a room without one. During busy times, hotel rates usually rise 30%. From November through April, many of the city's lodgings offer discount weekend packages and other promotions.

Highly recommended properties in each price category are indicated by a star ★.

Category	Cost*
$$$$	over $140
$$$	$85–$140
$$	$50–$85
$	under $50

**All prices are for a standard double room, excluding 7% federal sales tax, 4% provincial sales tax, and an optional service charge.*

$$$$

★ **Château Frontenac.** Towering above the St. Lawrence River, the Château Frontenac is indisputably Québec City's most renowned landmark. Although the Frontenac can no longer claim to be the city's top-rated hotel, the mystique of staying at "the Château" endures. Its public rooms—from the intimate piano bar to its 700-seat ballroom, reminiscent of the Versailles Hall of Mirrors—have the opulence of years gone by, and almost all the guest rooms offer excellent views. You must make a reservation in advance, as the average booking rate is 80% a year. A five-year, $60 million renovation was completed in 1993, in time for the hotel's 100th birthday. A new wing of rooms was added, as was a long-awaited health spa. The Frontenac has one of the finer restaurants in town, Le Champlain, where classic French cuisine is served by waiters dressed in traditional French costumes. The ground floor has several luxury shops and a restaurant, Le Café de la Terrasse (*see* Dining, *above*). *1 rue des Carrières, G1R 4P5, tel. 418/692–3861 or 800/441–1414, fax 418/692–1751. 610 rooms. Facilities: 3 restaurants, 2 bars, health spa, indoor pool. AE, DC, MC, V.*

★ **Hilton International Québec.** Just outside St-Jean Gate, the Hilton rises from the shadow of Parliament Hill as the city's finest luxury hotel. It has such spacious facilities and efficient services that it could easily cater exclusively to the convention crowd. Instead, it has adapted its renowned comfort and dependable service to tourists. The sprawling atrium lobby is flanked with a bar and an open-air restaurant, and it offers the added convenience of being connected with the mall, Place Québec, which offers 40 shops and boutiques. Ultramodern rooms with pine furniture have tall windows so that rooms on upper floors offer fine views of the Old City. *3 Pl. Québec, G1K 7M9, tel. 418/647–2411 or 800/445–8667, fax 418/647–6488. 565 rooms, 36 suites. Facilities: restaurant, piano bar, pool, health club, sauna, whirlpool. AE, DC, MC, V.*

Hôtel Radisson Gouverneurs Québec. Opposite the Parliament Buildings, this large, full-service establishment is part of a Québec chain. Formerly called Auberge des Gouverneurs when it opened in 1975, the hotel has upgraded its light and spacious rooms by furnishing them with luminous pastel decor, wood furniture, and marble bathrooms. VIP floors were designed to lure the business traveler, but there is also plenty of room for tourists. The hotel occupies the first 12 floors of a tall office complex; views of the Old City are limited to the higher floors. There's a year-round outdoor swimming pool, perfect for use even when the weather is frigid. *690 boul. René Levesque E, G1R 5A8, tel. 418/647–1717 or 800/333–3333, fax 418/647–2146. 377 rooms with private bath. Facilities: restaurant, piano bar, health club, heated outdoor pool, sauna, whirlpool. AE, DC, MC, V.*

★ **Hôtel Loews Le Concorde.** When Le Concorde was built in 1974, the shockingly tall concrete structure went up with controversy because it was taking the place of 19th-century Victorian homes. Yet of all the modern hotels outside the city gates, tourists will probably find that Le Concorde occupies one of the most convenient locations for city touring and nightlife. Inside the hotel there's almost as much going on as at the cafés and restaurants along the nearby Grande Allée; Le Concorde houses the revolving restaurant L'Astral (*see* Dining, *above*), a sidewalk café, and a bar. Rooms have good views of Battlefields Park, and nearly all have been redone in modern decor combined with traditional furnishings. Amenities for business travelers have expanded; one of the new VIP floors is reserved for female executives. *1225 Pl. Montcalm, G1R 4W6, tel. 418/647–2222 or 800/463–5256; in the U.S., tel. 800/23–LOEWS; fax 418/647–4710. 424 rooms. Facilities: 2 restaurants, bar, heated outdoor pool, health club, sauna, whirlpool. AE, DC, MC, V.*

$$$

Château Bonne Entente. If you have a car, you may want to stay at this sprawling resort located 10 minutes from the airport and 20 minutes from the walled city. The hotel is more commonly called "The Other Château," the country cousin of the urban Frontenac. It was a private mansion until 1940, when it became a hotel; a $7 million renovation several years ago has helped this establishment to become a popular spot for the well-heeled. In 1993, a spa and exercise room—known as the relaxarium—was added. In the newer section, rooms are decorated in contemporary style with fine wood, plush carpeting, and all the modern amenities. The other rooms are furnished with antiques, and a rustic atmosphere prevails. The property encompasses 11 acres of land with a main complex as well as separate cottage rooms in back. *3400 chemin Ste-Foy, Sainte-Foy G1X 1S6, tel. 418/653–5221 or 800/463–4390, fax 418/653–3098. 163 rooms. Facilities: restaurant, bar, spa, pool, tennis court, trout fishing in back pond, ice-skating in winter, full day care. AE, DC, MC, V.*

Le Château de Pierre. Built in 1853 and converted from a private residence in 1960, this tidy Victorian manor on a picturesque street has kept its English origins alive. The high-ceiling halls have ornate chandeliers. The rooms are imaginatively decorated with floral themes, and each usually has some special added feature—a balcony, fireplace, or vanity room—to lend some extra charm. Rooms in the front face imposing old stone buildings across the way that date from the English regime. *17 av. Ste-Geneviève, G1R 4A8, tel. 418/694–0429, fax 418/694–0153. 15 rooms with private bath and air-conditioning. MC, V.*

L'Hôtel du Théâtre. There's much history that accompanies this hotel, located in the Capitole Building just outside the St-Jean Gate. In 1903 this property opened as an avant-garde theater, then, in the 1920s—the era of silent films—it became a movie house, and some 12 years ago the doors closed in ruin. However, in 1992 the hotel came back to life, following a $15 million restoration, which transformed this historic building into an exclusive 40-room lodging, Italian bistro, and an elaborate 1920s cabaret-style dinner theater (*see* Arts and Nightlife, *below*). A glitzy show-biz theme is prevalent throughout the hotel, with stars on carpets, doors, and keys. Rooms are small and simple, highlighted with a few rich details. Ceilings are painted within sculpted moldings with a blue-and-white sky motif; beds are adorned with white down-filled comforters, and plush terry-cloth bathrobes await guests in every room. *972 rue St-Jean, G1R 1R5, tel. 418/694–4040, fax 418/694–1916. 40 rooms. Facilities: restaurant, bar, theater. AE, MC, V.*

L'Hôtel du Vieux Québec. Located in the heart of the Latin Quarter on rue St-Jean, this hotel's brick exterior is surrounded by more striking historic structures. The establishment was once an apartment building and still has the long-term visitor in mind. The interior design is simple, featuring sparsely decorated but comfortable rooms decorated in pastel colors. The hotel recently added five new rooms on the main floor, overlooking Québec's busy main street. Many rooms have a full kitchenette with a stove, cabinets, a sink, and a refrigerator; all have cable TV. Dishes and cooking utensils can be rented for $10. Some rooms are air-conditioned. *1190 rue St-Jean, G1R 1S6, tel. 418/692–1850, fax 418/692–5637. 42 units with private bath. AE, MC, V.*

★ **Manoir d'Auteuil.** Originally a private home, this lodging is one of the more lavish manors in town, artfully revamped at great expense. An ornate sculpted iron banister wraps around four floors; guest rooms feature detailed trimmings in mahogany and marble and blend modern design with the art deco structure. Each room differs in shape and design; one room was formerly the residence's chapel, while another has become a duplex with a luxurious marble bathroom on the second floor. Some rooms look out onto the wall between the St-Louis and St-Jean gates. A complimentary Continental breakfast awaits guests each morning. *49 rue d'Auteuil, G1R 4C2, tel. 418/694–1173, fax 418/694–0081. 16 rooms with private bath. AE, MC, V.*

Manoir Sainte-Geneviève. This quaint and elaborately decorated hotel dating from 1880 stands near the Château Frontenac, on the southwest corner of the Jardin des Governeurs. A plush Victorian ambience is created with fanciful wallpaper and rooms decorated with precious stately English manor furnishings, such as marble lamps, large wooden bedposts, and velvet upholstery; you'll feel as if you are staying in a secluded country inn. A hidden porch facing the Citadel is perfect for relaxing and soaking in the atmosphere of Upper Town. Service here is personal and genteel. One suite on the ground floor has a private entrance. *13 av. Ste-Geneviève, G1R 4A7, tel. and fax 418/694–1666. 9 rooms with private bath; 7 rooms have air-conditioning, color TV. No credit cards.*

$$

Château de la Terrasse. Although this four-story inn may not have the same charm as others in the city, it does have something that the others in the area lack: a view of the St. Lawrence River. However, only half of the rooms face the river; others in the rear look out onto the backs of buildings. While the interior hints at having once possessed a refined and elegant decor, with its high ceilings and stained glass lining the large bay windows, the furnishings these days are plain and unremarkable. *6 Pl. Terrasse Dufferin, G1R 4N5, tel. 418/694–9472, fax 418/694–0055. 18 rooms with private bath. V.*

★ **L'Auberge du Quartier.** This small, amiable inn, situated in a house dating from 1852, will please those seeking moderately priced lodging with a personal touch. Proprietors Lise Provost and Pierre Couture are highly attentive to their guests' needs. The cheerful rooms, without phones or televisions, are modestly furnished but well maintained; two of them have fireplaces. A suite of rooms on the third floor can accommodate a family at a reasonable cost. This is one of the few inns in the area that offers a tasty Continental breakfast—warm croissants, homemade banana bread, cheese, preserves, strong coffee, and fresh fruit. A 20-minute walk west from the Old City, L'Auberge du Quartier is convenient to avenue Cartier and Grande Allée nightlife; joggers can use Battlefields Park across the street. *170 Grande Allée O, G1R 2G9, tel. 418/525–9726. 13 rooms, 11 with private bath. Free parking. AE, DC, MC, V.*

L'Auberge Saint-Louis. If you're looking for convenience, this inn's central location on the main street of the city can't be beat. A lobby resembling a European pension and tall staircases lead to small guest rooms with comfortable but bare-bones furniture. The ultrabudget room on the fourth floor is just big enough for a bed. The service here is friendly and hospitable. Most guest rooms share floor bathrooms or have a semibathroom. *48 rue St-Louis, G1R 3Z3, tel. 418/692–2424, fax 418/692–3797. 27 rooms, 13 with private bath. MC, V.*

Le Manoir Lafayette. In 1882, this gray stone building was a lavish, private home; over a century later, it is a simple hotel. Considering the location on Grande Allée—a street crowded with restaurants and trendy bars—the clean, comfortable accommodations are reasonably priced. The lobby is open and welcoming, with floral sofas surrounding a fireplace and television. In 1992 the hotel underwent a massive renovation, adding 53 rooms to the existing 14. Rooms in the new wing—although fresher— resemble those in the old part: each is quite small, with high ceilings, wooden furniture, floral bed spreads and drapes, a television, and phone. Rooms facing Grande Allée may be noisy; older rooms cost a little less. *661 Grande Allée E, G1R 2K4, tel. 418/522–2652 or 800/363–8203, fax 418/522–2652. 67 rooms. Facilities: bistro, baby-sitting. AE, DC, MC, V.*

$

Manoir des Remparts. There's nothing fancy about this hotel, which is on a residential street bordering the north side of Québec City's natural cliff. But this manor offers just enough to attract the budget-conscious traveler: spacious and clean rooms with basic old-time furnishings. The halls are well lighted and considered large for a residence in the Old City. Guest rooms have private bath or share a bath on the floor but don't have telephones or televisions. A Continental breakfast, which includes croissants, cereal, juice, and coffee, is included in the price of the room. *3½ rue des Remparts, G1R 3R4, tel. 418/692–2056, fax 418/692–1125. AE, MC, V.*

Bed-and-Breakfasts

Québec City has a large number of bed-and-breakfast and hostel accommodations. To guarantee a room during peak season, be sure to reserve in advance. **Québec City Tourist Information** (60 rue d'Auteuil, G1R 4C4, tel. 418/692–2471) has B&B listings. **Bed and Breakfast–Bonjour Québec** (450 rue Champlain, G1K 4J3, tel. 418/524–0524) has several B&Bs to choose from. Prices range from $45 for a single room to $75 for a double. Apartments are available starting at $75.

The Arts and Nightlife

For a place its size, Québec City boasts a wide variety of cultural events, from the reputable Québec Symphony Orchestra to several small theater companies. The arts scene changes significantly depending on the season. From September to May, a steady repertoire of concerts, plays, and performances is presented in theaters and halls around town. In summer, indoor theaters close to make room for several outdoor stages.

For arts and entertainment listings in English, consult the *Québec Chronicle-Telegraph,* published on Wednesday. Each day in the French-language daily newspaper, *Le Soleil,* listings appear on a page called "Où Aller à Québec" ("Where to Go in Québec"). *Voilà Québec* and *Hospitalité Québec* are bilingual quarterly entertainment guides distributed free in tourist information areas.

Tickets for most shows can be purchased through **Billetech,** whose main outlet is the Grand Théâtre de Québec (269 boul. René Levesque E, tel. 418/643–8131). Other outlets are located at Bibliothèque Gabrielle-Roy, Colisée, Implanthéâtre, Palais Montcalm, Salle Albert-Rousseau, La Baie department store (Place Laurier, tel. 418/627–5959), and Provigo supermarkets. Outlet hours vary, depending on the location.

The Arts

Dance **Grand Théâtre de Québec** (269 boul. René Levesque E, tel. 418/643–8131) presents a dance series with both Canadian and international companies. Dancers also appear at Bibliothèque Gabrielle-Roy, Salle Albert-Rousseau, and the Palais Montcalm (*see* Theater, *below*).

Film Most theaters present French films and American films dubbed into French. Two popular theaters are **Cinéma de Paris** (966 rue St-Jean, tel. 418/694–0891) and **Cinéma Place Charest** (500 rue du Pont, tel. 418/529–9745). **Cinémas Sainte-Foy** (Place Sainte-Foy, Sainte-Foy, tel. 418/656–0592) almost always features films in English. **Le Clap** (2360 chemin Ste.-Foy, Ste.-Foy, tel. 418/650–2527) offers a repertoire of foreign, off-beat, and art films.

Music **L'Orchestre Symphonique de Québec** (Québec Symphony Orchestra) is Canada's oldest. It performs at Louis-Frechette Hall in the **Grand Théâtre de Québec** (269 boul. René Levesque E, tel. 418/643–8131).
Bibliothèque Gabrielle-Roy (350 rue St-Joseph E, tel. 418/529–0924). Classical concerts are performed at the Auditorium Joseph Lavergne. Tickets must be purchased in advance at the library.
Colisée de Québec (2205 av. du Colisée, Parc de l'Exposition, tel. 418/691–7211). Popular music concerts are often booked here.

Theater All theater productions are in French. The following theaters schedule shows from September through April:

Grand Théâtre de Québec (269 boul. René Levesque E, tel. 418/643–8131). Classic and contemporary plays are staged by the leading local theater company, le Théâtre du Trident (tel. 418/643–5873).
Palais Montcalm (995 Pl. d'Youville, tel. 418/670–9011). This municipal theater outside St-Jean Gate presents a broad range of productions.
Salle Albert-Rousseau (2410 chemin Ste-Foy, Sainte-Foy, tel. 418/659–6710). A diverse repertoire, from classical to comedy, is staged here.

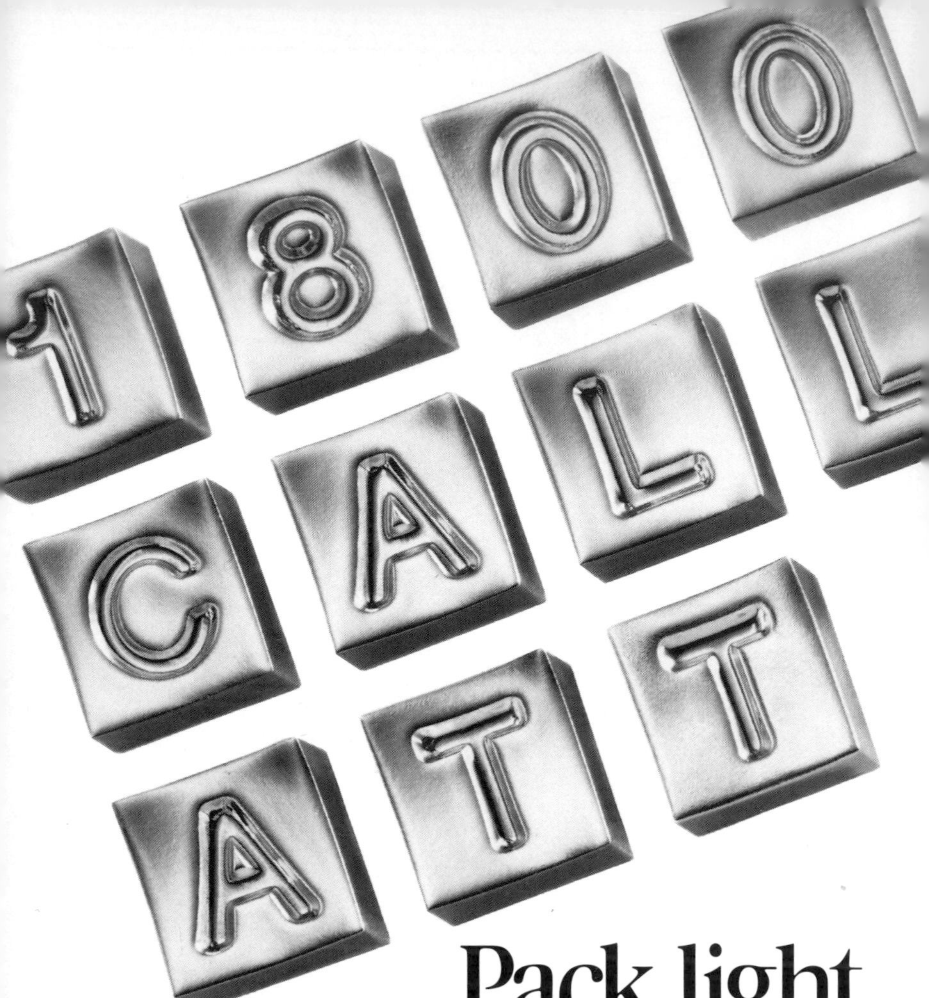

Pack light.

Take the one number you need for any kind of call, anywhere you travel.

Checking in with your family back home? Calling for a tow truck? When you're on the road, the phone you use might not accept your calling card. Or you might get overcharged by an unknown telephone company. Here's the solution: dial 1 800 CALL ATT.[sm] You'll get flawless AT&T service, competitive calling card prices, and the lowest prices for collect calls from any phone, anywhere. Travel light. Just bring along this one simple number: 1 800 CALL ATT.

AT&T

Théâtre Capitole (972 rue St-Jean, tel. 418/694–4444). This recently restored turn-of-the-century cabaret-style theater offers a diverse repertoire of classical and pop music, plays, and comedy shows.
Théâtre de la Bordée (1143 rue St-Jean, tel. 418/694–9631). This local company presents small-scale productions.
Théâtre Périscope (2 rue Crémazie E, tel. 418/529–2183). This multipurpose, experimental theater stages about 200 presentations a year, including performances for children.

Summer Theater

Place d'Youville (tel. 418/670–9011). During the summer, open-air concerts are presented here, just outside St-Jean Gate. Recent renovations have madc this spot quite enjoyable.

Nightlife

Nightlife in Québec City is centered on the clubs and cafés of rue St-Jean, avenue Cartier, and Grande Allée. In the winter, evening activity is livelier toward the end of the week, beginning on Wednesday. But as the warmer temperatures set in, the café-terrace crowd emerges, and bars are active seven days a week. Most bars and clubs stay open until 3 AM.

Bars and Lounges

Le Central (1200 rue St-Jean, tel. 418/694–0618). At this stylish piano bar at Serge Bruyère's restaurant complex, you can order from the restaurant's sophisticated haute-cuisine menu.
Le Pub Saint-Alexandre (1087 rue St-Jean, tel. 418/694–0015). This popular English-style pub, formerly a men-only tavern, is a good place to look for your favorite brand of beer. There are approximately 135 different kinds.
Vogue and **Sherlock Holmes** (1170 d'Artigny, tel. 418/529–9973). You'll find mainly Yuppies at these two bars stacked one on top of the other. Sherlock Holmes is a pub-restaurant downstairs; for dancing, try Vogue upstairs.

Disco

Chez Dagobert (600 Grande Allée E, tel. 418/522–0393). You'll find a little bit of everything—live rock bands to loud disco—at this large and popular club.
Merlin (1179 av. Cartier, tel. 418/529–9567). This one-room disco is packed nightly. It's a favorite Québecois hangout.

Folk, Jazz, and Blues

Chez Son Père (24 St-Stanislas, tel. 418/692–5308). French Canadian folk songs fill this smoky pub on the second floor of an old building in the Latin Quarter. Singers perform every Wednesday through Friday night.
Le d'Auteuil (35 rue d'Auteuil, tel. 418/692–2263). Rhythm and blues, jazz, and blues emanate from this converted church across from Kent Gate.
L'Emprise at Hôtel Clarendon (57 rue Ste-Anne, tel. 418/692–2480). The first jazz bar in Québec City is the preferred spot for enthusiasts. The art deco decor sets the mood for Jazz Age rhythms.

6 Excursions from Québec City

Côte de Beaupré

As legend tells it, when explorer Jacques Cartier first gained sight of the north shore of the St. Lawrence River in 1535, he exclaimed, "*Quel beau pré!*" ("What a lovely meadow!"), because the area was the first inviting piece of land he had spotted since leaving France. Today this fertile meadow, first settled by French farmers, is known as Côte de Beaupré (Beaupré Coast), stretching 40 kilometers (25 miles) from Québec City to the famous pilgrimage site of Sainte-Anne-de-Beaupré. The impressive Montmorency Falls are located midway between these two points.

Tourist Information

Beaupré Coast Interpretation Center, housed in the old mill Petit-Pré, built in 1695, features displays on the history and development of the region. *7007 av. Royale, Château-Richer, tel. 418/824–3677. Admission: $1. Open late June–Labor Day, daily 9–noon and 1–5.*
Beau Temps, Mauvais Temps, offers guided bus tours of the Côte de Beaupré. *22 rue du Quai, Suite 101, Saint-Pétronille, Ile d'Orléans, tel. 418/828–2275.*
The offices of the **Québec City Region Tourism and Convention Bureau** (tel. 418/692–2471) can provide information on tours of the Côte de Beaupré (*see* Essential Information *in* Chapter 5).

Guided Tours

Québec City touring companies, such as **Gray Line** (tel. 418/622–7420) and **Maple Leaf Sightseeing Tours** (tel. 418/649–9226), lead day excursions along the Côte de Beaupré, with stops at Montmorency Falls and the Sainte-Anne-de-Beaupré Basilica.

Arriving and Departing

By Car To reach Montmorency Falls, take Route 440 (Dufferin Montmorency Autoroute) northeast from Québec City. Approximately 9.6 kilometers (6 miles) east of the city is the exit for Montmorency Falls. To drive directly to Sainte-Anne-de Beaupré, continue northeast on Route 440 for approximately 29 kilometers (18 miles) and exit at Sainte-Anne-de-Beaupré.

An alternative way to reach Sainte-Anne-de-Beaupré is to take Route 360 or avenue Royale. Take Route 440 from Québec City, turn left at d'Estimauville, and right on boulevard des Chutes until it intersects with Route 360. Also called "le chemin du Roi" (the King's Road), this panoramic route is one of the oldest in North America, winding 30 kilometers (18.8 miles) along the steep ridge of the Côte de Beaupré. The road borders 17th- and 18th-century farmhouses, historic churches, and Normandy-style homes with half-buried root cellars. Route 360 goes past the Sainte-Anne-de-Beaupré Basilica.

Montmorency Falls

Begin this excursion with a visit to **Montmorency Falls.** The Montmorency River, named after Charles de Montmorency who was a governor of New France, cascades over a coastal cliff and is one of the most beautiful sights in the province. The falls, which are actually 50% higher than the wider Niagara Falls, measure 83 meters (274 feet) in height. During very cold weather conditions, the falls' heavy spray freezes and forms a giant loaf-shape ice cone known to

Québecois as the Pain du Sucre (Sugarloaf); this phenomenon attracts sledders and sliders from Québec City. In the warmer months, a park in the river's gorge leads to an observation terrace that is continuously sprayed by a fine drizzle from water pounding onto the cliff rocks. The top of the falls can be observed from avenue Royale. *Admission free. Open daily.*

Time Out **Restaurant Baker** (8790 av. Royale, Château-Richer, tel. 418/824-4478), on the way to Sainte-Anne-de Beaupré on Route 360, is a good, old-fashioned rustic restaurant that serves such hearty traditional French Canadian dishes as meat pie, pea soup, pâtés, and maple-sugar pie.

Basilique Sainte-Anne-de-Beaupré

The monumental and inspiring **Basilique Sainte-Anne-de-Beaupré** (Sainte-Anne-de-Beaupré Basilica) is located in a small town with the same name. The basilica has become a popular attraction as well as an important shrine: More than half a million people visit the site each year.

The French brought their devotion to Saint Anne with them when they sailed across the Atlantic to New France. In 1650, Breton sailors caught in a storm vowed to erect a chapel in honor of this patron saint at the exact spot where they would land. The present-day neo-Roman basilica constructed in 1923 was the fifth to be built on the site where the sailors first touched ground.

According to local legend, Saint Anne was responsible over the years for saving voyagers from shipwrecks in the harsh waters of the St. Lawrence. Tributes to her miraculous powers can be seen in the shrine's various mosaics, murals, altars, and church ceilings. A bas-relief at the entrance depicts Saint Anne welcoming her pilgrims, and ceiling mosaics represent details from her life. Numerous crutches and braces posted on the back pillars have been left by those who have felt the healing powers of Saint Anne.

The basilica, which is in the shape of a Latin cross, has two granite steeples jutting from its gigantic structure. Its interior has 22 chapels and 18 altars, as well as round arches and numerous ornaments in the Romanesque style. The 214 stained-glass windows by Frenchmen Auguste Labouret and Pierre Chaudière, finished in 1949, tell a story of salvation through personages who were believed to be instruments of God over the centuries. Other features of the shrine include intricately carved wood pews decorated with various animals and several smaller altars (behind the main altar) that are dedicated to different saints.

The original wood chapel built in the village of Sainte-Anne-de-Beaupré during the 17th century was situated too close to the St. Lawrence and was swept away by flooding of the river. In 1676, the chapel was replaced by a stone church that was visited by pilgrims for more than a century, but this structure was also demolished in 1872. The first basilica, which replaced the stone church, was destroyed by a fire in 1922. The following year architects Maxime Rosin from Paris and Louis-N. Audet from Québec province designed the basilica that now stands. *10,018 av. Royale, Sainte-Anne-de-Beaupré, tel. 418/827–3781. Admission free. Reception booth open mid-May–mid-Oct., daily 8:30–7:30. Tours daily in summer at 1 PM start at the information booth at the southwest corner of the court-*

yard outside the basilica. Guided tours during the off-season (Sept.–mid-May) can be arranged by phoning in advance.

Across the street from the basilica on avenue Royale is the **Commemorative Chapel,** designed by Claude Bailiff and built in 1878. The memorial chapel was constructed on the location of the transept of a stone church built in 1676 and contains the old building's foundations. Among the remnants housed here are the old church's bell dating from 1696, an early 18th-century altar designed by Vezina, a crucifix sculpted by François-Noël Levaseur in 1775, and a pulpit designed by François Baillargé in 1807.

Ile d'Orléans

Ile d'Orléans, an island slightly downstream in a northeasterly direction from Québec City, exemplifies the historic charm of rural Québec province with its quiet, traditional life-style. A drive around the island will take you past stone churches that are among the oldest in the region and centuries-old houses amid acres of lush orchards and cultivated farmland. Horse-drawn carriages are still a means of transport. Ile d'Orléans is also an important marketplace that provides fresh produce daily for Québec City; roadside stands on the island sell a variety of local products, such as crocheted blankets, woven articles, maple syrup, homemade bread and jams, and fruits and vegetables.

The island was discovered at about the same time as Québec City in 1535. Explorer Jacques Cartier noticed an abundance of vines on the island and called it the "Island of Bacchus," after the Greek god of wine. In 1536, Cartier renamed the island in honor of the duke of Orléans, son of the king of France, François I. Long considered part of the domain of Côte de Beaupré, the island was not given its seignorial autonomy until 1636, when it was bought by La Compagne des Cents Associés, a group formed by Louis XIII to promote settlement in New France.

Ile d'Orléans, about 9 kilometers (5 miles) wide and 34 kilometers (21 miles) long, is now composed of six small villages. These villages have sought over the years to remain relatively private residential and agricultural communities; the island's bridge to the mainland was built only in 1935.

Important Addresses and Numbers

Tourist Information

Beau Temps, Mauvais Temps has a tourist office located in Sainte-Pétronille. *22 rue du Quai, suite 101, tel. 418/828–2275. Open Feb.–May, weekdays 8:30–4; June–Sept., daily 8:30–8; Oct.–Jan., will respond to messages left on answering machine.*

The island's **Chamber of Commerce** operates a tourist information kiosk situated at the west corner of côte du Pont and chemin Royal. *490 côte du Pont, Saint-Pierre, tel. 418/828–9411. Open June–Sept., daily 10–7; Oct.–May, weekdays (no fixed schedule).*

Medical Clinic

Centre Médical (1015 rte. Prévost, Saint-Pierre, tel. 418/828–2213) is the only medical clinic on the island.

Guided Tours

Beau Temps, Mauvais Temps (22 rue du Quai, suite 101, Sainte-Pétronille, Ile d'Orléans, tel. 418/828–2275) offers guided walking tours of three villages: Sainte-Pétronille, Saint-Jean, and Saint-Laurent. River excursions departing from Saint-Laurent are available from mid-May–mid-September. In addition, the company is a referral service for lodging.

Beau Temps, Mauvais Temps also sells dinner-theater packages, which include a meal at one of the island's restaurants, followed by a play at one of three theaters on Ile d'Orléans and Ancienne Lorette. *Available mid-May–Labor Day. Cost: Wed. and Thurs. $45–$60, Fri.–Sun. $47–$62.*

Québec City touring companies, including **Maple Leaf Sightseeing Tours** (tel. 418/649–9226), **Gray Line** (tel. 418/622–7420), and **Visite Touristiques de Québec** (tel. 418/653–9722) offer full- and half-day bus tours of the western tip of the island, combined with sightseeing along the Côte de Beaupré.

Any of the offices of the **Québec City Region Tourism and Convention Bureau** can provide information on tours and accommodations on the island (*see* Essential Information *in* Chapter 5).

Arriving and Departing

By Car Ile d'Orléans has no public transportation; cars are the only way to get to and around the island, unless you take a guided tour (*see* Guided Tours, *above*). Parking on the island is never a problem; you can always stop and explore the villages on foot. The main road, chemin Royal (Route 368), extends 67 kilometers (40 miles) through the island's six villages; street numbers along chemin Royal begin at No. 1 for each municipality.

From Québec City, take Route 440 (Dufferin-Montmorency Autoroute) northeast. After a drive of approximately 10 kilometers (7 miles) take the bridge, Pont de l'Ile d'Orléans, to reach the island. Before you get to the island's only traffic light, turn right heading west on chemin Royal to begin the exploring tour, *below*.

Exploring Ile d'Orléans

Numbers in the margin correspond to points of interest on the Ile d'Orléans map.

Start your tour heading west on chemin Royal to **Sainte-Pétronille,** the first village to be settled on the island. Founded in 1648, the community was chosen in 1759 by British General James Wolfe for his headquarters. With 40,000 soldiers and a hundred ships, the English bombarded French-occupied Québec City and Côte de Beaupré.

During the late-19th century, the English population of Québec developed Sainte-Pétronille into a resort village. This section is considered by many to be the island's most beautiful area, not only because of the spectacular views it offers of Montmorency Falls and Québec City but also for the stylish English villas and exquisitely tended gardens that can be seen from the roadside.

On the left at 20 chemin Royal is the **Plante family farm,** where you can stop to pick apples (in season) or buy some of the island's fresh fruits and vegetables.

❶ Farther along on the right is the **Maison Gourdeau de Beaulieu House** (137 chemin Royal), the island's first home, built in 1648 for Jacques Gourdeau de Beaulieu, who was the first seigneur of Sainte-Pétronille. Today this white building with blue shutters is still

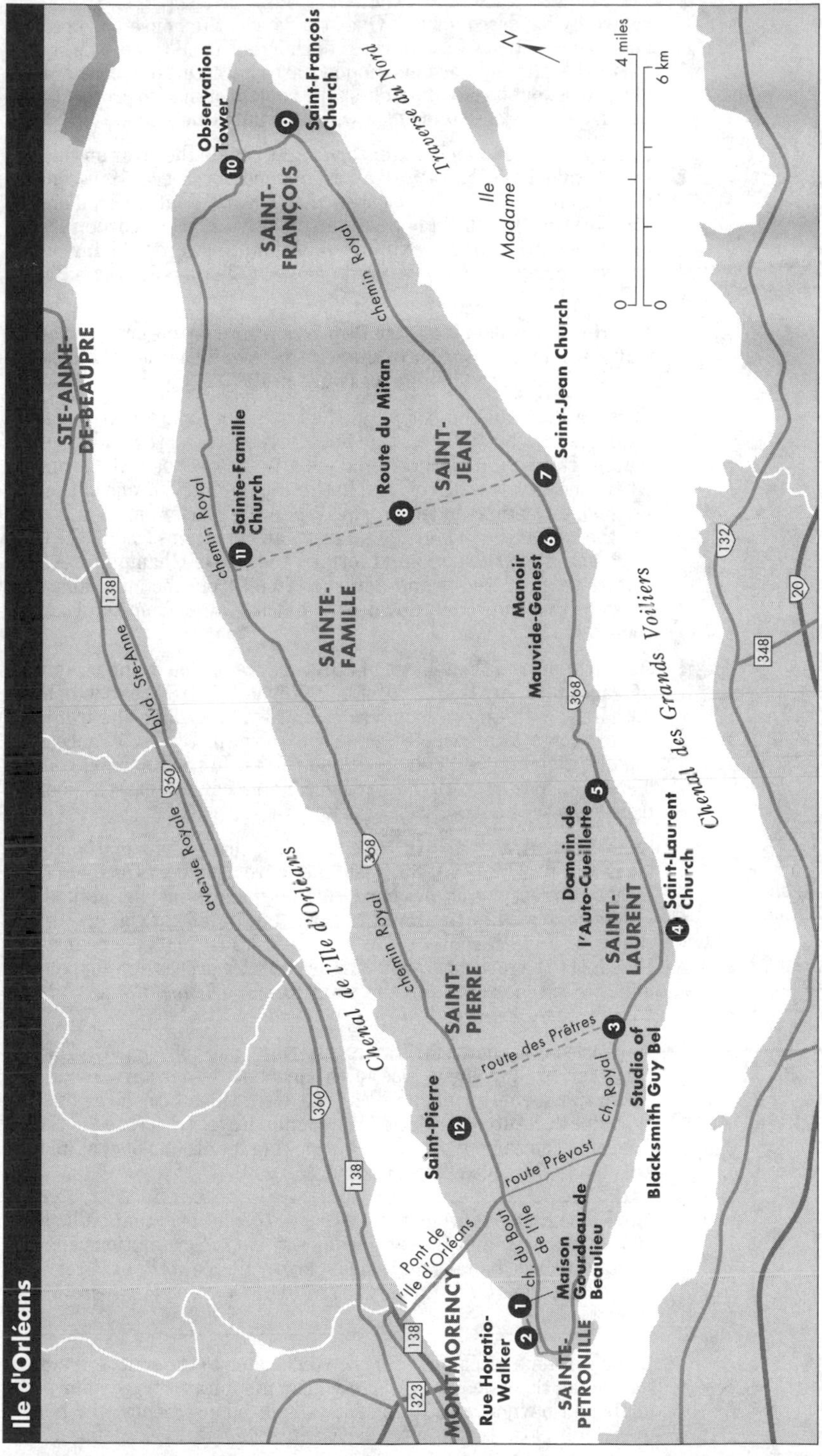
Ile d'Orléans
STE-ANNE-DE-BEAUPRE
MONTMORENCY
SAINTE-PETRONILLE
SAINT-PIERRE
SAINT-LAURENT
SAINTE-FAMILLE
SAINT-JEAN
SAINT-FRANÇOIS
1 Maison Gourdeau de Beaulieu
2 Rue Horatio-Walker
3 Studio of Blacksmith Guy Bel
4 Saint-Laurent Church
5 Domain de l'Auto-Cueillette
6 Manoir Mauvide-Genest
7 Saint-Jean Church
8 Route du Mitan
9 Saint-François Church
10 Observation Tower
11 Sainte-Famille Church
12 Saint-Pierre
Pont de l'Ile d'Orléans
ch. du Bout de l'Ile
route Prévost
route des Prêtres
ch. Royal
chemin Royal
avenue Royale
blvd. Ste-Anne
Chenal de l'Ile d'Orléans
Chenal des Grands Voiliers
Traverse du Nord
Ile Madame
138
323
360
350
368
132
20
348
N
0
4 miles
0
6 km

owned by his descendants. Over the years, the house has been remodeled and it now incorporates both French and Québecois styles. Its thick walls and dormer windows are characteristic of Breton architecture, but its sloping bell-shape roof, designed to protect buildings from large amounts of snow, is typically Québecois.

2 After you descend an incline, turn right beside the river on the tiny street called **rue Horatio-Walker,** named after the 19th-century painter known for his landscapes of the island. Walker lived on this street from 1904 until his death in 1938. Around the corner are his home and studio, where exhibits of his paintings are held during the summer. *Open by reservation with Beau Temps, Mauvais Temps (tel. 418/828–2275).*

Rue Horatio-Walker was also the place where people crossed the St. Lawrence by an ice path in the winter to go from the island to the mainland before the bridge was built in 1935.

Farther along chemin Royal, at the border of Sainte-Pétronille and Saint-Laurent, look for a large boulder situated in the middle of nowhere. The **roche à Maranda,** named after the owner of the property where the rock was discovered in the 19th century, is one of the oldest rock formations in the world. When the glaciers melted in 9000 BC, the land at the foot of the Laurentian mountains (today the Côte de Beaupré) was flooded and formed the Sea of Champlain. As the waters receded, the island detached itself from the land, and such rocks as this one rolled down with glacial water from the Laurentians, onto lower land.

3 As you approach the village of Saint-Laurent, you'll find the **studio of blacksmith Guy Bel** (2200 chemin Royal, tel. 418/828–9300), a talented and well-known local craftsman who has done the ironwork restoration for Québec City. He was born in Lyons, France, and studied there at the École des Beaux Arts. In the summer, you can watch him hard at work; his stylish candlesticks, mantels, and other ironworks are for sale.

Saint-Laurent, founded in 1679, is one of the island's maritime villages. Until as late as 1935, residents here used boats as their main means of transportation. Next to the village's marina stands the
4 tall, inspiring **Saint-Laurent Church.** Built in 1860, it was erected on the site of an 18th-century church that, because of its poor construction, had to be torn down. One of the church's procession chapels is a miniature stone replica of the church. *1532 chemin Royal. Admission free. Open summer, daily.*

Ile d'Orléans is known for its superb fruits, and you won't find better strawberries anywhere else in the province. There are about two dozen spots where you can pick your own. One of the larger fields,
5 **Domaine de l'Auto-Cueillette** (211 chemin Royal), is located in Saint-Laurent. You can buy a basket for picking for around 50¢; a full basket of strawberries will cost about $5.

Time Out **Moulin de Saint-Laurent** is an early 18th-century stone mill. Dine here in the herb-and-flower garden out back. Scrumptious snacks, such as quiches, bagels, and salads, are available at the café-terrace. *754 chemin Royal, tel. 418/829–3888. AE, DC, MC, V. Closed Nov.–Apr.*

If you continue on chemin Royal, you'll come to the southern side of the island, **Saint-Jean,** a village whose inhabitants were once river pilots and navigators. Most of its small, homogeneous row homes were built close to the river between 1840 and 1860. Being at sea most of the time, the sailors did not need large homes and plots of land as did the farmers. The island's sudden drop in elevation is most noticeable in Saint-Jean.

6 Saint-Jean's beautiful Normandy-style manor, **Manoir Mauvide-Genest,** was built in 1734 for Jean Mauvide—surgeon to Louis XV—and his wife, Marie-Anne Genest. Most notable about this house, which still has its original thick walls, ceiling beams, and fireplaces, is the degree to which it has held up over the years, in spite of being targeted by English guns during the 1759 siege of Québec City. The home is a pleasure to roam; all rooms are furnished with original antiques from the 18th and 19th centuries. It also offers an exhibit on French architecture and a downstairs restaurant that serves French cuisine. *1451 chemin Royal, tel. 418/829-2630. Open June–Aug., daily 10–5; Sept.–mid-Oct., weekends 10–5.*

North of the manor stands **Théâtre Paul-Hébert,** an indoor summer theater founded five years ago by an actor who lives on the island.

7 At the opposite end of the village, you'll see **Saint-Jean Church,** a massive granite structure with large red doors and a towering steeple built in 1749. The church bears a remarkable resemblance to a ship; it is big and round and appears to be sitting right on the St. Lawrence River. Paintings of the patron saints of seamen line the interior walls. The church's cemetery is also intriguing, especially if you can read French. Back in the 18th century, piloting the St. Lawrence was a dangerous profession; the boats could not easily handle the rough currents. The cemetery tombstones recall the tragedies of lives lost in these harsh waters. *2001 chemin Royal, tel. 418/829-3182. Admission free. Open summer, daily.*

As you leave Saint-Jean, chemin Royal mounts the incline and
8 crosses **route du Mitan.** In old French, *mitan* means "halfway." This road, dividing the island in half, is the most direct route from north to south. It is also the most beautiful on the island, with acres of tended farmland, apple orchards, and maple groves. If you're running out of time and want to end the tour here, take route du Mitan, which brings you to Saint-Pierre and the bridge to the mainland.

When you come to 17th-century farmhouses separated by sprawling open fields, you know you've reached the island's least-toured and most rustic village, **Saint-François.** At the eastern tip of the island, this community is the one situated farthest from the St. Lawrence River and was originally settled mainly by farmers. Saint-François is also the perfect place to visit one of the island's *cabanes à sucre* (maple-sugaring huts) found along chemin Royal. Stop at a hut for a tasting tour; sap is gathered from the maple groves and boiled until it turns to a syrup. When it is poured on ice, it tastes like a delicious toffee. The maple season is late March through April.

9 Straight on chemin Royal is **Saint-François Church,** built in 1734 and one of eight provincial churches dating from the French regime. At the time the English seized Québec in 1759, General Wolfe knew Saint-François to be among the better strategic points along the St. Lawrence. Consequently, he stationed the British troops here and used the church as a military hospital. In May 1988, a fatal car crash set the church on fire. Although it is in the process of being rebuilt, most of the interior treasures were lost.

10 About a mile down the road is a picnic area with a wood **observation tower** situated for perfect viewing of the majestic St. Lawrence at its widest point, 10 times as wide as it is near Québec City. During the

spring and autumn months, you can observe wild Canadian geese here.

Heading west on chemin Royal, you'll come to one of the island's earliest villages, Sainte-Famille, which was founded in 1661. The scenery is exquisite here; there are abundant apple orchards and strawberry fields with a view of Côte de Beaupré and Mont Sainte-Anne in the distance. But the village also has plenty of man-made historic charm; it has the area's highest concentration of stone houses dating from the French regime.

11 Take a quick look at **Sainte-Famille Church,** which was constructed in 1749, later than some of the others on the island. This impressive structure is the only church in the province to have three bell towers at the front. Its ceiling was redone in the mid-19th century with elaborate designs in wood and gold. The church also holds a famous painting, *L'Enfant Jésus Voyant la Croix,* done in 1670 by Frère Luc (Father Luc), who was sent from France to decorate churches in the area. *3915 chemin Royal. Admission free. Open summer, daily.*

The next village situated on the north side of the island,
12 **Saint-Pierre,** was established a bit later than Sainte-Famille, in 1679. Its church, though, is older—dating back to 1717—and is officially the oldest on the island. **Saint-Pierre Church** is no longer open for worship, but it was restored during the 1960s and is open to tourists. Many of its original components are still intact, such as benches with compartments below, where hot bricks and stones were placed to keep people warm during winter services. *1243 chemin Royal. Admission free. Open summer, daily.*

Because Saint-Pierre is situated on a plateau with the island's most fertile land, the village has long been the center of traditional farming industries. The best products grown here are potatoes, asparagus, and corn, and the many dairy farms have given the village a renowned reputation for butter and other dairy products. At 2370 chemin Royal is the former home of Felix Leclerc, one of the many artists who have made the island their home. Leclerc, the father of Québecois folk singing, lived here until he died in August 1988.

If you continue west on chemin Royal, just up ahead are the bridge back to the mainland and Route 440.

Dining and Lodging

For price categories, *see* Québec City Dining and Lodging, *above*.

Dining

$$$ **La Goéliche.** The first rule of the kitchen is that only the freshest ingredients from the island's farms can be used. The menu is classic French and depends upon the fruits and vegetables in season. Lunch is a moderately priced à la carte selection of salads, quiches, and omelets. The evening's menu is more expensive and features such specialties as quail with red vermouth and chicken with pistachio mousseline. The desserts, such as maple syrup mousse with strawberry syrup, have a regional flavor. This rustic inn has a romantic dining room with windows overlooking the St. Lawrence River and a view of Québec City. *22 chemin du Quai, Sainte-Pétronille, tel. 418/828–2248. Reservations advised. Dress: casual but neat. MC, V. Closed Jan.*

$$$ **L'Atre.** After you park your car, you'll take a horse-drawn carriage to a 17th-century Normandy-style house furnished with Québecois pine antiques. True to the establishment's name, which means "hearth," all the traditional dishes are cooked and served from a fireplace. The menu emphasizes hearty fare, such as beef

Bourguignon and *tourtière* (meat pie), with maple-sugar pie for dessert. La Grande Fête (The Big Feast) is a nine-course dinner that costs about $60. Half way through the meal, guests visit the attic for a nip of maple syrup liqueur. *4403 chemin Royal, Sainte-Famille, tel. 418/829–2474. Reservations required. Dress: casual but neat. AE, MC, V. Open mid-May–mid-Oct.; occasionally in winter; call ahead.*

Lodging
$$ **Auberge le Chaumonot.** This medium-size hotel in rural Saint-François is right near the St. Lawrence River's widest point. The inn's large bay windows capitalize on the view of the river and neighboring islands, but the decor is uninspired, with simple wood furniture of the island. The service here is efficient and friendly. The restaurant serves Continental cuisine, with table d'hôte and à la carte menus. *425 chemin Royal, Saint-François, G0A 3S0, tel. 418/829–2735. 8 rooms with private bath and air-conditioning. Facilities: restaurant, pool. AE, MC, V. Closed Nov.–Apr.*

$$ **La Goéliche.** This 1890 Victorian country inn stands just steps away from the St. Lawrence River in the village of Sainte-Pétronille. Québecois antiques decorate light and spacious rooms with their original wood floors. Rooms are on the second and third floors, and half of them look out across the river to Québec City. The rooms have no television, but they do have phones. *22 chemin du Quai, Sainte-Pétronille, G0A 4C0, tel. 418/828–2248. 22 rooms, 18 with private bath. Facilities: 2 restaurants. MC, V.*

You can get to know the island by staying at one of its 30 bed-and-breakfasts. Reservations are necessary. The price for a room, double occupancy, runs about $45–$90. **Beau Temps, Mauvais Temps** (tel. 418/828–2275) is a referral service for these accommodations.

French Vocabulary

Words and Phrases

	English	*French*	*Pronunciation*
Basics	Yes/no	Oui/non	wee/no
	Please	S'il vous plait	seel voo play
	Thank you (very much)	Merci (beaucoup)	mare-**see** (boh-**koo**)
	You're welcome	De rien	deh ree-**en**
	That's all right	Il n'y a pas de quoi	eel nee ah pah deh kwah
	Excuse me, sorry	Pardon	pahr-**doan**
	Sorry!	Désolé(e)	day-zoh-**lay**
	Good morning/afternoon	Bonjour	bone-**joor**
	Good evening	Bonsoir	bone-**swar**
	Goodbye	Au revoir	o ruh-**vwar**
	Mr. (Sir)/ Mrs. (Ma'am)	Monsieur/madame	meh-see-**ur**/mah-**dahm**
	Miss	Mademoiselle	mad-mwah-**zel**
	Pleased to meet you	Enchanté(e)	on-shahn-**tay**
	How are you?	Comment allez-vous?	ko-men-tahl-ay-**voo**
	Very well, thanks	Très bien, merci	tray bee-**en,** mare-**see**
	And you?	Et vous?	ay voo?
Numbers	one	un	un
	two	deux	dew
	three	trois	twa
	four	quatre	**cat**-ruh
	five	cinq	sank
	six	six	seess
	seven	sept	set
	eight	huit	wheat
	nine	neuf	nuf
	ten	dix	deess
	eleven	onze	owns
	twelve	douze	dues
	thirteen	treize	trays
	fourteen	quatorze	ka-**torz**
	fifteen	quinze	cans
	sixteen	seize	sez
	seventeen	dix-sept	deess-**set**
	eighteen	dix-huit	deess-**wheat**
	nineteen	dix-neuf	deess-**nuf**
	twenty	vingt	vant
	twenty-one	vingt-et-un	vant-ay-**un**
	thirty	trente	trahnt
	forty	quarante	ka-**rahnt**
	fifty	cinquante	sang-**kahnt**
	sixty	soixante	swa-**sahnt**

	seventy	soixante-dix	swa-sahnt-**deess**
	eighty	quatre-vingts	cat-ruh-**vant**
	ninety	quatre-vingt-dix	cat-ruh-vant-**deess**
	one-hundred	cent	sahnt
	one-thousand	mille	meel
Colors	black	noir	nwar
	blue	bleu	blu
	brown	brun	brun
	green	vert	vair
	orange	orange	o-**ranj**
	pink	rose	rose
	red	rouge	rouge
	violet	violette	vee-o-**let**
	white	blanc	blahnk
	yellow	jaune	jone
Days of the Week	Sunday	dimanche	dee-**mahnsh**
	Monday	lundi	lewn-**dee**
	Tuesday	mardi	mar-**dee**
	Wednesday	mercredi	mare-kruh-**dee**
	Thursday	jeudi	juh-**dee**
	Friday	vendredi	van-dra-**dee**
	Saturday	samedi	sam-**dee**
Months	January	janvier	jan-**vyay**
	February	février	feh-vree-**ay**
	March	mars	mars
	April	avril	a-**vreel**
	May	mai	may
	June	juin	jwan
	July	juillet	jwee-**ay**
	August	août	oot
	September	septembre	sep-**tahm**-bruh
	October	octobre	**oak-toe**-bruh
	November	novembre	no-**vahm**-bruh
	December	décembre	day-**sahm**-bruh
Useful Phrases	Do you speak English?	Parlez-vous anglais?	par-lay vooz ahng-**glay**
	I don't speak French	Je ne parle pas français	jeh nuh parl pah fraun-**say**
	I don't understand	Je ne comprends pas	jeh nuh kohm-prahn **pah**
	I understand	Je comprends	jeh kohm-**prahn**
	I don't know	Je ne sais pas	jeh nuh say **pah**
	I'm American/British	Je suis américain/anglais	jeh sweez a-may-ree-**can**/ ahng-**glay**
	What's your name?	Comment vous appelez-vous?	ko-mahn voo za-pel-ay-**voo**
	My name is . . .	Je m'appelle . . .	jeh muh-**pel** . . .
	What time is it?	Quelle heure est-il?	kel ur et-**il**
	How?	Comment?	ko-**mahn**

	When?	Quand?	kahnd
	How much is it?	C'est combien?	say comb-bee-**en**
	It's expensive/cheap	C'est cher/pas cher	say sher/pa sher
	A little/a lot	Un peu/beaucoup	un puh/bo-**koo**
	More/less	Plus/moins	ploo/mwa
	Enough/too (much)	Assez/trop	a-**say**/tro
	I am ill/sick	Je suis malade	jeh swee ma-**lahd**
	Please call a doctor	Appelez un docteur	a-pe-lay un dohk-**tore**
	Help!	Au secours!	o say-**koor**
	Stop!	Arrêtez!	a-ruh-**tay**
	Fire!	Au feu!	o fuw
	Caution!/Look out!	Attention!	a-tahn-see-**own**
Dining Out	A bottle of . . .	une bouteille de . . .	ewn boo-**tay** deh
	A cup of . . .	une tasse de . . .	ewn tass deh
	A glass of . . .	un verre de . . .	un vair deh
	Ashtray	un cendrier	un sahn-dree-**ay**
	Bill/check	l'addition	la-dee-see-**own**
	Bread	du pain	due pan
	Breakfast	le petit déjeuner	leh pet-**ee** day-zhu-**nay**
	Butter	du beurre	due bur
	Cheers!	A votre santé!	ah-vo-truh sahn-**tay**
	Cocktail/aperitif	un apéritif	un ah-pay-ree-**teef**
	Dinner	le dîner	leh dee-**nay**
	Dish of the day	le plat du jour	leh pla do **zhoor**
	Enjoy!	Bon appétit!	bone a-pay-**tee**
	Fixed-price menu	le menu	leh may-**new**
	Fork	une fourchette	ewn four-**shet**
	I am diabetic	Je suis diabétique	jeh swee-dee-ah-**bay-teek**
	I am on a diet	Je suis au régime	jeh sweez o ray-**jeem**
	I am vegetarian	Je suis végétarien (ne)	jeh swee vay-jay-ta-ree-**en**
	I cannot eat . . .	Je ne peux pas manger de . . .	jeh nuh puh pah mahn-**jay** deh
	I'd like to order	Je voudrais commander	jeh voo-**dray** ko-mahn-**day**
	I'd like . . .	Je voudrais . . .	jeh voo-**dray**

I'm hungry/thirsty	J'ai faim/soif	jay fam/swahf
Is service/the tip included?	Est-ce que le service est compris?	ess keh leh sair-veess ay comb-**pree**
It's good/bad	C'est bon/mauvais	say bon/mo-**vay**
It's hot/cold	C'est chaud/froid	say sho/frwah
Knife	un couteau	un koo-**toe**
Lunch	le déjeuner	leh day-juh-**nay**
Menu	la carte	la cart
Napkin	une serviette	ewn sair-vee-**et**
Pepper	du poivre	due **pwah**-vruh
Plate	une assiette	ewn a-see-**et**
Give me . . .	Donnez-moi . . .	doe-nay-**mwah**
Salt	du sel	dew sell
Spoon	une cuiller	ewn kwee-**ay**
Sugar	du sucre	due **sook**-ruh
Waiter!/Waitress!	Monsieur!/ Mademoiselle!	meh-see-**ur** /mad-mwah-**zel**
Wine list	la carte des vins	la cart day **van**

Index

Personal Itinerary

Departure *Date*

Time

Transportation

Arrival *Date* *Time*

Departure *Date* *Time*

Transportation

Accommodations

Arrival *Date* *Time*

Departure *Date* *Time*

Transportation

Accommodations

Arrival *Date* *Time*

Departure *Date* *Time*

Transportation

Accommodations

Personal Itinerary

Arrival *Date* *Time*

Departure *Date* *Time*

Transportation

Accommodations

Arrival *Date* *Time*

Departure *Date* *Time*

Transportation

Accommodations

Arrival *Date* *Time*

Departure *Date* *Time*

Transportation

Accommodations

Arrival *Date* *Time*

Departure *Date* *Time*

Transportation

Accommodations

Addresses

Name

Address

Telephone

Name

Address

Telephone

Name

Address

Telephone

Name

Address

Telephone

Name

Address

Telephone

Name

Address

Telephone

Name

Address

Telephone

Name

Address

Telephone

Name

Address

Telephone

Name

Address

Telephone

Name

Address

Telephone

Name

Address

Telephone

Name

Address

Telephone

Name

Address

Telephone

Name

Address

Telephone

Name

Address

Telephone

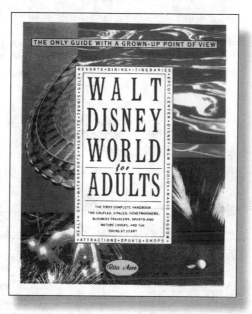

Special Series

Fodor's Affordables

Caribbean

Europe

Florida

France

Germany

Great Britain

Italy

London

Paris

Fodor's Bed & Breakfast and Country Inns Guides

America's Best B&Bs

California

Canada's Great Country Inns

Cottages, B&Bs and Country Inns of England and Wales

Mid-Atlantic Region

New England

The Pacific Northwest

The South

The Southwest

The Upper Great Lakes Region

The Berkeley Guides

California

Central America

Eastern Europe

Europe

France

Germany & Austria

Great Britain & Ireland

Italy

London

Mexico

Pacific Northwest & Alaska

Paris

San Francisco

Fodor's Exploring Guides

Australia

Boston & New England

Britain

California

The Caribbean

Florence & Tuscany

Florida

France

Germany

Ireland

Italy

London

Mexico

New York City

Paris

Prague

Rome

Scotland

Singapore & Malaysia

Spain

Thailand

Turkey

Fodor's Flashmaps

Boston

New York

Washington, D.C.

Fodor's Pocket Guides

Acapulco

Bahamas

Barbados

Jamaica

London

New York City

Paris

Puerto Rico

San Francisco

Washington, D.C.

Fodor's Sports

Cycling

Golf Digest's Best Places to Play

Hiking

The Insider's Guide to the Best Canadian Skiing

Running

Sailing

Skiing in the USA & Canada

USA Today's Complete Four Sports Stadium Guide

Fodor's Three-In-Ones (guidebook, language cassette, and phrase book)

France

Germany

Italy

Mexico

Spain

Fodor's Special-Interest Guides

Complete Guide to America's National Parks

Condé Nast Traveler Caribbean Resort and Cruise Ship Finder

Cruises and Ports of Call

Euro Disney

France by Train

Halliday's New England Food Explorer

Healthy Escapes

Italy by Train

London Companion

Shadow Traffic's New York Shortcuts and Traffic Tips

Sunday in New York

Sunday in San Francisco

Touring Europe

Touring USA: Eastern Edition

Walt Disney World and the Orlando Area

Walt Disney World for Adults

Fodor's Vacation Planners

Great American Learning Vacations

Great American Sports & Adventure Vacations

Great American Vacations

Great American Vacations for Travelers with Disabilities

National Parks and Seashores of the East

National Parks of the West

The Wall Street Journal Guides to Business Travel

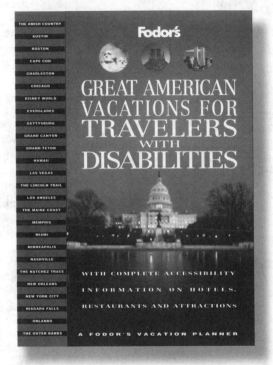

Personalized:
Prepared expressly
for you.

Up-to-the-minute:
Includes the most current
information available.

Your travel dates:
Covers only days
when you will be
there.

June 1

Fodor's/Worldview presents a Travel Update for:

Mr. Gavin Lynch
201 East 50th Street
New York, New York, 10022

Fodor's
WORLDVIEW

LONDON, UK

ARRIVE 23 Jun DEPART: 21 Jul

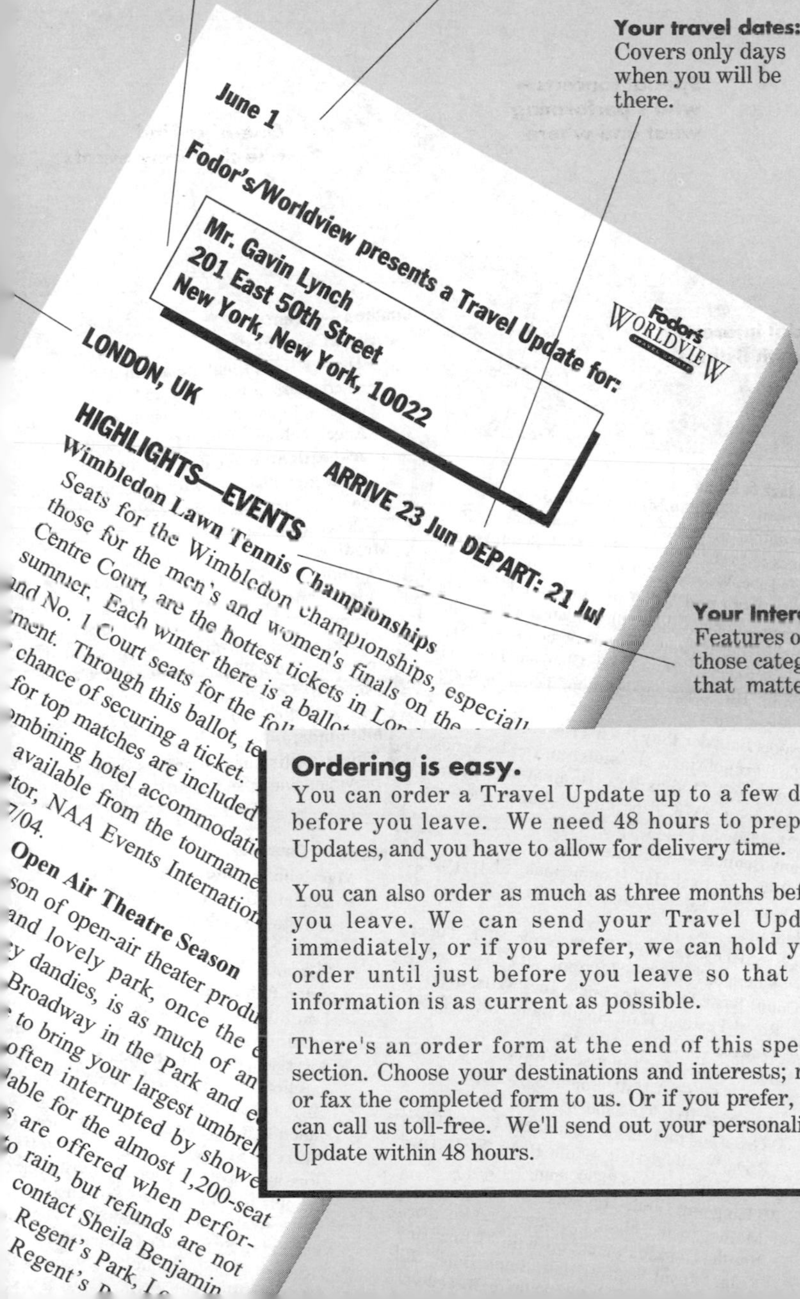

Your Interests:
Features only
those categories
that matter to you.

HIGHLIGHTS—EVENTS

Wimbledon Lawn Tennis Championships

Seats for the Wimbledon championships, especially
those for the men's and women's finals on the
Centre Court, are the hottest tickets in Lon
summer. Each winter there is a ballo
and No. 1 Court seats for the fol
ment. Through this ballot, te
chance of securing a ticket.
for top matches are included
combining hotel accommodati
available from the tourname
tor, NAA Events Internatio
7/04.

Open Air Theatre Season

son of open-air theater produ
and of lovely park, once the e
y dandies, is as much of an
Broadway in the Park and e
to bring your largest umbrel
often interrupted by showe
able for the almost 1,200-seat
s are offered when perfor-
to rain, but refunds are not
contact Sheila Benjamin
Regent's Park, L
Regent's P

Ordering is easy.

You can order a Travel Update up to a few days
before you leave. We need 48 hours to prepare
Updates, and you have to allow for delivery time.

You can also order as much as three months before
you leave. We can send your Travel Update
immediately, or if you prefer, we can hold your
order until just before you leave so that the
information is as current as possible.

There's an order form at the end of this special
section. Choose your destinations and interests; mail
or fax the completed form to us. Or if you prefer, you
can call us toll-free. We'll send out your personalized
Update within 48 hours.

Interest Categories

For your personalized Travel Update, choose the categories you're most interested in from this list. Every Travel Update automatically provides you with *Event Highlights* - the best of what's happening during the dates of your trip.

1.	**Business Services**	Fax & Overnight Mail, Computer Rentals, Photocopying, Protocol, Secretarial, Messenger, Translation Services
	Dining	
2.	**All Day Dining**	Breakfast & Brunch, Cafes & Tea Rooms, Late-Night Dining
3.	**Local Cuisine**	In Every Price Range—from Budget Restaurants to the Special Splurge
4.	**European Cuisine**	Continental, French, Italian
5.	**Asian Cuisine**	Chinese, Far Eastern, Japanese, Other
6.	**Americas Cuisine**	American, Mexican & Latin
7.	**Nightlife**	Bars, Dance Clubs, Casinos, Comedy Clubs, Ethnic, Pubs & Beer Halls
8.	**Entertainment**	Theater—Comedy, Drama, English Language, Musicals, Dance, Ticket Agencies
9.	**Music**	Country/Western/Folk, Classical, Traditional & Ethnic, Opera, Jazz & Blues, Pop, Rock
10.	**Children's Activities**	Events, Attractions
11.	**Tours**	Local Tours, Day Trips, Overnight Excursions, Cruises
12.	**Exhibitions, Festivals & Shows**	Antiques & Flower, History & Cultural, Art Exhibitions, Fairs & Craft Shows, Music & Art Festivals
13.	**Shopping**	Districts & Malls, Markets, Regional Specialities
14.	**Fitness**	Bicycling, Health Clubs, Hiking, Jogging
15.	**Recreational Sports**	Boating/Sailing, Fishing, Golf, Ice Skating, Skiing, Snorkeling/Scuba, Swimming, Tennis & Racquet
16.	**Spectator Sports**	Auto Racing, Baseball, Basketball, Boating & Sailing, Football, Golf, Horse Racing, Ice Hockey, Rugby, Soccer, Tennis, Track & Field, Other Sports

Please note that interest category content will vary by season, destination, and length of stay.

Destinations

The Fodor's/Worldview Travel Update covers more than 160 destinations worldwide. Choose the destinations that match your itinerary from this list. (Choose bulleted destinations only.)

Europe
- • Amsterdam
- • Athens
- • Barcelona
- • Berlin
- • Brussels
- • Budapest
- • Copenhagen
- • Dublin
- • Edinburgh
- • Florence
- • Frankfurt
- • French Riviera
- • Geneva
- • Glasgow
- • Istanbul
- • Lausanne
- • Lisbon
- • London
- • Madrid
- • Milan
- • Moscow
- • Munich
- • Oslo
- • Paris
- • Prague
- • Provence
- • Rome
- • Salzburg
- * Seville
- • St. Petersburg
- • Stockholm
- • Venice
- • Vienna
- • Zurich

United States (Mainland)
- • Albuquerque
- • Atlanta
- • Atlantic City
- • Baltimore
- • Boston
- * Branson, MO
- * Charleston, SC
- • Chicago
- • Cincinnati
- • Cleveland
- • Dallas/Ft. Worth
- • Denver
- • Detroit
- • Houston
- * Indianapolis
- • Kansas City
- • Las Vegas
- • Los Angeles
- • Memphis
- • Miami
- • Milwaukee
- • Minneapolis/St. Paul
- * Nashville
- • New Orleans
- • New York City
- • Orlando
- • Palm Springs
- • Philadelphia
- • Phoenix
- • Pittsburgh
- • Portland
- * Reno/Lake Tahoe
- • St. Louis
- • Salt Lake City
- • San Antonio
- • San Diego
- • San Francisco
- * Santa Fe
- • Seattle
- • Tampa
- • Washington, DC

Alaska
- • Alaskan Destinations

Hawaii
- • Honolulu
- • Island of Hawaii
- • Kauai
- • Maui

Canada
- • Quebec City
- • Montreal
- • Ottawa
- • Toronto
- • Vancouver

Bahamas
- • Abaco
- • Eleuthera/Harbour Island
- • Exuma
- • Freeport
- • Nassau & Paradise Island

Bermuda
- • Bermuda Countryside
- • Hamilton

British Leeward Islands
- • Anguilla
- • Antigua & Barbuda
- • St. Kitts & Nevis

British Virgin Islands
- • Tortola & Virgin Gorda

British Windward Islands
- • Barbados
- • Dominica
- • Grenada
- • St. Lucia
- • St. Vincent
- • Trinidad & Tobago

Cayman Islands
- • The Caymans

Dominican Republic
- • Santo Domingo

Dutch Leeward Islands
- • Aruba
- • Bonaire
- • Curacao

Dutch Windward Island
- • St. Maarten/St. Martin

French West Indies
- • Guadeloupe
- • Martinique
- • St. Barthelemy

Jamaica
- • Kingston
- • Montego Bay
- • Negril
- • Ocho Rios

Puerto Rico
- • Ponce
- • San Juan

Turks & Caicos
- • Grand Turk/Providenciales

U.S. Virgin Islands
- • St. Croix
- • St. John
- • St. Thomas

Mexico
- • Acapulco
- • Cancun & Isla Mujeres
- • Cozumel
- • Guadalajara
- • Ixtapa & Zihuatanejo
- • Los Cabos
- • Mazatlan
- • Mexico City
- • Monterrey
- • Oaxaca
- • Puerto Vallarta

South/Central America
- * Buenos Aires
- * Caracas
- * Rio de Janeiro
- * San Jose, Costa Rica
- * Sao Paulo

Middle East
- * Jerusalem

Australia & New Zealand
- • Auckland
- • Melbourne
- * South Island
- • Sydney

China
- • Beijing
- • Guangzhou
- • Shanghai

Japan
- • Kyoto
- • Nagoya
- • Osaka
- • Tokyo
- • Yokohama

Pacific Rim/Other
- * Bali
- • Bangkok
- • Hong Kong & Macau
- • Manila
- • Seoul
- • Singapore
- • Taipei

* Destinations available by 1/1/95

Fodor's WORLDVIEW TRAVEL UPDATE

Order Form

THIS TRAVEL UPDATE IS FOR (Please print):

Name ______________________________

Address ______________________________

City ________ State ________ Country ________ ZIP ________

Tel # ( ) - Fax # ( ) -

Title of this Fodor's guide: ______________________________

Store and location where guide was purchased: ______________________________

INDICATE YOUR DESTINATIONS/DATES: You can order up to three (3) destinations from the previous page. Fill in your arrival and departure dates for each destination. **Your Travel Update itinerary (all destinations selected) cannot exceed 30 days from beginning to end.**

		Month / Day		Month / Day
(Sample) LONDON	From:	6 / 21	To:	6 / 30
1	From:	/	To:	/
2	From:	/	To:	/
3	From:	/	To:	/

CHOOSE YOUR INTERESTS: Select up to eight (8) categories from the list of interest categories shown on the previous page and circle the numbers below:

1 2 3 4 5 6 7 8 9 10 11 12 13 14 15 16

CHOOSE WHEN YOU WANT YOUR TRAVEL UPDATE DELIVERED (Check one):

❑ Please send my Travel Update immediately.

❑ Please hold my order until a few weeks before my trip to include the most up-to-date information.

Completed orders will be sent within 48 hours. Allow 7-10 days for U.S. mail delivery.

ADD UP YOUR ORDER HERE. ***SPECIAL OFFER FOR FODOR'S PURCHASERS ONLY!***

	Suggested Retail Price	Your Price	This Order
First destination ordered	~~$ 9.95~~	$ 7.95	$ 7.95
Second destination (if applicable)	~~$ 6.95~~	$ 4.95	+
Third destination (if applicable)	~~$ 6.95~~	$ 4.95	+

DELIVERY CHARGE (Check one and enter amount below)

	Within U.S. & Canada	Outside U.S. & Canada
First Class Mail	❑ $2.50	❑ $5.00
FAX	❑ $5.00	❑ $10.00
Priority Delivery	❑ $15.00	❑ $27.00

ENTER DELIVERY CHARGE FROM ABOVE: + ________

TOTAL: $ ________

METHOD OF PAYMENT IN U.S. FUNDS ONLY (Check one):

❑ AmEx ❑ MC ❑ Visa ❑ Discover ❑ Personal Check (U. S. & Canada only)

❑ Money Order/ International Money Order

Make check or money order payable to: Fodor's Worldview Travel Update

Credit Card _/_/_/_/_/_/_/_/_/_/_/_/_/_/_/_/ **Expiration Date:**____/____

Authorized Signature ______________________________

SEND THIS COMPLETED FORM WITH PAYMENT TO:

Fodor's Worldview Travel Update, 114 Sansome Street, Suite 700, San Francisco, CA 94104

OR CALL OR FAX US 24-HOURS A DAY

Telephone **1-800-799-9609** • Fax **1-800-799-9619** (From within the U.S. & Canada)

(Outside the U.S. & Canada: Telephone 415-616-9988 • Fax 415-616-9989)

(Please have this guide in front of you when you call so we can verify purchase.)

Code: FTG

Offer valid until 12/31/95.

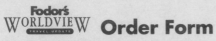